Fodor's
MONTRÉAL &
QUÉBEC CITY

5

MAPS

Contents

Welcome to Montréal and Québec City

France's old-world charm lives on in Montréal and Québec City, two enchanting Canadian cities with rich pasts. Their French heritage is ever-present, from the language to wonderful food to pockets of cobblestoned streets. Cosmopolitan Montréal rocks with lively cultural and shopping scenes; smaller Québec City is jam-packed with history. Visits are lovely year-round: summer brings festivals galore; spring and fall are perfect for city strolls and countryside jaunts; and winter, despite the cold, heats up with Winter Carnival, hot chocolate, and snow sports.

TOP REASONS TO GO

★ **French food:** *Haute* to hearty—including *poutine,* fries with cheese curds and gravy.

★ **Shopping:** Fashion-forward local designers, top-notch cold-weather wear, Inuit art.

★ **Festivals:** From Winter Carnival to Jazz Fest, Quebecers throw great parties all year.

★ **History:** Museums, monuments, and ancient fortifications bring the past to life.

★ **Hockey:** Tickets for Habs games are hard to get, but catch a game on TV at a local bar.

★ **Fun in the snow:** Winter brings ice-skating, tobogganing, skiing, and snowshoeing.

Chapter 1

EXPERIENCE MONTRÉAL AND QUÉBEC CITY

22 ULTIMATE EXPERIENCES

Montréal & Québec City offer terrific experiences that should be on every traveler's list. Here are Fodor's top picks for a memorable trip.

1 Exploring the Old Port

One of the city's most popular parks, Montréal's Old Port is the place to gallery-hop, cycle, stroll, take a jet boat ride on the Lachine Rapids, or just explore the waterfront at your leisure. *(Ch. 3)*

2 Strolling Rue du Petit-Champlain

Take the funicular down to explore lamp-lit Rue du Petit-Champlain, North America's oldest commercial street. *(Ch. 5)*

3 Carnaval de Québec

One of the world's biggest winter celebrations, this midwinter fête encompasses scores of activities that are bound to make you forget it's below zero. *(Ch. 5)*

4 Saluting the Citadel

La Citadelle is home to Canada's Royal 22nd Regiment, who turn out in bearskin caps and scarlet tunics for the daily changing of the guard. *(Ch. 5)*

5 Crossing Montmorency Falls

Ride an aerial cable car to admire the chute from above, or—if you're really daring—cross the suspension bridge above the breathtaking falls. *(Ch. 6)*

6 Visiting Île d'Orléans

This so-called Garden of Québec is a bucolic wonderland of centuries-old summer cottages, ancient churches, wineries, cider mills, culinary artisans, and produce stands. *(Ch. 6)*

7 Cheering the Habs

Nothing is more Canadian than hockey, and the fan energy and enthusiasm at a Canadiens (aka "Habs") game provide sport for even the most reluctant sports fan. *(Ch. 3)*

8 Bowing to the Basilique Notre Dame de Montréal

Everything about this magnificent Roman Catholic basilica is grand, from the 228-foot twin steeples to the 7,000-pipe organ to the 24-carat gold stars on the ceiling. *(Ch. 3)*

9 Posing on Dufferin Terrace

The long boardwalk in front of the Château Frontenac is one of Québec City's most romantic—and photogenic—spots. *(Ch. 5)*

10 Partying in the Gay Village

Once a tiny nook carved out of Downtown, The Village is great for shopping, strolling, people-watching, and partying. *(Ch. 3)*

11 Ferrying to Lévis

Treat yourself to views of a lifetime by taking the quick (and inexpensive) 20-minute trip aboard the commuter ferry to the town of Lévis. *(Ch. 5)*

12 Climbing Parc du Mont Royal

Snowshoe, ski, or hike a network of trails leading through the dense wooded areas of this hill overlooking the city. *(Ch. 3)*

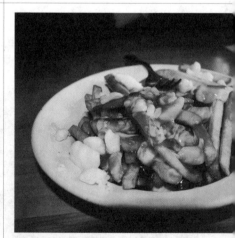

13 Eating poutine

Québec City has some of the best spots to sample poutine (fries drenched in gravy and cheese curds) including the Chez Ashton chain. *(Ch. 5)*

14 Musée de Beaux Arts de Montréal

One of Canada's oldest museums has an exceptional collection of art including works by Rembrandt, Renoir, and Picasso, all housed in a former church. *(Ch. 3)*

15 Shopping at Marché du Vieux Port

At this foodies' haven, you'll be tempted by maple syrup products, chocolates, iced cider, and other local specialties. *(Ch. 5)*

16 Reflecting at the Plains of Abraham

Filled with runners, picnickers, and cyclists, it's hard to imagine the fierce battles between empires that unfolded on this very spot in the 18th century. *(Ch. 5)*

17 Taking in Old Montréal

Shops and restaurants are touristy in this part of town, so your time is best spent winding through the old lamp-lit streets and marvelling at the architecture. *(Ch. 3)*

18 Eating up Jean Talon Market

As well as flowers, fruits, and vegetables, this European-style open market has food stands with crêpes, samosas, Turkish pastries, and more. *(Ch. 3)*

19 Skiing Mont-Tremblant

With 662 acres of skiable terrain, this towering peak of the Laurentian Mountains, northwest of Montréal, is one of North America's top ski resorts. *(Ch. 4)*

20 Grooving to Jazz Fest

Montréal's annual International Jazz Festival is the largest in the world, attracting millions of fans for more than 400 (mostly free!) concerts every summer. *(Ch. 2,3)*

21 Praising Oratoire Saint-Joseph

The oratory, gardens, and copper dome of the world's largest and most popular shrine to St. Joseph are a sight to behold. *(Ch. 3)*

22 Wandering Old Québec

A UNESCO World Heritage site, the enchanting Old City (Vieux Québec) features cobblestone streets lined with cafés, shops, galleries, and cathedrals. *(Ch. 5)*

What to Eat and Drink

POUTINE

Canada's national dish, poutine (from Quebecois slang meaning "mess"), is a mushy mess of fries covered in melty cheese curds and dark gravy. The take-out mishmash was traditionally a bumpkin's meal until it was named Canada's national dish in 2010.

JULIETTE & CHOCOLAT

Chocolate is celebrated in all its chocolate-y forms at this beloved dessert shop in Montréal, where highlights include crepe soufflé, bite-size brownies, candy, milkshakes, and rich hot chocolate, all made from cocoa beans sourced in Peru, Madagascar, and Uganda.

TOURTIÈRE

This rib-sticking meat-and-potatoes pie is a tabletop staple during the cold Québec winters. Named after the old-fashioned cooking vessel that was once used to bake it, tourtière is a dish recognized across the province and everybody's grandma has a different recipe.

MONTRÉAL BAGELS

It's the ultimate rivalry among Montrealers : who makes the better bagel, St. Viateur or Fairmont? Both shops famously sell Montréal bagels, made by hand with sourdough and malt, boiled in honey-sweetened water, wood-fired and sprinkled with sesame seeds. The result is a firmer, denser bagel than what European Jewish immigrants also brought over to the Big Apple.

SMOKED-MEAT SANDWICH

Smoked-meat sandwiches, like bagels, are another much-loved and much-argued-over classic Montréal eat. Sliced by hand and served over deli countertops, these juicy beef brisket sandwiches, feature cured, spiced meat that is hot-smoked, stacked onto rye bread, and completed with a squirt of yellow mustard.

BOULANGERIE BREAD

In Québec City, there's no better morning start than Le Paingrüel, a longstanding artisan bakery with daily specials including bread with dark chocolate and dried pear and cranberry-chocolate buns. In Montréal, Plateau-Mont-Royal is known for its croissant shops, and the La Petite-Patrie neighborhood has several, like the popular Le pain les voiles.

ÎLE D'ORLÉANS

An island just a 15-minute drive from Downtown Québec City, l'Île d'Orléans is home to the Chocolaterie de l'Île d'Orléans, known

The Boulangerie

for insanely delicious chocolate-dipped soft ice cream cones that have a cult following throughout the province. It's also home to sprawling fruit orchards, producing a bounty of ciders, liqueurs, pies, and pastries that can be purchased at roadside stalls.

ICE CIDER
A Quebec specialty, ice cider is a sweet, delicate liqueur that is produced through the alcoholic fermentation of juice from slowly pressed frozen apples. It's a must-try in Quebec if only because it is so complex and complicated to produce.

ARTISAN CHEESES
Québec is home to more than half of Canada's artisan cheese-makers. As such, there's a wealth of craftsman fromage to feast on here. Stock up at farmers' markets.

CRAFT BREWS
Québéc takes microbrewing very seriously, specializing in strong beers that'll knock you over faster than you can say, "Sante!" Montréal's first craft brewpub, Le Cheval Blanc, opened 30 years ago, well before the global craft beer revolution, and these days there are several more to choose from.

MAPLE SYRUP
Québec produces more than three-quarters of the world's maple syrup, and you'll find it right next to the salt and pepper on most table setups for breakfast, lunch, and dinner. Its origins date to the 1800s when the French learned how to tap trees from the First Nations.

STREET FOOD AT FIRST FRIDAYS
On the first Friday of every month from May to October, around 50 food trucks park at Montréal's Olympic Park and dole out their goodies to the hungry masses.

Cool Things to Do in Montréal and Québec City

CROSS-COUNTRY SKIING, SNOWSHOEING, AND SLEDDING ON THE MOUNTAIN

Take a guided nighttime snowshoe climb through the snow-covered forest of Mount Royal. By day, make the summit to Beaver Lake where a skating rink, tubing lanes, and ski trails facilitate the snow sport of your choice.

DANCING UP A STORM AT IGLOOFEST

Why should below freezing temperatures stop anyone from having an outdoor dance party? Just as the glitter from New Year's parties and resolutions begins to dull, Igloofest takes over the Old Port for nine days and heats things up with electronic sets spun by the hottest local and international DJs. Thousands bundle up and head to Igloo Village to shake off their hats and scarfs on the dance floor under the snow and stars.

COZYING UP AT CRAFT BEER BARS

Montrealers have long been spoiled for choice when it comes to finding warm watering holes with quality brews on tap. Like a hot chocolate but better, Dieu du Ciel!'s dark Aphrodisiaque stout is brewed with cocoa and vanilla beans, creating bourbon and toasty malt notes that will chase the winter blues away. Vices & Versa, L'Amère à Boire, Broue Pub Brouhaha, and MaBrasserie lead a long list of local craft breweries to hunker down in when the forecast reads hyperborean degrees.

PACKING IN THE POUTINE

When it comes to winter comfort foods, poutine reigns supreme in la belle province. Served with crispy fries, homemade gravy, and requisite squeaky cheese, the carb-heavy medley never fails to grease the arteries and warm the belly. Numerous establishments are dedicated to the dish—including La Banquise, Chez Claudette, Poutineville, and Paul Patates—but it can also be found on the menu at nearly every casse-croûte (greasy spoon). For an elevated take, there's Au Pied du Cochon's foie gras poutine and Garde Manger's lobster-heaped frites. Also, look out for La Poutine Week, an annual fry fest that takes place every February in restaurants across the city.

LIGHTING UP WITH MONTRÉAL EN LUMIÈRE AND LUMINOTHÉRAPIE

A little light therapy goes a long way to combat the season's shorter days and longer nights. Every February, Quartier des Spectacles is illuminated with Montréal en Lumière's light projects and installations, bright revolving Ferris wheel, flood-lit toboggan run, and the bundled-up masses, crowding in for the winter fair. Before that, Luminothérapie illumines the square with light art exhibitions from November to January.

Igloofest Music Festival

SKATING IN WINTER WONDERLANDS

Whether for an improvised game of shinny (pick-up hockey), attempts at the quad, there's ample ice space in the city for every skill level. Outdoor ice rinks can be found in the parks of every neighborhood, like Plateau's Parc La Fontaine pond, or the Old Port's Natrel Rink. If you don't have your own blades to cut the ice with, most places have them for rent. For those who prefer to keep indoors, Atrium Le 1000 brings the best of both worlds together with its large inside rink and centerpiece skylight.

GOING FOR A DIP IN THERMAL SPAS

A warm bath is one of the best antidotes for the chill that settles into your bones midwinter, and a little massage therapy doesn't hurt either. Visit Bota Bota, a lakeside boat spa located in the Old Port, for a steamy thermotherapy session to relieve aches and pains and release toxins in the body. In Plateau, St. Jude Spa repurposes a church into an urban oasis, with dry and wet saunas, a Nordic bath, and two rooftop hot tubs, open in the winter thanks to heated decks.

PARTYING WITH THE FAMILY AT FÊTE DES NEIGES

Pack the kids into snowsuits and hop across the river to Parc Jean Drapeau for Fête des Neiges' outdoor snow festival. Among the many attractions are dog sled rides, a 50-foot-high zipline, ice sculptures, a scenic skating path, giant foosball, and a 10-lane tube slide that includes two super-slides and one fitted for a four-seat tube. Plus, a packed program of games and performances for children is sure to keep les enfants terribles off thin ice and out of snowball fights during the cold weather season.

SWEETENING UP AT SUGAR SHACKS

Before the season melts into spring, head to the sugar bush to tap Canadian maples for their syrupy gold. To enjoy the late winter harvest, Montrealers congregate in a cabane à sucre (aka sugar shack), log cabins with long communal tables made for plate passing and syrup swapping. More than just a breakfast garnish, maple is drizzled into courses of the meal, which typically begins with yellow pea soup and is followed with savory traditional dishes such as tourtière meat pies, baked beans, and plenty of pork. The featured ingredient is the star of dessert, too, used generously in supersweet treats like maple pies, taffy, and donuts.

Best Spa Experiences in Montréal & Québec City

BOTA BOTA, SPA SUR L'EAU

A unique concept in this Nordic city, this spa is set on a repurposed ferry-boat in Old Montréal. The floating spa features a garden, pool, terraces, and hammocks. Other facilities include a sauna, steam room, a water circuit (cold bath, exterior cold shower, lukewarm bath, jet bath). Silence and or whispering is required everywhere on the boat.

SPA WILLIAM GRAY

This luxury spa (in an old colonial home in Old Montréal) is a local favorite. Highlights include warm quartz massages, a Spa Wave sound therapy system, an herbal sauna, and a Himalayan salt room with walls of Himalayan salt bricks.

SPA BOLTON

This spa in the Eastern Townships, set amid natural waterfalls from the Missisquoi River, allows for polar plunging in winter. Guests lie on beds in yurts for massages, while in summer only tent flaps stand between you and the sound of the river. A highlight is the Finnish wood-burning smoke sauna, or Savusauna, the only one of its kind in Canada.

SIBERIA SPA

Located in a peaceful woodsy setting a 20-minute drive from Vieux-Québec, Sibéria Spa offers the opportunity to escape the daily urban grind. Guests can enjoy the hot and cold baths — or for the more daring, there's the invigorating river, choose between 12 massages, and re-energize with a snack or light meal at the spa's adorable café, housed in an A-frame chapel.

BALNÉA SPA ET RÉSERVE THERMALE

This contemporary spa in the Bromont ski resort is surrounded by trees and overlooks a lake. In addition to treatments and wraps, guests can float outdoors on airbeds among the lily pads, soak up the sun on tiers of sundecks, bliss out in one of the hot or cold pools, or practice yoga by the lake.

STROM SPA—NUN'S ISLAND

This peaceful respite located minutes from Downtown Montréal boasts outdoor whirlpools, hot and cold baths, Finnish saunas, a eucalyptus-scented steam bath, thermal and Nordic waterfalls, indoor and outdoor fireplaces, and a massage rooms on stilts.

STROM SPA—VIEUX QUÉBEC

Overlooking the St. Lawrence River, this spa in Old Québec offers a thermal experience that takes you through outdoor whirlpools, thermal and Nordic baths, Finnish saunas, a eucalyptus steam bath, and indoor and outdoor relaxation areas with fireplaces.

The Nordik Spa-Nature

SCANDINAVE SPA

Located in Old Montréal, Scandinave Spa offers hot and cold baths, a waterfall, and a range of therapeutic massages, including Thai, Swedish, and a fusion of the Hawaiian lomilomi and the re-harmonizing Japanese shiatsu.

THE NORDIK SPA

The Nordik Spa-Nature in the Outaouais region is the largest spa in North America and its vast catalog of facilities impress. It's got 10 outdoor baths, nine saunas, an infinity pool, a saltwater flotation pool, a yoga and meditation room, an outdoor massage pavilion, and four restaurants, including a biergarten with an outdoor terrace and panoramic view.

SPA NORDIQUE LE GERMAIN

Part of Le Germain Hotel in Charlevoix's Baie St-Paul, Spa Nordique Le Germain provides the usual menu of thermal, hydrotherapy, and beauty treatments, but you'll also find a Nordic shower and a "Snow Fountain" producing finely crushed ice that you rub all over your body.

Best Side Trips from Montréal and Québec City

FARM-HOPPING ON ÎLE D'ORLÉANS

Thousands of tourists visit this island every year to go farm-hopping, savoring along the way the local produce and food products, such as maple syrup, fruit jams, apple cider, wine, black currant liqueur, chocolate, bread, pastries, and more.

WENDAKE, HURON-WENDAT NATION VILLAGE

Just half an hour outside Québec City, the village of Wendake transports you to the world of the Huron Nation before colonization.

EASTERN TOWNSHIPS VILLAGES

The area is known for its green mountains and forests, spas, wineries, ski hills, and charming Loyalist-era towns and villages strung out along the Québec-Vermont border.

ROUTES DES VINS

The official Route des Vins organization of the Brome-Missisquoi area includes 20 wineries and suggests four scenic road trip itineraries and four cycling routes for your Québec wine tasting adventure.

CHUTE MONTMORENCY

Plunging 272 feet from the top of a cliff, the spectacular Montmorency Falls stand a full 98 feet higher than Niagara Falls. Daredevils and more active types may prefer to enjoy the falls by zipline, via Ferrata, or from the stairway climbing up the side of the promontory.

KAMOURASKA AND THE BAS SAINT-LAURENT

With its expansive meadows and farmlands sweeping down to the water, three archipelagos welcoming thousands of seabirds, painted wooden Victorian homes, and a lively main street, Kamouraska is without a doubt the prettiest village in the region.

CHARLEVOIX AND THE NORTH SHORE

The Charlevoix is a year-round destination beloved for its painterly landscapes, its ski resort, Le Massif de Charlevoix, its maritime atmosphere in summer, its appeal as a whale-watching destination, and, last but not least, its epicurean trail, La Route des Saveurs.

Abbaye St-Benoît-du-Lac

ABBAYE ST-BENOÎT-DU-LAC

Built by the Benedic-tines in 1912 on a wooded peninsula overlooking Lac Memphremagog, the abbey is inhabited by more than 50 monks. Plan a retreat, pick-your-own apples in season, take a tour, shop the delicious homemade cheeses and jellies in the store, and hike the trails.

THE OUTAOUAIS

Less than two hours north-east of Montréal lies the Outaouais, a 33,000 square-mile natural playground numbering 20,000 lakes, 249 miles of hiking trails, and countless rivers. It's beauti-ful year-round but easier to explore in summer. Be sure to visit Montebello and Gatineau.

ASTROLAB IN PARC DU MONT-MÉGANTIC

Located in a wild and mountainous area, the Parc du Mont-Mégantic features 31 miles of hiking, snowshoeing and cross-country skiing trails and the most powerful observa-tory in Canada. In 2007, the remote park became the world's first-ever Interna-tional Dark Sky Reserve.

WHAT'S WHERE

1 Montréal. This is a bustling, multiethnic city of neighborhoods, from the historic Old City to the hip Plateau.

2 The Laurentians. The Laurentians (les Laurentides) encompass thousands of miles of forests, mountains, and lakes, but for many people the draw is Mont-Tremblant and its world-class ski slopes.

3 The Eastern Townships. Called les Cantons de l'Est in French, the Eastern Townships region has quaint architecture and rolling hills that might remind you of New England. Atop imposing Mont-Mégantic, you're 3,150 feet closer to the heavens. Far from city lights, the sky here is ideal for stargazing. Indeed, the park received its certification as an International Dark Sky Reserve in 2007.

4 The Outaouais. Bordering the Ottawa River, the Outaouais is known for its many lakes, majestic views, hiking trails, and interesting wildlife, as well as the imposing Château Montebello.

5 Québec City. The capital of the province of Québec is the most French city in North America. Québec's Old City (Vieux Québec) is split into two tiers, separated by steep rock against which are more than 25 *escaliers* (staircases) and a funicular. The surrounding cluster of small, low-rise neighborhoods all have their own charm and flavor.

6 Île d'Orléans. Famed for its wine and cider as well as its strawberry crop and other local produce, the Île d'Orléans is often called the "Garden of Québec." Made up of six small villages, this charming island has several bed-and-breakfasts and fabulous farm stands.

7 Côte-de-Beaupré. The coast hugged by the St. Lawrence River embraces the thundering Montmorency Falls and the impressive Ste-Anne-de-Beaupré shrine. It leads to Mont-Sainte-Anne, famous for its skiing, golfing, and mountain biking.

8 Charlevoix. The big bang of an ancient meteor created picturesque valleys, cliffs, and mountains that brush the St. Lawrence River. This Canadian Switzerland has inspired painters, poets, and musicians for generations.

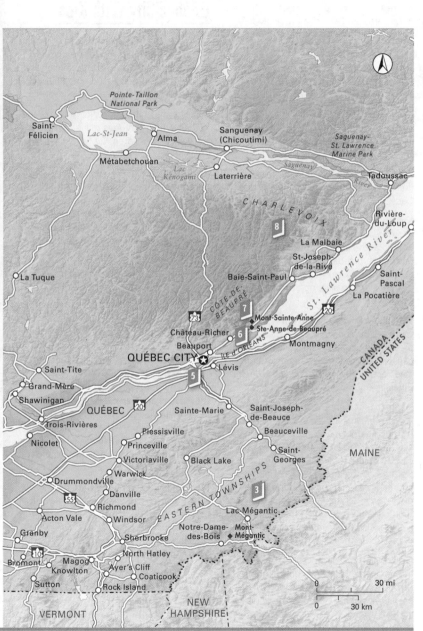

Pointe-Taillon
National Park

Saint-
Félicien

Lac-St-Jean

Alma

Sanguenay
(Chicoutimi)

Saguenay-
St. Lawrence
Marine Park

Métabetchouan

*Lac
Kénogami*

Laterrière

Saguenay

Tadoussac

River

CHARLEVOIX

8

La Malbaie

Rivière-
du-Loup

St-Joseph-
de-la-Rive

La Tuque

Baie-Saint-Paul

St. Lawrence River

Saint-
Pascal

La Pocatière

CÔTE-DE-BEAUPRÉ

73

7

Mont-Sainte-Anne

20

Château-Richer

6

Ste-Anne-de-Beaupré

ÎLE d'ORLÉANS

Beauport

Montmagny

QUÉBEC CITY ★

CANADA
UNITED STATES

5

Lévis

Saint-Tite

Grand-Mère

Shawinigan

QUÉBEC   20

Sainte-Marie

Saint-Joseph-
de-Beauce

MAINE

Trois-Rivières

Nicolet

Plessisville

Beauceville

Princeville

Victoriaville

Black Lake

Saint-
Georges

Warwick

EASTERN TOWNSHIPS

Drummondville

55

Danville

Richmond

3

Acton Vale

Windsor

Lac-Mégantic

Granby

Sherbrooke

Notre-Dame-
des-Bois

Mont-
Mégantic

10

Magog

North Hatley

Bromont

Knowlton

Ayer's Cliff

Sutton

Coaticook

Rock Island

NEW
HAMPSHIRE

VERMONT

0   30 mi

0   30 km

Montréal and Québec City with Kids

There's no shortage of fantastic activities in Montréal and Québec City for kids. Here's a sampling of what the little ones might enjoy during a visit.

Montréal with Kids

Montréal's popular rent-a-bicycle system, **Bixi**, is a great way for families to see the city. The expanding network of car-free cycling paths now meanders around Parc du Mont-Royal and through Old Montréal, across Parc Jean-Drapeau on Île Notre-Dame, and along the Lachine Canal.

Kids who've had their fill of churches and museums can expend some pent-up energy at the adjacent **Old Port,** which has boats to pedal, a clock tower to climb, and a maze. There's also a water-front beach, but alas, no swimming is allowed.

For culturally adventurous youngsters, there are outdoor dance and theater presentations at **Parc Lafontaine.** Kids can also explore the mysteries of bonsai trees and Chinese gardens at the **Jardin Botanique**.

What soccer is to Brazilians and baseball is to Americans, hockey is to Canadians. It's not a game, it's a religion! If you can score tickets (best to order in advance), catch a **Montréal Canadiens** game at the Centre Bell. A night with the "Habs" and their lively fans is a riveting family experience. Alternatively, take a one-hour tour (ages five and up) of the **Centre Bell**, which includes access to the Canadiens dressing room.

On hot summer days, spend some time at the Quartier des Spectacles, where the large fountains spread along the street will provide some fun and surely cool off your kids. You may even see some adults jumping in, too.

Québec City With Kids

Ice-cream stands, street performers, and (in winter) a thrilling toboggan run make **Terrasse Dufferin** as entertaining for children as for adults, as do the **Plains of Abraham's** open spaces.

Place Royale in the Lower Town brings the 17th and 18th centuries to life for even the youngest children.

La Citadelle's Changing of the Guard ceremony, complete with the Royal 22e Régiment's mascot, Batisse the Goat, has lots of kid appeal. The hands-on exhibits at the **Musée de la Civilisation** and the 19th-century jail cells preserved in the **Musée de Québec** are both must-see attractions.

And for a little animal fun, polar bears, seals, and walruses are the stars of the city's **Aquarium du Québec.**

Outside Montréal and Québec City with Kids

In the Laurentians, the gentle rides of the **Au Pays des Merveilles** and the **Village du Père Noël** (Santa's Village) are perfect for younger children. There are plenty of thrills at the **Water Parks** at Mont-St-Sauveur in the Laurentians and Bromont in the Eastern Townships.

Montmorency Falls, on the Côte-de-Beaupré, aren't as grand as Niagara, but they're higher, and crossing the suspen-sion bridge above the spectacular chutes of water is a thrill. Farther along the St. Lawrence coast in **Tadoussac,** you can take a boat ride for an up-close encounter with whales (be careful not to get saltwa-ter in your camera or phone).

Free and Cheap

There might be no such thing as a free lunch in Montréal or Québec City, but plenty of other things are free, or nearly so.

ART

Admission to the permanent collections of Montréal's Musée des Beaux-Arts (⊕ www.mbam.qc.ca) and Québec City's Musée National des Beaux-Arts (⊕ www.mnbaq.org) is always free. The Musée d'Art Contemporain (⊕ www.macm.org) is half price on Wednesday nights. Every summer the city of Montréal mounts an outdoor exhibit of art or photographs on the sidewalks of avenue McGill College between rues Ste-Catherine and Sherbrooke.

CONCERTS

Montréal's Christ Church Cathedral (✉ 635 rue Ste-Catherine Ouest, ☎ 514/843–6577), a magnificent neo-Gothic treasure, and Oratoire St-Joseph (✉ 3800 Chemin Queen-Mary, ☎ 514/733–8211) offer free organ recitals on Sunday afternoons at 3:30 pm and 4:30 pm throughout the year. And Les Petits Chanteurs du Mont-Royal, one of the finest boys' choirs in North America, sings the 11 am mass at the Oratoire every Sunday from March to December 24. They also perform several free concerts throughout the year.

Montréal's Festival Internationale de Jazz every June and Québec City's Festival d'Été in July have dozens of free, open-air concerts. These huge happenings bring thousands, and tens of thousands, of revelers to the streets.

FIREWORKS

From mid-June through July, the sky comes alive with light and color on most Wednesday and Saturday evenings when fireworks teams from around the world compete in the spectacular L'International des Feux Loto-Québec. You can pay for a seat at La Ronde amusement park, or join thousands of Montrealers in the Old Port, on the Jacques Cartier Bridge, and in Parc Champlain on the South Shore and watch for free.

POLITICS

Political junkies can join free guided tours of North America's only French-speaking legislature, the Assemblée Nationale du Québec (☎ 418/643–7239). The parliamentary debates are on Tuesday to Thursday from August to November and February to May.

SCIENCE

McGill University's Redpath Museum (✉ 859 rue Sherbrooke Ouest, ☎ 514/398–4086) houses an eclectic collection of dinosaur skeletons, seashells, fossils, minerals, Egyptian mummies, and Stone Age tools in a beautiful 19th-century building. Watch for free lectures.

SIGHTSEEING

For one of the best views of Québec City, take the C$3.35 ferry (✉ 10 rue des Traversiers, ☎ 418/643–8420) for a minicruise across the St. Lawrence River to Lévis and back. Or for C$2.25, ride the Funiculaire du Vieux-Québec (✉ 16 rue Petit-Champlain, ☎ 418/692–1132), the sharply vertical railway that creaks along the cliff from Lower Town to Upper Town.

What to Read and Watch Before Your Trip

THE APPRENTICESHIP OF DUDDY KRAVITZ BY MORDECAI RICHLER

Duddy Kravitz is a scrappy kid, determined to fight his way out of the Jewish tenements of 1950s Montréal, and this novel is full of colorful characters and classic Montréal neighborhood institutions. The book covers much of the city, and expanses of Québec countryside, from the "cold-water flats" of rue St-Urbain, to the lakes of Québec's Laurentian region. A 1974 movie version stars Richard Dreyfus. Mordecai Richler's other popular novel, *Barney's Version,* is set in Montreal as well, and was adapted into a movie with Paul Giomatti and Rosamund Pike.

SWEET AFFLICTION BY ANNA LEVENTHAL

A series of interweaving, loosely connected stories make up this fresh, funny work of fiction, starring a youthful cast of characters quintessential to Montréal: members of the LGBTQ community, writers, artists, bohemians, and anarchists. Here you'll get slices of Montréal contemporary life, such as in "Moving Day": a story dedicated to Montréal's unique tradition and once-official law in the province, decreeing that any lease in Montréal must end on July 1st, Canada Day—thus forcing all of the city's residents to share the same moving day.

MÃN BY KIM THÚY

Like Thúy's first novel, *Ru, Mãn* is about the Vietnamese immigrant experience in Montréal: this time, with an intimate personal story centered largely around cooking and food. Aside from writing fiction, author Kim Thúy has been a lawyer, cookbook author, and restaurant owner, and her restaurant Ru de Nam was a longtime favorite Vietnamese eatery in Montréal. Ru de Nam is no longer open, but this novel is sure to get you excited about the other great choices in Montréal's Vietnamese dining scene—only some of the great international eating experiences the city has to offer.

THE ARMAND GAMACHE SERIES BY LOUISE PENNY

Chief Inspector Armand Gamache is the hero of Louise Penny's popular mystery crime series, about a provincial police chief solving crimes in the fictional Québec village of Three Pines. The author herself is a longtime resident of Québec's Eastern Townships, just outside Montréal, and bases this beloved series' setting on her own rustic life. Penny's books are a bountiful reading choice for the Québec traveler, as there are fifteen total installments in the series; including and, most recently, *A Better Man.*

THE PEOPLE'S HISTORY OF QUÉBEC BY JACQUES LACOURSIÈRE AND ROBIN PHILPOT

A concise, well-written account of Québec's long history, this book is great preparation before exploring the region. The book touches on the main lives and historical events in this province's rich and complicated past, spanning over 450 years of history: from early French explorers arriving to Gaspé Peninsula in the 14th century (and their dealings with the Iroquois, Cree, and other native groups), to the forming of a constitution, ongoing fights for sovereignty, and the creation of a modern society.

COCKROACH BY RAWI HAGE

Canadian author Rawi Hage's second novel is about a cynical, downtrodden man living in Montréal, who often feels—both (meta)physically and metaphorically—as if he is a cockroach. Hage, born in Beirut, introduces the reader to a community of Middle Eastern and European immigrants making life in their adopted city. The story is told through the narrator's dark wit and dry humor, as he struggles with hunger and poverty, desire and pain—and the long, unforgiving Montréal winter.

JESUS OF MONTRÉAL

Jesus of Montréal—along with *The Fall of the American Empire, The Decline of the American Empire,* and *Barbarian Invasions*—is just one of several great films from acclaimed Quebecois director Denys Arcand, who makes French-language movies that deal in smart social commentary and Montréal-area settings. In this film, a group of actors are hired by the Catholic Church to create a modernized "Passion of the Christ" play—and end up radicalizing themselves and the audience more than was intended.

LÉOLO

Touching and surreal, this French-Canadian film has plenty of fantasy and enjoyable strangeness (backed up by a Tom Waits' soundtrack), telling the story of a boy named Léolo as he comes of age in a very chaotic family. Based in Montréal's Mile End neighborhood, where Léolo's family lives, this critically acclaimed film is full of symbolism and spirituality, with some more realistic commentary on mental illness and familial relations.

THE SCORE

The plot formula in *The Score* will seem familiar: a lone wolf, a convincing rogue sidekick, the big, last job before getting out "for good"—but typical elements are pulled off well here, with plenty of action and entertainment. The target of this classic heist movie (starring Robert De Niro as a Montréal jazz club owner and grand thief) is a $4 million French sceptre stored in the basement of the Montréal Customs House, the most guarded building in Québec, according to the script.

Marlon Brando makes a great cameo as an old-time Montréal gangster, and Angela Bassett and Edward Norton complete the cast, in a fun picture with plenty of shots of Montréal's Downtown.

C.R.A.Z.Y.

Often considered one of the most popular Canadian films of all time, Jean Marc Vallée (director of *Dallas Buyer's Club* and *Wild*) directs this colorful drama, about a young homosexual man growing up in a conservative Catholic French Canadian family in the 1960s and 70s. This poignant coming-of-age tale is uniquely Quebecois—but the late 60s fashion and soundtrack strike a more universal note.

How to Speak Quebecois

Français, S'il Vous Plaît

Anytime you visit a foreign country, being familiar with the local language is sure to win you friends. Learn a few phrases, regardless of whether you pronounce them correctly, and the locals will appreciate it. More than 80% of Quebecers claim French as their mother tongue, and while many Quebecers are bilingual or know at least a little English, plenty more don't, especially outside Downtown Montréal and the less touristy areas of the province. Rest assured that you will come across more than a few unilingual Francophones.

As in France, accents and colloquialisms vary widely from region to region. Still, there are several commonly used, uniquely Quebecois words and expressions.

Everyday Terms

For starters, Montréal's impressive subway system is known as *le métro*. If you go around asking francophone Quebecers where the closest subway station is, you'll likely be greeted with a blank stare followed by a "*Je m'excuse, mais je ne parle pas l'anglais*" ("I'm sorry, but I don't speak any English"). Similarly, don't go looking for a "convenience store" when you need some last-minute item. Here, even Anglophones call them *dépanneurs*, or "deps" for short.

While here you'll probably spend a lot of time in the *centre-ville* (Downtown) checking out splendid sights like the *Palais de Justice* (not a palace at all, but a courthouse). Except in order to do so you're likely going to need some *argent* (money), or better, *un peu de cash*, which is *franglais* (a curious yet distinct local hybrid of French and English) for "a bit of money." And where will you be getting that money? Nowhere if you start asking people for the closest ATM. In Québec a bank machine is called a *guichet* (the *gui* pronounced like guitar, the *chet* like "shea").

Dining Out

Of course, many things in Québec, like the menus in most restaurants, will be in both French and English, but you'll impress the waitstaff if you order a *steak-frites avec un verre de vin rouge* when you want steak with French fries and a glass of red wine. Later, when you ask for *la facture* or *l'addition* (your bill), and your waiter inquires if you've enjoyed your meal, tell him it was *écoeurant* (the literal translation is disgusting, or nauseating, but it's akin to saying something is "sick" for great) and you'll likely see a big amused grin come over his face. It's the rare tourist who's in the know when it comes to Quebecois slang and/ or colloquialisms, so locals will certainly be impressed if they hear you coming out with the occasional *mon char* (my car) when talking about your wheels or, *ma blonde*, or *ma copine* (girlfriend), when introducing somebody to your female significant other. Conversely, if you're talking about a boyfriend, *mon chum,* or *mon copain,* is how the locals would say it.

Holy Swear Words

Almost all Quebecois swear words—aka *sacres*—come courtesy of the Catholic Church, so while the literal translation of words like *tabarnac* (tabernacle) or *câlice* (chalice) might seem pretty tame or nonsensical in English, here they're the equivalent of the dreaded F word.

Chapter 2

TRAVEL SMART MONTRÉAL AND QUEBÉC CITY

Updated by
Barbara Woolsey

2

POPULATION
Montreal: 1,700,000

Quebec City: 500,000

LANGUAGE
French

$ CURRENCY
Canadian dollar

AREA CODE
Quebec has nine area codes:
354, 367, 418, 438, 450, 514,
579, 581, 819, 873.

EMERGENCIES
911

DRIVING
On the left

ELECTRICITY
110-120V/60Hz; electrical
plugs have two flat prongs
and a round prong in a V

TIME
Same as New York

WEB RESOURCES
www.mtl.org/en

www.quebec-cite.com/en

www.mtlblog.com

What You Need to Know Before You Go

You know about poutine and Céline Dion—what else is there? Well, the Canadian province fascinates with a rich culture and history that's been earnestly preserved. Here's what you should know to make the most of your visit.

HISTORY = CONTEXT

The short version: After the English victory in 1759, the francophone people became a minority in the New World. During the 1960s Quiet Revolution, they resolved to uphold their unique culture or risk it being forgotten—defining Quebecois identity as separate from that of either English-speaking Canada or France. Quebecers are fiercely proud and protective of their traditions as a result. Remembering this helps to put a lack of English representation into perspective.

BRUSH UP ON YOUR FRENCH

For historical reasons, Québec is very conscious of retaining its language. According to law, French must be the predominant language on retail and road signs, and shop and restaurant employees must greet customers first in French. Particularly in rural areas, you may encounter people who speak little to no English—and in the capital city, locals might just simply be reluctant to. In Montréal, bilingualism is more common and most people will quickly switch to English for you. Nonetheless, attempting a few French phrases is appreciated by locals, and might make traveling easier.

THEY DON'T SPEAK FRENCH FRENCH

The French language spoken in Québec is a little different than the French you'll hear on the streets of France. Mostly it comes down to intonation and accent, but there are many uniquely Quebecois words and expressions, too. There are a few that could be helpful like "dépanneur" or "dep" for short: a neighborhood convenience store, or "cinq-à-sept" (also written out as "5-à-7"), which is what the locals call a happy hour.

TIPS ARE APPRECIATED

Servers earn minimum wage, so tips make all the difference. In Québec, tipping is generally 15%—the same amount as the local GST and QST taxes, which makes it easy to just quickly match whatever appears under that amount on your bill. Feel free to tip up to 20% for exceptional service; that would generally be the maximum. A 10% tip is usually customary for taxi drivers.

DOWNLOAD A RIDE-SHARING APP

Having Uber's or its Montréal-based competitor Eva's app on your smartphone will save you a little money and a lot of peace of mind. Montréal's subway only runs until 12:30 am on weekdays and 1:30 am on weekends; starting service again at 5:30 am daily, while Québec City busses and express shuttles always finish at midnight. Particularly in the capital, it might be helpful for those who might get stumped by French signs on public transport.

BRACE YOURSELF FOR BAD ROADS AND CONSTRUCTION

Québec's roads are in abominable shape. In 2018, it was estimated that over C$15 billion in repairs were necessary. The government is investing C$20 billion over the next few years, so all those cracks and potholes won't be disappearing anytime soon. Drive carefully, particularly in winter when weather and road conditions are even worse, and in spring when the snow starts melting. In summer, factor road closures and construction detours into itineraries.

NO TURNING RED IN MONTRÉAL

The Island of Montréal is the only place in North America, aside from New York City, where it's not permitted to turn right on a red light (unless otherwise indicated). Changing the law is still being debated in local government, but that won't save you from a fine of up to $200. The

SAAQ government website states that elsewhere in Québec, it's not mandatory to turn right on red—in fact, it's a driver's right not to. If you honk at someone for staying put, that can also rack up a $200 fine if unlucky!

DRINKING IN PUBLIC ISN'T ALWAYS ILLEGAL

Unlike elsewhere in Canada, you are allowed to drink alcohol in public in Québec—but not everywhere. The rule is you must be in a public park and consuming food at the same time so that the liquor is accompanying your meal. A bag of chips won't suffice; the law calls for a picnic-style spread and that you be sitting at a picnic table to do so. The latter caveat is laxer; as long as you're behaving respectfully, authorities will usually turn a blind eye.

GET OUTDOORS IN WINTER

Don't shy away from the chills, as some of Québec's finest joie de vivre happens at -30° Celsius (-22° Fahrenheit). There's skating on the St. Lawrence or at rinks, and festivals like the famed Carnaval de Québec or Igloofest, an electronic music party where guests sport neon snowsuits. Wonderful memories are to be made in the cold.

DRESS FOR THE ELEMENTS—AND COBBLESTONE

Loading up on layers is essential as you never know what Mother Nature's up to. Temperatures can start to plummet as early as October and linger on until March. Québec winter is notorious for gusty winds and icy sidewalks. Slipping and falling is a Montrealer's rite of passage, but can be avoided by a pair of sturdy shoes. Similarly, the cobblestone streets in historic areas can wreak havoc on high heels, so you may just be better off with flats.

THERE'S AN UNDERGROUND CITY

Montréal's mammoth underground city – known locally as the RÉSO – connects museums, universities, office towers, shopping plazas, hotels, and salons, while providing a welcome escape from the cold or heat and serving as a transport link for 500,000 people per day beneath the city's streets. As well as linking museums like the Place des Arts and the Musée d'art contemporain, the 20 miles of underground is an art network itself. Look for the Art Souterrain festival which showcases contemporary art every February or March in the corridors of Montréal's underground city.

QUÉBEC BEER IS BOOZIER

Québec beers are probably stronger than you're used to unless you're already a craft beer enthusiast. Local and regional microbreweries are known for producing brews with a considerably higher alcohol level, such as darker beers that make the cheeks rosy during winter. Typically, these local beers can be 6% and even rise into the double digits. Know your tipsy limit!

THE LEGAL DRINKING AGE IS 18

In Québec and one other Canadian province, Alberta, the drinking age is 18. That makes Québec a destination for partying, particularly for those who haven't had too much practice doing it yet. Of course, bars and nightclubs cater to different age demographics and crowds—do your research in case you aren't up for getting rowdy.

HAVE THE RIGHT DOCUMENTS

Those with non-U.S. citizenship will likely need to apply for an Electronic Travel Authorization (eTA) from the Canadian government's website. Nationalities which are not eligible for eTAs must apply for visas. Naturalized U.S. residents should carry their naturalization certificate and passport. Permanent residents who aren't citizens should carry their "green card." U.S. residents entering Canada from a third country must have a valid passport, naturalization certificate, or "green card."

Getting Here and Around

✈ Air Travel

Flying time (gate to gate) to Montréal is about 1½ hours from New York, 2½ hours from Chicago, 4 hours from Dallas, and 6 hours from Los Angeles. Flying time to Québec City is about 2 hours from New York, 3 hours from Chicago, 5 hours from Dallas, and 7 hours from Los Angeles.

Trudeau Airport offers self-serve check-in and boarding passes at electronic kiosks throughout the airport. Make sure you arrive at the airport two hours before your flight's scheduled departure.

Security measures at Canadian airports are similar to those in the United States.

AIRPORTS

For service to Montréal, Montréal–Pierre Elliott Trudeau International Airport is 20 km (12.5 miles) west of the city. Québec City's Jean Lesage International Airport is about 13 km (9 miles) northwest of Downtown. Both airports handle domestic and international flights.

GROUND TRANSPORTATION

In Montréal, a taxi from Trudeau International to Downtown costs C$40. All taxi companies must charge the same rate for travel between the airport and Downtown. Taking an Uber might be slightly cheaper.

The least expensive way to get from Trudeau International Airport into the city is to take the 747 Express Bus, operated by Société de transport de Montréal. Shuttles leave from Montréal Central Bus Station, which is connected to Berri–UQAM métro station. They run 24/7—from noon to midnight, they leave every 10 minutes or less while you may wait up to an hour in the early morning hours. The cost is C$10 one-way, payable by card from automated dispensers in the international arrivals area or on the bus in coins only (no bills). The ticket is valid for unlimited travel on the entire Montréal bus and métro system for a 24-hour period.

In Québec City, taxis are available immediately outside the airport exit near the baggage-claim area. A ride into the city costs a flat rate of C$35.10. Taxi Coop Québec is the largest taxi company in the city. You can also take an Uber; depending on the traffic it may save you a few dollars.

FLIGHTS

All the major U.S. airlines, including American, Delta, and United, serve Montréal and Québec City.

Regularly scheduled flights from the United States to Montréal and Québec City as well as flights within Canada are available on Air Canada and the regional airlines associated with it, including Air Canada Express (reservations are made through Air Canada). Porter Airlines also has connecting service to Montréal and Québec City from select U.S. cities, via Toronto's Billy Bishop Airport.

🚲 Bicycle Travel

Québec continues to expand its Route Verte (Green Route), North America's largest network of bike trails totaling over 5,000 km (more than 3,100 miles). Covering the southern half of the province, the bikeways link to Canadian provinces Ontario and New Brunswick, as well as New England and New York. For information and a route planner, head to Route Verte's website or contact Vélo Québec.

🚢 Boat and Ferry Travel

The Québec–Lévis ferry, which crosses the St. Lawrence River, gives you a magnificent panorama of Old Québec on its trips to and from Lévis. Although the crossing takes only 12 minutes, the waiting time can increase the trip to an hour. The cost is C$3.65. The first ferry from Québec City leaves weekdays at 6:20 am from the pier at rue Dalhousie, opposite Place Royale. Crossings run every half an hour during weekdays until 6:30 pm. It then runs hourly until 2:20 am. On weekends and holidays, the ferry leaves hourly from 6:30 am to 2:20 am. Schedules can change, so be sure to check the ferry website or call ahead.

🚌 Bus Travel

Several private bus lines serve the province. Orléans Express is probably the most convenient, as it offers regular service between Montréal and Québec City and its buses are clean and comfortable. The trip takes a little over three hours. Limocar, another bus line, serves the Eastern Townships, while Greyhound Lines provides interprovincial service. Megabus offers somewhat more luxurious service to the province of Ontario and the city of Buffalo.

Bus terminals in Montréal and Québec City offer service all week. In some small towns the bus station is simply a counter in a local gas station. In rural Québec it's a good idea to bring along a French–English dictionary, although merchants can handle a simple ticket sale in English.

Buses from Montréal to Québec City depart 17 times daily between 6 am and 11 pm. A one-way ticket booked at least a week in advance starts at C$25. All intercity bus lines servicing Montréal arrive at and depart from the city's downtown bus terminal, the Gare d'Autocars de Montréal, which is conveniently located next to the Berri-UQÀM métro station.

Many bus companies offer discounts if you book in advance, usually either 7 or 14 days ahead. Discounts are available for kids.

Most bus lines don't accept reservations for specific seats. You should plan on picking up your tickets at least 45 minutes before the bus's scheduled departure time.

🚗 Car Travel

Montréal is accessible from the rest of Canada via the Trans-Canada Highway, which crosses the southern part of the island as Autoroute 20, with Autoroute 720 leading into Downtown. From New York, take I–87 north until it becomes Autoroute 15 at the Canadian border; continue for another 47 km (29 miles) to the outskirts of Montréal. From I–91 through Massachusetts via New Hampshire and Vermont, you can take Route 55 to Autoroute 10.

■TIP→ At the border you must clear Canadian Customs, so be prepared with your passport and car registration. On holidays and during the peak summer season, expect to wait a half hour or more at the major crossings. Border wait times can be checked on the Transport Québec website.

Montréal and Québec City are linked by Autoroute 20 on the south shore of the St. Lawrence River and by Autoroute 40 on the north shore. On both highways, the ride between the two cities is about 240 km (149 miles) and takes about three hours.

Getting Here and Around

In Québec the road signs are in French, but the important ones have pictograms. Keep in mind the following terms: *centre-ville* (Downtown), *arrêt* (stop), *détenteurs de permis* (permit holders only), *gauche* (left), *droit* (right), *ouest* (west), and *est* (east).

Drivers must carry vehicle registration and proof of insurance coverage, which is compulsory in Canada. Québec drivers are covered by the Québec government no-fault insurance plan. Drivers from outside Québec can obtain a Canadian Non-Resident Inter-Provincial Motor Vehicle Liability Insurance Card, available from any U.S. insurance company, as evidence of financial responsibility in Canada. The minimum liability in Québec is C$50,000. If you are driving a car that isn't registered in your name, carry a letter from the owner that authorizes your use of the vehicle.

PARKING

Expect on-street parking in Montréal to be hard to find; your best bet is to leave the car at your hotel garage and take public transportation or a cab. If you must drive, ask your concierge to recommend a garage near your destination. Be extra careful where you park if it snows, to avoid getting towed. Parking in Québec City is much less stressful, although it's also advisable to leave the car at the hotel and walk—especially if you're heading to Vieux-Québec.

The narrow streets of the Old City leave few two-hour metered parking spaces available. Nevertheless, several parking garages at central locations charge about C$12 a day on weekdays or C$7 for 12 hours on weekends. Main garages are at Hôtel de Ville (City Hall), Place d'Youville, Edifice Marie-Guyart, Place Québec, Château Frontenac, rue St-Paul, and the Old Port.

ROAD CONDITIONS

In Montréal and Québec City the jumble of bicycle riders, delivery vehicles, taxis, and municipal buses can be chaotic. In the countryside at night, roads are lighted at exit points from major highways but are otherwise dark. Roads in the province aren't very good, especially during the spring pothole season—be prepared for some spine-jolting bumps and potholes, and check tire pressure once in a while.

In winter, Montréal streets are kept mostly clear of snow and ice, but outside the city the situation can deteriorate. Locals are notorious for exceeding the speed limit, so keep an eye on your mirrors. For up-to-date reports on road conditions throughout the province, go to Transport Québec's website.

ROADSIDE EMERGENCIES

Dial 911 in an emergency. Contact CAA, the Canadian Automobile Association, in the event of a flat tire, dead battery, empty gas tank, or other car-related mishap. Automobile Association of America membership includes CAA service.

RULES OF THE ROAD

By law, you're required to wear seat belts even in the backseat. Infant seats also are required. Radar-detection devices are illegal in Québec; just having one in your car is punishable by fine. Speed limits, given in kilometers, are usually within the 90 kph–100 kph (50 mph–60 mph) range outside the cities.

Right turns on a red light are allowed in most of the province, the island of Montréal being the notable exception, where they're prohibited. Driving with a blood-alcohol content of 0.08% or higher is illegal and can earn you a stiff fine and jail time. Headlights are compulsory in inclement weather. Drivers aren't permitted to use handheld cell phones. The laws here are similar to the rest of North America.

CAR RENTAL

Rates in Montréal start from about C$20 a day for an economy car with air-conditioning and unlimited kilometers. If you prefer a manual-transmission car, check whether the rental agency offers stick shifts; many agencies in Canada don't.

You must be at least 21 years old to rent a car in Québec, and some car-rental agencies don't rent to drivers under 25. Most rental companies don't allow you to drive on gravel roads. Child seats are compulsory for children ages five and under.

Rentals at the airports near Québec City and Montréal are usually more expensive than neighborhood rentals.

🚆 Train Travel

Amtrak offers its daily Adirondak service from New York City's Penn Station to Montréal, although the train sometimes arrives too late to make any connecting trains that evening. Connections are available, often the next day, to Canadian rail line VIA Rail's Canadian routes. The ride takes up to 11 hours, and one-way tickets start at C$92.

VIA Rail trains run from Montréal to Québec City in three hours, arriving at the 19th-century Gare du Palais in Lower Town. Trains on the Montréal—Québec City route run five times daily on weekdays, three to four times daily on weekends. Tickets can be purchased in advance at the station prior to departure or on the VIA Rail website. If you're lucky you can sometimes find discounted fares online for as little as C$37. They are usually nonrefundable.

Business class tickets start at C$104 each way and include early boarding, seat selection, and a three-course meal with wine.

To save money, look into rail passes. But be aware that if you don't plan to cover many miles, you may come out ahead by buying individual tickets. Senior citizens (60 and older), children (11 and under), and students are often entitled to discounts.

The Train de Charlevoix train system takes you from Québec City to Baie-St-Paul and stops in between, priced at C$88 round-trip. From Baie St-Paul, one can go on to La Malbaie, Charlevoix for C$54 round-trip. The small villages and the natural beauty along the route are impressive.

Essentials

Activities

BASEBALL

There is currently one major league baseball team in Canada, the Toronto Blue Jays, founded in 1977. Canada's first major league team, the Montréal Expos, formed in 1969, relocated to Washington, D.C., in 2005. There are proposals to bring the Expos back to Montréal, even part-time, but in the meantime, baseball fans can take in a Capitales game at Québec's Canac stadium. Games are affordable and lively and the stadium, built in 1939, is set in the middle of the city and has trees that are over 200 years old in the outfield. There's also an inflatable dome, affordable concessions, and nice views. ⊕ *capitalesdequebec.com*

BIKING

Weather permitting, one of the best ways to discover Montréal is on a bicycle. This is an incredibly bike-friendly metropolis, and there are thousands of designated bike paths connecting diverse neighborhoods across the island, running along the river, and through parks and forests. The most popular cycling trail on the island begins at the Old Port and winds its way to the shores of Lac St-Louis in Lachine. Pack a picnic lunch; there are plenty of green spaces where you can stop and refuel along the way. If you like to bike but would rather not do it on city streets, ferries at the Old Port can take you to Île Ste-Hélène and the south shore of the St. Lawrence River, where riders can connect to hundreds of miles of trails in the Montérégie region.

HIKING

Canada's second-largest province is packed with hiking trails revealing nature's splendor. The Eastern Townships has a good mix of paths for all fitness levels, including over mountain landscapes with campsites or inns along the way. National parks like La Mauricie and Forillon offer more challenging, remote treks while the Magdalen Islands are perfect for those seeking short and scenic routes.

GOLF

Montréal golf enthusiasts have several excellent golf courses available to them, many less than a half-hour drive from Downtown. If you're willing to trek a bit farther (about 45 minutes), you'll find some of the best golfing in the province. For a complete listing of the many golf courses in the area, Tourisme Québec (⊕ *www.bonjourquebec.com*) is the best place to start.

HOCKEY

Ice hockey is nothing short of an institution in Montréal, the city that arguably gave birth to the sport back in the late 19th century. Although variations of the game are said to have been played in other U.S. and Canadian cities as early as 1800, the first organized game of modern hockey was played in Montréal in 1875, and the first official team, the McGill University Hockey Club, was founded in Montréal in 1880. The city's beloved Montréal Canadiens ⊕ *canadiens.nhl.com* is the oldest club in the National Hockey League and, as Montrealers are keen to tell you, one of the most successful teams in North American sports history. Tickets tend to sell out well before the game—especially if the Habs, as they're nicknamed, play their arch rivals, the Toronto Maple Leafs. You can buy tickets on the NHL website starting from C$54 or show up to the Bell Centre on game day, when scalpers usually drop stubs to half price after the puck drops. During playoffs, the city sets up a massive tailgate party called Fan Jam.

SKIING AND SNOWBOARDING

There are pros and cons to skiing in the Eastern Townships and the Laurentians. The slopes in the Townships are generally steeper and slightly more challenging, but it requires more time to get out to them. Also, the Townships' centers tend to be quieter and more family-oriented, so if it's après-ski action you're looking for, you might prefer heading out to a Laurentian hill like Mont St-Sauveur where, for many, partying is as much the experience as is conquering the slopes.

Skiing makes for a great day trip from either Montréal or Québec City. Near Montréal, is Ski Bromont, a year-round resort with runs for different experience levels, and Mont Saint-Saveur, offering night skiing. As for cross-country skiing, you needn't even leave the city to find choice locations to pursue the sport. There's a network of winding trails stretching throughout Parc du Mont-Royal, and the Lachine Canal offers a 12-km (7-mile) stretch of relatively flat terrain, making for both a scenic and relatively simple cross-country excursion. There are pros and cons to skiing in the Eastern Townships and the Laurentians. The slopes in the Townships are generally steeper and slightly more challenging, but it requires more time to get out to them. Also, the Townships' centers tend to be quieter and more family-oriented, so if it's après-ski action you're looking for, you might prefer heading out to a Laurentian hill like Mont St-Sauveur where, for many, partying is as much the experience as is conquering the slopes.

Québec City has several lodges only an hour's drive or less from Old Québec. Le Relais and Le Massif de Charlevoix are popular with locals, particularly families, while Stoneham Mountain Resort features challenging freestyle runs and outdoor hot tubs for a soothing après-ski.

SWIMMING

Most of the city's municipal outdoor pools are open from mid-June through August. Admission is free on weekdays. On weekends and holidays there's a small fee of no more than C$4 at some pools, depending on the borough. The city's man-made beach, Parc-Plage l'Île Notre-Dame, on the west side of Île Notre-Dame probably has the cleanest water (tested and monitored) in Montréal.

Accommodations

In Montréal and Québec City you have a choice of luxury hotels, moderately priced modern properties, and small older hotels with fewer conveniences but sometimes more charm. Options in small towns and in the country include large, full-service resorts; small, privately owned hotels; roadside motels; and bed-and-breakfasts. Even outside the cities it's a good idea to make reservations.

Expect accommodations to cost more in summer than in the colder months (except for places such as ski resorts, where winter is high season). When making reservations, ask about special deals and packages. Big-city hotels that cater to business travelers often offer weekend packages, and many city hotels offer rooms at up to 50% off in winter. If you're planning to visit Montréal or Québec City or a resort area in high season, book well in advance. Also be aware of any special events or festivals that may coincide with your visit and fill every room for miles around.

APARTMENT AND HOUSE RENTALS

Airbnb (⊕ *www.montrealgazette.com*) has a wide selection of cabins and chalets for rent.

Essentials

BED-AND-BREAKFASTS

B&Bs, which are also known as *gîtes* in Québec, can be found in both the country and the cities. For assistance in booking these, be sure to check out B&B websites (⊕ *www.gitesetaubergesdupassant.com* and ⊕ *www.bedandbreakfast.com* are good resources for B&Bs throughout the province). Room quality varies from house to house as well, so ask to see a few rooms before making a choice.

The nonprofit organization Association de l'Agrotourisme et du Tourisme Gourmand du Québec has extensive listings of B&Bs, both urban and rural, as well as farms that take paying guests.

HOTELS

Canada doesn't have a national rating system for hotels, but Québec's tourism ministry rates the province's hotels and bed-and-breakfasts; the stars are more a reflection of the number of facilities and amenities than of the hotel's performance. Hotels are rated zero to three stars (B&Bs, zero to four suns), with zero stars or suns representing minimal comfort and few services and three stars or four suns being the very best. All hotels listed have private baths unless otherwise noted.

Montréal is always hosting a festival or an international convention, so the hotels are consistently booked. This takes visitors by surprise. Many of the quaint auberges have a small number of rooms, so they fill up fast. It's necessary to book months ahead for the Grand Prix, the Jazz Festival, the World Film Festival, and all holiday weekends.

⊗ Customs and Duties

U.S. Customs and Immigration has preclearance services at **Pierre Elliott Trudeau International Airport,** which serves Montréal. This allows U.S.-bound air passengers to depart their airplane directly on arrival at their U.S. destination without further inspection and delays.

American visitors may bring in, duty-free, for personal consumption, 200 cigarettes, 50 cigars, 7 ounces of tobacco, and 1 bottle (1.5 liters or 40 imperial ounces) of wine or liquor respectively or up to 8.5 liters of beer or ale. Any alcohol and tobacco products in excess of these amounts are subject to duty, provincial fees, and taxes. You can also bring in gifts for friends or family duty-free, as long as each gift does not exceed C$60 in value.

Cats and dogs must have a certificate issued by a licensed veterinarian that clearly identifies the animal and vouches that it has been vaccinated against rabies during the preceding 36 months. Certificates aren't necessary for Seeing Eye dogs. Plant material must be declared and inspected. There may be restrictions on some live plants, bulbs, and seeds. You may bring food for your own use, as long as the quantity is consistent with the duration of your visit and restrictions or prohibitions on some fruits and vegetables are observed.

Canada's firearms laws are significantly stricter than those in much of the United States. All handguns and semiautomatic and fully automatic weapons are prohibited and cannot be brought into the country. Sporting rifles and shotguns may be imported provided they are to be used for sporting, hunting, or competing while in Canada. All firearms must be declared to Canada Customs at the first point of entry. Failure to declare firearms will result in their seizure, and criminal charges may be made. Regulations require visitors to have a confirmed Firearms Declaration to bring any guns into Canada; a fee of C$25 applies, valid for 60 days but good for one year if renewed before it expires. For more information, contact the Canadian Firearms Centre.

⊕ Emergencies

All embassies are in Ottawa. The U.S. consulate in Montréal is open weekdays 7:30 am–5 pm, while in Québec City it's open weekdays 9 am–4 pm. The U.S. Consulate maintains a list of medical specialists in the Montréal area.

In Montréal, the main English-language hospital is the Montréal General Hospital (McGill University Health Centre). Many pharmacies in Montréal stay open until midnight, including Jean Coutu and Pharmaprix stores. Some are open around the clock, including the Pharmaprix on chemin de la Côte-des-Neiges.

In Québec City, the Centre Hospitalier Universitaire de Québec is the city's largest institution and incorporates the teaching hospitals Pavillon CHUL in Ste-Foy and Pavillon Hôtel-Dieu, the main hospital in Vieux-Québec. Most outlets of the big pharmacy chains in the region (including Jean Coutu, Brunet and Uniprix) are open every day and offer free delivery.

🍴 Dining

French-Canadian fast food follows the same concept as American fast food, though barbecue chicken is also popular. Local chains to watch for include St-Hubert, which serves rotisserie chicken; Chez Cora, which specializes in breakfasts; and La Belle Province, Lafleur, and Valentine, all of which serve hamburgers,

hot dogs, and fries. For a vegetarian option, try the excellent Montréal chain Resto Végo.

Many restaurants post their *menu du jour* outside, so you can stroll along and let your cravings guide the way. Nevertheless, bear in mind that reservations are a must at most restaurants during holidays, Winter Carnival, and in the summer months, when the coveted outdoor terraces open. The *table d'hôte*, a cost-cutting special, is a regular at many Montréal restaurants. Upscale restaurants serve elaborate lunch tables d'hôte at reduced prices.

WINES, BEER, AND SPIRITS

Some of the best local microbreweries include Unibroue (Fin du Monde, U Blonde, U Rousse), Brasseurs du Nord (Boréale), and McAuslan (Griffon, St. Ambroise). The local hard cider P.O.M. is also excellent. Caribou, a traditional concoction made from red wine, vodka (or some other liquor), spices, and, usually, maple syrup, is available at many winter events and festivals throughout the province, such as Québec City's winter carnival. Small bars may also offer the drink in season.

The province's liquor purveyor, SAQ, stocks a wide choice of wines (with a heavy emphasis on those from France) and is also the only place you can buy hard liquor; most SAQ stores are open regular business hours. Supermarkets and convenience stores carry lower-end wines at notably higher prices but they can sell wine and beer until 11 pm all week (long after SAQ stores have closed). The minimum legal age for alcohol consumption is 18.

In Québec, it is illegal to drink alcohol in public with one key exception: in public parks, when consumed with food as part of a meal.

Essentials

Holidays

Canadian national holidays are as follows: New Year's Day (January 1), Good Friday (late March or early April), Easter Monday (the Monday following Good Friday), Victoria Day (called Fête des Patriotes in Québec; late May), Canada Day (July 1), Labor Day (early September), Thanksgiving (mid-October), Remembrance Day (November 11), Christmas, and Boxing Day (December 26). St. Jean Baptiste Day (June 24) is a provincial holiday.

Money

Throughout this book, prices are given in Canadian dollars, which at this writing are worth roughly 75¢ to the American dollar. The price of a cup of coffee ranges from C$2.50 or more, depending on how upscale or downscale the place is; beer costs C$3 to C$7 in a bar; a smoked-meat sandwich costs about C$8 to C$10; and museum admission can cost anywhere from nothing to C$20.

Prices throughout this guide are given for adults. Substantially reduced fees are almost always available for children, students, and senior citizens.

CURRENCY AND EXCHANGE

U.S. dollars are sometimes accepted in Canada, especially in communities near the border. Major U.S. credit cards are accepted in most areas.

The units of currency in Canada are the Canadian dollar (C$) and the cent, in almost the same denominations as U.S. currency ($5, $10, $20, 5¢, 10¢, 25¢, etc.). The exception is 1¢ coins, which are no longer minted and circulated, so expect to pay and receive change rounded up or down by 5¢ accordingly. The $1 and $2 bill are also no longer used in Canada; they have been replaced by $1 and $2 coins (known as "loonies," because of the loon that appears on the coin, and "toonies," respectively).

At this writing, the exchange rate is US$1 to C1.3375¢.

Bank cards are widely accepted in Québec and throughout Canada. There are many branches of Québec's financial cooperative, La Caisse populaire Desjardins (a "Caisse Pop" as it's locally referred to), as well as bank machines (ATMs), throughout the region.

Nightlife

If nightlife in Montréal could be distilled into a cocktail, it would be one part sophisticated New York club scene (with the accompanying pretension), one part Parisian joie-de-vivre (and, again, a dash of snobbery), and one part Barcelonan stamina (which keeps the clubs booming until dawn). Montréal's nightlife swings with a robust passion. From the early evening "5-à-7" after-work cocktail circuit, to the slightly later concerts and supper clubs (restaurant–dance club hybrids where people dance on the tables after eating off them), on into the even later dance club scene, all tastes, cultural backgrounds, and legal ages join the melee. Clubbing is, to say the least, huge in Montréal. Some restaurants are even installing discotheques in their basements.

Québec City has a variety of cultural institutions for a town of its size, from the symphony to small theater companies. To sample the nightlife, you'll need to head to the clubs and cafés of rue St-Jean, avenue Cartier, and Grande-Allée, as well as Lower Town. Most bars and clubs stay open until 3 am.

Packing

If you're visiting Montréal anytime between November and May, be sure to bring some warm clothes, or be prepared to purchase some while you're here. Come winter Montréal gets cold—very cold—with temperatures almost always dipping below the freezing mark from December until late March. A good winter coat, scarf, hat (locally called a "tuque"), gloves, and warm winter boots are pretty much a necessity in Québec if you want to be comfortable going outside in the winter months. In summer, however, temperatures regularly rise above 86°F (30°C) and Downtown Montréal in particular can get very humid, so bring a few pairs of shorts, sandals, and warm weather clothes.

Passports and Visas

All travelers will need a passport or other accepted secure documents to enter or reenter the United States. Naturalized U.S. residents should carry their naturalization certificate. Permanent residents who aren't citizens should carry their "green card." U.S. residents entering Canada from a third country must have a valid passport, naturalization certificate, or "green card."

⚠ All American visitors require an Electronic Travel Authorization (eTA) if arriving by plane (an eTA is not necessary if arriving by land or sea).

Safety

Montrealers are keen to boast they can walk the streets of their city at any time of day or night without fear of incident. And although both Montréal and Québec City are among the safest cities in North America, travelers should nevertheless be on their guard for pickpockets and other petty criminals, especially when traveling on Montréal's often-crowded métro system.

Taxes

A goods and services tax (GST or TPS in Québec) of 5% applies on virtually every transaction in Canada except for the purchase of basic groceries. In addition to imposing the GST, Québec levies a provincial sales tax of 9.975% on most goods and services as well.

Departing passengers in Montréal pay a C$30, plus tax, airport-improvement fee that's included in the cost of an airline ticket.

Time

Montréal and Québec City are both in the eastern standard time zone. Los Angeles is three hours behind local time and Chicago is one hour behind.

Tipping

Tips and service charges aren't usually added to a bill in Canada. In general, tip at least 15% of the total bill. This goes for waiters and waitresses, barbers and hairdressers, and taxi drivers. Porters and doormen should get about C$2 a bag. For maid service, leave at least C$2 per person a day (C$3 to C$5 in luxury hotels).

Essentials

Tours

DAY TOURS AND GUIDES

In Montréal, from May through October, Bateau-Mouche runs four harbor excursions and an evening supper cruise daily. The boats are reminiscent of the ones that cruise the canals of the Netherlands—wide-beamed and low-slung, with a glassed-in passenger deck. Boats leave from the Jacques Cartier Pier at the foot of Place Jacques-Cartier in the Vieux-Port.

Gray Line has nine different types of tours of Montréal from June through October and one tour the rest of the year. There are also day trips to Mont Tremblant and Québec City. The company offers pickup service at the major hotels and at Centre Infotouriste (✉ *1001 Dorchester Square*).

In Québec City, Autocar Dupont/Old Québec Tours runs bus tours of the city, departing across the square from the Hôtel Château Laurier (✉ *1230 pl. Georges V*); you can buy tickets at most major hotels. The company runs guided tours in a minibus as well as tours of Côte-de-Beaupré and Île d'Orléans, and whale-watching excursions to Charlevoix. Tours run year-round and cost C$36–C$140. Call for a reservation and the company will pick you up at your hotel.

Croisières AML has day and evening cruises, some of which include dinner, on the St. Lawrence River aboard the MV *Louis-Jolliet*. The 1½- to 4-hour cruises run from May through mid-October and start at C$35 plus tax.

Visitor Information

In Montréal, Centre Infotouriste, on Dorchester Square, has extensive tourist information on Montréal and the rest of the province of Québec, as well as a currency-exchange service and Internet café. It's open from 9 am to 6 pm daily. The Vieux-Montréal branch is open 9–7 in high season, and 10–6 in low season.

In Québec City, the Québec City Region Tourism and Convention Bureau's visitor information center in Montcalm is open June 21–to August 31, daily 9–7; September through October, daily 9–6; and November 1–June 20, daily 9–5. A mobile information service operates between mid-June and September 7 (look for the mopeds marked with a big question mark).

The Québec government tourism department, Tourisme Québec, has a center open September–June 20, daily 9–5; and June 21–August 31, daily 8:30–7. Tourisme Québec can provide information on specific towns' tourist bureaus.

Montréal and Québec City's Best Festivals

JANUARY AND FEBRUARY
Carnaval de Québec (*Québec Winter Carnival*). The biggest winter carnival in the world takes place on the Plains of Abraham over three weekends from the end of January to mid-February, with winter sports competitions, ice-sculpture contests, and parades. ⊠ *Parc de la Francophonie, Québec City* ☎ *866/422-7628* ⊕ *www.carnaval.qc.ca.*

Fête des Neiges de Montréal. Over four weekends from mid-January to mid-February, Montréal celebrates its winter festival at Parc Jean Drapeau across the Port from Old Montréal. Hockey games, tubing, skiing, dog sledding, and a Himalayan zipline are perfect activities to enjoy in the cold winter weather, but don't forget your toque, pronounced *took* with long Os. ⊠ *Montréal* ☎ *514/872–6120* ⊕ *www.parcjeandrapeau.com/events/fete-des-neiges-de-montreal* Ⓜ *Jean-Drapeau.*

Montréal en Lumière (*Montréal Highlights*). This festival brightens the bleak days of February with fabulous food and cultural activities. Leading chefs from around the world give demonstrations and take over the kitchens of top restaurants for special dinners. "Nuit Blanche," held on the last Saturday of this festival, lets you explore the city until the wee hours of the morning. Many of the events are free, and there are shuttle services to take you to the locations. Dress extra warmly. ☎ *514/288–9955, 855/864–3737* ⊕ *www.montrealenlumiere.com.*

MARCH
Art Souterrain. Art Souterrain offers an annual free exhibition of contemporary art in an unlikely place: the public corridors of Montréal's Underground City. The ingenious location puts art in front of a prospective daily audience of the nearly 500,000 people that walk beneath Downtown Montréal through vast corridors that connect office towers, shopping centers, hotels, convention halls, universities, restaurants, museums and performing arts venues. Along over three miles linking the Complexe Guy Favreau to the 1000 de la Gauchetière (as well as nine additional satellite venues aboveground), Art Souterrain exhibits 70 contemporary works in various mediums (sculpture, performance, photography, video, audio, painting), all tied together by a theme that addresses a modern-day social issue. ⊠ *RÉSO Underground City, Montréal* ☎ *800/565-5068* ⊕ *artsouterrain.com.*

APRIL
The **Blue Metropolis Montréal International Literary Festival** (⊕ *www.bleumetropolis.org*) presents more than 200 writers for readings and discussions in English, French, and other languages.

Blue Met (Metropolis Bleu) Festival. Taking place in late April/early May, this multicultural literary festival presents more than 200 reading, writing, and discussion workshops in English, French, Spanish, Portugese, and other languages. ⊠ *Montréal* ☎ *514/932–1112* ⊕ *bluemetropolis.org.*

MAY
Féria de Vélo de Montréal (*Montréal Bike Festival*) The biggest bike celebration in North America includes the **Tour la Nuit**, a 22-kilometer (14-mile) nighttime ride through the city. The weeklong festival culminates in as many as 50,000 cyclists taking over the streets for the **Tour de l'Île**, a 50-km (31-mile) ride along a route encircling Montréal. ⊠ *Montréal* ☎ *514/521–8356, 800/567–8356* ⊕ *www.velo.qc.ca/en/govelo/Go-bike-Montreal-festival.*

JUNE
Fringe Festival. Open to playwrights, acting troupes, dancers, comics, and musicians, the Fringe Festival, during

Montréal and Québec City's Best Festivals

the first three weeks of June, is run on a lottery system to determine which performers get onstage. ☎ 514/849–3378 ⊕ www.montrealfringe.ca.

Les FrancoFolies de Montréal. Such major Quebecois stars as Isabelle Boulay, Les soeurs Boulay, Coeur de Pirate, Paul Piché, and Nicola Ciccone play to packed concert halls, while lesser-known artists play free outdoor concerts during this mid-June festival celebrating the art of French songwriting. More than 1,000 musicians, many from France, Belgium, Senegal, and Haiti, perform rock, hip-hop, jazz, funk, and Latin. ☎ 514/876–8989, 855/372–6267 ⊕ www.francofolies.com.

Mondiale de la Bière. In Montréal, for five days every June, this beer festival transforms the exhibition hall of Palais des Congrès into a giant indoor beer garden serving some 600 ales, lagers, and ciders from nearly 100 microbreweries from Québec and around the world. Admission is free, tasting coupons are $1 each. ☎ 514/722–9640 ⊕ www.festivalmondial-biere.qc.ca/en/.

JULY

Festival d'Été de Québec (*Québec City Summer Festival*). This exuberant 11-day music extravaganza in Québec City features rock, folk, hip-hop, and world-beat music. The main concerts rock nightly with 10 indoor and outdoor stages in early July in or near Old Québec, including one on the Plains of Abraham. ☎ 418/529–5200, 888/992–5200 ⊕ www.infofestival.com.

Festival International de Jazz de Montréal (*Montréal International Jazz Festival*). This major event, now in its 41st year, attracts more than 1,000 musicians for more than 400 concerts held over a period of nearly two weeks from the end of June through the beginning of July. Past stars have included B.B. King, Ella Fitzgerald, Lauryn Hill, Wynton Marsalis, Chick Corea, Dave Brubeck, and Canada's most famed singer-pianist, Diana Krall. You can also hear blues, Latin rhythms, gospel, Cajun, and world music. ☎ 514/871–1881, 855/299–3378 ⊕ www.montrealjazzfest.com/en.

Festival International Nuits d'Afrique. From France to Jamaica to Cabo Verde, from traditional to contemporary sounds, this eclectic two-week music and dance festival brings together over 700 artists from 30 countries, for the biggest world music gathering in the Americas. At the outdoor stages in the Quartier des Spectacles, you'll find an appealing selection of pop-up restaurants and bars, a family area, open-air workshops with master dancers and drummers, and a Timbuktu market. ✉ Montréal ☎ 514/499-9239 ⊕ www.festivalnuitsdafrique.com/en/.

Festival OFF. A sidekick of the Festival d'Été International de Québec, this music event takes to the stage in July at the same time as its big brother. Most of the shows are free and take place in offbeat spaces such as in front of Église St-Jean-Baptiste, Bar Le Sacrilège, and the Musée de l'Amérique Française, just to name a few. ☎ 418/529–5200, 888/992–5200 ⊕ www.quebecoff.org.

Juste pour Rire (*Just for Laughs*). Montréal's world-famous comedy festival hosts international comics, in French and English, from the second through third weeks of July. There are tons of shows to watch, from big concert halls to quaint bars. Walk around the Quartier des Spectacles during the festival and giggle your way from one outdoor act to another. The twins parade is not to be missed. ☎ 514/845–2322 ⊕ www.hahaha.com.

L'International des Feux Loto-Québec (*International Fireworks Competition*). Join the thousands heading to Montréal's Jacques Cartier Bridge or the Old Port to watch the free fireworks show most Wednesday and Saturday nights in late June and July. The launch site for this high-in-the-sky show, set off by competing international teams, is La Ronde, on Île Ste-Hélène. ☎ 514/397–2000 ⊕ www.laronde.com/fr/larondefr/linternational-des-feux/accueil.

AUGUST

Festival International des Films du Monde (*World Film Festival*). For several days in Montréal from late August to early September, this festival presents about 400 films from all over the world, including feature films, documentaries, shorts, animation, and student productions. During the festival, Cinema Under the Stars, in the Quartier des Spectacles, screens foreign films outdoors. Go early to grab a seat or bring your own blanket. ☎ 514/848–3883 ⊕ www.ffm-montreal.org.

Fêtes de la Nouvelle France (*New France Festival*). During this five-day festival, in early to mid-August, Québec City's centuries-old heritage comes alive. The streets of Lower Town are transported back in time, and events range from an old-time farmers' market to games and music—all done in period costume. ☎ 418/694–3311 ⊕ www.nouvellefrance.qc.ca/en/.

St-Jean-sur-Richelieu's Hot-Air Balloon Festival (*International des Montgolfières St-Jean-sur-Richelieu*). This colorful airborne event, the largest gathering of hot-air balloons in Canada, takes flight about 25 minutes' drive southeast of Montréal. The balloons are so vivid and plentiful that you can sometimes see them from Downtown. ☎ 450/346–6000 ⊕ www.ballooncanada.com.

OCTOBER

Black and Blue Festival. Organized by the Bad Boy Club Montréal, this festival started more than 25 years ago as a gay community fundraiser for AIDS charities. It has grown to be a gay and gay-friendly week (in mid-October) of intense partying, featuring soirées like the Leather Ball, the Military Ball, and the Black and Blue Ball. ☎ 514/875–7026 ⊕ www.bbcm.org.

Festival of Colors. Farmers' markets, arts-and-crafts fairs, and weekend hikes are part of this festival, which celebrates the fall throughout Québec. If you head to a ski resort you can get a bird's-eye view of the splendid and vibrant red, orange, and yellow foliage from the chairlifts.

NOVEMBER AND DECEMBER

Marché de Noël allemand de Québec (*German Christmas Market of Québec City*) In the large plaza fronting city hall, as well as the little park across the street, neat rows of darling little wooden huts exactly like those you'd find in Germany proffer stollen, steaming hot pretzels, gingerbread, mulled wine, roasted chestnuts, and other aromatic foods, while jewelry designers, wood sculptors, glassmakers, and other artisans chat animatedly with customers, as German Christmas carols play in the background. If you can't get to Europe for the holidays, Québec City's German Christmas market is probably the most magical and most authentic you'll find in North America. The market opens in the third week of November and lasts until Decembr 23rd. ⊕ www.noelallemandquebec.com/en.

2

Travel Smart Montréal and Québec City MONTRÉAL AND QUÉBEC CITY'S BEST FESTIVALS

48

Helpful French Phrases

BASICS

Hello	Bonjour	bohn- zhoor
Yes/No	Oui/non	wee/nohn
Please	S'il vous plaît	seel voo play
Thank you	Merci	mair- see
You're welcome	De rien	deh ree- ehn
I'm Sorry (apology)	Pardon	pahr- don
Good morning	Bonjour	bohn- zhoor
Good evening	Bonsoir	bohn- swahr
Goodbye	Au revoir	o ruh- vwah
Mr. (Sir)	Monsieur	muh- syuh
Mrs.	Madame	ma- dam
Miss	Mademoiselle	mad-mwa- ze
Pleased to meet you	Enchanté(e)	ohn-shahn- tay
How are you?	Comment allez-vous?	kuh-mahn- tahl-ay voo

NUMBERS

one-half	un demi	uhn de-mee
one	un	uhn
two	deux	deuh
three	trois	twah
four	quatre	kaht-ruh
five	cinq	sank
six	six	seess
seven	sept	set
eight	huit	wheat
nine	neuf	nuf
ten	dix	deess
eleven	onze	ohnz
twelve	douze	dooz
thirteen	treize	trehz
fourteen	quartorze	kah-torz
fifteen	quinze	kanz
sixteen	seize	sez
seventeen	dix-sept	deez-set
eighteen	dix-huit	deez-wheat
nineteen	dix-neuf	deez-nuf
twenty	vingt	vehn
twenty-one	vingt-et-un	vehnt-ay-uhn
thirty	trente	trahnt
forty	quarante	ka-rahnt
fifty	cinquante	sang-kahnt
sixty	soixante	swa-sahnt
seventy	soixante-dix	swa-sahnt-deess
eighty	quante-vingts	kaht-ruh-vehn
ninety	quatre-vingts-dix	kaht-ruh-vehn-deess
one hundred	cent	sahn
one thousand	mille	meel
one million	million	meel-ion

COLORS

black	noir	nwahr
blue	bleu	bleuh
brown	brun	bruhn
green	vert	vair
orange	orange	o-rahnj
red	rouge	rouge
white	blanc	blahnk
yellow	jaune	zhone

DAYS OF THE WEEK

Sunday	Dimanche	dee-mahnsh
Monday	Lundi	luhn-dee
Tuesday	Mardi	mahr-dee
Wednesday	Mercredi	mair-kruh-dee
Thursday	Jeudi	zhuh-dee
Friday	Vendredi	vawn-druh-dee
Saturday	Samedi	sahm-dee

MONTHS

January	Janvier	zhahn-vee-ay
February	Février	feh-vree-ay
March	Mars	marce
April	Avril	a-vreel
May	Mai	meh
June	Juin	zhwehn
July	Juillet	zhwee-ay
August	Août	ah-oo
September	Septembre	sep-tahm-bruh
October	Octobre	oc-to-bruh
November	Novembre	no-vahm-bruh
December	Décembre	day-sahm-bruh

USEFUL WORDS AND PHRASES

Do you speak English?	Parlez-vous anglais?	par-lay voo ahn-glay
I don't speak [Language].	Je ne parle pas . . .	zhuh nuh parl pah
I don't understand	Je ne comprends pas.	zhuh nuh kohm-prahn pah
I don't know.	Je ne sais pas.	zhuh nnuh say pah
I understand.	Je comprends	zhuh kohm-prahn
I'm American.	Je suis américain.	a-may-ree-kehn
I'm British.	Je suis anglais.	ahn-glay
What's your name?	Comment vous appelez-vous?	ko-mahn voo za-pell-ay-voo
My name is . . .	Mon nom est...	zhuh ma-pell
What time is it?	Quelle heure es-il	kel air eh-teel
How?	Comment?	ko-mahn
When?	Quand?	kahn
Yesterday	Hier	yair

Today	Aujourd'hui	o-zhoor-dwee
Tomorrow	Demain	duh-mehn
This morning	Ce matin	suh mah-tin
This afternoon	Cet après-midi	set a-pray mee-dee
Tonight	Ce Soir	suh swahr
What?	Quoi?	kwah
What is it?	Qu'est-ce que c'est?	kess-kuh-say
Why?	Pourquoi?	poor-kwa
Who?	Qui?	kee
Where is ...	Où est	oo ay
...the train station?	la gare?	la gar
...the subway station?	la station de metro?	la sta-syon duh may-tro
...the bus stop?	l'arrêt de bus?	la-ray duh booss
...the airport	l'aéroport?	la-ay ro-porr
...the post office?	la poste?	la post
...the bank?	la banque?	la bahnk
...the hotel?	l'hôtel?	lo-tel
...the museum?	le musée?	luh mew-zay
...the hospital?	l'hôpital?	lo-pee-tahl
...the elevator?	l'ascenseur?	la-sahn-seuhr
Where are the restrooms?	Où sont les toilettes?	oo sohn lay twah- let
Here/there	Ici/là	ee- see /la
Left/right	à gauche/à droite	a goash/a draht
Is it near/far?	Est-ce que c'est près/loin?	say pray/lwehn
I'd like ...	Je voudrais...	zhuh voo- dray...
...a room	une chambre	ewn shahm-bruh
...the key	la clé	la clay
...a newspaper	un journal	uhn zhoor- nah
...a stamp	un timbre	uhn tam-bruh
I'd like to buy ...	Je voudrais acheter...	zhuh voo- dray ahsh-tay...
...a city map	un plan de la ville	uhn plahn de veal
...a road map	une carte routière	ewn cart roo-tee- air
...a magazine	une revue	ewn reh- vu
...envelopes	des enveloppes	dayz ahn-veh-lope
...writing paper	du papier à lettres	dew pa-pee- ay a let-ruh
...a postcard	une carte postale	ewn cart pos- tahl
...a ticket	un billet	uhn bee-yeah
How much is it?	C'est combien?	say comb-bee- ehn
It's expensive/cheap	C'est cher/pas cher	say sher/pa sher
A little/a lot	Un peu/beaucoup	uhn peuh/bo- koo
More/less	Plus/moins	plus/mwehn

Enough/too (much)	Assez/trop	a-say/tro
I am ill/sick	Je suis malade.	zhuh swee ma- lahd
Call a doctor	Appelez un docteur	a-play uhn dohk- tehr
Help!	Au secours!	o suh- koor
Stop!	Arrêtez!	a-reh- tay

DINING OUT

A bottle of ...	une bouteille de...	ewn boo- tay duh
A cup of ...	une tasse de...	ewn tass duh
A glass of ...	un verre de...	uhn vair duh
Beer	une bière	ewn bi- yair
Bill/check	l'addition	la-dee-see- ohn
Bread	du pain	dew pan
Breakfast	le petit-déjeuner	luh puh- tee day-zhuh- nay
Butter	du beurre	dew burr
Cocktail/apéritif	un apéritif	uhn ah-pay-ree- teef
Coffee	un café	uhn ca- fay
Dinner	le dîner	luh dee- nay
Fixed-price menu	la table d'hôte	la ta- bleh doe- teh
Fork	une fourchette	ewn four- shet
I am a vegetarian	Je suis végétarien(ne)	zhuh swee vay-zhay-ta-ree- en
I cannot eat ...	Je ne peux pas manger de...	zhuh nuh puh pah mahn- jay deh
I'd like to order ...	Je voudrais commander...	zhuh voo- dray ko-mahn- day...
Is service included?	Est-ce que le service est compris?	ess kuh luh sair- veess ay comb- pree
I'm hungry/thirsty	J'ai faim/soif	zay fehn / sua- f
It's good/bad	C'est bon/mauvais	say bohn/mo- vay
It's hot/cold	C'est chaud/froid	say sho/frwah
Knife	un couteau	uhn koo- toe
Lunch	le déjeuner	luh day-zhuh- nay
Menu	la carte	la cart
Napkin	une serviette	ewn sair-vee- et
Pepper	du poivre	dew pwah-vruh
Plate	une assiette	ewn a-see- et
Please give me ...	Donnez-moi...	doe-nay- mwah...
Salt	du sel	dew sell
Spoon	une cuillère	ewn kwee-air
Tea	du thé	dew tay
Water	de l'eau	duh lo
Wine	du vin	dew vehn

Great Itineraries

ESSENTIAL MONTRÉAL IN A DAY

Start with a stroll to the peak of Mont-Royal, the city's most enduring natural symbol. Afterward, wander south on avenue du Parc and through McGill University's leafy campus to Downtown. The Musée des Beaux-Arts de Montréal, on rue Sherbrooke, was once the bastion of the Anglo-Canadian establishment, and is worth a visit.

For a more francophone perspective, head from Mont-Royal (the mountain) along rue Mont-Royal (the street) to rue St-Denis, below rue Sherbrooke, home to funky boutiques and a boisterous strip of bars near the Université du Québec à Montréal.

In the late afternoon, head down to Old Montréal and pop into the Basilique Notre-Dame-de-Montréal before getting in some nightlife, as in the summer months the Old City is one of the most popular places to party. There are dozens of restaurants to choose from, as well as clubs and bars.

DAY TRIPS AND OVERNIGHTS FROM MONTRÉAL

If you have only a couple of days for a visit and you need to concentrate on one area, the Laurentians are a good choice. Less than an hour's drive from Downtown Montréal, this resort area has recreational options (depending on the season) that include golf, hiking, and superb skiing, both Alpine and cross-country.

Pick a resort town to stay in and use that as a base for visiting some of the surrounding towns. Each town has its own style and appeal: St-Sauveur-des-Monts is lively, Morin Heights is tranquil, and Ste-Adèle, along with the nearby towns of Val Morin and Val David, are a center of gastronomy. Mont-Tremblant, a sophisticated ski and golf resort, is worth a trip,

particularly for the picturesque gondola ride to the summit.

You can combine a taste of the Eastern Townships with a two-day visit to the Laurentians. After an overnight stay in the Laurentians, head back south of Montréal to the Townships, which extend to the east along the border with New England. Overnight in Bromont, which is known for golf, skiing, and its water park.

The next day, you can shop in attractive Knowlton (look for signs to Lac Brome) and explore regional history in such towns as Valcourt. Spend a night or two in the resort town of Magog, along Lac Memphrémagog, or in the quieter, and far prettier, North Hatley, on Lac Massawippi. You'll have good dining in either. Save some time for outdoor activities, whether it's golfing, skiing, biking, or hiking.

ESSENTIAL QUÉBEC CITY IN A DAY

It's inspiring to start your day in Québec's Lower Town, the earliest site of French civilization in North America. Stroll along the narrow streets of the Quartier Petit-Champlain, visit the Maison Chevalier, and browse the craft stores and boutiques. From there, head to Place Royale, making a stop at the Église Notre-Dame-des-Victoires, and continue on to Terrasse Dufferin. In the afternoon, when the crowds thin out, check out the Musée National des Beaux-Arts du Québec or the Musée Canadien de l'Histoire.

Catch a gorgeous sunset from the Plains of Abraham—site of the battle that ended France's colonial dreams in North America and marked the beginning of British rule in Canada—before dining anywhere on rue St-Jean, one of the best streets in the city for restaurants and nightlife.

DAY TRIPS AND OVERNIGHTS FROM QUÉBEC CITY

If you want to get out of Québec City for a day or two, take a 20-minute drive to Île d'Orléans, a picturesque island called the "Garden of Québec." In summer, you can explore this idyllic island's boutiques, galleries, and food stands, then dine in a vineyard at Panache Mobile. Stay over in a cozy B&B, or continue on Route 138 northeast to Côte de Beaupré. Here you can visit the impressive Montmorency Falls and the ornate shrine at Ste-Anne-de-Beaupré. Don't miss the classic Québec cuisine of roast goose, *tourtière* (meat pie), and sugar pie at the historical Auberge Baker on Côte-de-Beaupré.

Another option is to take the Train du Massif de Charlevoix, which departs from the spectacular Parc de la Chute-Montmorency outside Québec City. It follows the St. Lawrence shore and the dramatic mountainous landscapes of Charlevoix. You'll visit the artistic community of Baie St-Paul, the impressive mountain Le Massif, and the cliff-top village of La Malbaie. You can do the two-segment rail trip in one day or stay overnight at the castlelike Fairmont Le Manoir Richelieu.

From La Malbaie, it's an hour by car to Tadoussac, at the confluence of the Saguenay and St. Lawrence rivers, where you can hop on a boat for a whale-watching excursion.

MONTRÉAL AND QUÉBEC CITY OVER A LONG WEEKEND

Looking for an ideal four-day getaway? It's possible to see the best of both cities without feeling rushed. Here's one expedient itinerary: Fly into Montréal's Trudeau International Airport on a Thursday evening, take a cab to your Downtown hotel, put down your bags, and head out to grab a bite at a late-night bistro like L'Express. Spend Friday seeing the city's top sites, hit Old Montréal in the evening for dinner and nightlife, and enjoy a leisurely brunch on Saturday morning.

Rent a car from one of the many downtown rental agencies, then pack up and drive north to Québec City, which takes about three hours. Check into a B&B or boutique hotel in the Old City and spend the rest of the day exploring sites there. Spend Sunday morning in the Old City and dedicate the afternoon to the Fortifications, or take a day trip to the Côte-de-Beaupré or Île d'Orléans. On Monday, fly out of Québec City's Jean Lesage International Airport.

A Food Lover's Tour of Montréal

Many Montrealers are true gourmets, or at least enthusiastic food lovers. And, indeed, the city has thousands of restaurants, markets, and food boutiques catering to just about every conceivable taste, from Portuguese barbecue to Tonkinese soup. Most menus are posted outside.

DOWNTOWN

Although you can't go wrong starting the day with a bowl of steaming café au lait at **Café Myriade** Downtown, for something a little different head over to Chinatown for a dim sum breakfast at **Maison Kam Fung,** a neighborhood institution.

THE PLATEAU

Fortified with filling dumpling dough, walk up through the streets of the Latin Quarter on rue St-Denis and you'll hit Square St-Louis.

Turn west, then north on boulevard St-Laurent and browse through dozens of ethnic food shops and delis, inhaling the aromas from the Caribbean, the Middle East, Asia, and Eastern Europe. If that reanimates your appetite, stop at the iconic **Schwartz's Delicatessen** and split one of the world's best smoked-meat sandwiches, served piled high on rye (it's best slathered with spicy deli mustard), with your walking companion.

Next work up an appetite for lunch with a walk. Head east along avenue Duluth and take a stroll through Parc Lafontaine. There are two options for a bite to eat: exit the park on the southwest corner to rue Rachel and turn left for **La Banquise,** one of Montréal's top poutine spots (so popular you may have to wait in line to get in); or go northwest on rue de la Roche until you reach avenue Mont-Royal, a spirited stretch of terrasses, tattoo parlors, and thrift shops. Stop for a bagel

A Food Lover's Tour of Montréal

HIGHLIGHTS
A fat smoked-meat sandwich at Schwartz's Delicatessen; walking around the Marché Jean-Talon tasting vendors' samples.

WHERE TO START
Chinatown, located in Downtown, at the ornately decorated red gate on St-Laurent off boulevard René-Lévesque.

LENGTH
About 5.5 km (3.5 miles) walking, plus the métro from Laurier to Marché Jean-Talon on the Orange Line.

WHERE TO END
Little Italy. From here, you can walk back to the Orange Line that runs through Downtown.

BEST TIME TO GO
Busy summer Saturday (the crowds are half the entertainment).

WORST TIME TO GO
Dull winter Monday.

EDITOR'S CHOICES
Walking up boulevard St-Laurent, peeking in the delis and offbeat boutiques; the colorful streets of the Plateau; the maple ice cream at Le Glacier Bilboquet.

Side tab text (vertical):

Travel Smart Montréal and Quebec City A FOOD LOVER'S TOUR OF MONTRÉAL

---

sandwich on a hot and sweet Montréal-style bagel at **St-Viateur Bagel & Café.** In summer, stop for some ice cream at **Le Glacier Bilboquet,** on avenue Laurier Est, or try the Outremont location on rue Bernard.

LITTLE ITALY

Time to cheat. Hop on the métro at Laurier station and head north to the Jean-Talon stop for an afternoon visit to one of Canada's best markets, **Marché Jean-Talon.** You can spend hours browsing fish, sausage, and cheese shops and sampling everything from smoked buffalo to seasonal produce like heirloom tomatoes.

There's no leaving this area without stopping for dinner, so stroll over to boulevard St-Laurent and find a place to eat in Pétite-Italie (Little Italy). Two restaurants to try are **Inferno** and **Bottega Pizzeria.** Finish with a bracing espresso at **Café Italia,** where neighborhood men huddle around the TV to watch soccer.

From here, it's an easy walk back to the Jean-Talon métro stop for a ride back to Old Montréal or Downtown.

A Walk Through Québec City's History

Exploring Québec City's history can be an all-consuming pastime—and a rewarding one. The walk outlined here takes you through much of it, but feel free to pursue the Old City's inviting little detours.

OUTSIDE THE OLD CITY

The best place to begin a journey through the history of New France is at the end. Start your tour at the **Wolfe-Montcalm Monument,** on the far west side of the **Plains of Abraham.** It was here in 1759 that British general James Wolfe extinguished France's dreams of a North American empire and set off the English-French divergence that has both enriched and plagued Canada's history.

The Plains of Abraham was where the famous Battle of Québec (also called Battle of the Plains of Abraham) took place, in which General Wolfe's forces were victorious against Marquis de Montcalm's surprised French troops. Today this hilltop patch of green is a pleasant and expansive city park with trees, lawns, and meandering paths with sweeping views of the St. Lawrence River.

Make your way over to the Fortifications and the Old City via the northern side of the Plains of Abraham, along the **Grande Allée,** through the residential neighborhood of **Montcalm,** home to gorgeous 19th-century neo-Gothic and Queen Anne–style mansions and **Hôtel du Parlement.**

THE FORTIFICATIONS

The end of the Grand Allée is Porte St-Louis. Turn right down the Côte de la Citadelle, which leads to **La Citadelle.** Something of a microcosm of Canada's sometimes contrarian cultural character, the fortress is home to the Royal 22e Régiment, a crack military unit that speaks French but dresses in the

A Walk Through Québec City's History

HIGHLIGHTS
Exploring La Citadelle; leisurely strolling along the Terrasse Dufferin; walking along rue du Petit-Champlain in the Old City.

WHERE TO START
The Wolfe-Montcalm Monument, on the far western side of the Plains of Abraham outside the walls of the city.

LENGTH
About 3 km (2 miles).

WHERE TO END
On rue du Petit-Champlain, in the Lower Town section of the Old City.

BEST TIME TO GO
A weekday summer morning.

WORST TIME TO GO
A cold winter day.

EDITOR'S CHOICE
Strolling along the tree-lined streets off Grande Allée in Montcalm; riding the funicular from Upper Town to Lower Town; standing in historic Place Royale.

bearskin hats and red tunics of a British guards unit for ceremonial parades. Don't miss the daily Changing of the Guard ceremony.

UPPER TOWN

Beyond **Porte St-Louis,** you can imagine yourself in 17th- and 18th-century France. Steep-roofed houses with small windows crowd a tangle of narrow, curving streets and the rattle of horse-drawn carriages on ancient cobblestones adds to the illusion.

The **Maison Jacquet** on rue St-Louis looks exactly as it did when it was built in 1677 and the **Maison Kent** was once the home of Queen Victoria's father, the Duke of Kent. **Le Couvent des Ursulines** at 12 rue Donnacona has a museum featuring an exhibit of magnificent lace embroidery created by Ursuline nuns in the 19th and early 20th centuries.

Québec City's most famous building, the **Fairmont Le Château Frontenac,** is at the beginning of **Terrasse Dufferin,** which is worth a stroll for sweeping views of the St. Lawrence River before you get on the funicular to reach Lower Town.

LOWER TOWN

Once at the base of this cable-connected elevator, you end up in the 17th-century **Maison Louis-Jolliet,** built before he paddled off to explore the Mississippi River. From here, it's a short walk to **Place Royale,** a square graced by a statue of the Sun King Louis XIV, and considered to be the birthplace of New France. The last jaunt is along **rue du Petit-Champlain,** the oldest street in the city, lined with shops and cafés.

Montréal and Québec City's Best Walking Tours

Circuit des Fantômes du Vieux Montréal
(*Old Montréal Ghost Trail*). From mid-April to mid-November, you can join these street theater walking tours through the Old City, where a host of spirits are said to still roam the streets. Tours begin at 8:30 pm and the haunted journey lasts about 90 minutes. Reservations are required. ⊠ *360 rue St-François-Xavier, Old Montréal* ☎ *514/844–4021, 800/363–4021* ⊕ *www.fantommontreal.com* ⊠ *C$22* ☞ *Private tours only in winter* Ⓜ *Place-d'Armes.*

Ghost Tours of Québec. Costumed actors lead ghoulish 90-minute evening tours of Québec City murders, executions, and ghost sightings. The tours (C$22) are available in English or French, from May through October. After the walk, you can buy a copy of *Ghost Stories of Québec*, which has stories not told on the tours. ⊠ *34 boul. Champlain, Lower Town* ☎ *855/692–9770* ⊕ *www.ghosttour-sofquebec.com.*

Guidatour. You can walk through various historic, cultural, or architecturally diverse areas of the city with a costumed guide. Popular tours include Old Montréal, the Underground City, the Christmas Secrets of Old Montréal, and the elite 19th-century neighborhood known as the Golden Square Mile. ▪TIP➜ **Res-ervations are necessary.** ⊠ *360 rue St-François-Xavier , Suite 400, Old Mon-tréal* ☎ *514/844–4021, 800/363–4021* ⊕ *www.guidatour.qc.ca/en/?* ⊠ *From C$14* Ⓜ *Place-d'Armes.*

Kaleidoscope. This company offers a range of 60 different guided tours, from architecture tours to Montréal's Red Light district, and the city's many culturally diverse neighborhoods can be explored by foot, bike, or bus. ⊠ *Mon-tréal* ☎ *514/277–6990* ⊕ *www.tourskalei-doscope.com* ⊠ *C$15–C$55.*

Tours Voir Québec. This tour company offers English- and French-language (and Spanish from June to September) walking tours of the Old City, starting at C$23. Other tours include a "Bury Your Dead" murder mystery tour based on the novels of Louise Penny, as well as a popular food tour with tastings at various establishments for C$55. ⊠ *12 rue St-Anne, Upper Town* ☎ *418/694–2001, 866/694–2001* ⊕ *www.toursvoirquebec. com.*

Contacts

✈ Air Travel

AIRPORT INFORMATION Montréal–Pierre Elliott Trudeau International Airport. (*YUL*). ✉ *975 Roméo-Vachon Blvd. North, Dorval* ☎ *800/465–1213, 514/633–3333* ⊕ *www.admtl.com.* **Jean Lesage International Airport.** (*YQB*). ✉ *505 rue Principale, Québec City* ☎ *418/640–3300, 877/769–2700* ⊕ *www.aeroportdequebec.com.*

AIRLINE CONTACTS Air Canada. ☎ *888/247–2262* ⊕ *www.aircanada.com.* **American Airlines.** ☎ *800/433–7300* ⊕ *www.aa.com.* **Delta Airlines.** ☎ *800/221–1212 for U.S. reservations, 800/241–4141 for international reservations* ⊕ *www.delta.com.* **Porter Airlines.** ☎ *888/619–8622* ⊕ *www.flyporter.com.*

᠔ Bike Travel

Bixi. ☎ *514/789–2494, 877/820–2453* ⊕ *montreal.bixi.com.* **Vélo Montréal.** ✉ *3880 rue Rachel Est, Hochelaga-Maisonneuve* ☎ *514/259–7272* ⊕ *www.velomontreal.com* *Pie-IX.*

🚌 Bus Travel

Gare d'autocars de Montréal. ✉ *1717 rue Berri, Montréal* ☎ *514/842–2281* ⊕ *www.gamtl.com.* **Gare du Palais Bus Station.** ✉ *320 rue Abraham-Martin, Québec City* ☎ *418/525–3000.* **Greyhound Lines.** ☎ *800/231–2222 in the U.S., 800/661–8747 in Canada* ⊕ *www.greyhound.com.* **Limocar.** ☎ *866/692–8899* ⊕ *www.limocar.ca.* **Orléans Express.** ☎ *833/449–6444, 450/640–1477* ⊕ *www.orleansexpress.com.*

🚗 Car Travel

EMERGENCY SERVICES CAA. ☎ *800/222–4357, 800/686–9243, 800/222–4357 Roadside assistance* ⊕ *www.caaquebec.com.*

MAJOR RENTAL AGENCIES Alamo. ☎ *844/357–5138* ⊕ *www.alamo.com.* **Avis.** ☎ *800/879–2847* ⊕ *www.avis.com.* **Budget.** ☎ *800/268–8900 from Canada, 800/218–7992 from U.S.* ⊕ *www.budget.com.* **Hertz.** ☎ *800/654–3001* ⊕ *www.hertz.com.* **National Car Rental.** ☎ *844/382–6875 in the U.S., 844/307-8014 in Canada* ⊕ *www.nationalcar.com.*

🚆 Train Travel

INFORMATION Amtrak. ☎ *800/872–7245* ⊕ *www.amtrak.com.* **Train de Charlevoix.** ☎ *844/737–3282, 418/240–4124* ⊕ *www.traindecharlevoix.com.* **VIA Rail Canada.** ☎ *888/842–7245 from U.S.* ⊕ *www.viarail.ca.*

🛏 Accommodations

BED AND BREAKFASTS Association de l'Agrotourisme et du Tourisme Gourmand du Québec. ☎ *514/252–3138* ⊕ *www.agrotourismeettourismegourmand.com.* **BB Canada.** ⊕ *www.bbcanada.com.* **Bed and Breakfasts Québec.** ⊕ *www.bedbreakfastsquebec.com.*

➕ Emergencies

FOREIGN EMBASSIES AND CONSULATES U.S. Consulate General. ✉ *1155 rue St-Alexandre, Montréal* ☎ *514/398–9695* ⊕ *ca.usembassy.gov/embassy-consulates/montreal.* **U.S. Consulate General.** ✉ *2 pl. Terrasse Dufferin, Québec City* ☎ *418/692–2095* ⊕ *ca.usembassy.gov/embassy-consulates/quebec.* **U.S. Embassy.** ✉ *490 Sussex Dr., Ottawa* ☎ *613/688–5335* ⊕ *ca.usembassy.gov.*

Contacts

HOSPITALS Centre Hospitalier Universitaire de Québec. ✉ *2705 boul. Laurier, Ste-Foy* ☎ *418/525–4444, 418/654–2114 emergencies* ⊕ *www.chuq.qc.ca.* **Centre Hospitalier Universitaire de Québec, Pavillon Hôtel-Dieu.** ✉ *11 côte du Palais, Upper Town* ☎ *418/525–4444, 418/691–5042 emergencies* ⊕ *www.chuq.qc.ca/fr/le_chuq/nos_etablissements/hdq.* **Montréal General Hospital (McGill University Health Centre).** ✉ *1650 av. Cedar, Downtown* ☎ *514/934–1934* ⊕ *www.muhc.ca/mgh* Ⓜ *Guy-Concordia.*

🧭 Tours

CONTACTS Bateau-Mouche. ☎ *514/849–9952, 800/361–9952* ⊕ *www.bateaumouche.ca.* **Croisières AML.** ✉ *10 rue Dalhousie, Lower Town* ☎ *866/856–6668* ⊕ *www.croisieresaml.com.* **Fitz and Follwell Co.** ✉ *115 av. du Mont-Royal Ouest, The Plateau* ☎ *514/840–0739* ⊕ *www.montreal.fitz.tours.* **Gray Line.** ☎ *800/472–9546* ⊕ *www.grayline.com.* **Old Québec Tours.** ☎ *418/664–0460, 800/267–8687* ⊕ *www.oldquebectours.com.*

📍 Visitor Information

CONTACTS Association Touristique des Cantons de l'Est. ✉ *20 rue Don Bosco Sud, Sherbrooke* ☎ *819/820–2020 administration, 800/355–5755* ⊕ *www.cantonsdelest.com.* **Association Touristique des Laurentides.** ✉ *La Porte-du-Nord rest area, Autoroute des Laurentides, Exit 51* ☎ *450/224–7007, 800/561–6673* ⊕ *www.laurentides.com.* **Association Touristique Régionale de Charlevoix.** ✉ *495 boul. de Comporté, C.P. 275, La Malbaie* ☎ *418/665–4454, 800/667–2276* ⊕ *www.tourisme-charlevoix.com.* **Canadian Tourism Commission.** ☎ *604/638–8300* ⊕ *www.travelcanada.ca.* **Centre d'Interpretation de la Côte-de-Beaupré. (***Beaupré Coast Interpretation Center***).** ✉ *7976 av. Royale, C.P. 40, Château-Richer* ☎ *418/824–3677, 877/824–3677* ⊕ *www.histoire-cotedebeaupre.org.* **Centre Info-Touriste.** ✉ *1255 rue Peel, suite 100, Downtown* ☎ *514/873–2015, 877/266–5687* ⊕ *www.bonjourquebec.com* Ⓜ *Peel or Bonaventure* ✉ *174 rue Notre-Dame Est, at pl. Jacques-Cartier, Old Montréal* ☎ *514/873–2015* Ⓜ *Champ-de-Mars.* **Parks Canada.** ☎ *819/420–9486, 888/773–8888* ⊕ *www.pc.gc.ca.* **Québec City Tourist Information.** ✉ *12 rue Sainte-Anne, Upper Town* ☎ *418/641–6290, 877/266–5687* ⊕ *www.quebec-cite.com/en.* **Sépaq.** ☎ *800/665–6527* ⊕ *www.sepaq.com.* **Terroir & Saveurs.** ☎ *514/252–3138* ⊕ *www.terroiretsaveurs.com.* **Tourisme-Montréal.** ☎ *877/266–5687* ⊕ *www.tourisme-montreal.org.*

Chapter 3

MONTRÉAL

3

Updated by
Elizabeth Warkentin

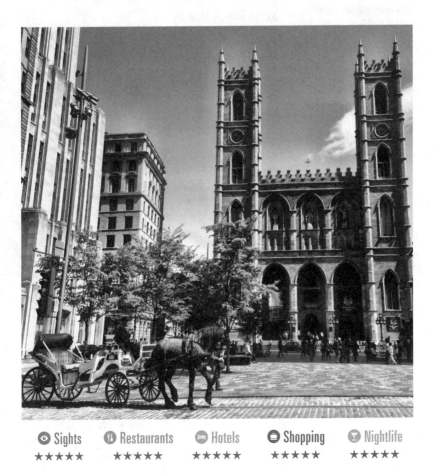

◉ Sights	🍴 Restaurants	🛏 Hotels	🛍 Shopping	🍸 Nightlife
★★★★★	★★★★★	★★★★★	★★★★★	★★★★★

WELCOME TO MONTRÉAL

TOP REASONS TO GO

★ **Browse public markets:** Amble through Marché Atwater, one of the city's oldest public markets, and the bustling Marché Jean-Talon, the largest open-air market in North America.

★ **Check out the nightlife:** Enjoy Canada's unrivalled party capital at famous nightlife spots that include rue Crescent, boulevard St-Laurent, and the Latin Quarter, as well as Old Montréal and the Village, Montréal's gay epicenter.

★ **Get a dose of multiculturalism:** Explore ethnic neighborhoods and sample global cuisine.

★ **Celebrate Jazz Fest:** Montréal's biggest musical event, Jazz Fest, happens every year in late June and early July. Reserve early: hotels book up months in advance.

★ **Stroll Old Montréal:** Historic Vieux-Montréal has cobblestone streets, a great waterfront, fine restaurants and bed-and-breakfasts, and the Old Port, which buzzes with nightlife.

1 **Old Montréal (Vieux-Montréal).** The oldest part of the city.

2 **Downtown.** Montréal's largest shopping district.

3 **Westmount.** An affluent suburb.

4 **The Latin Quarter.** People-watching is the order of the day here.

5 **The Village.** Lively, diverse, and great nightlife.

6 **The Plateau Mont-Royal and Mile End.** Trendy cafés and upscale boutiques and galleries.

7 **Outremont.** Chic fashion boutiques and stylish cafés.

8 **Little Italy.** All the best pastry shops and grocery stores.

9 **Parc du Mont-Royal.** The Central Park of Montréal.

10 **Côte-des-Neiges.** A vibrant and ethnically diverse neighborhood.

11 **Hochelaga-Maisonneuve.** See the site of the 1976 Olympics.

12 **Sud-Ouest and Lachine.** A magnet for creatives and foodies.

13 **The Islands.** Île Ste-Hélène and Île Notre-Dame.

KEY

Ⓜ Métro Stations

🚲 Route Verte Bike Route

LITTLE ITALY ↑
av. du Parc
8
Marché Jean-Talon

BEAUBIEN
r. De Bellechasse

OUTREMONT
OUTREMONT
7 rue Bernard
av. St-Viateur

ROSEMONT

UNIVERSITÉ-DE-MONTRÉAL
ÉDOUARD-MONTPETIT
blvd. Mont-Royal
av. Fairmont

Côte-Ste-Catherine
av. Laurier
r. Villeneuve
blvd. St-Laurent

LAURIER
MILE END

r. St-Denis
r. De St-Vaillier
r. Boyer

MONT-ROYAL
6
av. du Mont-Royal
r. Marie-Anne

Cimetière Mont-Royal

St-Urbain
THE PLATEAU
av. Duluth
av. du Parc
av. Laval
rue Berri
r. St-Denis
de Bullion
r. Roy

Chemin Remembrance
Voie C. Houde
Parc du Mont-Royal

Côte-des-Neiges
9
PARC DU MONT-ROYAL
av. Cedar

av. des Pins
av. Docteur-Penfield
r. Prince-Arthur
r. Jeanne-Mance
r. Milton

r. Rachel
Parc Lafontaine
r. Sherbrooke
Calixa-Lavallée
av. du Parc Lafontaine
av. Papineau
Panet
Beaudry
r. Fabre
r. Hochelaga
av. Papineau
r. de Rouen
Parthenais
r. Chapleau

SHERBROOKE

ATWATER
av. Atwater
GUY-CONCORDIA
r. Peel
r. Crescent
r. St-Marc
r. du fort
r. St-Mathieu

PLACE-DES-ARTS
ST-LAURENT
r. Ontario
BERRI-UQAM
BEAUDRY
PAPINEAU

PEEL
MCGILL
Côte Beaver Hall
blvd. de Maisonneuve
r. Ste-Catherine
HOCHELAGA-MAISONNEUVE
11

DOWNTOWN
2
blvd. René-Lévesque
THE VILLAGE
5
autoroute Ville-Marie

autoroute Ville-Marie
BONAVENTURE
CHINATOWN
r. de la Gauchetière
CHAMP-DE-MARS
4
r. Notre-Dame

GEORGES-VANIER
LUCIEN-L'ALLIER
SQ.-VICTORIA
LATIN QUARTER
Jacques-Cartier

r. St-Jacques
r. Notre-Dame
r. Guy
r. St-Jacques
r. Peel
1
PL.-D'ARMES
OLD MONTRÉAL

Lachine Canal
r. St-Patrick
OLD PORT
ÎLE STE-HÉLÈNE
La Ronde

r. Ctre
r. Mullins
r. Shearer
r. Peel
av. Pierre-Dupuy
r. Mill
Route Verte Bike Route
THE ISLANDS
13
Parc Jean-Drapeau

r. Wellington
autoroute Bonaventure
r. d'Hibernia
112
Pont de la Concorde

Parc Leber
Route Verte Bike Route
St. Lawrence River
ÎLE NOTRE-DAME

Pont Victoria
Parc Floral
Casino de Montréal
20

0   1/2 mile
0   500 meters

15/20

Canada's most diverse metropolis, Montréal is an island city that favors style and elegance over order or even prosperity, a city where past and present intrude on each other daily. In some ways it resembles Vienna—well past its peak of power and glory, perhaps, yet still vibrant and grand.

But don't get the wrong idea. Montréal has always had a bit of an edge. During Prohibition, thirsty Americans headed north to the city on the St. Lawrence for booze, music, and a good time, and people still come for the same things. Summer festivals celebrate everything from comedy and French music and culture to beer and fireworks, and, of course, jazz. And on those rare weeks when there isn't a planned event, the party continues. Clubs and sidewalk cafés are abuzz from late afternoon to the early hours of the morning. Montréal is also a city that knows how to mix it up even when it's 20 below zero. Rue St-Denis is almost as lively on a Saturday night in January as it is in July, and the festival Montréal en Lumière, or Montréal Highlights, enlivens the dreary days of February with concerts, balls, and fine food.

Montréal takes its name from Parc du Mont-Royal, a stubby plug of tree-covered igneous rock that rises 764 feet above the surrounding cityscape. Although its height is unimpressive, "the Mountain" forms one of Canada's finest urban parks, and views from the Chalet du Mont-Royal atop the hill provide an excellent orientation to the city's layout and major landmarks.

Old Montréal is home to museums, the municipal government, and the magnificent Basilique Notre-Dame-de-Montréal within its network of narrow cobblestone streets. Although Montréal's centre-ville, or Downtown, bustles like many other major cities on the surface, it's active below street level as well, in the so-called Underground City—the underground levels of shopping malls and food courts connected by pedestrian tunnels and the city's subway system, or métro. Residential Plateau Mont-Royal and trendy neighborhoods like Griffintown/St-Henri thrum with the kinetic energy of restos, boîtes de nuit (nightclubs), bars, art galleries, and cafés. The greener areas of town are composed of Parc du Mont-Royal, Parc Lafontaine, and the Jardin Botanique.

Planning

Getting Here and Around

AIR TRAVEL

Montréal's Trudeau International Airport (also often referred to by its previous name, Dorval) is about 24 km (15 miles) west of the city center.

Montréal's History

Montréal is the second-largest French-speaking city in the Western world, but it's not only francophone culture that thrives here. About 14% of the 3.3 million people who call Greater Montréal home claim English as their mother tongue.

Yet the two cultures are not as separate as they once were. Chatter in the bars and bistros of rue St-Denis east of boulevard St-Laurent still tends to be in French, and crowds in restaurants on rue Crescent in the Downtown core speak English. But the lines have blurred, with more conversations taking place in a uniquely Montréal mixture of the two languages.

Both linguistic groups have had to come to grips with no longer being the only player. So-called *allophones*—people whose mother tongue is neither French nor English—make up 19% of the city's population.

The first European settlement on Montréal island was Ville-Marie, founded in 1642 by 54 men and women under the leadership of Paul de Chomedey, Sieur de Maisonneuve, and Jeanne Mance, a French noblewoman, who hoped to create a new Christian society. The settlement's location near the confluence of the St. Lawrence and Ottawa rivers also meant a lucrative trade in beaver pelts, as the fur was a staple of European hat fashion for nearly a century.

The French regime in Canada ended with the Seven Years' War, also known as the French and Indian War. The Treaty of Paris ceded all of New France to Britain in 1763.

American troops under generals Richard Montgomery and Benedict Arnold occupied the city during their 1775–76 campaign to conquer Canada, but their efforts failed and troops withdrew. Soon invaders of another kind—English and Scottish settlers—poured into Montréal. By 1832 the city became a colonial capital. But 1837 brought anti-British rebellions, and this led to Canada's becoming a self-governing dominion in 1867.

The city's ports continued to bustle until the St. Lawrence Seaway opened in 1957, allowing ships to sail from the Atlantic to the Great Lakes without having to stop in Montréal to transfer cargo.

The opening of the métro in 1966 changed the way Montrealers lived, and the next year the city hosted the World's Fair. But the rise of Québec separatism in the late 1960s under René Lévesque created political uncertainty, and many major businesses moved to Toronto. By the time Lévesque's separatist Parti Quebecois won power in Québec in 1976—the same year the summer Olympics came to the city—Montréal was clearly Canada's No. 2 city.

Uncertainty continued through the 1980s and '90s, with the separatist Parti Quebecois and the federalist Liberals alternating in power in Québec City. Since 1980 the city has endured two referenda on the future of Québec and Canada. In the cliff-hanger of 1995, just 50.58% of Quebecois voted to remain part of Canada. Montréal bucked the separatist trend and voted nearly 70% against independence.

Money-Saving Tips

There are several good ways to save money during your trip. If you'll be visiting three or more of the city's museums, consider buying a museum pass. It's available for C$75 for three days, but the better deal is the C$80 pass, which also includes unlimited access to Montréal's transportation system, including the métro and buses. ⊕ www.museesmontreal.org/en/passes/the-passes.

Tourist passes, which give you unlimited access to the transit system, also may be worth your while; one-day passes are C$10 while three-day passes will set you back C$18. Weekly passes cost C$25.75 but they're loaded electronically on a special Opus card that costs C$6.

Hitting the town earlier in the evening is a good way to save as well, by stopping into cafés and bars for food and drink specials offered during cinq-à-sept (5-to-7), Montréal's happy hour.

GROUND TRANSPORTATION

The easiest way to get in is to take a cab for a fixed fare of C$40 or a limousine for about C$55, unless your hotel provides transportation. The cheapest way to get into town is the 747 express bus, a 24-hour shuttle service from the airport to the main bus terminal with stops at the Lionel-Groulx métro station and several additional stops near Downtown hotels. The one-way fare is C$10 (accepted in coins only) —with 24 hours of unlimited bus and métro travel included in the price. Plan on it taking about a half hour outside rush hour to get to Downtown from the airport. Another alternative is the 204 bus, with a one-way fare of C$3.25, taking you from the Dorval train terminal straight to the airport.

BICYCLE TRAVEL

An extensive network of bike paths and relatively flat terrain make Montréal ideal for bicycles. The Bixi (a contraction of "bicycle" and "taxi") system—with more than 3,000 sturdy aluminum-frame bikes at more than 300 credit card–operated stands throughout the city—makes two-wheel exploring easy. For just C$5 you can take as many bike trips as you like over a 24-hour period, or for C$12 you can extend that to 72 hours. A one-way trip is C$2.75. Pay attention to the time, though: the system is designed for short hops; keep any one bike for more than 30 minutes, and you'll be charged extra.

CONTACTS Bixi. ☎ 514/789–2494, 877/820–2453 ⊕ montreal.bixi.com.

CAR TRAVEL

If you're driving in to the city, take I–91 or I–89 from Vermont, I–87 from New York, and Autoroute 20 (also known as Autoroute Jean-Lesage) from Québec City.

Having a car Downtown isn't ideal—garages are expensive and on-street parking can be a hassle. The city has a diligent tow-away and fine system for double-parking or sitting in no-stopping zones during rush hour, and ticket costs are steep. In residential neighborhoods, beware of alternate-side-of-the-street parking rules and resident-only parking. In winter, street plows are ruthless in dealing with parked cars in their way. If they don't tow them, they'll bury them.

PUBLIC TRANSPORTATION

The Société de transport de Montréal (STM) operates both the métro (subway) and the bus system. The métro is clean and quiet (it runs on rubber tires), and will get you to most of the places you want to visit. For those few places that are more than a 15-minute walk from the nearest métro station, bus connections are available.

Métro hours on the Orange, Green, Blue, and Yellow lines are weekdays 5:30 am to 12:30 am and weekends 5:30 am to 12:30, 1, or 1:30 am (it varies by line). Trains run every three minutes or so on the most crowded lines—Orange and Green—at rush hours. The cash fare for a single ticket is C$3.25. One- and three-day unlimited-use cards are also available for C$10 and C$18.

TAXI TRAVEL

Taxis in Montréal all run on the same rate: C$3.45 minimum and C$1.70 per kilometer (roughly ½ mile). They're usually easy to hail on the street, outside train stations, in shopping areas, and at major hotels. You can also call a dispatcher to send a driver to pick you up at no extra cost. A taxi is available if the white or orange plastic rooftop light is on.

⇨ *For more information on getting here and around, see Travel Smart.*

Planning Your Time

Put Old Montréal and the Old Port at the top of your sightseeing list. Spend a full day walking around this area, head back to your hotel for a late-day break, and return for dinner. Aside from finding several of the city's top restaurants here, city hall, Marché Bonsecours, and other grand and charming buildings are illuminated at night. Also dedicate a full day to wandering around Downtown, rue Ste-Catherine, and Chinatown. Visit the Latin Quarter and the area around McGill University—both have a busy student

life, but shouldn't be dismissed as places where only under-20s frequent. Even if you're too tired to go out on the town, take a nighttime walk down rue Crescent or rue St-Denis for a taste of the city's *joie de vivre.*

For browsing, shopping, and dining out, explore Outremont, Mile End/thePlateau, Griffintown/St-Henri and Westmount. For kid-friendly activities, check out Hochelaga-Maisonneuve and the Islands for the Biôdôme, La Ronde, and the Jardin Botanique.

And a city landmark not to miss is St. Joseph's Oratory, Canada's largest church, on the west end of the city.

When to Go

To avoid crowds and below-freezing temperatures, Montréal's short spring, which typically starts in late April or early May but doesn't normally end until early June, is ideal. Fall is gorgeous—and touristy—when the leaves change color, so expect traffic on weekends. Early September after Labor Day until the end of the month is another good time to visit.

Restaurants

Montréal has one of Canada's most cosmopolitan restaurant scenes with trendy new eateries popping up regularly, their menus heavily influenced by flavors from around the globe, and often with an added touch of French flair.

Montréal's top dining destinations are plentiful, especially as young chefs move to hip destinations in Mile End and the Plateau areas to open new restaurants. Downtown, convenient to many hotels, finds most of its restaurants clustered between rues Guy and Peel and on the side streets that run between boulevard René-Lévesque and rue Sherbrooke. Rue St-Denis and boulevard St-Laurent, between rues Sherbrooke and Jean

Talon, have long been, and continue to be, convenient and fashionable areas, with everything from sandwich shops to high-price gourmet shrines. Old Montréal, too, has a collection of well-regarded restaurants, most of them clustered on rue St-Paul, avenue McGill, and place Jacques-Cartier.

You can usually order à la carte, but make sure to look for the table d'hôte, a two- to four-course package deal. It's often more economical, offers interesting specials, and may also take less time to prepare. For a splurge, consider a *menu dégustation,* a five- to seven-course tasting menu that generally includes soup, salad, fish, sherbet (to cleanse the palate), a meat dish, dessert, and coffee or tea. A *menu dégustation* for two, along with a good bottle of wine, will cost around C$250.

Most restaurants will have an English menu or, at the very least, a bilingual menu—but some might only be in French. If you don't understand what a dish is, don't be too shy to ask; a good server will be happy to explain. If you feel brave enough to order in French, remember that in Montréal an *entrée* is an appetizer, and what Americans call an entrée is a *plat principal,* or main dish.

What It Costs in Canadian Dollars

$	$$	$$$	$$$$
RESTAURANTS			
under C$12	C$12–C$20	C$21–C$30	over C$30

Hotels

Montréal is a city of neighborhoods with distinct personalities, which creates a broad spectrum of options when it comes to deciding on a place to stay. The Downtown core has many of the big chain hotels you'd find in any city, while Old Montréal, the Plateau, and other surrounding areas have unique *auberges* (inns) and boutique hotels.

Most of the major hotels in Downtown—the ones with big meeting rooms, swimming pools, and several bars and restaurants—are ideal for those who want all the facilities along with easy access to the department stores and malls on rue Ste-Catherine, the museums of the Golden Square Mile, and nightlife on rues Crescent and de la Montagne. If you want something a little more historical, consider renting a room in one of the dozen or so boutique hotels that occupy the centuries-old buildings lining the cobbled streets of Old Montréal. Most of them offer all the conveniences along with the added charm of stone walls, casement windows, and period-style furnishings.

If your plans include shopping expeditions to avenue Mont-Royal and rue Laurier with maybe a few late nights at the jazz bars and dance clubs of Boulevard St. Laurent and rue St-Denis, then the place to bed down is in one of Plateau Mont-Royal's small but comfortable hotels. Room rates in the area tend to be quite reasonable, but be careful: the hotels right in the middle of the action—on rue St-Denis, for example—can be noisy, especially if you get a room fronting the street.

What It Costs in Canadian Dollars

$	$$	$$$	$$$$
HOTELS			
under C$200	C$200–C$300	C$301–C$400	over C$400

Nightlife

If nightlife in Montréal could be distilled into a cocktail, it would be one part sophisticated New York club scene (with the accompanying pretension), one part Parisian joie-de-vivre (and, again, a dash

	Neighborhood Vibe	Pros	Cons
Old Montréal	Cobblestone streets, boutique hotels, designer clothes, and historic architecture; very touristy, especially at the eastern end, although it quiets down at night.	Quaint; easy access to bike paths; nice to walk along the waterfront; hip restaurants and mixology options are in the Old Port.	Can be desolate in the late evening outside hotel lobbies; parking is scarce; depending on the exact location, métro and bus access can be limited.
Downtown	Montréal's center for hustle and bustle, mostly on rue Sherbrooke, rue Ste-Catherine, and boulevard de Maisonneuve.	Extremely convenient; big-name hotel chains and luxury hotels; central location; pools; garage parking; perfect for families as well as business travelers; near the outdoor Quartier des spectacles.	Traffic congestion is relentless; not as many dining options as other neighborhoods, and what is there tends to be at either extreme—fast food or very pricey (and not always worth it).
The Latin Quarter	Hopping with university kids and moviegoers, this area boasts a crazy mix of cafés, bars, handmade-chocolate shops, and folks carrying library books.	Festival central; easy métro access; right between the Plateau and Downtown; local characters abound.	Uneven gentrification means dodgy pockets; litter; bad roads.
The Plateau Mont-Royal and Mile End	Scattered auberges, Airbnb rentals, and B&Bs host the artsy crowd and academics, with streets filled with local boutiques and hip restaurants; perfect for strolling.	Stumbling distance to the best bistros and pubs; unique shopping that focuses on local designers and craftspeople.	Limited métro and taxi access; limited hotel selections; can be noisy at night; panhandlers galore.

3

Montréal PLANNING

of snobbery), and one part Barcelonan stamina (which keeps the clubs booming until dawn).

Hot spots are peppered throughout the city. There are compact clusters along rue Crescent, boulevard St-Laurent (known as "The Main"), avenue Mont-Royal, and rue St-Denis. Prominent rue Ste-Catherine plows through town, connecting most of these nighttime niches, and farther east, near Beaudry métro station, it becomes the main drag for the Village, also called Gay Village. For whatever reason, the streets named after saints contain most of the clubs: rue Ste-Catherine, boulevard St-Laurent, rue St-Paul, and rue St-Denis. The Old Port is currently Montréal's hottest neighborhood, with a steady stream of chic venues opening in this cobblestone district.

Montréal's nightlife swings with a robust passion. From the early evening "5-à-7" after-work cocktail circuit, to the slightly later concerts and supper clubs (restaurant–dance club hybrids where people dance on the tables after eating off them), on into the even later dance club scene, all tastes, cultural backgrounds, and legal ages join the melee. Clubbing is, to say the least, huge in Montréal. Some restaurants are even installing discotheques in their basements.

The bars stop serving around 3 am and shut down shortly thereafter (with the exception of sanctioned "after-hour" haunts). On the weekends, expect them to be packed to the gills until closing. The club scene picks up right after the bars close, and then extends until dawn.

Performing Arts

Montréal is the home of nearly a dozen professional companies and several important theater schools, but there's also a lively English-language theater scene and one of the few remaining Yiddish theaters in North America. As for venues, the Quartier des Spectacles is a 70-acre theater district in Downtown with stages for outdoor performances and nearly 80 venues for dance, music, theater, and art.

For a city its size, Montréal offers a remarkable number of opportunities for fans of classical music to get their fill, from operas and symphonies to string quartets.

As for dance, there are several modern dance companies of note, including Montréal Danse and Québec's premier ballet company Les Grands Ballets Canadiens.

Shopping

Montrealers *magasinent* (shop) with a vengeance, whether they're scurrying down busy Ste-Catherine Downtown checking out department store bargains, hunting for Danish antiques in the Gay Village, browsing designer wares on St-Laurent, or sampling gourmet eats at one of the city's markets. For many locals, doing the *magasinage* is practically an art form.

Yet one of North America's top shopping cities is in a state of flux. Where, until recently, boulevard St-Laurent and rue St-Denis, were the "it" streets to shop, increasingly this honor is now being shared with Old Montréal, an area that has been enjoying a renaissance. In the last decade or so, Montréal's patron saint of shopping streets, Ste-Catherine, has been undergoing a metamorphosis as a significant cohort of young, educated professionals moves into condos Downtown and retailers scramble to meet their needs and tastes. The changing face of retail and the prevalence of online shopping has also contributed to the transformation of Ste-Catherine and other Downtown streets, with the corresponding downward slide of many traditional brick-and-mortar stores. That being said, Montréal's most important shopping street has also welcomed new arrivals such as the trendy Vancouver-based Aritzia; Lolë, Montréal's more stylish version of Lululemon; an elegant Club Monaco spread out over two floors of the Beaux Arts–style Dominion Square Building; and a branch of hip Montréal-brand, Frank and Oak, initially an online-only retailer. Moreover, the city's two luxury department stores, Ogilvy and Holt Renfrew, are set to merge into one mammoth luxury department store and Four Seasons Hotel complex slated to open by late 20120.

Meanwhile, city hall is planning (and has been for a while now) an epic—and highly controversial—face-lift for Ste-Catherine. If implemented, the commercial epicenter will be reimagined into a new outdoor pedestrian shopping mall with heated sidewalks and longer shopping hours. For now, the Downtown core, including Old Montréal, Chinatown, and the Quartier des Spectacles, is a tourist zone, and as such, stores are permitted to stay open 24/7.

Activities

Most Montrealers would probably claim they hate winter, but the city is full of cold-weather sports venues—skating rinks, cross-country ski trails, and toboggan runs—that see plenty of action. During warm-weather months, residents head for the tennis courts, bicycle trails, golf courses, and two lakes for boating and swimming.

You don't have to travel far from Montréal to find good downhill skiing or snowboarding. The many ski centers in the Laurentians and Eastern Townships are within an hour's drive from the city. As for cross-country, excellent trails can be found right in Parc du Mont-Royal, or on the Islands (Île Ste-Hélène and Île Notre-Dame).

Despite the bitter winters (or perhaps because of them), Montréal has fallen in love with the bicycle, with enthusiasts cycling year-round. More than 600 km (372 miles) of bike paths crisscross the metropolitan area, and bikes are welcome on the first car of métro trains during off-peak hours.

The city is truly passionate about Canada's national sport, hockey. If you're here during hockey season, try to catch a Montréal Canadiens game at Centre Bell, or at the very least find yourself a good sports bar.

Old Montréal (Vieux-Montréal)

Old Montréal, which was once enclosed by thick stone walls, is the oldest part of the city. It runs roughly from the waterfront in the south to ruelle des Fortifications in the north and from rue McGill in the west to rue Berri in the east. The churches and chapels here stand as testament to the religious fervor

that inspired the French settlers who landed here in 1642 to build a "Christian commonwealth" under the leadership of Paul de Chomedey, Sieur de Maisonneuve, and the indomitable Jeanne Mance. Stone warehouses and residences are reminders of how quickly the fur trade commercialized that lofty ideal and made the city one of the most prosperous in 18th-century Nouvelle France. And finally, the financial houses along rue St-Jacques, bristling with Victorian ornamentation, recall the days when Montrealers controlled virtually all the wealth of the young Dominion of Canada.

History and good looks aside, however, Old Montréal still works for a living. Stockbrokers and shipping companies continue to operate out of the old financial district. The city's largest newspaper, *La Presse,* has its offices here. Lawyers in black gowns hurry through the streets to plead cases at the Palais de Justice or the Cour d'Appel, the city council meets in the Second Empire city hall on rue Notre-Dame, and local shoppers hunt for deals in the bargain clothing stores just off rue McGill.

GETTING HERE AND AROUND
The easiest way to get from Downtown to Old Montréal is aboard Bus 515, a shuttle that provides a quick direct link to several sites in the Old City and Old Port. It runs from 7 am to midnight. You can also take the métro Orange line to the Place-d'Armes and Square-Victoria stations, or you can walk, but the primary routes from Downtown go through some drab and somewhat seedy, although not especially dangerous, areas. If you feel like biking, it's better to rent a Bixi bicycle at a Downtown stand and drop it off at one in Old Montréal. Biking to Old Montréal is a breeze because it's all downhill, but the return trip to Downtown is a challenging workout.

Taxis can whisk you here from Downtown in about 10 minutes.

The best way to get around the Old City is on foot, but wear good shoes because the cobbles can be hard on the feet.

TIMING

Having enough time to see the sights, stroll around, and try some of the area's notable restaurants means dedicating at least one day. If it's your first time in the city and you're only here for an extended weekend, consider staying in one of Old Montréal's auberges or boutique hotels.

◉ Sights

★ **Basilique Notre-Dame-de-Montréal** (*Our Lady of Montréal Basilica*)
HISTORIC SITE | Few churches in North America are as wow-inducing as Notre-Dame. Everything about the Gothic Revival–style church, which opened in 1829, seems designed to make you gasp—from the 228-foot twin towers out front to the tens of thousands of 24-karat gold stars that stud the soaring blue ceiling.

Nothing in a city renowned for churches matches Notre-Dame for sheer grandeur—or noise-making capacity: its 12-ton bass bell is the largest in North America, and its 7,000-pipe Casavant organ can make the walls tremble. The pulpit is a work of art in itself, with an intricately curving staircase and fierce figures of Ezekiel and Jeremiah crouching at its base. The whole place is so overwhelming it's easy to miss such lesser features as the stained-glass windows from Limoges and the side altars dedicated to St. Marguerite d'Youville, Canada's first native-born saint; St. Marguerite Bourgeoys, Canada's first schoolteacher; and a group of Sulpician priests martyred in Paris during the French Revolution.

For a peek at the magnificent baptistery, decorated with frescoes by Ozias Leduc, you'll have to tiptoe through the glassed-off prayer room in the northwest corner of the church. Every year dozens of brides—including Céline Dion, in

1994—march up the aisle of **Chapelle Notre-Dame-du-Sacré-Coeur** (Our Lady of the Sacred Heart Chapel), behind the main altar, to exchange vows with their grooms before a huge modern bronze sculpture that you either love or hate.

Notre-Dame is an active house of worship, so dress accordingly. The chapel can't be viewed weekdays during the 12:15 pm mass, and is often closed Saturday for weddings. ■TIP→ **Don't miss the 45-minute multimedia spectacle,"Aura," which celebrates the basilica's exquisite features through light and sound.** See website for schedule (⊕ *www.aurabasiliquenotredame.com/en*). ⊠ *110 rue Notre-Dame Ouest, Old Montréal* ☎ *514/842–2925, 866/842–2925 for Aura tickets* ⊕ *www.basiliquenddm.org* ⊠ *C$8 (with or without tour); multimedia show "Aura" C$26.50* Ⓜ *Place-d'Armes.*

Centre des Sciences de Montréal
MUSEUM | FAMILY | You—or more likely, your kids—can design an energy-efficient bike, create a television news report, explore the impact that manufacturing one T-shirt has on the environment, find out what it's like to ride a unicycle 20 feet above the ground, create an animated film, or just watch an IMAX movie on a giant screen at Montréal's interactive science center. A recent addition, Clic! The Zone for Curious Young Minds, is a colorful and fun area for four- to seven-year-olds. Games, puzzles, and hands-on experiments make it an ideal place for rainy days or even fair ones. The center also has a bistro serving light meals, a coffee and pastry shop, and a food court. ⊠ *Quai King Edward, Old Montréal* ☎ *514/496–4724, 877/496–4724* ⊕ *www.centredessciencesdemontreal.com* ⊠ *C$22, IMAX C$12* Ⓜ *Place-d'Armes.*

Chapelle Notre-Dame-de-Bon-Secours (*Our Lady of Perpetual Help Chapel*)
ARCHAEOLOGICAL SITE | Mariners have been popping into Notre-Dame-de-Bon-Secours for centuries to kneel before a little 17th-century statue of the Virgin Mary

72

and pray for a safe passage—or give thanks for one. Often, they've expressed their gratitude by leaving votive lamps in the shape of small ships, many of which still hang from the barrel-vaulted ceiling. This is why most Montrealers call the chapel the Église des Matelots (the Sailors' Church), and why many people still stop by to say a prayer and light a candle before leaving on a long trip.

These days, the statue of Our Lady of Perpetual Help guards the remains of St. Marguerite Bourgeoys, who had the original chapel built in 1657 and is entombed in the side altar next to the east wall of the chapel. The current chapel dates from 1771; a renovation project in 1998 revealed some beautiful 18th-century murals that had been hidden under layers of paint.

The 69-step climb to the top of the steeple is worth the effort for the glorious view of the harbor, as is the equally steep climb down to the archaeological excavations under the chapel for a glimpse into the history of the chapel and the neighborhood. The dig is accessible through the adjacent **Musée Marguerite Bourgeoys,** which also has exhibits on the life of St. Marguerite and the daily lives of the colonists she served. The chapel is closed mid-January through February except for the 10:30 am mass on Sunday. ⊠ *400 rue St-Paul Est, Old Montréal* ☎ *514/282–8670* ⊕ *www.marguerite-bourgeoys.com* ✉ *Museum (includes archaeological site) and tower C$12; Chapel free* ⊗ *Closed Mon. Nov.–April* Ⓜ *Champ-de-Mars.*

Hôtel de Ville (*City Hall*)
GOVERNMENT BUILDING | President Charles de Gaulle of France marked Canada's centennial celebrations in 1967 by standing on the central balcony of Montréal's ornate city hall on July 24 and shouting "*Vive le Québec libre*" ("Long live free Québec"), much to the delight of the separatist movement and to the horror of the federal government that had invited him over in the first place. Perhaps he got

carried away because he felt so at home: the Second Empire–style city hall, built in 1878, is modeled after the one in Tours, France. Free guided tours are available (reservations required). ⊠ *275 rue Notre-Dame Est, Old Montréal* ☎ *514/872–0077 for guided tours* ⊕ *www.ville.montreal.qc.ca* ✉ *Free* Ⓜ *Champ-de-Mars.*

Maison St-Gabriel
HISTORIC SITE | Thick stone walls, a steep roof, and mullioned windows mark the Maison St-Gabriel as one of Montréal's rare surviving 17th-century houses. But it's the interior and the furnishings that will sweep you back to the colonial days when Sainte-Marguerite Bourgeoys and the religious order she founded used this house to train *les filles du roy* (king's daughters) in the niceties of home management. Les filles were young women without family or fortune but plenty of spunk who volunteered to cross the Atlantic in leaky boats to become the wives and mothers of New France. It wasn't an easy life, as the Maison's hard, narrow beds, primitive utensils, and drafty rooms attest—but it had its rewards, and the prize at the end was a respectable, settled life. Ste-Marguerite also had some state-of-the-art domestic equipment—the latest in looms and butter churns, labor-saving spit turners for roasting meat, and an ingenious granite sink with a drainage system that piped water straight out to the garden. Located on the little island of New France and deep in the working-class neighborhood of Pointe St-Charles, Maison St-Gabriel is off the beaten path, but it's well worth a 10-minute taxi ride from Old Montréal. ⊠ *2146 pl. Dublin, Pointe-St-Charles* ☎ *514/935–8136* ⊕ *www.maisonsaint-gabriel.qc.ca* ✉ *C$15 weekdays; C$20 weekends* ⊗ *Closed Mon.* Ⓜ *Square-Victoria, then Bus 61.*

Marché Bonsecours (*Bonsecours Market*)
BUILDING | You can't buy fruits and vegetables in the Marché Bonsecours anymore, but you can view an exhibit, shop for local

fashions, crafts, and souvenirs in the row of upscale boutiques that fill its main hall, lunch in one of several restaurants, or grab a craft beer. But the Marché is best admired from the outside. Built in the 1840s as the city's main market, it is possibly the most beautifully proportioned neoclassical building in Montréal, with its six cast-iron Doric columns and two rows of meticulously even sashed windows, all topped with a silvery dome. Perhaps the marché was too elegant to be just a farmers' market. ⊠ *350 rue St-Paul Est, Old Montréal* ☎ *514/872–7730* ⊕ *www.marchebonsecours.qc.ca* Ⓜ *Champ-de-Mars.*

★ **Musée d'Archéologie et d'Histoire Pointe-à-Callière (PAC)** (*Pointe-à-Callière Archaeology and History Museum*) **ARCHAEOLOGICAL SITE** | The modern glass building is impressive, and the audiovisual show is a breezy romp through Montréal's history from the Ice Age to the present. The museum presents new local and international temporary exhibitions each year, but the real reason to visit the city's most ambitious archaeological museum is to take the elevator ride down to the 17th century.

It's dark down there, and just a little creepy thanks to the 350-year-old tombstones teetering in the gloom, but it's worth the trip. This is a serious archaeological dig that takes you to the very foundations of the city. A more lighthearted exhibit explores life and love in multicultural Montréal. For a spectacular view of the Old Port, the St. Lawrence River, and the Islands, ride the elevator to the top of the tower, or stop for lunch in the museum's glass-fronted café. In summer there are re-creations of period fairs and festivals on the grounds near the museum.

The Fort Ville-Marie pavilion showcases the remains of the forts and artifacts from the first Montrealers. The 360-foot underground William collector sewer, built in the 1830s and considered a

masterpiece of civil engineering at that time, connects the original museum space with the new pavilion and features a sound-and-light show projected onto the walls of the collector sewer. ⊠ *350 pl. Royale, Old Montréal* ☎ *514/872–9150* ⊕ *www.pacmuseum.qc.ca* 🎟 *C\$22* Ⓜ *Place-d'Armes.*

Musée du Château Ramezay
HISTORIC SITE | Claude de Ramezay, the city's 11th governor, was probably daydreaming of home when he built his Montréal residence, which is on UNESCO's list of "1001 historic sites you must see before you die." Its thick stone walls, dormer windows, and steeply pitched roof make it look like a little bit of 18th-century Normandy dropped into the middle of North America—although the round, squat tower is a 19th-century addition. The extravagant mahogany paneling in the Salon de Nantes was installed when Louis XV was still king of France. The British used the château as headquarters after their conquest in 1760, and so did the American commanders Richard Montgomery and Benedict Arnold. Benjamin Franklin, who came north in a failed attempt to persuade the Quebecois to join the American Revolution, stayed here during that winter adventure.

Most of the château's exhibits are a little staid—guns, uniforms, and documents on the main floor and tableaux depicting colonial life in the cellars—but they include some unexpected little eccentricities that make it worth the visit. Head outside, through the back door, and you'll enter gardens full of 18th-century tranquility. ⊠ *280 rue Notre-Dame Est, Old Montréal* ☎ *514/861–3708* ⊕ *www.chateauramezay.qc.ca* 🎟 *C\$11* 🕙 *Closed Mon. late Oct. to late May* Ⓜ *Champ-de-Mars.*

Old Port (*Vieux Port*)
CITY PARK | FAMILY | Montréal's favorite waterfront park is your ideal gateway to the St. Lawrence River. Rent a pedal boat, take a ferry to **Île Ste-Hélène,** sign

Built on the actual foundations of the city, the impressive Pointe-à-Callière museum takes visitors back in time to 17th-century Montréal.

up for a dinner cruise, or, if you're really adventurous, ride a raft or a jet boat through the turbulent Lachine Rapids. If you're determined to stay ashore, however, there's still plenty to do, including riding the Grande Roue, the tallest Ferris wheel in Canada; soaking in the rays at the Clock Tower Beach (you can't swim, though); and enjoying street performances, sound-and-light shows, or art displays and exhibitions. Visiting warships from the Canadian navy and other countries often dock here and open their decks to the public. You can rent a bicycle or a pair of in-line skates at one of the shops along rue de la Commune and explore the waterfront at your leisure. In winter, rent a pair of skates and glide around the outdoor rink. You can also, quite literally, lose the kids in **Shed 16's Labyrinthe,** a maze of alleys, surprises, and obstacles built inside an old waterfront warehouse. ⊠ *Old Montréal* ☎ *514/496–7678, 800/971–7678* ⊕ *www. oldportofmontreal.com* Ⓜ *Place-d'Armes or Champ-de-Mars.*

Place-d'Armes

HISTORIC SITE | When Montréal was under attack, citizens and soldiers would rally at Place-d'Armes, but these days the only rallying is done by tourists, lunching office workers, calèche drivers, and flocks of voracious pigeons. The pigeons are particularly fond of the triumphant statue of Montréal's founder, Paul de Chomedey, with his lance upraised, perched above the fountain in the middle of the cobblestone square. Tunnels beneath the square protected the colonists from the winter weather and provided an escape route; unfortunately, they are too small and dangerous to visit. ⊠ *Bordered by rues Notre-Dame Ouest, St-Jacques, and St-Sulpice, Old Montréal* Ⓜ *Place-d'Armes.*

Place de la Grande-Paix

HISTORIC SITE | If you're looking for peace and quiet, the narrow strip of grass and trees on Place d'Youville just east of Place Royale is an appropriate place to find it. It was here, after all, that the French signed a major peace treaty with dozens of aboriginal nations in 1702. It was also here that the first French colonists to settle in Montréal landed their four boats on May 17, 1642. An obelisk records the settlers' names. ✉ *Between pl. d'Youville and rue William, Old Montréal* Ⓜ *Place-d'Armes.*

Place Jacques-Cartier

PLAZA | FAMILY | The cobbled square at the heart of Old Montréal is part carnival, part flower market, and part sheer fun. You can pause here to have your portrait painted, buy an ice cream or watch the street performers. If you have more time, try to get a table at one of the sidewalk cafés, order a beer or a glass of wine, and watch the passing parade. At Christmastime you can order a mulled wine in the market and warm up by one of the wood-burning stoves from your perch on an Adirondack chair. The 1809 monument honoring Lord Nelson's victory over Napoléon Bonaparte's French navy at Trafalgar angers some modern-day Québec nationalists. The campaign to raise money for it was led by the Sulpician priests, who were engaged in delicate land negotiations with the British government at the time and were eager to show what good subjects they were. ✉ *Bordered by rues Notre-Dame Est and de la Commune, Old Montréal* Ⓜ *Champ-de-Mars.*

Place Royale

HISTORIC SITE | The oldest public square in Montréal, dating to the 17th century, was a market during the French regime and later became a Victorian garden. ✉ *Bordered by rues St-Paul Ouest and de la Commune, Old Montréal* Ⓜ *Place-d'Armes.*

Square Victoria

PLAZA | Although Square Victoria officially lies within the Quartier International, or International District, Montrealers consider it a part of Old Montréal. The square nicely blends its French and English heritage with an 1872 statue of Queen Victoria on one side and an authentic Parisian métro entrance and a flower market on

the other. Both are framed by a two-block stretch of trees, benches, and fountains that makes a pleasant place to relax and admire the handsome 1920s office buildings on the east side. The art nouveau métro entrance, incidentally, was a gift from the French capital's transit commission. ✉ *Rue du Square Victoria, between rues Viger and St-Jacques, Old Montréal* Ⓜ *Square-Victoria.*

🍴 Restaurants

Old Montréal is home to some of the city's hippest and most charming bistros and fine-dining restaurants—all tucked into heritage buildings. Foodies eat wild game and fresh seafood while drinking imported wine. Many of the better restaurants have a reasonable table d'hôte at lunch. Daily changing menus written on chalkboards are a common sight, since market-fresh food is popular.

Boris Bistro

$$$ | FRENCH | Behind a freestanding facade (the remains of a burned-out historic building) is one of the best alfresco dining areas in Montréal. Like an enchanted forest, the tree-shaded terrace draws crowds to sip glasses of kir royale or munch on locally sourced cheese plates. **Known for:** organic wines; outdoor terrace; gluten-free cuisine. ⑤ *Average main: C$24* ✉ *465 rue McGill, Old Montréal* ☎ *514/848–9575* ⊕ *www. borisbistro.com* ☉ *Closed Sun. fall–spring* Ⓜ *Square-Victoria.*

Brasserie 701

$$$ | BRASSERIE | Inspired by Paris's golden-age brasseries, Brasserie 701's spectacular setting features high ceilings, neoclassical architecture, giant arched windows, and lovely chandeliers. The menu incudes the usual suspects expected at a brasserie, from tartares, filet mignon, and bavette to merguez sausage, Alsatian salad, and escargot. **Known for:** salmon and beef tartare; homemade wild mushroom ravioli; seared duck

Old Montréal (Vieux Montréal)

Sights ▼

1	Basilique Notre-Dame-de-Montréal	E6
2	Centre des Sciences de Montréal	F7
3	Chapelle Notre-Dame-de-Bon-Secours	I5
4	Hôtel de Ville	H5
5	Maison St-Gabriel	A9
6	Marché Bonsecours	H6
7	Musée d'Archéologie et d'Histoire Pointe-à-Callière (PAC)	D7
8	Musée du Château Ramezay	H5
9	Old Port	H7
10	Place d'Armes	E5
11	Place de la Grande-Paix	D7
12	Place Jacques-Cartier	H5
13	Place Royale	E6
14	Square Victoria	B4

Restaurants ▼

1	Boris Bistro	B6
2	Brasserie 701	E5
3	Brit & Chips	B6
4	Club Chasse et Pêche	H5
5	Crew Collective Café	C5
6	Da Emma	A9
7	Garde Manger	D6
8	Gibbys	C7
9	Hambar	B7
10	Ikanos	B7
11	L'Assommoir	D5
12	L'Auberge Saint-Gabriel	G5
13	Le Cartet	B8
14	Le Petit Dep	D6
15	Le Serpent	A7
16	Les 400 Coups	I5
17	Maison Christian Faure	E6
18	Olive + Gourmando	C6
19	Restaurant Helena	B6
20	Toqué!	C4
21	Verses	E6

Hotels ▼

1	Auberge Bonaparte	D6
2	Auberge du Vieux-Port	G6
3	Hôtel Épik Montréal	D6
4	Hôtel Gault	C6
5	Hôtel Le St-James	C5
6	Hôtel Nelligan	E6
7	Hôtel St. Paul	B7
8	Hôtel William Gray	G5
9	InterContinental Montréal	C4
10	Le Petit Hôtel	D6
11	Le Place d'Armes Hôtel & Suites	E5
12	Le Saint-Sulpice	E6
13	LHotel	C5
14	Springhill Suites by Marriott	F6
15	W Montréal	B4

breast with Quebec pattypan. $ *Average main:* ⊠ *701 côte de la Place-d'Armes, Old Montréal* ☎ *514/904–1201* ⊕ *www. brasserie701.com/en* Ⓜ *Place-d'Armes.*

Brit & Chips

$$ | BRITISH | FAMILY | There's no need to cross the pond to find perfectly battered fish and delicious chips, as they can be found right here in Old Montréal. The cod is a staple, but the salmon dipped in beer batter is also a menu favorite, and for a Canadian touch, try the haddock covered in golden maple syrup batter. **Known for:** fish-and-chips; maple syrup batter; long lines at weekday lunch. $ *Average main: C$12* ⊠ *433 rue McGill, Old Montréal* ☎ *514/840–1001* ⊕ *www.britandchips. com* Ⓜ *Square-Victoria.*

Club Chasse et Pêche

$$$$ | CANADIAN | Despite the name— French for "Hunting and Fishing Club"—this isn't a hangout for the local gun-and-rod set. Impeccable service and top-notch ingredients have made this one of the best restaurants in the city; the name is simply referencing the wood-and-leather decor. **Known for:** chasse (filet mignon) et pêche (lobster) dish; impeccable service; terroir cuisine. $ *Average main: C$38* ⊠ *423 rue St-Claude, Old Montréal* ☎ *514/861–1112* ⊕ *www. leclubchasseetpeche.com* ⊘ *Closed Sun. and Mon.* Ⓜ *Champ-de-Mars.*

★ Crew Collective Café

$ | CAFÉ | Undoubtedly the most strikingly beautiful coffee shop in Montréal, perhaps even in North America, Crew Collective & Café is housed inside a former 1920s-era bank that's fitted with 50-foot-high vaulted ceilings, intricate tiling, and bronze chandeliers. The café doubles as a co-working space for Web start-ups, so it's only fitting that patrons be able to order their coffee and nibbles directly online, in real-time, without ever having to queue. **Known for:** architectural, lavish space; curated coffee beans; cold brew. $ *Average main: C$6* ⊠ *360 rue Saint-Jacques,*

The City's Oldest Patisserie 🍴

A light croissant or rich pastry from **Duc de Lorraine**, the city's oldest patisserie, makes for a nice break. Try to snag an almond paste croissant before the store runs out. For lunch, try one of the quiches, sandwiches, or the soupe du jour followed by a scoop of homemade ice cream or a *tartelette poire et amande* (pear and almond tart). ⊠ *5002 Côte-des-Neiges* ☎ *514 731–4128* ⊕ *www.ducdelorraine.ca.*

Old Montréal ⊕ *crewcollectivecafe.com* Ⓜ *Place-d'Armes.*

Da Emma

$$$$ | ITALIAN | The cellar of what used to be Montréal's first women's prison hardly sounds like the ideal setting for an Italian eatery, but grandma Emma's cooking hushes any bad vibes from the 1800s. Stone walls and heavy beams serve as backdrop for Roman dishes like roasted lamb, fettuccine *con funghi porcini* and pasta *al vongole*, which have all foregone fussy presentation to focus on superior fixings. **Known for:** 300-year-old stone walls; friendly ambience; rustic, authentic dishes. $ *Average main: C$35* ⊠ *777 rue de la Commune Ouest, Old Montréal* ☎ *514/392–1568* ⊘ *Closed Sun. No lunch Mon.* Ⓜ *Square-Victoria.*

Garde Manger

$$$$ | CANADIAN | Popular options at this see-and-be-seen locale, steered by local celebrity chef Chuck Hughes, include bountiful platters of seafood, rich lobster poutine, and hearty braised short ribs. The bar, where flirting is in high gear, is a fun option for dining and hanging out. **Known for:** seafood platter; lively atmosphere; lobster poutine. $ *Average main: C$35* ⊠ *408 rue St-François-Xavier, Old*

Montréal ☎ 514/678–5044 ⊕ gardeman-ger.ca ⊗ Closed Mon. Ⓜ Place-d'Armes.

Gibbys

$$$$ | STEAKHOUSE | A culinary landmark like few others in the city, Gibbys is one of Montréal's most famous steak hous-es. Part of what makes it so attractive is the 200-year-old historic building in which it's located, with vaulted-ceilinged, wood-beamed, stone-walled, and candlelit dining rooms. **Known for:** aged steaks; historic building; extensive wine list. ⑤ Average main: C$48 ✉ 298 pl. d'Youville, Old Montréal ☎ 514/282–1837 ⊕ www.gibbys.com Ⓜ Square-Victoria.

Hambar

$$$$ | CANADIAN | As the name suggests, the focus of this restaurant is ham in all its many incarnations. The menu changes seasonally but charcuteries and marinat-ed vegetables imported from Europe are ever-present. **Known for:** extensive by-the-glass wine list; brunch on weekends; rib steak. ⑤ Average main: C$35 ✉ Hotel St. Paul, 355 rue McGill, Old Montréal ☎ 514/879–1234 ⊕ www.hambar.ca.

★ Ikanos

$$$$ | MODERN GREEK | A far cry from the cliché-clad tavernas found elsewhere in the city, Ikanos serves refined Aegean gastronomy in an elegant and sleek envi-ronment. No blue-and-white checkered tablecloths in sight; the muted neutral palette puts the spotlight on the food. **Known for:** mezzes (Greek tapas); Greek wines; loukoumades. ⑤ Average main: C$45 ✉ 112 rue McGill, Old Montréal ☎ 514/842–0867 ⊕ www.restauranti-kanos.com ⊗ No lunch on weekends Ⓜ Square-Victoria.

L'Assommoir

$$$ | CANADIAN | The cocktail menu originally put this hip bistro on the map, drawing crowds for creative martinis (think cucumber and basil), and now the food holds its own. The house specialty is tartares—the menu lists four varia-tions of marinated raw fish—and heaps of grilled meat, fish, or tempeh served on wooden chopping blocks. **Known for:** tartares; lively crowd; inventive cocktails. ⑤ Average main: C$25 ✉ 211 rue Notre-Dame Ouest, Old Montréal ☎ 514/272–0777 ⊕ www.assommoir.com Ⓜ Place-d'Armes.

L'Auberge Saint-Gabriel

$$$$ | BISTRO | Stone walls and wood-beamed ceilings give this restaurant located inside the "first inn in North America" an appropriate dash of dra-ma. The funky overlapping decor and eclectically surprising elements—hanging fireplaces, stained-glass windows, tap-estries on the walls—make it absolutely extraordinary. **Known for:** desserts; cheese fondue; outdoor patio. ⑤ Aver-age main: C$35 ✉ 426 rue St-Gabriel, Old Montréal ☎ 514/878–3561 ⊕ www.lesaint-gabriel.com ⊗ Closed Sun. and Mon. Ⓜ Place-d'Armes.

Le Cartet

$$ | FRENCH | As a gourmet grocery shop, takeout counter, and French restaurant rolled into one, this splendid space was quickly adopted by local foodies. Instead of being dejected by the brunch queues on Saturday and Sunday, visitors should take advantage of that time to browse the restaurant's inviting grocery shop for gourmet souvenirs to take home. **Known for:** brunch; mimosas; gazpa-cho. ⑤ Average main: C$15 ✉ 106 rue McGill, Old Montréal ☎ 514/871-8887 Ⓜ Square-Victoria.

★ Le Petit Dep

$ | CANADIAN | This adorable little gourmet convenience store and café with a mint-green facade serves single origin coffee, prêt-à-manger soups, salads, and comfort foods such as chili, pasta, and vegan shepherd's pie. There are also mouth-watering home-baked goods and candy in bulk. **Known for:** prêt-à-manger meals; delightful setting; delicious sweets. ⑤ Average main: C$6 ✉ 179 rue St-Paul Ouest, Old Montréal ☎ 514/284-9162 Ⓜ Place-d'Armes or Square-Victoria.

3

Montréal OLD MONTRÉAL (VIEUX-MONTRÉAL)

★ Le Serpent

$$$ | **MODERN ITALIAN** | The expertise and irreproachable service at Le Serpent truly make it an essential stop on any Montréal foodie itinerary. The industrial-looking space caters to trendy diners, and almost paradoxically, serves sublime Italianate plates that could be mistaken for comfort food if they weren't so elegantly presented. **Known for:** good food; industrial chic vibe; friendly service. $ *Average main: C$30* ✉ *257 rue Prince, Old Montréal* ☎ *514/316–4666* ⊕ *www.leserpent.ca* ⊘ *Closed Sun.* Ⓜ *Square-Victoria.*

Les 400 Coups

$$$ | **CANADIAN** | This low-key destination is the perfect spot for an intimate yet elevated meal, where diners can safely anticipate irreproachable dishes (including the $125, five-course tasting menu with wine pairing) and a finely curated wine list. The decor is grandiose and includes a very large mural taking up one long wall, a vintage tin ceiling, and floor-to-ceiling doors and windows. **Known for:** tasting menu; curated wine list; intimate setting. $ *Average main: C$27* ✉ *400 Notre-Dame Est, Old Montréal* ☎ *514/985–0400* ⊕ *www.les400coups.ca* ⊘ *Closed Sun. and Mon.*

Maison Christian Faure

$ | **BAKERY** | **FAMILY** | The upscale bakery has made its elegant home inside a historic, beautifully renovated three-story grayston in Old Montréal. Baskets of buttery brioches and flaky croissants await, and the prominent pastry display holds rows of seasonal fruit tarts and classic French desserts like *mille-feuilles* (made of delicate layers of puff pastry and airy vanilla-scented custard) and Paris-Brest (made of choux pastry and a praline-flavored cream). **Known for:** French-style pâtisseries; historic building; acclaimed pastry chef. $ *Average main: C$7* ✉ *355 Place Royale, Old Montréal* ☎ *514/508–6453* ⊕ *maisonchristianfaure.ca/en* Ⓜ *Place-d'Armes.*

★ Olive + Gourmando

$$ | **CAFÉ** | **FAMILY** | Influential types arrive at lunchtime en masse for a table at this bustling bakery and sandwich shop where vegetables are organically grown in a nearby garden and fresh crab is flown in for salads. Crowd pleasers include Le Cubain panini (pancetta, roasted pork, Gruyère with lime, cilantro, and chipotle and the vegan sandwich with chickpea and harissa spread, pickled beets, creamy sauce, and minty slaw. **Known for:** organic produce; affordable sandwiches; popular brunch. $ *Average main: C$15* ✉ *351 rue St-Paul Ouest, Old Montréal* ☎ *514/350–1083* ⊕ *www.oliveetgourmando.com* ⊘ *No dinner* Ⓜ *Square-Victoria.*

Restaurant Helena

$$$$ | **PORTUGUESE** | Housed inside a welcoming space with alcove windows and stone walls, this airy, colorful restaurant serves traditional Portuguese with plenty of seafood dishes. Share a few tapas plates, like the grilled sardines fillets, cod fritters, the grilled asparagus, or the baby potatoes with herbs before delving into the main course. **Known for:** historic building; Portuguese tapas; lunchtime prix-fixe. $ *Average main: C$36* ✉ *438 McGill, Old Montréal* ☎ *514/878–1555* ⊕ *www.restauranthelena.com* ⊘ *Closed Sun. No lunch Sat.* Ⓜ *Square-Victoria.*

★ Toqué!

$$$$ | **FRENCH** | Frequently named one of Montréal's best restaurants and Canada's third best by canadas100best.com, a meal at Toqué! is not so much about sustenance but rather experience. Toqué is slang for "a little stubborn," as in the chef's insistence on using fresh, local ingredients; consequently, the menu changes daily in accordance with market offerings but foie gras, duck and wild venison are on constant rotation. **Known for:** tasting menu; market cuisine; wine pairings. $ *Average main: C$54* ✉ *900 pl. Jean-Paul-Riopelle, Old Montréal* ☎ *514/499–2084* ⊕ *www.*

restaurant-toque.com ⊗ *Closed Sun. and Mon. No lunch Sat.* Ⓜ *Square-Victoria.*

Verses

$$$$ | **MODERN CANADIAN** | The setting—a stone-walled room overlooking the hubbub of rue St-Paul—may be the most romantic in the Old City, and the food here is almost poetic. There are a few vegetarian/vegan options such as the cauliflower steak with ras el hanout, the fennel and greens in a white balsamic vinaigrette with marinated peppers, and the truffle linguini. **Known for:** cauliflower steak; crab risotto; truffle linguini. Ⓢ *Average main: C$37* ⊠ *Hôtel Nelligan, 100 rue St-Paul Ouest, Old Montréal* ☎ *514/788–4000* ⊕ *www.versesrestaurant.com* Ⓜ *Place-d'Armes.*

 ## Hotels

Let's start with the name. Nobody says "Old Town." That's an American phrase. You may call it Old Montréal, but street signs are in French and say "Vieux-Montréal." Either way, it's full of charm—from narrow, cobblestone streets to quaint outdoor terraces, or *terrasses* in French. You can find boutique hotels, auberges, and cozy bed-and-breakfasts nestled inside heritage buildings. Most properties have exposed beams, stone walls, wooden floors, and thick, casement windows. History buffs find this area pleasing, as do people who want to wander around boutiques and art galleries. But know that this is no place for stilettos. Bring your walking shoes and expect to stumble on film crews and the occasional Hollywood actor taking a smoke break. We're talking to you, Brad Pitt.

Auberge Bonaparte

$$$ | **B&B/INN** | Stately and distinguished inside a 19th-century building, the freshly updated Auberge Bonaparte is a true gem, with old-world charm. **Pros:** excellent location; some rooms have balconies; perfect for theater lovers— the Centaur Theatre is next door. **Cons:**

downstairs restaurant can be a bit noisy on weekends; not family-friendly; parking lot is down the street. Ⓢ *Rooms from: C$329* ⊠ *447 rue St-François-Xavier, Old Montréal* ☎ *514/844–1448* ⊕ *www.bonaparte.ca* ⊷ *31 rooms* ⦿ *Free breakfast* Ⓜ *Place-d'Armes.*

★ Auberge du Vieux-Port

$$$ | **B&B/INN** | This showcase for 19th-century architecture—think casement windows, exposed beams and brick—is the gold standard for intimate boutique hotels, attracting A-listers and well-heeled romantics with its mix of old-world charm and modern comfort. **Pros:** new loft options offer more space and high ceilings; expansive rooftop deck; some rooms have decks and fireplaces. **Cons:** sometimes noisy in street-facing rooms; some rooms are very small; breakfast not included in base price. Ⓢ *Rooms from: C$315* ⊠ *97 rue de la Commune Est, Old Montréal* ☎ *514/876–0081, 888/660–7678* ⊕ *www.aubergeduvieuxport.com* ⊷ *75 rooms* ⦿ *No meals* Ⓜ *Place-d'Armes or Champ-de-Mars.*

★ Hôtel Épik Montréal

$$$ | **B&B/INN** | With its rustic stone walls and exposed beams, this inn was the first of its kind in the Old Port when it opened in the late 1980s, and the new owners continue to honor its tradition of calm excellence while adding modern comfort and contemporary design accents throughout. **Pros:** refrigerator downstairs for guest to use in a pinch (if there's space); soundproof shutters; bountiful breakfast. **Cons:** rooms need to be booked far in advance; lobby's chic cocktail bar isn't suitable for kids; king-size beds are pricey. Ⓢ *Rooms from: C$329* ⊠ *171 rue St-Paul Ouest, Old Montréal* ☎ *514/842–2634, 877/841–2634* ⊕ *www.epikmontreal.com* ⊷ *10 rooms* ⦿ *Free breakfast* Ⓜ *Place-d'Armes.*

★ Hôtel Gault

$$$$ | **HOTEL** | Once a cotton factory in the 1800s, this five-story heritage boutique

hotel has loftlike rooms with soaring ceilings, cast-iron columns, and an artsy vibe that doesn't sacrifice comfort for style. **Pros:** some rooms have private terraces; 24/7 room service; quiet location. **Cons:** a bit hard to find; $35 valet; no pool. $ *Rooms from: C$400* ⊠ *449 rue Ste-Hélène, Old Montréal* ☎ *514/904–1616, 866/904–1616* ⊕ *www.hotelgault.com* ⟿ *30 suites* ¦○¦ *No meals* Ⓜ *Square-Victoria.*

★ Hôtel Le St-James
$$$$ | HOTEL | FAMILY | Civility reigns at one of the city's most celebrated Grande Dame hotels, a member of the Leading Hotels of the World group and popular with celebrities (from Hollywood moguls to European nobility) who appreciate the splendor of this former Mercantile bank and its discrete staff. **Pros:** 20-foot ceilings; luxurious experience and stately lobby; most rooms have fireplaces. **Cons:** lacks curb appeal; expensive daily pet fees; no pool. $ *Rooms from: C$475* ⊠ *355 rue St-Jacques, Old Montréal* ☎ *514/841–3111, 866/841–3111* ⊕ *www.hotellestjames.com* ⟿ *60 rooms* ¦○¦ *No meals* Ⓜ *Square-Victoria.*

★ Hôtel Nelligan
$$$$ | HOTEL | There's a cultivated air of refinement echoing through this landmark on rue St. Paul, named for Quebec's most passionate poet, Emile Nelligan, and known for its romance-inspiring lobby atrium and rooftop terrace offering views of the Old City and the harbor. **Pros:** cozy rooms with king-size beds and enormous bathrooms; breakfast with a view on the rooftop terrace; excellent pub grub at the resto-bar, Méchant Bœuf. **Cons:** popular event space; pricey valet parking; no pool. $ *Rooms from: C$400* ⊠ *106 rue St-Paul Ouest, Old Montréal* ☎ *514/788–2040, 877/788–2040* ⊕ *www.hotelnelligan.com* ⟿ *105 rooms* ¦○¦ *No meals* Ⓜ *Place-d'Armes.*

Hôtel St. Paul
$$$ | HOTEL | Forget fussy oil paintings or rococo furniture—behind its 19th-century Beaux-Arts facade, the St. Paul has a chic new lobby furnished with jewel-toned velvet sofas and a giant alabaster fireplace built of backlit blocks of "ice." **Pros:** newly renovated rooms; fashionable lobby design; great location on a north–south artery. **Cons:** underlighted hallways and elevators can be spooky; modern furniture and bright colors not for everyone; no pool. $ *Rooms from: C$310* ⊠ *355 rue McGill, Old Montréal* ☎ *514/380–2222, 866/380–2202* ⊕ *www.hotelstpaul.com* ⟿ *119 rooms* ¦○¦ *No meals* Ⓜ *Square-Victoria.*

Hôtel William Gray
$$$$ | HOTEL | Popular with A-listers and the millennial crowd, the Hotel William Gray marries the deep history and contemporary cool of Old Montréal, with its two 18th-century stone buildings topped by a new eight-story glass tower. **Pros:** magnificent views of Old Montréal and Jacques Cartier bridge from popular rooftop terrace; small, tranquil outdoor pool, a rarity in Old Montréal hotels; Himalayan salt room in the spa. **Cons:** older travelers may not appreciate the trendy scene, especially at two rooftop bars; pool too small for laps; most rooms don't have bathtubs. $ *Rooms from: C$416* ⊠ *421 rue Saint Vincent, Old Montréal* ☎ *514/656–5600* ⊕ *www.hotelwilliamgray.com* ⟿ *127 rooms* ¦○¦ *No meals* Ⓜ *Champ-de-Mars.*

InterContinental Montréal
$$$ | HOTEL | After extensive room renovations in 2016, the InterContinental definitely got its groove back, catering to a variety of travelers—from families and their pets, to the business and fitness cliques. **Pros:** saltwater swimming pool; easy underground access to shopping and nightlife; trendy, locally owned café in lobby. **Cons:** gets the convention crowd; dull ground-floor entry; 1990 building lacks character. $ *Rooms from: C$329* ⊠ *360 rue St-Antoine Ouest, Old Montréal* ☎ *514/987–9900, 877/660–8550* ⊕ *www.montreal.intercontinental.*

Biking in Montreal

Weather permitting, one of the best ways to discover Montréal is on a bicycle. This is an incredibly bike-friendly metropolis, and there are thousands of designated bike paths connecting diverse neighborhoods across the island, running along the river, and through parks and forests. If you like to bike but would rather not do it on city streets, ferries at the Old Port can take you to Île Ste-Hélène and the south shore of the St. Lawrence River, where riders can connect to hundreds of miles of trails in the Montérégie region.

Féria de Vélo de Montréal. *(Montréal Bike Festival)* The biggest bike celebration in North America includes the **Tour la Nuit**, a 22-kilometer (14-mile) nighttime ride through the city. The weeklong festival culminates in as many as 50,000 cyclists taking over the streets for the **Tour de l'Île**, a 50-km (31-mile) ride along a route encircling Montréal. ⌧ *Montréal* ☎ *514/521–8356, 800/567–8356* ⊕ *www.velo.qc.ca/en/govelo/Go-bike-Montreal-festival.*

Fitz & Follwell Co. This company's bike tour of Montréal highlights is popular, but go deeper and try "Hoods & Hidden Gems" to really learn what makes the city tick. They also offer bike rentals, walking tours, and snow tours in winter. ⌧ *115 av. du Mont-Royal Ouest, The Plateau* ☎ *514/840–0739* ⊕ *www.fitzandfollwell.ca.*

Lachine Canal. The most popular cycling trail on the island begins at the Old Port and winds its way to the shores of Lac St-Louis in Lachine. Pack a picnic lunch; there are plenty of green spaces where you can stop and refuel along the way. ⌧ *Montréal.*

Le Pôle des Rapides. This 100-km (62-mile) network of bicycle trails follows lakefronts, canals, and aqueducts. The trails are open April 15 to October 15. ⌧ *Montréal* ☎ *514/732–7303* ⊕ *www.pistescyclables.ca* Ⓜ *Verdun, Angrignon, LaSalle, Charlevoix, Lionel-Groulx.*

Vélo Montréal. For longer cycling excursions, renting a bike from this company is your best bet. Each rental includes a bicycle helmet, bottle cage, lock, and rear carrier rack. Packages start at C$15 for two hours and go all the way to C$120 for a full week or C$165 for two weeks. They also lease tandem bikes, a fun alternative for couples. ⌧ *3880 rue Rachel Est, Hochelaga-Maisonneuve* ☎ *514/259–7272* ⊕ *www.velomontreal.com* Ⓜ *Pie-IX.*

com ⌑ *357 rooms* ⧈ *No meals* Ⓜ *Square-Victoria or Place-d'Armes.*

★ Le Petit Hôtel
$$$$ | **HOTEL** | **FAMILY** | The hip little sister of the Auberge du Vieux Port, this boutique hotel marries creative design with old stone walls, exposed beams, a narrow lobby with a counter coffee bar and a seven-foot orange sculpture, and—contrary to its name—not-so-petite rooms. **Pros:** bicycles to borrow; chic lobby café; cribs, playpens, and babysitters available. **Cons:** small bathrooms have no tubs; steep fee for valet parking; lobby not especially elegant or cozy. ⑤ *Rooms from: C$430* ⌧ *168 rue St-Paul Ouest, Old Montréal* ☎ *514/940–0360, 877/530–0360* ⊕ *www.petithotelmontreal.com* ⌑ *28 rooms* ⧈ *Free breakfast* Ⓜ *Square-Victoria.*

★ Le Place d'Armes Hôtel & Suites
$$$ | **HOTEL** | **FAMILY** | Four splendidly ornate Victorian commercial buildings

were merged to create Old Montréal's largest boutique hotel, pleasing honeymooners and business execs alike with its old-fashioned grandeur, exposed brick walls in rooms, *hammam* (Middle Eastern–style steam bath), rooftop terrace, and unobstructed views of the Basilique Notre-Dame-de-Montréal. **Pros:** best (Turkish) spa in town; Japanese tavern (hamachi bibibap [marinaded yellowtail]); rooftop bar. **Cons:** late sleepers may be disturbed by the noontime Angelus bells at the basilica; steep approach from métro is slippery in winter; rooms in new building have no bathtubs, only multijet showers. ⑤ *Rooms from: C$329* ✉ *55 rue St-Jacques, Old Montréal* ☎ *514/842–1887, 888/450–1887* ⊕ *www.hotelplacedarmes.com* ⇝ *169 rooms* ⑩ *No meals* Ⓜ *Place-d'Armes.*

Le Saint-Sulpice

$$$ | **HOTEL** | With its sought-after address beside the basilica's chapel, this boutique hotel is blessed with a magical garden terrace, casement windows that actually open, luxurious suites—both in space and decor—and a lively lobby restaurant with one of the city's best menus. **Pros:** in-room massage service; celebrity-spotting; proximity to the Basilique Notre-Dame de Montréal. **Cons:** church bells may disturb late sleepers; too posh for comfort with kids; pricey summer rates. ⑤ *Rooms from: C$385* ✉ *414 rue St-Sulpice, Old Montréal* ☎ *514/288–1000, 877/785–7423* ⊕ *www.lesaintsulpice.com* ⇝ *108 rooms* ⑩ *No meals* Ⓜ *Place-d'Armes.*

LHotel

$$$ | **HOTEL** | Housed in a stately 19th-century bank in the financial district, the dignified facade accurately suggests its grand and elegant interior with high ceilings, antique furnishings, and large windows, but the iconic Robert Indiana Love sculpture sitting outside also hints at the colorful rooms, bright art deco breakfast room, and extraordinary contemporary art collection within, including works by

Jasper Johns, Andy Warhol, and Damien Hirst. **Pros:** Botero wine bar has distinct character; spacious high-ceiling rooms; excellent art collection and close to other galleries. **Cons:** some rooms are dated; buffet continental breakfast is pricey and not included; rue St-Jacques is dull after 6 pm. ⑤ *Rooms from: C$369* ✉ *262 rue St-Jacques Ouest, Old Montréal* ☎ *514/985–0019, 877/553–0019* ⊕ *www. lhotelmontreal.com* ⇝ *59 rooms* ⑩ *No meals* Ⓜ *Square-Victoria.*

Springhill Suites by Marriott

$$$ | **HOTEL** | **FAMILY** | Convenient and quiet, with large rooms and underground parking—rarities in Old Montréal—this all-suites hotel attracts families and business travelers who return for the free breakfast buffet, lobby market, saltwater pool, and fitness center. **Pros:** free, bountiful breakfast with healthy options; saltwater pool; well-stocked lobby store. **Cons:** popular with families so pool can be crowded; difficult access on a narrow street; poor views. ⑤ *Rooms from: C$335* ✉ *445 rue St-Jean-Baptiste, Old Montréal* ☎ *514/875–4333, 888/287–9400* ⊕ *www.springhillsuites. com* ⇝ *124 rooms* ⑩ *Free breakfast* Ⓜ *Champ-de-Mars.*

★ W Montréal

$$$ | **HOTEL** | A chic showcase for your Prada luggage, the W Montréal lives up to the brand's reputation for a hip take on luxury and style, providing its A-list clientele with excellent service and sleek, modern decor, notably peekaboo bathrooms, a trendy bar, and a lobby designed for lingering and entertaining. **Pros:** bright, airy rooms; well-connected concierge; luxe pet program ($100 + $25 daily fee). **Cons:** nonmember fee for in-room Wi-Fi (free in the lobby); lobby noisy at night; showers afford no privacy. ⑤ *Rooms from: C$370* ✉ *901 Square Victoria, Old Montréal* ☎ *514/395–3100* ⊕ *www.whotels.com/montreal* ⇝ *152 rooms* ⑩ *No meals* Ⓜ *Square-Victoria.*

ⓨ Nightlife

Once a tourist trap full of overpriced souvenirs, Old Montréal is now home to a mix of top-notch restaurants and chic lounges. During the summer you can enjoy stunning views of the river from some of the city's best rooftop terraces. Excellent dining can be found along rue St-Paul, while rue McGill is a big part of the 5-à-7 scene.

BARS AND LOUNGES
Maison St-Paul

WINE BARS—NIGHTLIFE | Sharpen your swords! This chic bar for champagne and other sparklers is the perfect place to break open a bottle—literally. The staff like to open the bottles of bubbly with sabers, a practice that adds an element of fun to an accessible venue. Finger foods include oysters, steak (and other kinds of) tartares, and caviar. ⊠ *343 rue St-Paul Est, Old Montréal* ☎ *514/504–2319* ⊕ *www.maisonsaintpaul.ca* ⊗ *Closed Mon.* Ⓜ *Champs-de-Mars.*

Philémon Bar

BARS/PUBS | You can grab a glass of one of Philémon's well-priced private import cavas, proseccos, or champagnes to accompany the menu at this sleek bar, which serves more than the usual pub fare (oysters, anyone?). It's packed with locals Thursday through Saturday—in fact, it's become quite the singles hangout. Bouncers keep the ratio of guys to gals at a comfortable level. ⊠ *111 rue St-Paul Ouest, Old Montréal* ☎ *514/289–3777* ⊕ *www.philemonbar. com* Ⓜ *Place-d'Armes.*

Terrasse sur l'Auberge

BARS/PUBS | For an unbeatable view of the Old Port and numerous Montréal landmarks, head to this unpretentious patio on the roof of the Auberge du Vieux-Port Hotel. Open from the end of May through mid-October (2–11 weekdays, 1–11 on weekends), it's a great place to watch the International Fireworks Festival—if you're early enough to snag

a table—and enjoy cocktails and a light tapas menu. ■TIP➜ **Try the clear sangria (made with peach Ciroc, Cointreau, white wine, and Sprite).** ⊠ *97 rue de la Commune Est, Old Montréal* ☎ *514/876–0081* ⊕ *www.terrassesurlauberge.com* Ⓜ *Place-d'Armes or Champs-de-Mars.*

LIVE MUSIC
Modavie Wine Bar

WINE BARS—NIGHTLIFE | With a Mediterranean menu, an attractive sidewalk terrasse, and a sophisticated interior that places dark wood against stone walls, this jazz bar is pleasing to the eyes *and* ears. Despite being spread out over two floors, the space still feels cozy. Live duos play during the first part of the week, while weekends showcase full bands. There's never a cover charge. ⊠ *1 rue St-Paul Ouest, Old Montréal* ☎ *514/287–9582* ⊕ *www.modavie.com* Ⓜ *Champ-de-Mars.*

🎭 Performing Arts

THEATER
Centaur Theatre

THEATER | Montréal's best-known English-language theater company stages everything from frothy musical revues to serious works, and prominently features works by local playwrights. Its home is in the former stock-exchange building in Old Montréal. ⊠ *453 rue St-François-Xavier, Old Montréal* ☎ *514/288–3161* ⊕ *www.centaurtheatre. com* Ⓜ *Place-d'Armes.*

Centre Phi

ARTS CENTERS | Packed with intimate screening rooms, recording facilities, exhibition spaces, and a performance space, this center promotes artist-driven film, design, and music from locals as well as international artists. Films are in English and French. ⊠ *407 rue St-Pierre, Old Montréal* ☎ *514/225–0525, 855/526–8888* ⊕ *www.phi-centre.com* Ⓜ *Place-d'Armes or Square-Victoria.*

🛍 Shopping

The old part of the city has more than its share of garish souvenir shops, but fashion boutiques and shoe stores with low to moderate prices line rues Notre-Dame and St-Jacques, from rue McGill to Place Jacques-Cartier. With gentrification in the west end of the area, high-end fashion boutiques and spas abound, especially along rue St-Paul Ouest. The area is also rich in art galleries and crafts shops along rue St-Paul and tucked inside the narrow rue des Artistes. Use the Place-d'Armes, Champ-de-Mars, or Square-Victoria métro stations.

ART

★ **Boutique Métiers d'Art du Québec**

GIFTS/SOUVENIRS | Looking for that special handcrafted gift that can't be found anywhere else? A whimsical teapot straight out of a children's picture book, perhaps? A handpainted ceramic bead necklace? A wood-sculpted anthropomorphized bird that reminds you of your brother? A gold bracelet made of hundreds of miniscule seed-like beads? An adorable animal-shaped cushion? This Quebec artisans' guild boutique may have just what you're *not* looking for but find delight in nonetheless. ⊠ *20 rue Saint-Paul Ouest, Local 103, Old Montréal* ☎ *438 /385-7787* ⊕ *www.metiersdart.ca* Ⓜ *Place d'Armes.*

Fondation Phi pour l'art contemporain

ART GALLERIES | Housed in two heritage buildings, this nonprofit organization aims to showcase compelling contemporary art from around the world. The Fondation presents two to three major exhibitions a year in addition to a series of public events, special collaborative projects, and a forward-thinking education program. A free app takes you through the exhibits, and podcasts provide a fascinating look at the artists themselves. *Check the website or call before you visit as the Fondation Phi closes regularly for installations.* ⊠ *451–465 rue St-Jean, Old Montréal* ☎ *514/849-3742, 888/934-2278* ⊕ *www.fondation-phi.org/foundation* ⊙ *Closed Mon. and Tues.* Ⓜ *Square-Victoria or Place-d'Armes.*

Images Boréales

ART GALLERIES | If the friendly and knowledgeable staff doesn't win you over, the vast collection of Inuit and First Nations art certainly will. Images Boréales represents the best-known Inuit artists while also making a point of working with young, emerging Inuit talent with strong potential. With more than 2,000 pieces of sculpture in soapstone and serpentine, the store will give you the biggest challenge in deciding what to buy. ⊠ *4 rue St-Paul Est, Old Montréal* ☎ *514/439–1987* ⊕ *www.imagesboreales.com* Ⓜ *Champ-de-Mars.*

CLOTHING

Boutique Denis Gagnon

CLOTHING | This innovative designer, whose creations have been exhibited at the Montréal Museum of Fine Arts, is much loved on the Montréal fashion scene. In this sleek, subterranean boutique, Gagnon's couture designs stand alongside his ready-to-wear collection. He's also well-known for his shoes. ⊠ *170 rue St-Paul Ouest, Old Montréal* ☎ *514/935–6360* ⊕ *www.denisgagnon.ca* Ⓜ *Place-d'Armes.*

Boutique Philippe Dubuc

CLOTHING | One of the city's favorite menswear designers, Philippe Dubuc's collections are characterized by richly textured fabrics, exquisite tailoring, and lots of grays, blues, blacks, and beiges. ⊠ *417 rue St. Pierre, Suite 101, Old Montréal* ☎ *514/282–1465* ⊕ *www.dubucstyle.com* Ⓜ *Square Victoria.*

Delano Design

CLOTHING | Fashion, art, and design unite under one architecturally stunning roof. Sartorial offerings from Canadian and European designers hang alongside works from the contemporary painter Yunus Chkirate. ⊠ *70 rue St-Paul Ouest,*

Old Montréal ☎ *514/286–5005* ⊕ *www. delanodesign.com* Ⓜ *Place-d'Armes.*

★ Espace Pepin

CLOTHING | Talented owner and painter Lysanne Pepin has an eye for design. Her boutiques, located a few addresses apart on the same block, are beautiful and intriguing spaces to explore. They are filled with romantic clothes, funky shoes, and a carefully edited mix of local and international labels, as well as eclectic housewares and furniture for home and office. ⊠ *350 and 378 rue St-Paul Ouest, Old Montréal* ☎ *514/844–0114* ⊕ *www. pepinart.com* Ⓜ *Square-Victoria.*

Signatures québécoises

CLOTHING | Housing a streamlined selection of Quebecois fashion designers, the loftlike space inside Marché Bonsecours sells luxe lines that include Ricardo, Christian Chenail, and the fanciful creations of Ophelie Hats. It's the owner's own exotic kimonos that steal the show. ⊠ *Marché Bonsecours, 350 rue St-Paul Est, Old Montréal* ☎ *514/866–2006* ⊕ *signaturesquebecoises.com* Ⓜ *Champ-de-Mars.*

U&I

CLOTHING | Stylish locals flock to this sleek boutique in Old Montréal, which is stocked with unisex avant-garde finds from North America and Europe, with an emphasis on Montréal and Canadian brands. Cydwoq and Canada Goose hang alongside coats from the sleek Montréal label Mackage and pieces from U&I's own label. ⊠ *215 rue St. Paul Ouest, Old Montréal* ☎ *514/508–7704* ⊕ *www.boutiqueuandi.com* Ⓜ *Place-d'Armes.*

SPAS

Le Scandinave Les Bains Vieux-Montréal

SPA/BEAUTY | A bastion of urban chic in historic Old Montréal, this spa is especially popular on cold winter days. Inspired by the age-old tradition of public baths, the Scandinave prides itself on offering guests an authentic yet contemporary experience with an accent of privacy and total relaxation. The posh interior of slate, marble, and wood contrasts nicely with the bubbling pool and misty steam rooms. The ultimate meltdown is the zero-stress chamber of absolute quiet and darkness to intensify the peacefulness. All you need to bring along is your bathing suit; the spa provides sandals, bathrobes, and towels. For extra relaxation, sign up for a massage with one of their professional masseuses. ⊠ *71 rue de la Commune Ouest, Old Montréal* ☎ *844/220–2009* ⊕ *www. scandinave.com* Ⓜ *Place-d'Armes.*

🏃 Activities

BOATING

In Montréal you can climb aboard a boat at a Downtown wharf and be crashing through Class V white water minutes later.

Lachine Rapids Tours (*Jet Boating Montréal*)

BOATING | Discover the rapids on a large jet boat—and bring a change of clothes. There are daily departures (every two hours) May through October from Clock Tower Pier in the Old Port. The price includes all gear, and the trip lasts an hour. Another option is a 20-minute ride in a 12-passenger boat that reaches speeds up to 80 kph (50 mph). Boats leave the Old Port's Jacques Cartier Pier every half hour between 10 am and 6 pm from May to October. Trips are narrated in French and English. ⊠ *47 rue de la Commune Ouest, Old Montréal* ☎ *514/284–9607* 🚢 *Jet boat C$71; 20-minute speed boat ride C$23; 45-minute panoramic trip (much calmer) $46* Ⓜ *Champ-de-Mars.*

Downtown

The heart of Downtown (or *centre-ville* in French)—with department stores, boutiques, bars, restaurants, amusement arcades, theaters, cinemas, art galleries, bookstores, and even a few

Montréal's Best Shopping Streets

Most visitors to Montréal will have Downtown and Old Montréal on the itinerary, but for an authentic experience à la Montréalaise you should also venture into some of the other neighborhoods.

Avenue Laurier Ouest. Shops and boutiques along the eight blocks between boulevard St-Laurent and chemin de la Côte-Ste-Catherine sell medium- to high-end fashions, home furnishings, decorative items, artwork, books, kitchenware, toys and children's items, and gourmet food. There are plenty of restaurants, bars, and cafés in which to rest your feet and check out your purchases. The street is about a 10-minute walk from the Laurier métro station.

Boulevard St-Laurent. Affectionately known as The Main, St-Laurent has restaurants, boutiques, and nightclubs that cater mostly to an upscale clientele. Still, the area has managed to retain its working-class immigrant roots and vitality to some degree: high-fashion shops are interspersed with ethnic-food stores, secondhand clothing and decor boutiques, and hardware stores. Indeed, a trip up this street takes you from Chinatown to Little Italy.

Rue Amherst. Antiques shops began springing up in the Gay Village in the early 1990s, most of them on rue Amherst between rues Ste-Catherine and Ontario. Copious cafés and brunch spots nearby will fuel your quest. The area used to be less expensive than rue Notre-Dame, but it's not always the case these days. Use the Beaudry métro station.

Rue Bernard. Only a few blocks away from the Outremont métro station,

this chic villagey street is well worth a detour. The street boasts many sidewalk cafés—called *terrasses* in local parlance—for fine or casual dining, as well as specialty food stores, decor shops, and some of the best ice cream in Montréal at Le Glacier Bilboquet.

Rue Chabanel. The eight-block stretch of Chabanel just west of boulevard St-Laurent is the heart of the city's garment district. The goods seem to get more stylish and more expensive the farther west you go. If you're lucky, you might come across signs for designer sample sales. Many of the city's furriers have also moved into the area. A few places on Chabanel accept credit cards, but bring cash anyway. If you pay in cash, the price will often include the tax. From the Crémazie métro station, take Bus 53 north.

Rue Notre-Dame Ouest. The fashionable place for antiquing is a formerly run-down five-block strip of Notre-Dame between rue Guy and avenue Atwater. Most of the action is at the western end of the strip, as are many of the restaurants and cafés that have sprung up to cater to shoppers. Walk east from Lionel-Groulx métro station.

Victoria Village. The carriage-trade area for wealthy Westmount citizens, who live on the leafy slopes of Mont-Royal, has morphed into a shopping destination for all Montrealers with an eye for style. Independent boutiques offer distinctive home decor, shoes, gifts, stationery, and fashion along rues Victoria and Sherbrooke, with the epicenter between Victoria and Claremont. Cafés and fine specialty food shops also abound. Vendôme is the closest métro station.

Top Montréal Shopping Experiences

Some of the best deals can be found at **La Maison Simons** department store, where there's something cheap and chic for everyone, from teeny-boppers to mesdames and messieurs on a budget. Montréal's luxury lane runs from **Holt Renfrew Ogilvy**, the Saks 5th Avenue of Montréal, on rue Ste-Catherine, up rue de la Montagne to rue Sherbrooke, with local designer fashions such as **Marie Saint Pierre** lining the route.

The path of luxury continues west along rue Sherbrooke, where you'll find the Montréal Museum of Fine Arts, as well as high-end galleries and antiquarians such as **Galerie Alan Klinkhoff.**

Funky fashionistas will want to hit Mile End and the Plateau. In Mile End, hipster territory includes **General 54** and **Unicorn**, with **Citizen Vintage** for recycled fashions. Moving down Montréal's beloved Main—boulevard St-Laurent—check out vintage, decor, fashion, and design shops.

Closer to Downtown, **Boutique 1861** and **M0851** are worth the walk. One-of-a-kind independent shops line avenue Mont-Royal and rue St-Denis.

churches—runs from avenue Atwater to boulevard St-Denis. Ste-Catherine is also the main drag of the Quartier des Spectacles, which runs west to east from rue Bleury to rue St-Hubert. Inside this arts and entertainment district are the Place des Arts and several other cultural venues; it also serves as the Downtown home to most of Montréal's many summer festivals.

Walk farther north on rue Crescent to rue Sherbrooke and the lower slopes of Mont-Royal and you come to what was once the most exclusive neighborhood in Canada—the **Golden Square Mile.** During the boom years of the mid-1800s, baronial homes covered the mountain north of rue Sherbrooke. Many are gone, replaced by high-rises or modern town houses, but there are still plenty of architectural treasures to admire, most of them now foreign consulates or university institutes.

And underneath it all—the entire Downtown area and then some—is Montréal's **Underground City,** a vast network of more or less anything you'd find on the street above.

GETTING HERE AND AROUND
Getting to and around Downtown is easy, thanks to the métro. There are several stations along boulevard de Maisonneuve, which is a block away from and runs parallel to rue Ste-Catherine. Many of them link directly to the Underground City.

◉ Sights

Arsenal Art Contemporain
ARTS VENUE | Housed in a repurposed shipyard boasting 80,000 square feet of exhibition space, Arsenal Art Contemporain dedicates itself to the support, promotion, and development of contemporary art and has been credited with helping revitalize the old industrial area of Griffintown. The largest private art center in Canada, it was originally founded in Montréal in 2011 but also has locations in Toronto and New York City. ⊠ *2020 rue William, Downtown* ☎ *514/931–9978* ⊕ *www.arsenalcontemporary.com* Ⓜ *Georges-Vanier or Lionel-Groulx.*

Cathédrale Marie-Reine-du-Monde (*Mary Queen of the World Cathedral*)
RELIGIOUS SITE | The best reason to visit this cathedral is that it's a quarter-scale replica of St. Peter's Basilica in Rome— complete with a magnificent reproduction of Bernini's ornate baldachin (canopy) over the main altar and an ornately coffered ceiling. When Bishop Ignace Bourget (1799–1885) decided to build his cathedral in the heart of the city's Protestant-dominated commercial quarter, many fellow Catholics thought he was crazy. But the bishop was determined to assert the Church's authority—and its loyalty to Rome—in the British-ruled city. Bourget didn't live to see the cathedral dedicated in 1894, but his tomb holds a place of honor among those of his successors in the burial chapel on the east side of the nave. ✉ *1085 rue de la Cathédrale, Downtown* ✛ *Enter through main doors on boul. René-Lévesque.* ☎ *514/866–1661* 🏷 *Free* Ⓜ *Bonaventure.*

Centre Bell
ARTS VENUE | The Montréal Canadiens haven't won the Stanley Cup since 1993, and most of the team's fans can't remember the golden 1960s and '70s, when *Les Glorieux* virtually owned the trophy. The superstitious blame the team's fallen fortunes on its 1996 move from the hallowed Forum to the brown-brick Centre Bell arena. Still, Montréal is a hockey-mad city and the Habs, as locals call the team, are still demigods here, and there are even university courses based on this superstar team. (When they celebrated their 100th season in 2009–10, the city changed the name of the strip of rue de la Gauchetière in front of the Centre Bell to Avenue des Canadiens-de-Montréal.) The Bell Centre is also a venue for blockbuster acts like Coldplay, Drake, and Trevor Noah. ✉ *1260 av. des Canadiens-de-Montréal, Downtown* ☎ *877/668–8269, 514/790–2525 for hockey tickets, 800/663–6786 for more information, 514/932–2582 for other*

events ⊕ *www.centrebell.ca* Ⓜ *Bonaventure or Lucien-l'Allier.*

★ **Christ Church Cathedral**
RELIGIOUS SITE | The seat of the Anglican (Episcopalian) bishop of Montréal offers downtown shoppers and strollers a respite from the hustle and bustle of rue Ste-Catherine, with free noontime concerts and organ recitals. Built in 1859, the cathedral is modeled on Snettisham Parish Church in Norfolk, England, with some distinctly Canadian touches. The steeple, for example, is made with aluminum plates molded to simulate stone, and inside, the Gothic arches are crowned with carvings of the types of foliage growing on Mont-Royal when the church was built. The stained-glass windows behind the main altar, installed in the early 1920s as a memorial to the dead of World War I, show scenes from the life of Christ. On the wall just above and to the left of the pulpit is the Coventry Cross; it's made of nails taken from the ruins of Britain's Coventry Cathedral, destroyed by German bombing in 1940. *Free Saturday group tours can be arranged by calling the office.* ✉ *635 rue Ste-Catherine Ouest, Downtown* ☎ *514/843–6577 ext. 241* ⊕ *www.montrealcathedral.ca* 🏷 *Free* Ⓜ *McGill.*

Church of St. Andrew and St. Paul
RELIGIOUS SITE | Montréal's largest Presbyterian church—sometimes affectionately called the A&P—is worth a visit, if only to see the glorious stained-glass window of the risen Christ that dominates the sanctuary behind the white-stone communion table. It's a memorial to members of the Royal Highland Regiment of Canada (the Black Watch) who were killed in World War I. ✉ *3415 rue Redpath (main entrance on rue Sherbrooke), Downtown* ☎ *514/842–3431* ⊕ *www.standrewstpaul.com* 🏷 *Free* ☞ *For guided visit, phone in advance to make arrangements* Ⓜ *Guy-Concordia.*

McGill University

COLLEGE | Merchant and fur trader James McGill would probably be horrified to know that the university that he helped found in 1828 has developed an international reputation as one of North America's best party schools. McGill also happens to be one of the two or three best universities in Canada, and certainly one of the prettiest. Its campus is an island of grass and trees in a sea of traffic and skyscrapers. If you take the time to stroll up the drive that leads from the Greek Revival Roddick Gates to the austere neoclassical Arts Building, keep an eye out to your right for the life-size statue of McGill himself, hurrying across campus clutching his tricorn hat. If you have an hour or so, drop into the temple-like **Redpath Museum of Natural History** (⊕ www.mcgill.ca/redpath) to browse its eclectic collection of dinosaur bones, old coins, African art, and shrunken heads. ⊠ 859 rue Sherbrooke Ouest, Downtown ☎ 514/398–4455 main switchboard, 514/398–4086 museum ⊕ www.mcgill.ca ⊠ Suggested donation: C$10 Ⓜ McGill.

Musée d'Art Contemporain (Museum of Contemporary Art)

MUSEUM | If you have a taste for pastoral landscapes and formal portraits, you might want to stick with the Musée des Beaux-Arts, but for a walk on the wild side of art, head to the Musée d'Art Contemporain and see what you can make of the jagged splashes of color that cover the canvases of the "Automatistes," as Québec's rebellious artists of the 1930s styled themselves. The works of the Automatistes form the core of this museum's collection of 5,000 pieces. The museum often has weekend programs and art workshops, some of which are geared toward children, and almost all are free. And for a little romance and music with your art, try the Vendredi Nocturnes (Nocturnal Fridays) with live music, bar service, and guided tours of the exhibits. Hours for guided tours vary. ⊠ 185 rue Ste-Catherine Ouest,

Downtown ☎ 514/847–6226 ⊕ www.macm.org ⊠ C$15; half price 5–9 pm Wed. ☻ Closed Mon. Ⓜ Place-des-Arts.

★ Musée des Beaux-Arts de Montréal (Montréal Museum of Fine Arts)

MUSEUM | Not surprisingly, Canada's oldest museum has one of the finest collections of Canadian art anywhere. The works of such luminaries as Paul Kane, the Group of Seven, Paul-Émile Borduas, and Marc-Aurèle Fortin are displayed here in a space built onto the back of the neoclassical Erskine and American United Church, one of the city's most historic Protestant churches. The nave has been preserved as a meeting place and exhibition hall and also displays the church's 18 Tiffany stained-glass windows, the biggest collection of Tiffany's work outside the United States. The rest of the gallery's permanent collection, which includes works by everyone from Rembrandt to Renoir, is housed in its two other pavilions: the neoclassical **Michal and Renata Hornstein Pavilion**, across Avenue du Musée from the church, and the glittering, glass-fronted **Jean-Noël-Desmarais Pavilion**, across rue Sherbrooke. All three are linked by tunnels. If you visit the museum in summer, spring or fall, you'll be greeted outside the main entrance by The Sun, Seattle sculptor Dale Chihuly's bright, twisted glass sculpture, now part of the MMFA's permanent collection.

■TIP→ **Admission is free from 5 to 9 pm Wednesday.** ⊠ 1380 rue Sherbrooke Ouest, Downtown ☎ 514/285–2000 ⊕ www.mbam.qc.ca/en ⊠ C$24; half price on Wed. after 5 pm; Discovery exhibitions and collections free first Sun. of the month Ⓜ Guy-Concordia.

Musée McCord de l'Histoire Canadienne (McCord Museum of Canadian History)

MUSEUM | David Ross McCord (1844–1930) was a wealthy pack rat with a passion for anything that had to do with Montréal or Canadian history. His collection of paintings, costumes, toys, tools,

Montréal DOWNTOWN

Sights ▼

1 Arsenal Art
   Contemporain A8
2 Cathédrale Marie-Reine-
   du-Monde D5
3 Centre Bell.............. B5
4 Christ Church
   Cathedral E3
5 Church of St. Andrew
   and St. Paul............. A2
6 McGill University D1
7 Musée d'Art
   Contemporain H3
8 Musée des Beaux-Arts
   de Montréal A2
9 Musée McCord de
   l'Histoire Canadienne ... E2
10 Place des Arts H3
11 Place Ville-Marie and
   Observatoire Place
   Ville-Marie............... E4
12 Square Dorchester
   and Place du Canada ... C4
13 St George's
   Anglican Church......... C5
14 Saint Patrick's
   Basilica F5
15 The Underground City.. G6

Restaurants ▼

1 Bouillon Bilk............... I3
2 Brasserie T H3
3 Café Ferreira C3
4 Café Myriade............ A3
5 Café Parvis G3
6 Deville Dinerbar......... C3
7 Dominion Square
   Tavern................... D4
8 La Habanera.............. E4
9 Kazu A4
10 LOV B4
11 Le Taj C2
12 Mandys B2
13 Ryū C3

Hotels ▼

1 Château Versailles...... A2
2 Delta Montréal........... F2
3 Fairmont Le Reine
   Elizabeth D5
4 Four Seasons
   Montréal................. B3
5 Hôtel Birks............... F4
6 Hotel Bonaventure
   Montréal................. E6
7 Hôtel Chez Swann B3
8 Hôtel Le Crystal B4
9 Hôtel le Square-
   Phillips et Suites F4
10 Le Centre Sheraton...... C4
11 Le Mount Stephen
   Hotel..................... B3
12 Le St-Martin Hôtel
   Particulier D3
13 Loews Hôtel Vogue..... B3
14 Ritz-Carlton Montréal .. B2
15 Sofitel Montréal.......... C2

The Musée des Beaux-Arts has one of Canada's largest permanent collections of Canadian art, as well as a gallery where you can buy paintings by local artists.

drawings, and housewares provides a glimpse of what city life was like for all classes in the 19th century. If you're interested in the lifestyles of the elite, however, you'll love the photographs that William Notman (1826–91) took of the rich at play. One series portrays members of the posh Montréal Athletic Association posing in snowshoes on the slopes of Mont-Royal, all decked out in Hudson Bay coats and woolen hats. Each of the hundreds of portraits was shot individually in a studio and then painstakingly mounted on a picture of the snowy mountain to give the impression of a winter outing. There are guided tours (call for schedule), a reading room, a documentation center, a gift shop, a bookstore, and a café. ■ TIP → Admission is free from 5 to 9 pm Wednesday. ⊠ 690 rue Sherbrooke Ouest, Downtown ☎ 514/861-6701 ⊕ www.mccord-museum.qc.ca ⊠ C$19 Ⓜ McGill.

Place des Arts

ARTS VENUE | Montréal's primary performing-arts complex has been hosting performances since 1963, and since 2010 the complex has been undergoing a major makeover to stunning effect. The glass-walled Maison Symphonique 2,000-seat concert hall is the permanent home of the Montréal Symphony Orchestra; with state-of-the-art acoustics and only 75 feet between the end of the stage and the last row, it's an intimate place for concerts. The Salle Wilfrid Pelletier performance space is used by three resident companies: the Opéra de Montréal, Les Grands Ballets Canadiens, and the popular Jean Duceppe theater company. The venue's four other performance spaces host dance, theater, and festival events. Place des Arts is also the centerpiece of the city's **Quartier des Spectacles,** a square kilometer dedicated to arts and culture, with performance halls, dance studios, broadcasting facilities, and recording studios. The huge plaza, or esplanade, in front of the complex is a favorite gathering place for locals and visitors—especially during the Jazz Festival and Just for Laughs, when it's packed with free concerts and entertainment. *Even if you* *don't have tickets to something, you can walk around the quartier during festival season (pretty much all summer) to take in a variety of shows and concerts for free. ⊠ 175 rue Ste-Catherine Ouest, Downtown* ☎ *514/842–2112 tickets, 514/285–4200 administration* ⊕ *www. placedesarts.com* Ⓜ *Place-des-Arts.*

Place Ville-Marie and Observatoire Place Ville-Marie

STORE/MALL | Ride up an ear-popping elevator (the fastest in Montréal) to be rewarded with 360-degree views of the city at this building's newly opened rooftop observation deck. The cross-shaped 1962 office tower of Place Ville-Marie was Montréal's first modern skyscraper; the mall complex underneath it was the first link in the Underground City. The wide expanse of the building's plaza, just upstairs from the mall, makes a good place to relax with coffee or a snack from the food court below. Benches, potted greenery, and fine views of Mont-Royal make it popular with walkers, tourists, and office workers. On the observatory deck there's a gourmet brasserie, Les Enfants Terribles, boasting a year-round terrace. ⊠ *Bordered by boul. René-Lévesque and rues Mansfield, Cathcart, and University, Downtown* ☎ *514/866–6666* ⊕ *www.observatoire360.com/en* ⊠ *Observation Deck C$19* Ⓜ *McGill or Bonaventure.*

Square Dorchester and Place du Canada

CITY PARK | On sunny summer days you can join the office workers, store clerks, and Downtown shoppers who gather in these two green squares in the center of the city to eat lunch under the trees and perhaps listen to an open-air concert. If there are no vacant benches or picnic tables, you can still find a place to sit on the steps at the base of the dramatic monument to the dead of the Boer War. Other statues honor Scottish poet Robert Burns (1759–96); Sir Wilfrid Laurier (1841–1919), Canada's first French-speaking prime minister; and Sir John A. Macdonald

(1815–91), Canada's first prime minister. ⊠ *Bordered by boul. René-Lévesque and rues Peel, Metcalfe, and McTavish, Downtown* Ⓜ *Bonaventure or Peel.*

St. George's Anglican Church

RELIGIOUS SITE | This is possibly the prettiest Anglican (Episcopalian) church in Montréal. Step into its dim, candle-scented interior and you'll feel you've been transported to some prosperous market town in East Anglia (England). The double hammer-beam roof, the rich stained-glass windows, and the Lady Chapel on the east side of the main altar all add to the effect. It certainly seems a world away from Centre Bell, the modern temple to professional hockey that's across the street. ⊠ *1001 av. des Canadiens-de-Montréal, Downtown* ☎ *514/866–7113* ⊕ *www.st-georges.org* ⊠ *Free* Ⓜ *Bonaventure.*

St. Patrick's Basilica

RELIGIOUS SITE | Built in 1847, this is one of the purest examples of the Gothic Revival style in Canada, with a high-vaulted ceiling glowing with green and gold mosaics. The tall, slender columns are actually pine logs lashed together and decorated to look like marble, so that if you stand in one of the back corners and look toward the altar you really do feel as if you're peering at the sacred through a grove of trees. St. Pat's—as most of its parishioners call it—is to Montréal's Anglophone Catholics what the Basilique Notre-Dame is to their French-speaking brethren—the mother church and a monument to faith and courage. One of the joys of visiting the place is that you'll probably be the only tourist there, so you'll have plenty of time to check out the old pulpit and the huge lamp decorated with six 2-meter- (6-foot-) tall angels hanging over the main altar. And if you're named after some relatively obscure saint like Scholastica or Aeden of Fleury, you can search for your namesake's portrait among the 170 painted panels on the walls of the nave. ■TIP→ **For a solemn**

experience visit on the third Sunday of the month (September through June), when the mass is sung completely in Latin. ✉ *454 boul. René-Lévesque Ouest, Downtown* ☎ *514/866–7379* ⊕ *www.stpatricksmtl. ca* 🎫 *Free* ☉ *Closed Sat. before Easter* Ⓜ *Square-Victoria*.

The Underground City (*La ville souterraine*)
BRIDGE/TUNNEL | Place Ville-Marie, the cruciform skyscraper designed by I. M. Pei, was the tallest structure in the city when it opened in 1962. Located in the heart of downtown, it signaled the beginning of Montréal's subterranean city. Montrealers were skeptical that anyone would want to shop or even walk around in the new "down" town, but more than four decades later they can't live without it, especially in winter.

About half a million people use the 32-km (20-mile) Underground City, or *la ville souterraine*, daily. The tunnels link 10 métro stations, 7 hotels, 200 restaurants, 1,700 boutiques, and 60 office buildings—not to mention movie theaters, concert halls, convention complexes, the Centre Bell, two universities, and a college. In 2004 the Underground City was rebranded as the "RESO," a play on the word "réseau," which means network. You'll see the signs for it in the Downtown area and can find a map of the network at ⊕ *montrealvisitorsguide.com/ the-underground-city-map*. ✉ *Downtown*.

🍴 Restaurants

From top-quality steak to gourmet burgers, there's lots of meat in Downtown. Though vegans appreciate that new plant-based restaurants have entered the scene as well. There are rich Indian curries, simple Chinese dumplings, whole-animal cooking, dry-aged beef, designer hamburgers, and updated Italian dishes that stretch the definition. The dress code can be as formal as in Old Montréal or completely toned down and hip—it all depends on where you go.

Bouillon Bilk

$$$$ | MODERN FRENCH | The decor at this restaurant reflects its philosophy: fresh, thoughtful, and simplified (yet not simple). The market-based menu changes often and includes dishes that are just as beautiful to look at as they are delicious.
Known for: private-import wines; market cuisine; sleek and intimate decor. ⑤ *Average main: C$35* ✉ *1595 boul. St-Laurent, Downtown* ☎ *514/845–1595* ⊕ *www. bouillonbilk.com* ☉ *No lunch on weekends*. Ⓜ *St-Laurent*.

Brasserie T

$$$ | BRASSERIE | The informal sibling of Montréal's famous Toqué! restaurant, Brasserie T is a see-and-be-seen spot in the heart of Downtown. It's an excellent place to eat before or after a show at Place des Arts, as well as a budget-friendly way to experience Toqué's expertise. **Known for:** lively atmosphere; legendary salmon tartare; casual French. ⑤ *Average main: C$30* ✉ *1425 rue Jeanne-Mance, Downtown* ☎ *514/282–0808* ⊕ *www.brasserie-t.com* Ⓜ *Place-des-Arts*.

Café Ferreira

$$$$ | PORTUGUESE | The open-concept kitchen is renowned for its for "haute" Portuguese cuisine, including roasted salted cod, seafood bouillabaisse, and a whole array of appetizers like giant shrimp and grilled octopus or the roasted sardine fillets. Wine connoisseurs are attracted to the impressive list of Portuguese wines. **Known for:** seafood bouillabaisse; intimate Portuguese experience; late-night set menu. ⑤ *Average main: C$40* ✉ *1446 rue Peel, Downtown* ☎ *514/848–0988* ⊕ *www.ferreiracafe. com* ☉ *No lunch weekends* Ⓜ *Peel*.

Café Myriade

$ | CAFÉ | Aficionados are willing to wait for a seat at this small café, where the foam on your latte or café au lait is artfully arranged in waves, hearts, or curlicues. The delicious coffee is imported from Ethiopia, Guatemala, Brazil, Bolivia, and

elsewhere via the famed 49th Parallel Coffee Roasters in Vancouver. **Known for:** high-quality coffee; latte art; photogenic location inside Club Monaco. $ *Average main: C$5.50* ✉ *1432 rue Mackay, Downtown* ☎ *514/939–1717* ⊕ *www.cafemyriade.com* Ⓜ *Guy-Concordia.*

★ Café Parvis

$$ | ECLECTIC | What used to be a fur showroom in the 1970s now hosts Café Parvis, a stylish yet eclectic eatery with floor-to-ceiling windows, half-stripped mint-green paint, and luxuriant plants hanging from the ceiling. If morning visits are for artisan coffee and pâtisserie du jour, dinner is for ordering shareable wood-oven baked pizzas enhanced by fresh salads and the on-point selection of organic wines. **Known for:** photogenic setting; wood-oven baked pizzas; organic wines. $ *Average main: C$16* ✉ *403 rue Mayor, Downtown* ☎ *514/764–3589* ⊕ *cafeparvis.com* Ⓜ *Place-des-Arts.*

Deville Dinerbar

$$$ | DINER | FAMILY | Located in Montréal's Downtown core, Deville Dinerbar is a whimsical alternative to the otherwise rather serious dining options in the area. A palette of neon pink, white, and black keeps the dining room sleek, sexy, and exciting (but not diner-kitschy). **Known for:** Deville Food Cake; substantial burgers; diner-like decor. $ *Average main: C$30* ✉ *1425 rue Stanley, Downtown* ☎ *514/281–6556* ⊕ *www.devilledinerbar.com* Ⓜ *Peel.*

★ Dominion Square Tavern

$$$ | BRITISH | Antique chairs and a 40-foot brass bar, along with the original terrazzo flooring, ceiling lamps, aged mirrors, and ceramic walls from 1927, set the tone at this atmospheric British tavern. Everything on the menu is made from scratch. **Known for:** bangers and mash; atmospheric British tavern; prix-fixe dish of the day. $ *Average main: C$25* ✉ *1243 rue Metcalfe, Downtown* ☎ *514/564–5056* ⊕ *www.tavernedominion.com* ☉ *No lunch on weekends* Ⓜ *Peel.*

La Habanera

$$ | CUBAN | This ambience-driven Cuban restaurant is one of the most colorful spaces in Downtown Montréal and perhaps even one of the most festive. The neon "All you need is love & mojitos" sign, which hangs on a millennial-pink wall among a flock of plastic flamingos, sets the tone, as does the cocktail list. **Known for:** piñados; rum and dulce-de-leche-soaked shrimp; characterful small space. $ *Average main: C$15* ✉ *1216 av. Union, Downtown* ☎ *514/375-5355* ⊕ *www.lahabanera.ca* ☉ *Closed Sun. and Mon.* Ⓜ *McGill.*

Kazu

$$ | JAPANESE | You could almost walk right by this tiny establishment on this seedier stretch of Ste-Catherine St., but the line of people waiting to get in is a telltale sign. Popular plates include the tuna rice bowl or the messy barbecue pork neck—you'll be licking sauce off your hands, but you won't be sorry. The juicy shrimp burger and the veggie bowl with tofu, lettuce, tempura flakes, and a little chili oil on rice are both great options for lunch. **Known for:** long lines; housemade tofu; Japanese comfort food. $ *Average main: C$16* ✉ *1862 rue Ste-Catherine Ouest, Downtown* ☎ *514/937–2333* ⊕ *www.kazumontreal.com* ☉ *Closed Tues. No lunch Sat.* Ⓜ *Guy-Concordia.*

LOV

$$ | VEGETARIAN | With its all-white and green, plant-heavy decor and sustainable approach to food, fashionable and botanical LOV is the kind of vegan restaurant that even die-hard carnivores will line up to enter. Stéphanie Audet, one of the rare female chefs in Montréal, works tirelessly with local farmers to limit the restaurant's footprint. **Known for:** vegan poutine; biodynamic and natural wines; upscale vegan and vegetarian cuisine. $ *Average main: C$15* ✉ *1232 rue de la Montagne, Downtown* ☎ *514/287–1155* ⊕ *www.lov.com* Ⓜ *Peel.*

Le Taj

$$$ | INDIAN | FAMILY | Refined Le Taj carries a piece of Montréal's history with its ornate mud wall originally made for India's pavilion at World Expo '67. With northern Indian cuisine in mind, which isn't as spicy as its southern counterpart, *thalis*—platters comprising a variety of curries—are ideal for sampling unfamiliar flavors. **Known for:** vegetarian-friendly; multiflavored platters; all-you-can-eat lunch buffet. ⑤ *Average main: C$21* ✉ *2077 rue Stanley, Downtown* ☎ *514/845–9015* ⊕ *www.restaurantletaj. com* ⊘ *No lunch Sat.* Ⓜ *Peel.*

Mandy's

$$ | CONTEMPORARY | If you're in the mood for a big, nourishing, market-fresh salad served in a colorful ceramic bowl in a pastel setting, Mandy's is the place to go. Choose from among 15 different varieties of salads, such as the Habibi salad with quinoa, parsley, mint, chickpeas, roasted sweet potato, cherry tomatoes, red onion, and feta, mixed with tahini dressing; and the Clean Green with basil, cilantro, mint, broccoli, cucumber, edamame, purple cabbage, green onions, and pumpkin seeds, garnished with tamari dressing. **Known for:** nourishing salads; attractive setting in soothing colors; always fresh ingredients. ⑤ *Average main: C$15* ✉ *2067 rue Crescent, Downtown* ☎ *514/419–0779* ⊕ *www. mandys.ca* Ⓜ *Guy.*

Ryū

$$ | JAMAICAN | The salmon and avocado tartare is a must at this surprisingly affordable Japanese tapas restaurant and lounge. Carefully selected wines and classic cocktails combine with sleek lighting (the dragon changes color throughout the night) for a memorable dining experience. **Known for:** high-end sushi; traditional and contemporary dishes; omakase. ⑤ *Average main:* ✉ *1468 rue Peel, Downtown* ☎ *514/446–1468* ⊕ *www.ryupeel.com* Ⓜ *Peel.*

🛏 Hotels

The hub for countless festivals, Downtown Montréal is a convenient place to unpack your bags. This is where you'll find the major chain hotels, with underground parking, pools, and all the amenities that families enjoy. A few new boutique hotels have appeared in recent years, providing more options for couples without kids. From Downtown, it's just a short trip—via bike path, métro, or taxi—to the city's other neighborhoods of interest, so this is a good central point from which to see the city. Traffic often crawls in the city, and since the outdoor festival "quartier," Le Quartier des Spectacles, was renovated, even more people are attracted to Downtown's hotels. So leave your car at the hotel and go by foot or métro whenever possible.

Château Versailles

$$ | HOTEL | History lovers and lovers of the romantic variety, too, appreciate the luxury within the Versailles' two elegant beaux arts mansions, with high ceilings, plaster moldings, antique furnishings, and a twinkling chandelier in the entryway. **Pros:** elaborate decor and breakfast; spacious rooms with fireplaces; easy access to museum district and to nearby Westmount. **Cons:** at busy intersection; too staid for children—and possibly some adults; no elevator. ⑤ *Rooms from: C$255* ✉ *1659 rue Sherbrooke Ouest, Downtown* ☎ *514/933–3611, 888/933–8111* ⊕ *www.versailleshotels. com* ➫ *65 rooms* ⦿ *Free breakfast* Ⓜ *Guy-Concordia.*

Delta Montréal

$ | HOTEL | FAMILY | Business travelers and jazz festival performers cycle through the Delta's airportlike lobby every year, taking advantage of the hotel's minimalist and quiet rooms, saltwater pool, squash courts, high-tech gym, and family-friendly restaurant. **Pros:** two squash courts and saltwater pool; excellent soundproofing; kid-friendly amenities and deals. **Cons:**

drab lobby needs a makeover; no safes in room; restaurant is not great. $ *Rooms from: C$199* ✉ *475 av. du Président-Kennedy, Downtown* ☎ *514/286–1986, 877/286–1986* ⊕ *www.deltamontreal. com* ⇨ *456 rooms* ⦵ *No meals* Ⓜ *McGill or Place-des-Arts.*

⭐ Fairmont Le Reine Elizabeth
$$$ | HOTEL | Reopened in summer 2017 after a $140 million renovation, Le Reine Elizabeth's retro-chic makeover includes 1960s-inspired interiors; a huge market and food hall; a new spa; creative meeting hubs; and a variety of trendy dining and lounging options—all the while preserving the property's iconic heritage (John and Yoko's 1969 "bed-in" suite [1742] has been carefully restored and enhanced with artifacts from the day). **Pros:** craft cocktails at Nacarat Bar and outdoor terrace; excellent dining options; luxurious, contemporary rooms. **Cons:** daily fee for Wi-Fi unless you are a member; conventioneers abound; some bathrooms are small. $ *Rooms from: C$319* ✉ *900 boul. René-Lévesque Ouest, Downtown* ☎ *514/861–3511, 866/540–4483 reservations* ⊕ *www.fairmont.com/ queen-elizabeth-montreal* ⇨ *952 rooms* ⦵ *No meals* Ⓜ *Bonaventure.*

⭐ Four Seasons Montréal
$$$$ | HOTEL | The city's most highly anticipated hotel opening of the decade, the Four Seasons Montréal opened its doors in 2019 and offers all you would expect from the iconic brand: world-class design, luxurious rooms, gorgeous social areas, and impeccable service. **Pros:** celebrity chef restaurant and bar, MARCUS; elegant, contemporary bar and lounge; spa boasts Kneipp water therapy with hot and cold foot baths. **Cons:** only an indoor pool; exorbitant nightly rates; no outdoor spaces. $ *Rooms from: C$800* ✉ *1440 rue de la Montagne, Downtown* ☎ *514/843–2500* ⊕ *www. fourseasons.com/montreal* ⇨ *169 rooms* ⦵ *No meals* Ⓜ *Guy-Concordia or Peel.*

⭐ Hôtel Birks
$$$ | HOTEL | Opened in fall 2018, the glamorous Hôtel Birks was once the Canadian headquarters of the Birks jewelry empire, Canada's equivalent of Tiffany's, and it wisely preserved the jewelry store's original stained glass, pendant lamps, and ornate crown moldings. **Pros:** richly appointed lobby in historic building; stunning, atmospheric brasserie popular with locals; many rooms have gas fireplaces. **Cons:** not all rooms have bathtubs; parking can be a challenge; no pool. $ *Rooms from: C$306* ✉ *1240 rue du Square Phillips, Downtown* ☎ *514/370–3000* ⊕ *www.hotelbirksmontreal.com* ⇨ *132 rooms* ⦵ *No meals* Ⓜ *McGill.*

Hotel Bonaventure Montréal
$ | HOTEL | FAMILY | From the Brutalist concrete facade to its slick, modern new lobby, the Bonaventure delivers style and value, along with a heated outdoor pool, 2½ acres of rooftop gardens, and updated bedrooms with dark-wood furniture, mini-refrigerators, and granite countertops. **Pros:** almost every room has a view of the rooftop garden; easy access to the métro and the Underground City; year-round heated pool. **Cons:** high volume of business traffic; elevator ride to reception is not very welcoming; modernist exterior not for everyone. $ *Rooms from: C$199* ✉ *900 rue de la Gauchetière O., Downtown* ☎ *514/878–2332, 800/267–2575* ⊕ *www.hotelbonaventure.com* ⇨ *397 rooms* ⦵ *No meals* Ⓜ *Bonaventure.*

Hôtel Chez Swann
$$ | HOTEL | Drawn to its Baz Luhrmann-style flamboyance, young culture vultures love that Chez Swann fully commits to the idiosyncratic design, with swirly black ceilings in the hallways, original art, custom furniture, textured rugs, sink-in sofas, a spin room, and free calls within North America. **Pros:** quirky design; in-room spa treatments; Downtown location. **Cons:** no bathtubs; no pets; not suitable for kids. $ *Rooms*

from: C$230 ✉ 1444 rue Drummond,
Downtown ☎ 514/842–7070, 877/
568–7070 ⊕ www.hotelchezswann.com
▤ No credit cards ⇄ 23 rooms ◉ Free
breakfast Ⓜ Peel.

Hôtel Le Crystal

$$$ | HOTEL | Le Crystal's luxury suites
are all about dramatic style and comfort,
designed to showcase the rooms' sleek
kitchens, spa-style bathrooms, separate
soaking tubs, and floor-to-ceiling win-
dows. **Pros:** walking distance to Centre
Bell; saltwater pool; outdoor year-round
whirlpool hot tub. **Cons:** not suitable for
kids; only option is suites; right on the
sidewalk of a busy intersection. Ⓢ Rooms
from: C$340 ✉ 1100 rue de la Montagne,
Downtown ☎ 514/861–5550, 877/861–
5550 ⊕ www.hotellecrystal.com ⇄ 131
suites ◉ No meals Ⓜ Lucien-L'Aller.

Hôtel le Square-Phillips et Suites

$$ | HOTEL | FAMILY | Often accommodating
movie crews and performers who make
themselves at home in the sun-filled
laundry room and glassed-in rooftop
pool, this apartment-style hotel is full of
basic rooms and suites—all with fully
equipped kitchens and living rooms with
flat-screen televisions. **Pros:** full in-room
kitchens; excellent rooftop pool, gym,
and sunbathing; good shopping nearby.
Cons: uninspired lobby; not much nightlife
nearby; the nice bathrooms make the
rest of the room look drab. Ⓢ Rooms
from: C$240 ✉ 1193 Pl. Phillips, Down-
town ☎ 514/393–1193, 866/393–1193
⊕ www.squarephillips.com ⇄ 164 rooms
◉ Free breakfast Ⓜ McGill.

Le Centre Sheraton

$$ | HOTEL | FAMILY | At this magnet for
conventioneers, hockey fans, and busi-
nesspeople, the high-tech gym inspires
exercise with views of the city, the lobby
bar draws boisterous guests for drinks
and networking, and the morning crowd
shares newspapers at the in-house
Starbucks café. **Pros:** Sheraton Signa-
ture comforts; rooms have views of the
mountain or St. Lawrence River; close

to the Centre Bell. **Cons:** lobby marred
by convention signs; lively scene not for
everyone; executive club lounge on the
37th floor costs extra. Ⓢ Rooms from:
C$235 ✉ 1201 boul. René-Lévesque
Ouest, Downtown ☎ 514/878–2000
⊕ www.sheraton.marriott.com ⇄ 825
rooms ◉ No meals Ⓜ Bonaventure or
Peel.

★ Le Mount Stephen Hotel

$$$$ | HOTEL | Set in a restored neoclassi-
cal landmark once owned by a Canadian
railway pioneer, as well as a new 11-story
tower behind the original mansion, this
modern boutique hotel features contem-
porary guest rooms with state-of-the-art
comforts (chromatherapy showers, Jap-
anese [Toto] toilets, heated floors, and
Nespresso machines) as well as ornate
interiors that include original features like
300-year-old stained-glass windows and
intricate woodwork. **Pros:** unique historic
property with opulent interior; high-end
experience; Insta-worthy Bar George.
Cons: not family-friendly; rates match the
luxury; British-inspired restaurant may
be too proper for some. Ⓢ Rooms from:
C$450 ✉ 1440 Drummond St., Down-
town ☎ 514/313–1000, 844/838–8655
⊕ www.lemountstephen.com ⇄ 90
rooms ◉ No meals.

Le St-Martin Hôtel Particulier

$$$ | HOTEL | FAMILY | Sober and chic, this
tasteful hotel is in a great location for
shopping, museums, and restaurants,
and made special with features like
a year-round heated pool, hardwood
accents, fireplaces, soundproofed windows, and a French fusion restaurant.
Pros: windows are soundproof; soaker
tub and TV in bathrooms; very good restaurant with stylish decor. **Cons:** reception
is just steps from the sidewalk and gets
crowded at checkout; small outdoor pool
often in shade; guests must be over the
age of 25. Ⓢ Rooms from: C$323 ✉ 980
boul. de Maisonneuve Ouest, Downtown
☎ 514/843–3000, 877/843–3003 ⊕ www.

Old meets new at Le Mount Stephen, where sleek contemporary guest rooms are housed in a grand neoclassical building.

lestmartinmontreal.com ⊟ *No credit cards* ⋥ *123 rooms* |◯| *No meals* Ⓜ *Peel.*

★ Loews Hôtel Vogue

$$ | HOTEL | FAMILY | Committed shoppers like the location—just a five-minute walk from Holt Renfrew, La Maison Ogilvy, La Maison Simons, and other destinations boutiques—but the hotel's appeal multiplied tenfold with a multimillion dollar renovation that made the rooms and lobby more fitting (i.e. gorgeous) for regulars like Oscar winners and business elites. **Pros:** chic lobby; huge bathrooms with flat-screen TVs; toys available for kids. **Cons:** no spa; valet parking fee; no pool. Ⓢ *Rooms from: C$229* ✉ *1425 rue de la Montagne, Downtown* ☎ *514/285–5555, 855/977–8585* ⊕ *www.loewshotels.com* ⋥ *142 rooms* |◯| *No meals* Ⓜ *Peel.*

★ Ritz-Carlton Montréal

$$$$ | HOTEL | The legacy, the elegance, the celebrity chef, the new pool—all good reasons to splurge on a room at the fully renovated "Ritz," the city's grandest hotel and icon in the Golden Square Mile, near museums, McGill University, and all the best boutiques. **Pros:** revived style, but still plenty of history; state-of-the-art bathrooms and soundproof windows; high-end shopping and galleries within a five-minute walk; infinity pool with patio. **Cons:** poor métro access; Sherbrooke Street can be dull on weeknights; not all rooms have a picturesque view. Ⓢ *Rooms from: C$840* ✉ *1228 rue Sherbrooke Ouest, Downtown* ☎ *514/842–4212, 800/542–8680* ⊕ *www.ritzmontreal.com* ⋥ *129 rooms* |◯| *No meals* Ⓜ *Peel or Guy-Concordia.*

★ Sofitel Montréal

$$ | HOTEL | At the foot of Mont-Royal, in the heart of Downtown, this exquisite 17-story hotel uses its understated elegance (if the exquisite lobby carpets, made by the same company that carpeted Versailles for King Louis XIV can be called understated), excellent service and details, and convenient location to attract a well-heeled international crowd. **Pros:** bright and tailored rooms; chef Olivier Perret helms the exceptional restaurant; within walking distance of museums,

McGill, the Bell Centre, and destination boutiques. **Cons:** no pool; scarce street parking; obstructed views in the east-facing rooms. ⑤ *Rooms from: C$295* ✉ *1155 rue Sherbrooke Ouest, Downtown* ☎ *514/285–9000* ⊕ *www.sofitel.com* ⟿ *258 rooms* ⫶⚬⫶ *No meals* Ⓜ *Peel.*

▼ Nightlife

From expensive restaurants to lowly bars, Downtown offers something for every taste and budget. Rue Crescent, with its lively mix of restaurants, pubs, and clubs, is where you'll find most of the action, with neighboring rue Bishop and rue Mackay not far behind.

BARS AND LOUNGES
★ Brutopia

BARS/PUBS | House-brewed concoctions like Raspberry Blond Beer or Mango Session IPA attract locals and tourists alike, and lately the kitchen has been serving up delicious tapas-style pub food, including some healthy vegetarian and vegan options. In addition to the unique brews, check out the sprawling outdoor seating, the art gallery on the third floor, and nightly live music. A typical crowd at Brutopia is under 30, but older folk shouldn't feel out of place. With live music ranging from traditional Irish folk to the occasional punk or psychedelic '60s garage band, this pub serves as a refreshing alternative to the slightly more upscale, trendy bars and nightclubs that mark the Crescent Street strip. ✉ *1219 rue Crescent, Downtown* ☎ *514/393–9277* ⊕ *www.brutopia.net* Ⓜ *Guy-Concordia.*

Burgundy Lion

BARS/PUBS | This British pub serves food that's a notch above the usual. Scotch eggs and the ploughman's lunch are paired with an English take on Québec's beloved poutine—with Stilton cheese and caramelized onions—though it's the fish-and-chips that really shines. Be sure to grab a pint of the Burgundy Lion Ale, or any of the many other beers

on draft. Two patios are open in the summer for alfresco drinking. Note that it can get loud in the evenings. ✉ *2496 rue Notre-Dame Ouest, Downtown* ☎ *514/934–0888* ⊕ *www.burgundylion.com* Ⓜ *Lionel-Groulx.*

★ Dominion Square Tavern

BARS/PUBS | Busy nearly every night of the week, this bar with a relaxed 1920s atmosphere is one of the hottest spots Downtown for a drink after work, a tasty bite before a hockey game, or an old-fashioned cocktail to unwind and plan the rest of the evening. It opens at 11:30 am weekdays and 4:30 pm weekends. Kitchen closes at midnight daily. ✉ *1243 rue Metcalfe, Downtown* ☎ *514/564–5056* ⊕ *www.tavernedominion.com.*

★ Furco

BARS/PUBS | Making its name through word of mouth alone, Furco has become one of the trendiest Downtown bars, and for good reason. It's all about the industrial-chic interior, the warm amber lighting, and the relaxed, inviting vibe. A nice mix of clientele, great food (the menu changes weekly), and good pours also help make this a popular after-work hangout for locals, and the perfect retreat from the Quartier des Spectacles, a stone's throw away. ✉ *425 rue Mayor, Downtown* ☎ *514/764–3588* ⊕ *www.barfurco.com* Ⓜ *Place-des-Arts or McGill.*

Hurley's Irish Pub

BARS/PUBS | For years this pub has been serving up a bounty of whiskeys and brews (19 different beers on tap), with a healthy dose of Irish atmosphere on the side. Despite its cavernous size, the arrangement of seating areas, flanked by bars, makes it feel cozy, and there's a stage for live entertainment. It still fills up quickly, so unless you don't mind standing while you sip your Guinness, come early to snag a seat. ✉ *1225 rue Crescent, Downtown* ☎ *514/861–4111* ⊕ *www.hurleysirishpub.com* Ⓜ *Guy-Concordia.*

Le Sainte-Elisabeth
BARS/PUBS | In the Quartier des Spectacles (the local performing-arts district), this European pub is popular in part because of its friendly service and good selection of domestic and imported beers, as well as whiskey and cognac. With one of the city's most beautiful backyard terraces, this is a great place to enjoy the fall colors. ✉ 1412 rue Ste-Elisabeth, Downtown ☎ 514/286–4302 ⊕ www.ste-elisabeth.com Ⓜ Berri.

★ Pullman
WINE BARS—NIGHTLIFE | At this sophisticated yet relaxed wine bar, let yourself be guided by the expertise of the sommeliers. The tapas-style cuisine is top-notch, and the green beans with truffle oil and roasted almonds are scrumptious. During cooler months things get going at 4:30 pm, but in summer don't arrive until the sun starts to set. ✉ 3424 av. du Parc, Downtown ☎ 514/288–7779 ⊕ www.pullman-mtl.com Ⓜ Place-des-Arts.

Stogie's Lounge
BARS/PUBS | If the surprisingly trendy interior and views of rue Crescent aren't a big enough draw, then check out the conspicuous glass humidor housing a seemingly infinite supply of imported cigars. Thanks to being grandfathered in, the bar still allows smoking Cubans on-site, despite Québec's tough no-smoking law. ✉ 2015 rue Crescent, Downtown ☎ 514/848–0069, 877/848–0069 ⊕ www.stogiescigars.com Ⓜ Guy-Concordia or Peel.

COMEDY CLUBS
The Montréal Just For Laughs comedy festival, which takes place every July, has been the largest such festival in the world since its inception back in 1983.

But Montrealers don't have to wait until summer to get their comedy fix, as there are several Downtown clubs covering all things funny.

Comedy Nest
COMEDY CLUBS | For decades, this comedy club has been showering Montrealers with humor from some of the biggest names out there: Jim Carrey, Tim Allen, and Russell Peters included. For a mere $5, Newbie Tuesdays and Comedy Lab Wednesdays, when novice comedians and local comics work out new material, are always good for a laugh and will also secure you one free ticket for a Thursday or Friday late show. Arrive early to get a decent spot near the stage (or perhaps away from it). ✉ Pepsi Forum, 2313 rue Ste-Catherine Ouest , 3rd fl., Downtown ☎ 514/932–6378 ⊕ www.comedynest.com Ⓜ Atwater.

Montréal Improv
COMEDY CLUBS | The heart of the city's improv comedy scene offers shows in both English and French. The Friday night Main Event Smackdowns, where the audience determines the winner, are especially good for a laugh. ■TIP→ Get here early, as the $8 tickets usually sell out quickly. ✉ 3697 boul. St-Laurent, Downtown ☎ 514/507–3535 ⊕ www.montreal-improv.com Ⓜ Sherbrooke.

DANCE CLUBS
Club Electric Avenue
DANCE CLUBS | Generation X will get along just fine here, as classics from the '80s and '90s boom out over a devoted, nostalgic crowd. In the basement of the Newtown lounge, these digs have great sound, excellent service, and sexy interior design. It's open Thursday to Saturday from 10 pm. ✉ 1476 rue Crescent, Downtown ☎ 514/285–8885 ⊕ www.clubsmontreal.com/en Ⓜ Guy-Concordia.

Foufounes Electriques
BARS/PUBS |"Foufs," as it's affectionately known, has been going strong for almost 40 years. Attracting a cult following of alternative rock and heavy metal fans, it gets packed on weekends. You can enjoy a cheap beer on one of two summer terrasses under the playful eyes of skulls and spiders. ✉ 87 rue Ste-Catherine Est,

Downtown ☎ 514/844–5539 ⊕ www.
foufouneselectriques.com Ⓜ St-Laurent.

Salsathèque

DANCE CLUBS | Though neon lights and
disco balls abound, this flashy club is all
about the Latin lover—dance lover, that
is. Merengue, bachata, and salsa (of
course) are the specialties, but themed
evenings keep things interesting with
R&B, reggae, and Top 40 hits. Check the
website to learn the week's schedule
and sign up for the guest list to avoid
a cover. ⊠ 1220 rue Peel, Downtown
☎ 514/875–0016 ⊕ www.salsatheque.ca
⊘ Closed Mon. and Tues. Ⓜ Peel.

LIVE MUSIC

Club Soda

MUSIC CLUBS | The grandaddy of the city's
rock clubs has evolved into one of the
dominant venues for jazz, reggae, tech-
no, and rhythm and blues. Club Soda is
a tall, narrow concert hall with high-tech
design and 500 seats—all of them with
great sight lines. ⊠ 1225 boul. St-Laurent,
Downtown ☎ 514/286–1010 ⊕ www.
clubsoda.ca Ⓜ St-Laurent.

House of Jazz

MUSIC CLUBS | The food is good but the
music is outstanding. For more than 30
years, this institution has been plying
the city with the best in jazz, with a little
blues and soul thrown in for good meas-
ure. A flashy, over-the-top interior that
includes mirrored walls adds to the experience. Dress up and be prepared to pay
a cover. ⊠ 2060 rue Aylmer, Downtown
☎ 514/842–8656 ⊕ www.houseofjazz.ca
Ⓜ McGill or Place-des-Arts.

McKibbin's Irish Pub

MUSIC CLUBS | This beautiful old sandstone
mansion includes three floors of food,
drink, and good Irish craic (a Gaelic term
that means having fun with amiable
companions). This isn't hard to do with
more than 20 different stouts, lagers, and
ales on tap. There's live entertainment
nearly every night of the week, so head
to the basement if you're looking for a

bit of quiet (or a good chin-wag). The
house fries are excellent for noshing,
but beware of the Rim Reaper—chicken
wings made with the world's hottest
pepper. ⊠ 1426 rue Bishop, Downtown
☎ 514/288–1580 ⊕ www.mckibbinsirish-
pub.com Ⓜ Guy-Concordia.

★ Upstairs Jazz Bar & Grill

MUSIC CLUBS | Five nights a week, the
cheerful Joel Giberovitch greets you
personally near the entrance to his club,
which despite the name is actually
downstairs. Giberovitch loves what he
does, and the constant stream of local
and imported jazz musicians makes this
the favored jazz hangout in the city. The
eclectic menu makes a nice accompani-
ment to the live music—try the home-cut
fries with smoky mayo. Cover charges
start at C$6 and range up to C$45 for
big-ticket performers during Jazz Fest.
The third set is free (usually around 11
pm), and other sets are also free if you sit
on one of the cozy terraces. ■ TIP→ Parking costs $5. Ask your server for a
ticket. ⊠ 1254 rue Mackay, Downtown
☎ 514/931–6808 ⊕ www.upstairsjazz.
com Ⓜ Guy-Concordia.

🎭 Performing Arts

CLASSICAL MUSIC

Opéra de Montréal

MUSIC | This renowned opera company,
the largest francophone opera in North
America, has a varied schedule of
classics, including Le Nozze di Figaro,
Rigoletto, and Silent Night. Seventy-five
minutes before each show, the "pre-Op-
era" program, done in French with a
summary in English, gives attendees a
look at the history, music, and artists of
the Opéra de Montréal. ⊠ Place des Arts,
260 boul. de Maisonneuve, Downtown
☎ 514/985–2258, 877/385–2222 ⊕ www.
operademontreal.com Ⓜ Place-des-Arts.

Orchestre Métropolitain du Grand Montréal

MUSIC | The Met may lie in the shad-
ow of the Orchestre Symphonique de

Montréal, but its talented conductor and artistic director, Yannick Nézet-Séguin, continues to draw the spotlight. He's in high demand across the world; in addition to his role here, he's the musical director at the Philadelphia Orchestra and New York City's Metropolitan Opera, and honorary conductor at the Rotterdam Philharmonic. His charismatic approach has brought in the crowds since 2000 and produced highly acclaimed performances. Most shows take place at Place des Arts or Maison Symphonique de Montréal. ✉ *486 rue Ste-Catherine Ouest, #401, Downtown* ☎ *514/598–0870* ⊕ *www.orchestremetropolitain. com* Ⓜ *Place-des-Arts*.

★ Orchestre Symphonique de Montréal

MUSIC | Montréal's beloved OSM plays programs that include masterful renditions of the classics, with contemporary works thrown into the mix. The orchestra's home, the Maison symphonique de Montréal, is part of the Place des Arts complex. ✉ *1600 rue St-Urbain, Downtown* ☎ *514/842–9951, 888/842–9951* ⊕ *www.osm.ca* Ⓜ *Place-des-Arts*.

Pollack Concert Hall

CONCERTS | McGill University's concert hall showcases the best talents from its formidable music faculty, with concerts by the McGill Symphony, Opera McGill, the McGill Baroque Orchestra, and the Montréal Chamber Orchestra, among others. ✉ *555 rue Sherbrooke Ouest, Downtown* ☎ *514/398–4547* ⊕ *www. mcgill.ca/music* Ⓜ *McGill*.

DANCE
Agora de la Danse

DANCE | More than just a performance space for contemporary dance, this center actively works in the dance community to encourage creativity and experimentation. Hosting acclaimed artists and companies from around the world, the company is also affiliated with the Université du Québec à Montréal dance faculty. ✉ *1435 rue de Bleury, Downtown* ☎ *514/525–1500* ⊕ *www.agoradanse. com* Ⓜ *Place-des-Arts*.

BJM Danse Montréal

DANCE | Under artistic director Louis Robitaille, BJM Danse Montréal fuses contemporary music and visual arts with extraordinary technique. Performances are held at Place des Arts and Agora de la Danse, and there are free shows at Théâtre de Verdure in Parc Lafontaine during the summer months. ✉ *Downtown* ☎ *514/982–6771* ⊕ *www.bjmdanse.ca*.

La Fondation de Danse Margie Gillis

DANCE | Margie Gillis, one of Canada's most exciting and innovative soloists, works with her own company and guest artists to stage performances at Place des Arts, Agora de la Danse, and other area venues. ✉ *Downtown* ☎ *514/845–3115* ⊕ *www.margiegillis.org*.

★ Les Grands Ballets Canadiens de Montréal

DANCE | One of Canada's premier ballet companies, Les Grands have been moving audiences since 1957. Under the artistic direction of Louis Robitaille, the company has continued to evolve a rich body of both classic and contemporary work. Its annual presentation of *The Nutcracker*, which often sells out, has become a Christmas tradition. Performances take place at the Place des Arts. ✉ *Downtown* ☎ *514/849–8681 tickets* ⊕ *www.grandsballets.com*.

Montréal Danse

DANCE | Lavish sets and dazzlingly sensual choreography have helped make Montréal Danse one of Canada's most popular contemporary repertory companies. It has a busy touring schedule, but also regularly performs at Place des Arts, Agora de la Danse, and the Théâtre de Verdure. ✉ *Downtown* ☎ *514/871–4005* ⊕ *www.montrealdanse.com*.

Tangente

DANCE | For more than 35 years, Tangente has hosted weekly performances of contemporary and experimental dance

Classical Music

The performing arts thrive in Montréal, from dance troupes to classical music groups to theater. Place des Arts, Montréal's main concert hall in Downtown Montréal, is a popular venue for large-scale productions, but some groups, such as I Musici, perform at venues throughout town. *Note that many performing arts groups take to the road or are on hiatus in summer.*

I Musici de Montréal Chamber Orchestra. Arguably the best chamber orchestra in Canada, I Musici, under the direction of Jean-Marie Zeitouni, performs at several places around town. These include the Salle Bourgie at the Musée des Beaux-Arts and the Place des Arts' Nouvelle Salle, but its music is best suited to the wood-paneled **Tudor Hall**, atop the Holt Renfrew Ogilvy department store. There, about a dozen times a year, you can enjoy a coffee or aperitif while you listen to a late-morning or early-evening concert. ⊠ *4672 B rue Saint-Denis* ☎ *514/790–1111 tickets, 866/908–9090* ⊕ *www.imusici.com.*

between September and May on various Montréal stages (there are currently three venues in the city). It also acts as an archive for contemporary dance and experimental performance art, with more than 2,000 files focusing on major international dance schools and festivals, companies and choreographers. Tangente encourages national and international exchanges between dance companies and artists. ⊠ *The Wilder, 1435 rue de Bleury, Downtown* ✛ *rue De Bleury and rue Sainte-Catherine Ouest* ☎ *514/525–5584* ⊕ *www.tangentedanse. ca* Ⓜ *Station Place-des-Arts.*

FILM

★ Cinéma du Parc

FILM | A favorite of Montréal moviegoers for years, this theater focuses on first-run movies from around the world. Retrospectives based on interesting themes and prominent directors are also screened. Located inside the Galeries du Parc mall, near McGill University, it primarily caters to an Anglophone audience. ■ TIP➔ **The cinema offers parking at $3 for three hours. Just ask for your coupon at the box office.** ⊠ *Galeries du Parc Mall, 3575 av. du Parc , Suite 6100, Downtown*

☎ *514/281–1900* ⊕ *www.cinemaduparc. com* Ⓜ *Place-des-Arts.*

Cinéma Impérial

FILM | Recognized by the Québec government as a historical monument in 2001, this grand Renaissance-style movie theater, complete with ornate ceilings, decorative moulding, and red-velvet seats, screens independent films, though on a somewhat irregular basis. It plays host to many cultural events, including the Montréal World Film Festival. ⊠ *1432 rue de Bleury, Downtown* ☎ *514/884–7187* ⊕ *www.cinemaimperial.com* Ⓜ *Place-des-Arts.*

THEATER

Black Theatre Workshop

THEATER | The only black English-language company in Québec (and the longest-running in Canada) continues to support and nourish the careers of many prominent artists on the national scene. Expect innovative new productions performed alongside classic plays, such as *A Raisin in the Sun.* Shows take place at the Centaur Theatre and other venues around the city. ⊠ *Downtown* ☎ *514/932–1104* ⊕ *www.blacktheatreworkshop.ca.*

Geordie Productions

THEATER | Promoting itself as a theater for all audiences, this accomplished English company has been delighting kids and adults since 1982. The 2018–19 lineup featured productions that included adaptations of *Robin Hood, A Christmas Carol,* and *Around the World in 80 Days.* Most productions are performed at the Centaur Theatre. ✉ *Downtown* ☎ *514/845–9810* ⊕ *www.geordie.ca.*

Monument-National

THEATER | The highly regarded École Nationale de Théâtre du Canada—aka National Theatre School of Canada—supplies world stages with a steady stream of well-trained actors and directors. It works and performs in the historic and glorious old theater that has played host to such luminaries as Edith Piaf and Emma Albani. (Québec's first feminist rallies in the early 1900s also took place here.) Graduating classes perform professional-level plays in both French and English. The theater also plays host to an assortment of touring plays, musicals, and concerts. ✉ *1182 boul. St-Laurent, Downtown* ☎ *514/871–2224* ⊕ *www. monument-national.qc.ca* Ⓜ *St-Laurent.*

Théâtre Jean Duceppe

THEATER | Named for one of Québec's most beloved actors, this theater makes its home in the smallest and most intimate of the four auditoriums in Place des Arts. It primarily stages major French-language productions. ✉ *175 rue Ste-Catherine Ouest, Downtown* ☎ *514/842–2112* ⊕ *www.duceppe.com* Ⓜ *Place-des-Arts.*

★ Théâtre du Nouveau Monde

THEATER | A season's offerings at this theater might include works by locals Michel Tremblay and Patrice Robitaille, as well as works by Shakespeare, Molière, Camus, Ibsen, Chekhov, and Arthur Miller. ✉ *84 rue Ste-Catherine Ouest, Downtown* ☎ *514/866–8668* ⊕ *www. tnm.qc.ca* Ⓜ *St-Laurent.*

🛍 Shopping

Montréal's largest retail district takes in rues Sherbrooke and Ste-Catherine, boulevard de Maisonneuve, and the side streets between them. Because of the density and variety of the stores, it's the best shopping bet if you're in town overnight or for a weekend. The area bounded by rues Sherbrooke, Ste-Catherine, de la Montagne, and Crescent has antiques and art galleries in addition to designer salons. Fashion boutiques and art and antiques galleries line rue Sherbrooke. Rue Crescent holds a tempting blend of antiques, fashions, and jewelry displayed beneath colorful awnings. Rue de la Montagne is the corridor of chic, between the high-end Holt Renfrew and Ogilvy department stores, with designer boutiques—including top Québec labels—en route. Rue Ste-Catherine is the main shopping thoroughfare, with most of the chain stores and department stores. To get here, take the métro to the Peel, McGill, or Guy-Concordia stations.

ANTIQUES
Antiquités Pour La Table

ANTIQUES/COLLECTIBLES | Armoires and sideboards brimming with fine crystal and china line the walls at this beautiful store, while chandeliers, linens, and other vintage pieces make up the rest of the treasures. *Phone before you visit, as hours can vary.* ✉ *762 av. Atwater, Downtown* ☎ *514/989–8945* ⊕ *www. antiquesforthetable.com* ☉ *Closed Sun. and Mon.* Ⓜ *St-Henri.*

Grand Central

ANTIQUES/COLLECTIBLES | "Grand" is the right word to describe this antiques emporium—it's filled to the brim with elegant chandeliers and candelabras, armchairs and secretaries, and other decorative elements from the 18th and 19th centuries. These items would add a touch of refinement to almost any home. ✉ *2448 rue Notre-Dame Ouest, St-Henri, Downtown* ☎ *514/935–1467,*

514/935–1269 ⊕ www.grandcentralinc.ca ⊙ Closed Sun. Ⓜ Lionel-Groulx.

ART
Edifice Belgo
ART GALLERIES | Built more than a century ago, Edifice Belgo houses more than two dozen art galleries exhibiting the works of both established and emerging artists. Galerie Hughes Charbonneau and Galerie Bellemare Lambert feature the work of contemporary artists working in Quebec and Canada. For wearable art, visit designer Véronique Miljkovitch's atelier on the second floor. ■TIP➔ Each gallery or atelier maintains different hours, so it's best to call ahead. ⊠ 372 rue Ste-Catherine Ouest, Downtown ☎ 514/861–2953 Ⓜ Place-des-Arts.

Galerie Alan Klinkhoff
ART GALLERIES | The Klinkhoffs know art. Open since 1950, the gallery boasts several floors of Canadian works from both contemporary and historical artists. ⊠ 1448 rue Sherbrooke Ouest, Downtown ☎ 514/284–9339, 416/233–0339 Toronto office ⊕ www.klinkhoff.ca ⊙ Closed Sun. Ⓜ Guy.

BOOKS AND STATIONERY
Paragraphe
BOOKS/STATIONERY | This cornerstone of Montréal's English-language literary scene carries the usual selection of mysteries and thrillers, but it also stocks a wide range of Canadian works. It's a favorite with visiting authors, who stop by to read from their latest releases. Sip on a coffee from the adjacent Second Cup coffee shop while you peruse the stacks. ⊠ 2220 av. McGill College, Downtown ☎ 514/845–5811 ⊕ www.paragraphbooks.com Ⓜ McGill.

Renaud-Bray
BOOKS/STATIONERY | Tucked away in the basement level of the Complexe Desjardins shopping mall, this outlet of the vast French-language book chain is chockablock with French and English books, magazines, and music.

⊠ 150 Ste-Catherine Ouest, Downtown ☎ 514/288–4844 ⊕ www.renaud-bray.com Ⓜ Place-des-Arts.

★ The Word
BOOKS/STATIONERY | Deep in the heart of the McGill University neighborhood, or ghetto as it's known by locals, this small shop is bursting with used books (including first editions) and specializes in philosophy, poetry, and literature. The award-winning Montréal landmark, open since 1975, shunned modern technology (including a cash register) until just a few years ago. There's not even a sign, so keep your eyes peeled as you walk along Milton, though the bargain books lining the window are a good clue. ⊠ 469 rue Milton, Downtown ☎ 514/845–5640 ⊕ www.wordbookstore.ca ⊙ Closed Sun. Ⓜ McGill.

CLOTHING
Aritzia
CLOTHING | At more than 10,000 square feet, Aritzia's gleaming glass-fronted, two-story location on Ste-Catherine Street is the Vancouver brand's largest in Canada, opening its doors in 2015 to great fanfare among the twentysomething fashionista set. Offering pretty, minimalist classics like embroidered bib-front sleeveless white dresses, lightweight shirt dresses and slip dresses for summer, this is the place to shop if you're looking for on-trend women's clothing at reasonable prices. Along with its own collections, Aritzia also carries popular labels like Mackage, Citizens of Humanity, and AGOLDE. ⊠ 1125 rue Ste-Catherine Ouest, Downtown ☎ 514/285–0791 ⊕ www.aritzia.com Ⓜ Peel.

★ Arthur
CLOTHING | Everything about this shop, from the immaculate hardwood floors to the classic bespoke men's shirts featuring damask silk linings and hand-sewn button holes speaks of quality, tradition, and style. Armenian-Canadian tailor Arthur der Shahinian has been creating bespoke suits for men (and

some women) since 1978, first from his modest digs at Marché Jean-Talon, now from his elegant atelier-cum-boutique on Crescent Street. Still, Mr. der Shahinian and his son Tavit haven't compromised their principles of quality and friendly, professional service. At 68, der Shahinian is the youngest shirtmaker in Montréal, a fact that speaks volumes about what has been happening to the fashion industry in the last quarter decade or so. The der Shahinians also custom-make men's shoes. ✉ *2165 rue Crescent, Downtown* ☎ *514/843-0522* ⊕ *www.arthurmontreal. com* Ⓜ *Guy-Concordia.*

Café Boutique Eva B

CLOTHING | On the secondhand fashion map for decades, Eva B has all kinds of clothes, shoes, jewelry, and even eyeglasses on offer. Budget at least 30 minutes to scour the labyrinth of racks and the "pool," a large platform in the back where everything is a dollar. Just watch your step; the floor is uneven. If you get hungry in the process, nosh on a samosa or something else from the in-store café. ✉ *2015 boul. St-Laurent, Downtown* ☎ *514/849-8246* Ⓜ *St-Laurent.*

Editorial Boutique

CLOTHING | Designer duds happily share space with inexpensive but chic items at this low-key Downtown boutique with a devoted cult following. Brands include Citizens of Humanity, Erin Wasson, Luv U Always, For Love of Lemons, Unif, and Jeffrey Campbell. ✉ *1455 rue Stanley, Downtown* ☎ *514/849-3888* ⊕ *www. editorialboutique.com* Ⓜ *Peel.*

★ E.R.A. Vintage Wear

CLOTHING | With a reputation as the best vintage shop in the city, this upscale boutique specializes in vintage clothing, shoes, and accessories from the 1920s through the mid-1980s. Each handpicked item is carefully cleaned, repaired, and altered as necessary to give it a more contemporary flavor. High-profile clients like Julianne Moore and Cate

Blanchett have been known to drop by. This location is bright, spacious, and loaded with irresistible treasures. ✉ *999 rue du College , Loft 41, Downtown* ☎ *514/543-8750* ⊕ *www.eravintagewear. com* ☾ *Closed Sun.* Ⓜ *Place St-Henri.*

★ Frank and Oak

CLOTHING | This store outfits young, creative professionals in quality denim and plaid essentials as well as rich velvets and airy chiffons in contemporary styles, but it's so much more. The 5,000-square-foot Montréal flagship of this Canadian brand is an experience. It's a welcoming space where people can drink specialty coffee, meet friends, get a shave and haircut, attend regular events like whiskey tastings, and enjoy high-tech shopping. ✉ *1420 rue Stanley, Downtown* ☎ *514/228-3761* ⊕ *www.frankandoak. com* Ⓜ *Peel.*

Harricana

CLOTHING | Yesterday's old fur coats and stoles are transformed into everything from car coats and ski jackets to baby wraps and throw pillows at this designer shop. For summer, vintage scarves become flirty little tops. The recycled furs, leather, silks, and woolen items are sold at dozens of shops, but the best place to see what's available is this combination atelier and boutique. ✉ *416 rue McGill, Downtown* ☎ *514/282-1616* ⊕ *www.harricana.qc.ca* ☾ *Closed Sun.– Tues.* Ⓜ *Square Victoria.*

Harry Rosen

CLOTHING | This is Canada's premier high-end menswear destination. Stocked with both casual and formal attire, wallets, watches, and hats, this 22,000-square-foot flagship store caters to the classically tailored male. Brands include 7 For All Mankind, Michael Kors, Cole Haan, Tom Ford, and Armani. ✉ *Cours Mont-Royal, 1455 rue Peel, Downtown* ☎ *514/284-3315* ⊕ *www.harryrosen.com* Ⓜ *Peel.*

Montréal-based Frank and Oak is hugely successful in Canada with 23 boutiques and a thriving online presence.

★ Henri Henri

CLOTHING | The best men's hat store in Canada carries a huge stock of homburgs, fedoras, and derbies, as well as cloth caps and other accessories. Prices range from about C$155 to C$1,000, the top price fetching you a top-of-the-line Panama hat. ⊠ *189 rue Ste-Catherine Est, Downtown* ☎ *514/288–0109, 888/388–0109* ⊕ *www.henrihenri.ca* Ⓜ *St-Laurent or Berri-UQAM.*

La Senza

CLOTHING | This Québec-based chain is known for its bright, cheerful push-up bras, panties, and negligees. It also sells sleepwear and sportswear. ⊠ *Place Montréal Trust, 705 rue Ste-Catherine Ouest, Downtown* ☎ *514/288-8775* ⊕ *www.lasenza.com* Ⓜ *Peel.*

Lululemon

CLOTHING | This Canadian sports-and-yoga wear chain offers plenty of styles, colors, and cuts to please both guys and gals. You'll also find headbands, scarves, jewelry, and more. ⊠ *1232 rue Ste-Catherine Ouest, Downtown* ☎ *514/394–0770* ⊕ *www.lululemon.com* Ⓜ *Peel.*

L'Uomo Montréal

CLOTHING | You'll come to this store for the selection of European menswear and accessories, but you'll stay for the impeccable service and attention to detail. Expect suits from Kiton and Borrelli, bags from Prada, shoes from UK brand Edward Green, and ties from Massimo Bizzocchi. ⊠ *1452 rue Peel, Downtown* ☎ *514/844–1008, 877/844–1008* ⊕ *www.luomo-montreal.com* ⊙ *Closed Sun.* Ⓜ *Peel.*

★ Marie Saint Pierre

CLOTHING | The leading female designer in Québec (and one who's celebrated throughout Canada), Marie Saint Pierre is known for her signature pleats and ruffles—think sleek and sophisticated rather than frilly. Now she's lending her avant-garde touch to bridal, with a wedding collection that's available only at this flagship boutique. ⊠ *2081 rue de la Montagne, Downtown* ☎ *514/281–5547* ⊕ *www.mariesaintpierre.com* Ⓜ *Peel or Guy-Concordia.*

Olam

CLOTHING | The fashions here don't come cheap, but French-influenced owner Charles Abitbol believes in quality fashion for women of all ages. Abitbol sources funky and whimsical fashions for the younger set, as well as more classic pieces with clean lines from European, American, and local Québec designers such as Yumi, Sanctuary Clothing, Desigual, and Mélissa Nepton. The Fat Boy beanbag chairs may entice you to hang a while in the vast loftlike upstairs space, but like the Taschen design books and the colonial-inspired Québec and French-made wooden furniture, these are also for sale. ⊠ *1374 rue Ste-Catherine Ouest, Downtown* ☎ *514/875–9696* Ⓜ *Peel.*

Roots

CLOTHING | Bring the great outdoors in, courtesy of this beloved Canadian chain with a beaver emblem. There are lots of casual neutrals for men, women, and kids, with pops of colorful sportswear thrown in for good measure. Quality leather goods are also available. ⊠ *1025 rue Ste-Catherine Ouest, Downtown* ☎ *514/845–7995* ⊕ *www.roots.com* Ⓜ *Peel.*

★ Shan

CLOTHING | Designed in Montréal and sold around the world, this is couture swimwear at its finest. In a rainbow of colors, these sexy cuts are meant to be displayed—though one of the ethereal cover-ups just might make one reconsider. There's also a collection of men's swim trunks and briefs. ⊠ *2150 rue Crescent, Downtown* ☎ *514/287–7426* ⊕ *www.shan.ca* Ⓜ *Peel or Guy-Concordia.*

Tozzi

CLOTHING | Known around Montréal as one of the top menswear destinations, Tozzi is a one-stop shop for the dapper gentleman. Suits, polos, jeans, watches, sunglasses, and cologne—this boutique offers just about everything in a minimalist, serene environment. It also carries women's clothing and shoes. ⊠ *2085, 2095, and 2115 rue Crescent, Downtown* ☎ *514/285–2444* ⊕ *www.boutiquetozzi.com* Ⓜ *Guy-Concordia or Peel.*

Winners

CLOTHING | Tucked away on the lowest level of Place Montréal Trust lies this huge discount store stocked with clothing, shoes, housewares—you name it. Allow adequate time if you really want to rummage, but if you're not at leisure, head straight to the runway collections and the sale racks for the best bargains. The Alexis Nihon (Atwater métro) location, on the edge of Westmount, can also be a good bet for snagging a deal on designer labels and Italian shoes. ⊠ *Place Montréal Trust, 1500 av. McGill College, Downtown* ☎ *514/788–4949* ⊕ *www.winners.ca* Ⓜ *McGill.*

DEPARTMENT STORES
★ Holt Renfrew

DEPARTMENT STORES | This upscale department store is Canada's answer to Bergdorf Goodman. Gucci, Chanel, and all the usuals are complemented by up-and-coming designers and Holt's own in-house line. *Holt Renfrew purchased Ogilvy, Montréal's other chic department store on rue Ste-Catherine, and the two are currently in the process of merging into a megaluxury store and hotel (the brand-new Four Seasons). Holt Renfrew's move from rue Sherbrooke to Ste-Catherine should be complete sometime in 2020.* ⊠ *1300 rue Sherbrooke Ouest, Downtown* ☎ *514/842–5111* ⊕ *www.holtrenfrew.com* Ⓜ *Peel or Guy-Concordia.*

Holt Renfrew Ogilvy

DEPARTMENT STORES | This iconic Canadian luxury department store has been undergoing a monumental expansion and rebranding in the last few years. Holt Renfrew Ogilvy boasts a vast selection of clothing and accessories for men and women from the world's premier designer labels, with many housed in intimate boutiques settings within the larger department store. The new all-white Beauty Hall is now open, while the new

Colette Grand Café will be unveiled soon. *Ogilvy and Holt Renfrew, Montréal's two posh department stores, are in the process of merging into a megaluxury store on rue Ste-Catherine so expect some potential disruption during your visit.* ✉ *1307 rue Ste-Catherine Ouest, Downtown* ☎ *514/842–7711, 844/922–4658* ⊕ *www.holtrenfrew.com/en/stores/holt-renfrew-ogilvy* Ⓜ *Peel.*

Hudson's Bay (formerly La Baie)
DEPARTMENT STORES | Hudson's Bay department store is a descendant of the Hudson's Bay Company, the great 17th-century fur-trading company that played a pivotal role in Canada's development. The Bay, as it's known by Canadians, has been a department store since 1891 and is known for its duffel coats and signature red-, green-, and white-striped blankets. Besides fashions, housewares, and toys, there's also a portrait studio, beauty salon, and spa. ✉ *585 rue Ste-Catherine Ouest, Downtown* ☎ *514/281–4422* ⊕ *www.thebay.com* Ⓜ *McGill.*

La Maison Simons
DEPARTMENT STORES | Find the *trends du jour* at a great price from the youth-oriented labels on the ground floor of this bustling department store. Upstairs, the fare is more mature, ranging from respectable and affordable twin sets to luxe offerings from the likes of Chloé and Missoni. The store's fashion-forward men's suits and casual wear are also worth checking out. ✉ *977 rue Ste-Catherine Ouest, Downtown* ☎ *514/289–1840, 877/666–1840* ⊕ *www.simons.ca* Ⓜ *Peel.*

FOOD
Divine Chocolatier
FOOD/CANDY | Tucked away in a small basement space on Crescent Street, this adorable little chocolaterie owned by Belgian *maître chocolatier* Richard Zwierzynski has lived here for 25 years, and been in existence since 1976. With its stuffed teddy bears, shoe- and bottle-shaped chocolate decorations, and antique porcelain plates adorning the walls, a visit to Divine feels like stepping into a 19th-century ice-cream parlor. Chocolate massage oil and chocolate tablets made from the mold of an illustration from the Kama Sutra will tickle the fancy, but it's the chocolate truffles, assorted chocolates, and the dark chocolate ganache cheesecake that people come for again and again. ✉ *2158 rue Crescent, Downtown* ☎ *514/282–0829* ⊕ *www.divine-chocolatier.com* Ⓜ *Guy-Concordia.*

Marché Atwater
FOOD/CANDY | Heading down Atwater Avenue toward Lachine Canal, you can't miss the art deco tower of Atwater Market. This is the best spot to pick up local produce, fresh flowers, and gourmet meats and cheeses. In summer, bring a blanket and enjoy a perfect picnic by the canal or have a drink at the Canal Lounge, a café and bar on a barge. During the winter holidays there is now the added bonus of a Christmas market. ✉ *138 av. Atwater, Downtown* ☎ *514/937–7754 for all Montréal's public markets* ⊕ *www.marches-publics-mtl.com* Ⓜ *Lionel-Groulx.*

JEWELRY
Birks
JEWELRY/ACCESSORIES | The Canadian equivalent of Tiffany's (with its own version of the iconic blue box) has been selling diamond engagement rings, exquisite jewelry, and fine crystal since 1879. Recently renovated and redesigned and now part of the new Hôtel Birks, the luxury jewelry store now contains boutiques within a larger boutique and sells items by brands such as Messika, Van Cleef & Arpels, Rolex, Cartier, and Breitling, in addition to Birks Collections. Even if diamonds or watches aren't on your shopping list, it's still worth a visit to the elegant new hotel and the seriously stunning Henri Brasserie Française (restaurant and bar lounge), serving French-inspired cuisine highlighting seasonal Quebec and Canadian products (⊕ *www.restauranthenri.com*)

Ice-Skating in Montréal

Come the winter months, you don't have to look very far to find an ice-skating rink in Montréal. There are municipally run outdoor—and some indoor—rinks in virtually every corner of the city. Outdoor rinks are open from December until mid-March, and admission is free. The rinks on Île Ste-Hélène and at the Old Port are especially large, but note that there is a C$6.95 admission charge (free admission for children under 6) to skate at the Old Port one.

All in all, there are at least 195 outdoor and 21 indoor rinks spread across Montréal. So lace up those skates and make some figure eights!

For information on the numerous ice-skating rinks in the city, call or check the city's website: ☎ 514/872–1111, ⊕ www.ville.montreal.qc.ca.

✉ Hôtel Birks, 620 rue Ste-Catherine O., Downtown ☎ 514/397–2511 ⊕ www.maisonbirks.com/en/maison-birks-montreal-centre-ville Ⓜ McGill.

★ **Bleu Comme Le Ciel**
JEWELRY/ACCESSORIES | In French they call costume jewelry *bijoux de fantaisie,* and that's exactly what you'll find here: a fantastic array of colorful crystal baubles. Elegant lines from Ginette NY contrast with the bold designs of Reminiscence Paris. The glass-walled boutique is easy to miss, as it blends into the surrounding building. ✉ 1143 boul. de Maisonneuve Ouest, Downtown ☎ 514/847–1128 ⊕ www.bleucommeleciel.com Ⓜ Peel.

Château d'Ivoire
JEWELRY/ACCESSORIES | Whether you're considering a watch, diamond bracelet, or engagement ring, Château d'Ivoire might just have what you're looking for (as long as a significant price tag doesn't deter you). Luxury brands include Chopard, Piaget, IWC, and Cartier. ✉ 2020 rue de la Montagne, Downtown ☎ 514/845–4651, 888/883–8283 ⊕ www.chateaudivoire.com ⊙ Closed Sun. Ⓜ Peel or Guy-Concordia.

MALLS AND SHOPPING CENTERS
Centre Eaton de Montréal
SHOPPING CENTERS/MALLS | In addition to its 175 stores, the largest mall in Downtown Montréal has free Wi-Fi in the spacious lower-level food court. There's also Musée Grévin, a wax museum that replicates more than a hundred local and international celebrities and Time Out Market, a gourmet food hall featuring offerings from the owners of Toqué, Montréal Plaza, Le Club Chasse et Pêche, Moleskine (a pizza and pasta eatery owned by the owners of Pullman's wine bar), and more. ✉ 705 rue Ste-Catherine Ouest, Downtown ☎ 514/288–3708 ⊕ www.centreeatondemontreal.com Ⓜ McGill.

Les Cours Mont-Royal
SHOPPING CENTERS/MALLS | A variety of chic independent boutiques are mixed in with quality chains like DKNY and Desigual in this graceful mall, once a grand hotel. Drop by Spa Diva or the top-notch salon Pure if you're in need of a beauty break. The elegant atrium sometimes hosts runway shows. ■TIP➔ Be sure to stop by the Barbie Expo, a collection of more than 1,000 Barbie dolls rocking some of the biggest names in fashion, including Christian Dior, Donna Karen, Armani, Vera Wang, Oscar De La Renta, Christian Louboutin, Carolina

Herrera, and Zac Posen. ✉ *1455 rue Peel, Downtown* ☎ *514/842–7777* ⊕ *www.lcmr.ca* Ⓜ *Peel.*

Place Ville Marie
SHOPPING CENTERS/MALLS | Stylish shoppers head to the 80-plus retail outlets in Place Ville Marie, part of the city's vast underground network. After a shopping spree, check out the rooftop observation deck (⊕ *www.observatoire360.com*), where you'll get a 360-degree view of the city and find the restaurant/brasserie and terrace Les Enfants Terribles. ✉ *Boulevard René-Lévesque and rue University, Downtown* ☎ *514/861–9393* ⊕ *www.placevillemarie.com* Ⓜ *McGill or Bonaventure.*

Promenades Cathédrale
SHOPPING CENTERS/MALLS | There are 60 shops at this complex directly beneath Christ Church Cathedral, including Canada's largest Linen Chest outlet, with hundreds of bedspreads and duvets, plus aisles of china, crystal, linen, and silver. The food court is spacious and comfortable. ✉ *625 rue Ste-Catherine Ouest, Downtown* ☎ *514/845–8230* ⊕ *www.promenadescathedrale.com* Ⓜ *McGill.*

SHOES
Browns
SHOES/LUGGAGE/LEATHER GOODS | This local institution stocks fashionable footwear and accessories for men and women. Besides its own label, Browns carries shoes by Emporio Armani, Michael Kors, Cole Haan, Steve Madden, and Stuart Weitzman. Comfortable couches make shopping a pleasant experience inside this gleaming white-and-silver flagship. ✉ *1191 rue Ste-Catherine Ouest, Downtown* ☎ *514/987–1206, 866/720–7463* ⊕ *www.brownsshoes.com* Ⓜ *Peel.*

 Activities

HOCKEY
Ice hockey is nothing short of an institution in Montréal, the city that arguably gave birth to the sport back in the late 19th century. Although variations of the game are said to have been played in other U.S. and Canadian cities as early as 1800, the first organized game of modern hockey was played in Montréal in 1875, and the first official team, the McGill University Hockey Club, was founded in Montréal in 1880. The city's beloved Montréal Canadiens is the oldest club in the National Hockey League and, as Montrealers are keen to tell you, one of the most successful teams in North American sports history—even though they haven't won the Stanley Cup since 1993.

McGill University Redmen Hockey
HOCKEY | Formed in 1877, this was the first organized hockey club in Canada. It is now one of the top university men's ice hockey programs in Canada, and the Redmen were a Canadian University cup finalist in 2011. Games against crosstown rivals the Concordia Stingers or the UQTR Patriotes are always emotional duels. Home games take place at Percival Molson Stadium. *In November 2018, 79% of McGill students voted in favor of changing the team's name following a campaign by indigenous students to shed the moniker. Although the university says the name is a tribute to the team's red uniforms, indigenous students and many others argued it is a reference to aboriginal skin and, therefore, offensive. A committee has been set up to select a new name.* ✉ *475 av. des Pins Ouest, Downtown* ☎ *514/398–7006* ⊕ *www.redmenhockey.com* Ⓜ *McGill.*

Montréal Canadiens
HOCKEY | The Montréal Canadiens meet National Hockey League rivals at the Centre Bell from October through April (and even later if they make the playoffs). The "Habs" (the nickname's taken from Habitants, or early settlers) have won 24 Stanley Cups, although they've been struggling in the standings for several years now and haven't won a cup since the 1992–93 season. Nevertheless, Les Canadiens are a great source of pride

The Route Verte

Stretches of what's called the most extensive route of biking trails in North America pass right through the very heart of Downtown Montréal.

The Route Verte (Green Route) is a free 5,000-km (3,100-mile) network of paths, shared roadways, and paved shoulders that traverse the province of Québec.

The cycling group Vélo Québec began first talking about the possibility of a province-wide bike network back in the 1980s, but it wasn't until 1995 that the government announced it would fund the C$88.5-million project to be built over the next 12 years.

More than 320 km (200 miles) of the Route Verte cover the streets of the city. It passes through Downtown, stretches up Mont-Royal, hugs the coast near the Lachine Canal, and extends out to Parc Jean-Drapeau, to name just a few of the major areas covered.

For more information, including maps, suggested routes, and other trip-planning tools, check out ⊕ *www. routeverte.com*.

to the city's sports fans, and tickets for their local games continue to be a hot commodity. Buy tickets in advance to guarantee a seat. ⊠ *1909 av. des Canadiens-de-Montréal, Downtown* ☎ *877/463–2674, 514/989–2841* ⊕ *canadiens.nhl.com* Ⓜ *Lucien-L'Allier or Peel.*

ICE-SKATING

Atrium le 1000 de la Gauchetière

ICE SKATING | Inside the tallest building in Montréal, this skating rink lies under a glass atrium, allowing sunlight to shine down on the rink year-round. After working up an appetite, hit any one of the 14 restaurants in the surrounding food court. ⊠ *1000 rue de la Gauchetière, Downtown* ☎ *514/395–0555* ⊕ *www.le1000.com* ⚷ *C$8; skate rental C$7* Ⓜ *Bonaventure.*

Westmount

The upscale neighborhood of Westmont is predominantly Anglophone and it's a far cry from the French-speaking Montréal foreigners often picture. You'll see polished moms in Prada sunglasses and Lululemon leggings pushing strollers, as well as dressed-down locals walking their dogs along rue Sherbrooke and avenue Victoria. It has lovely parks for strolling, and the houses are beautiful, but there aren't many tourist sites around here. Nevertheless, it's the place to go for luxury boutique shopping. Rue Sherbrooke Ouest is a pleasant mix of hip shops, florists, and home decor stores. Avenue Victoria is a smaller version of the same, with a few grocery stores and vintage shops thrown in. Westmont also has some interesting dining choices.

The closest métro to Westmont is Vendôme, or you can take Bus 24 west from Downtown.

🍴 Restaurants

Westmount is a relatively new foodie destination, and provides much-needed sustenance after hitting the area's luxury boutiques.

Park

$$$$ | JAPANESE FUSION | Sustainable, organic, and fresh every day is the philosophy of this high-end sushi place. The menu is eclectic, with excellent sashimi—some specimens flown in directly from Japan—noodles, and Japanese dishes mixed with a variety

of influences from the chef's multiple backgrounds—Korean, Argentinian, and Canadian. **Known for:** creative menu; omakase; exquisite desserts. $ *Average main: C$40* ⊠ *378 av. Victoria, Downtown* ☎ *514/750–7534* ⊕ *www.parkresto.com* ⊘ *Closed Sun.* Ⓜ *Vendôme.*

Petros

$$$$ | **GREEK** | **FAMILY** | A local favorite in Westmount, this Greek *estiatorio* (more upscale than a taverna) specializes in seafood and has a warm, friendly atmosphere. With its Grecian-blue tiles and shutters, white walls, traditional Greek music, and überfriendly, bona-fide Greek waiters, Petros's makes you feel as if you've stepped through a portal straight onto a Cycladic isle. **Known for:** jumbo shrimp; excellent vegan and vegetarian meze; BYOB. $ *Average main: C$36* ⊠ *4785 rue Sherbrooke, Westmount* ☎ *514/938-5656* ⊕ *www.restaurantpetros.ca/en* Ⓜ *Vendôme, then bus 24.*

☕ Coffee and Quick Bites

Café Bazin

$$ | **FRENCH** | A melange between a patisserie, a café, and a French bistro, this little resto has been a darling of food critics since it opened in 2017. Serving deftly executed French dishes like ratatouille, coquilles St-Jacques, and tartines niçoises in a fresh, modern setting of white subway tiles, decorative brass struts, richly patinated wooden tables, and mint green–velvet seating, Café Bazin is a little corner of France in the heart of Anglo Westmount. **Known for:** French classics; exquisite pastries; charming decor. $ *Average main: C$18* ⊠ *380 av. Victoria, Westmount* ☎ *438/387-3070* ⊕ *www.cafebazin.com* ⊘ *Closed Sun.* Ⓜ *Vendôme.*

🛍 Shopping

Stylish locals, quaint architecture, and upscale boutiques make Westmount a chic shopping destination. Rue

Sherbrooke Ouest is a pleasant mix of hip shops, florists, and home decor stores. Avenue Victoria is a smaller version of the same, with a few grocery stores and vintage shops thrown in. The closest métro is Vendôme, or you can take Bus 24 west from Downtown.

★ Ruth Stalker Antiques

ANTIQUES/COLLECTIBLES | The original owner made her reputation finding and salvaging fine pieces of early Quebec and Canadian pine furniture, but she also developed a good instinct for such folk art as exquisitely carved hunting decoys, weather vanes, and pottery. Now her two children continue the tradition. ⊠ *4447 rue Ste-Catherine Ouest, Westmount* ☎ *514/931–0822* ⊘ *Closed Sun. and Mon.* Ⓜ *Atwater.*

ART
Ben & Tournesol

GIFTS/SOUVENIRS | Head to this boutique for plush pillows, linens, and duvets from Designers Guild, which may inspire you to redesign your bedroom (if not your whole house). There are also products by Hermès, Fred Perry, and others. Ask the friendly staff for guidance on the perfect gift. ⊠ *4937 rue Sherbrooke Ouest, Westmount* ☎ *514/481–5050* ⊕ *www.benandtournesol.com* Ⓜ *Vendôme.*

Galerie de Bellefeuille

ART GALLERIES | This gallery has a knack for discovering important new talents. It represents many of Canada's top contemporary artists as well as some international ones. Its 5,000 square feet hold a good selection of sculptures, paintings, and limited-edition prints. ⊠ *1366 and 1367 av. Greene, Westmount* ☎ *514/933–4406* ⊕ *www.debellefeuille.com* Ⓜ *Atwater.*

CLOTHING
James

CLOTHING | The home of hippie chic in Montréal, this boutique is packed with flowing tunics, embroidered blouses, and white-cotton dresses. Add a good mix of designer jeans and funky moccasins by Minnetonka and you'll understand why James is a Victoria Village mainstay. ✉ *4910 rue Sherbrooke Ouest, Westmount* ☎ *514/369-0700* Ⓜ *Vendôme.*

Oink Oink

CLOTHING | FAMILY | This pigtail-covered boutique offers three levels of fun for babies, kids, and young adults. Innovative and kooky gifts, books, clothing, and even scooters are available. ✉ *1343 av. Greene, Westmount* ☎ *855/939-2634, 514/939-2634* ⊕ *www.oinkoink.com* Ⓜ *Atwater.*

★ Pretty Ballerinas

SHOES/LUGGAGE/LEATHER GOODS | This little boutique showcases beautiful ballerina flats handmade in Spain. Available in a wide variety of colors and styles, you'll find it difficult to limit yourself to just one pair. You'll also find Barbour handbags—a canvas tote might be the perfect accessory to complement your new flats. ✉ *392 av. Victoria, Westmount* ☎ *514/489-3030* ⊕ *www.prettyballerinas. ca* ⊙ *Closed Sun.* Ⓜ *Vendôme.*

★ WANT Apothecary

CLOTHING | Set in pleasant surroundings inspired by a 19th-century pharmacy, this boutique keeps its customers coming back with interesting and quality goods and doting service. In addition to items from the local leather-goods label WANT, the shop stocks beauty and skin care products and clothing by Acne, Fillppa K, and Nudie Jeans. ✉ *4960 rue Sherbrooke Ouest, Westmount* ☎ *514/484-3555* ⊕ *www.wantapothecary.com* Ⓜ *Vendôme.*

SHOES

★ Tony's

SHOES/LUGGAGE/LEATHER GOODS | A fixture in Westmount since 1937, Tony's is one of the area's top shoe stores. It might seem small from the outside, but it's filled with fine specimens for men, women, and kids—and at reasonable prices, too. ✉ *1346 av. Greene, Westmount*

☎ *514/935-2993, 888/488-6697* ⊕ *www. tonyshoes.com* Ⓜ *Atwater.*

The Latin Quarter

The **Latin Quarter** (Quartier Latin), just south of the Plateau, has been a center of student life since the 18th century, when Université de Montréal students gave the area its name (courses were given in Latin), and today it continues to infuse the city with youthful energy. When night falls, its streets are filled with multinational hordes—young and not so young, rich and poor, established and still studying.

The Université de Québec à Montréal (UQAM) spreads across the district, along with theaters, bars, bookstores, and movie theaters. Some area businesses cater to a young clientele and their penchant for the loud and flashy, but the quarter is also home to some of the city's trendiest nightspots. In summer, the streets of the Latin Quarter are busy with summer festival events, such as the Jazz Fest in late June/early July and the Just for Laughs Festival in July.

GETTING HERE AND AROUND

The Latin Quarter is concentrated on boulevard de Maisonneuve and rue St-Denis. The busy Berri-UQAM métro station is the closest.

◉ Sights

Chapelle Notre-Dame-de-Lourdes (*Our Lady of Lourdes Chapel*)

RELIGIOUS SITE | Artist and architect Napoléon Bourassa called his work here *l'oeuvre de mes amours,* or a labor of love—and it shows. He designed the little Byzantine-style building himself and set about decorating it with the exuberance of an eight-year-old making a Mother's Day card. He covered the walls with murals and encrusted the altar and pillars with gilt and ornamental

Montréal's Chinatown

Chinese immigrants first came to Montréal in large numbers after 1880, following the construction of the transcontinental railroad, and there's been a steady influx of peoples from Asia and Southeast Asia—including the Vietnamese—since then. Now the city's Chinatown covers about an 18-block area between boulevard René-Lévesque and avenue Viger to the north and south, and near rue de Bleury and avenue Hôtel de Ville on the west and east.

The best way to enter Chinatown is through the ornate gates on boulevard St-Laurent—Place d'Armes is the closest métro station—then head for the hub at rue de la Gauchetière at the intersection of rue Clark. Chinatown has four gates or *paifangs*. The most prominent one is probably the South Gate at the corner of boulevard Saint-Laurent and avenue Viger.

Where to Eat

Maison Kam Fung. This family-run restaurant for three generations offers more than 60 dishes on rotation on any given day, making this *the* place for dim sum feasts. Waiters clatter up and down the aisles pushing a parade of trolleys bearing such treats as firm dumplings stuffed with pork and stir-fried squid and shrimp. **Known for:** dim sum; Peking duck; Cantonese and Szechuan dishes. ⊠ *1111 rue St-Urbain, Chinatown* ☎ *514/878–2888* ⊕ *www. restaurantchinatownkimfung.com* Ⓜ *Place-d'Armes.*

Noodle Factory. The dining room is small and not much to look at, but no matter—the food here is the main attraction, and locals come in droves for the homemade noodles and dumplings. If you time your visit right, you might see the staff through the huge kitchen window working on the dough. **Known for:** cash only; General Tao chicken; homemade noodles. ⊠ *1018 rue St-Urbain, Chinatown* ☎ *514/868–9738* ⊕ *www.restonoodle-factory.com* ➾ *No credit cards* Ⓜ *Places-d'Armes.*

Orange Rouge. More of a brasserie than a restaurant, Orange Rouge pays tribute to its neighborhood with creative interpretations of traditional dishes that might ruffle the feathers of authenticity sticklers but will please Asian food aficionados. The chef takes liberties by combining familiar flavors with a surprising twist like the unusual, slightly herbaceous chrysanthemum salad or the intriguing foie gras steam buns. **Known for:** roasted duck; inventive Asian food; trendy decor. ⊠ *106 rue de la Gauchetière Ouest, Chinatown* ☎ *514/861–1116* ⊕ *orangerouge.ca* ◷ *Closed Sun. and Mon. No lunch Sat.*

Qing Hua Dumplings. Groups of students and other budget-conscious connoisseurs of hearty chows crowd the tables at this hole-in-the-wall restaurant for soup dumplings just like they make them in northeast China with a price that's right: just C$9 for 15 dumplings. Demand is high for the lamb-and-coriander dumplings; the boiled shrimp, leek, and egg version; and the fried dumplings with chicken and curry. **Known for:** soup dumplings; cash only; affordable eats. ⊠ *1019 boul. St-Laurent, Chinatown* ☎ *514/903–9887* ➾ *No credit cards* Ⓜ *Place-d'Armes.*

The Latin Quarter and the Village

KEY

1 Sights

1 Restaurants

1 Hotels

M Métro Stations

Bike Route

carving. It's not Montréal's biggest monument to the Virgin Mary, but it's the most unabashedly sentimental. ✉ *430 rue Ste-Catherine Est, Latin Quarter* ☎ *514/845–8278* ⊕ *www.cndlm.org* 🎫 *Free* Ⓜ *Berri-UQAM.*

Square St-Louis

PLAZA | This large, leafy square is an oasis in the middle of Montréal's urban jungle of noise, traffic jams, and construction. Entering the square, which is surrounded by colorful and ornate Second Empire-style homes, feels a little like entering a children's picture book, especially in winter, when the ground and the houses are blanketed with snow and the white stuff muffles all sound. In summer, locals spread out on the grass by the fountain or take a bistro table at the little gray kiosk (formerly a public toilet) that serves sandwiches, salads, ice cream, and other cold refreshments—it even offers a book exchange. And for an unexpected bonus, some of the lanes to the side and rear of the square's beautiful houses have been lovingly "greened up" with street art and vegetation, thanks to a lot of hard work and effort on the part of the neighbors. ✉ *Bordered by av. Laval and rue St-Denis between rue Sherbrooke Est and av. des Pins Est, Latin Quarter* Ⓜ *Sherbrooke.*

🍴 Restaurants

Institut de tourisme et d'hôtellerie du Québec

$$$ | **CONTEMPORARY** | Long held in disdain by Montréal food critics, the restaurant at the Institut de tourisme et d'hôtellerie du Québec (ITHQ) has recently upped its epicurean game. These days the resto's top-notch cuisine pays homage to Québec's terroir with enticingly

Montréal Jazz Fest offers a series of ticketed concerts that take place at a dozen or so Montréal venues as well as six stages of free diverse programming in the heart of Downtown Montréal.

presented dishes served in a contemporary yet elegant setting (think white table cloths, cloche plate covers, and impeccable service. **Known for:** mushroom dashi with king oyster mushrooms and green onions; smoked porcelet shoulder with blood pudding purée; veal tartare. $ *Average main: C$28* ⊠ *3535 rue St-Denis, Latin Quarter* ☏ *514/282–5155* ⊕ *www.ithq.qc.ca/en/restaurants/restaurant-de-lithq/.*

Juliette & Chocolat

$$ | CONTEMPORARY | This popular Québec restaurant/chocolate bar chain is the brainchild of Juliette Brun, a self-confessed chocoholic since she was a child. First opened in 2003 when Juliette was only 22, there are now nearly 30 locations across the province. **Known for:** all things chocolate; crepes and waffles; brunches. $ *Average main: C$16* ⊠ *1615 rue St-Denis, Latin Quarter* ☏ *514/287–3555* ⊕ *www.julietteetchocolat.com.*

★ Labo Culinaire Foodlab

$$$ | ECLECTIC | Take cutting-edge experimental art and mix it up with food and what you get is Labo Culinaire Foodlab. Located on the third floor of Montréal's Society of Arts and Technology (SAT), Foodlab is an ongoing culinary experiment with rotating themes that range from destinations (i.e., Jerusalem) to dishes inspired by chefs (i.e., Julia Child's cookbook). **Known for:** trendsetting chefs; lovely terrace; natural wines. $ *Average main: C$22* ⊠ *Société des Arts Technologiques building, 1201 boul. St-Laurent, Latin Quarter* ☏ *514/844–2033* ⊕ *www.sat.qc.ca/en/restaurant-food-lab-labo-culinaire* ☾ *Closed Sun. and Mon. No lunch* Ⓜ *St-Laurent.*

🛏 Hotels

Bustling with moviegoers and university kids rushing to cafés and libraries, the Quartier Latin is alive with expectation. No, it isn't as pristine as the Old Port, since gentrification has been slow and

Ruelles Vertes

Almost as emblematic of Montréal as its winding staircases fronting duplexes and triplexes, are the city's back alleys, or *ruelles*, with their jumble of ramshackle tin and wood sheds, circular staircases, and rambunctious kids playing hockey. Originally intended for back door coal and heating oil deliveries, garbage pickups, and telephone line and electrical services, they fell out of use by the "70s. But in the last 15 or so years, many of these back alleys have been lovingly embellished with plants, flowers, murals, and other art work, thanks to a lot of hard work and dedication on the part of residents. In some cases, asphalt has given way to grassy paths, giving an even greater impression of being in the countryside. In French, these vibrant and imaginative green spaces are known as *Ruelles Vertes*. There are currently more than 400 officially designated *ruelles vertes*, representing about 43 miles in terms of distance, and making Montréal one of the world's top cities for green laneways.

Green laneways and *éco-quartiers* (eco-neighborhoods) can be found all over the city, but the prettiest tend to be located around the Plateau, the Latin Quarter, Mile End, Outremont, Parc Extension, Rosemont—La Petite-Patrie, and NDG. If you're in the Latin Quarter, be sure to visit the one between rues Drolet and Henri-Julien and av. des Pins and Square St-Louis or Ruelle Demers, between rues Henri-Julien and Hôtel-de-Ville. In the Plateau try Ruelle Milton between rues Clark and Saint-Urbain. More information about the green laneway and *éco-quartier* citywide initiative can be found, in French only, at ⊕ *www.eco-quartiers.org/les-eco-quartiers*.

uneven, but it's full of local flavor—artisanal chocolate shops, gastropubs, and hippie shops. The panhandlers are funny, not dangerous, and beg in two languages.

Auberge le Jardin d'Antoine

$ | B&B/INN | Budget travelers flock to this small, shabby-chic hotel for its free Wi-Fi, métro access, kitchenettes, and deluxe continental breakfast, but its best-selling point is its location right on rue St-Denis, among the Latin Quarter's trendy restaurants, movie theaters, and poutine joints. **Pros:** lively neighborhood; budget and standard rooms have been upgraded; breakfast buffet goes way beyond the call of duty. **Cons:** a quarter of the rooms are outdated; the lively location means it can be noisy; panhandlers near the front door. $ *Rooms from: C$155 ⊠ 2024 rue St-Denis, Latin Quarter* ☎ *514/843–4506,* 800/361–4506 ⊕ *www.aubergelejardindantoine.com* ⟲ *25 rooms* ❍❙ *Free breakfast* Ⓜ *Berri-UQAM.*

★ Hotel 10

$ | HOTEL | Its exterior may be part art nouveau classic from 1914 and part brick-and-concrete contemporary, but the hip clientele, sleek and modern interiors, and contemporary furnishings and art throughout, make this centrally located hotel *all* cool. **Pros:** rooms are bright and modern; on-site car-rental; proximity to nightlife on the main. **Cons:** drivers must choose between iffy street parking or C$30 valet; weekend party atmosphere can be alienating for some; trendy is not everyone's cup of tea. $ *Rooms from: C$199 ⊠ 10 rue Sherbrooke Ouest, Latin Quarter* ☎ *514/843–6000, 855/390–6787*

⊕ www.hotel10montreal.com ⇆ 136 rooms ⦿ No meals Ⓜ St-Laurent.

Le Loft Hotel

$$ | HOTEL | Inside an art deco landmark, this chic hotel has loftlike rooms with high ceilings and lots of space, as well as sleek IKEA kitchens, king beds, funky art, leather sectionals, and expansive views of the cityscape. **Pros:** 10-foot ceilings; good for longer stays; superior soundproofing. **Cons:** street parking is scarce; a bit hard to find; dark hallway—some complaints about lack of security. Ⓢ Rooms from: C$249 ⊠ 334 Terrasse St-Denis, Latin Quarter ☎ 514/439–1818 ⊕ www.lofthotel.ca ⇆ 30 rooms ⦿ Free breakfast Ⓜ Berri-UQAM.

🍸 Nightlife

Though tiny, the Quartier Latin is known for its theaters, cafés, and student population. (One of the major French universities, UQAM, is located here.) Concentrated on lower rue St-Denis, there are copious bars if you're looking for some nightlife.

BARS AND LOUNGES

Le Cheval Blanc

BREWPUBS/BEER GARDENS | Unchanged for three decades and showing its age, this hole-in-the-wall-with-atmosphere is Montréal's first brew pub. It's a lively pub, where music combines with the buzz of arty and political dialogue. There is outdoor seating and it often hosts art exhibits. ⊠ 809 rue Ontario Est, Latin Quarter ☎ 514/522-0211 ⊕ www.lechev-alblanc.ca Ⓜ Berri-UQAM.

★ Le Lab

BARS/PUBS | Fabien Maillard is Montréal's mixologist extraordinaire, and the name of his unpretentious bar is entirely apt. Creating cocktails is his passion and it's shared by the friendly, skilled staff. The potent potions are inspired by everything from old, classic recipes to the fruits of the season. The entire menu changes twice a year, and there

are also monthly specials. ■TIP→ **Book a spot online, because the place gets busy.** ⊠ 279 rue Ste-Catherine E., Latin Quarter ☎ 514/903–6522 ⊕ www.barlelab.com ⊙ Closed Mon. Ⓜ Berri-UQAM.

🎭 Performing Arts

FILM

Bibliothèque et Archives Nationales du Québec

FILM | Spread over five floors, Montréal's largest public library is a modern, light-filled, and spacious place to while away an afternoon perusing an impressive film collection. With 18 screening stations and new titles acquired monthly, they offer a wide range of genres to suit film buffs. ⊠ Grande Bibliothèque, 475 boul. de Maisonneuve Est, Latin Quarter ☎ 514/873–1100 ⊕ www.banq.qc.ca ⊙ Closed Mon. Ⓜ Berri-UQAM.

Cinémathèque Québécoise

FILM | With more than 35,000 films in its collection, and a ticket price of just C$10, Montréal's Museum of the Moving Image is the best place in the city to catch a foreign flick in its original language (with subtitles), in addition to Quebecois and other Canadian productions. The museum also stocks scripts, television shows, and various new media, with a permanent display of vintage cinema equipment. ⊠ 335 boul. de Maisonneuve Est, Latin Quarter ☎ 514/842–9763 ⊕ www.cinematheque.qc.ca Ⓜ Berri-UQAM.

THEATER

Théâtre Ste-Catherine

THEATER | With approximately 100 comfortable seats, this independent alternative theater features comedy and improv shows most nights. On Sunday there's a free improv workshop that's open to all, with participants later showing off what they learned as that evening's entertainment. The theater also houses a café/bar as well as Le Nouveau International, a nonprofit organization run by a thriving

The projections on the wall at the pavilion of the Université du Québec à Montréal (UQÀM) change according to the different festivals happening there year-round.

community of artists working year-round to produce theater, comedy, improv, films, a bimonthly magazine, and sketch shows. ✉ *264 rue Ste-Catherine Est, Latin Quarter* ☎ *514/284–3939* ⊕ *www.theatresaintecatherine.com* Ⓜ *Berri-UQAM.*

Théâtre St-Denis

CONCERTS | This is one of several theaters hosting events that are part of the Just for Laughs Festival, and touring Broadway productions, concerts, musicals, and dance performances can often be seen here. ✉ *1594 rue St-Denis, Latin Quarter* ☎ *514/849–4211* ⊕ *www.theatrestdenis. com* Ⓜ *Berri-UQAM.*

The Village

Often called **Gay Village,** this area is the center of one of the most vibrant gay communities in the world, widely supported by residents of this proudly liberal, open-minded city. In recent years the municipal, federal, and provincial governments have taken it upon themselves

to promote the Village and Montréal's gay-friendly climate as a reason for tourists to visit, but its restaurants, antiques shops (on rue Amherst, now renamed to rue Atateken), and bars make it a popular destination for visitors of all persuasions. The lively strip of rue Ste-Catherine running east of the Latin Quarter is the backbone of the Village.

In late July, the Village's Pride Parade, widely considered the biggest and most outrageous party of the year, attracts more than a million people.

GETTING HERE AND AROUND

The Village centers on the Beaudry métro station, which has its entrance adorned with rainbow pillars. Its borders are considered rue Ste-Catherine Est from Amherst to de Lorimier, and on the north–south axis from René-Lévesque to Sherbrooke.

🍴 Restaurants

A little outside the hustle and bustle of the busy Downtown Montréal core, the Village is quite charming. Primo people-watching can be done at the many cafés in the area. During the summer months (May to September), rue Ste-Catherine in the Village is closed off to cars, which makes it pleasant to explore the shops and restaurants.

★ Agrikol

$$ | **CARIBBEAN** | Co-owned by Win Butler and wife Régine Chassagne of famed Montréal band Arcade Fire, this popular Haitian rum house with tropical décor is flanked by the most fabulous patio in the city, bar none. Besides the views, the main draw here is the make-your-own Ti' Punch setup—a bottle of rum, ice cubes, sugar cane juice, lime wedges, and other fixings. **Known for:** make-your-own Ti' Punch; Creole classics; groovy Haitian atmosphere. $ *Average main: C$19* ✉ *1844 rue Amherst, The Village* ☎ *514/903–6575* ⊕ *www.agrikol.ca* Ⓜ *Beaudry.*

Le Mousso

$$$$ | **MODERN CANADIAN** | Regularly lauded on Canadian best-of dining lists, Le Mousso is run by chef Antonin Mousseau-Rivard, who dreams up beautifully plated, northern European-inspired dishes that are as much works of art as they are imaginative combinations of flavor and texture for the taste buds. Using mostly local and seasonal ingredients, the seven-course tasting menu might feature dishes such as bortsch *décomposé* (beet soup), grilled scallops lightly smoked with fir and served on coals with wild plum butter, or tataki Wagyu beef accompanied by cream, New Brunswick caviar, and nasturtium leaves. **Known for:** tasting menus only; minimalist decor; innovative cuisine highlighting the terroir. $ *Average main: C$70* ✉ *1023 rue Ontario Est, The Village* ☎ *438/384–7410* ⊕ *www.lemousso.com* ⊗ *Closed Sun.–Tues.* Ⓜ *Berri-UQAM.*

🍸 Nightlife

Head east along rue Ste-Catherine to enjoy the colorful Gay Village—you'll know you've arrived when you're amid a sea of pretty pink balls and rainbow flags hung in the streets. It's developing a bit of a reputation for fine dining as of late, though it's still mainly known as a place for late-night partying.

GAY AND LESBIAN NIGHTLIFE

Cabaret Mado

CABARET | Makeup, glitter, and glamorous costumes abound at this nightclub with drag-queen entertainment. Mado herself is a Québec celebrity (so much so that she's immortalized in wax at the Grévin museum inside the Centre Eaton). During karaoke and improv evenings, even the clientele can get involved. ✉ *1115 rue Ste-Catherine Est, The Village* ☎ *514/525–7566* ⊕ *www.mado.qc.ca* Ⓜ *Beaudry.*

★ Club Unity

BARS/PUBS | Small, semiprivate lounges are scattered throughout the two-story complex, and the beautiful rooftop terrace is one of the finest in the Village. Unity is one of the longest running, most popular gay dance clubs in town—although, despite some complaints, you'll often find as many straight girls here as you will gay men. Open weekends from 10 pm to 3 am. ✉ *1171 rue Ste-Catherine Est, The Village* ☎ *514/523–2777* ⊕ *www.clubunity.com* Ⓜ *Beaudry.*

Le Stud

BARS/PUBS | Once a men-only establishment, Le Stud has been known to let in some women. A small dance floor and trance music have brought in a whole different crowd. It's packed most nights. ✉ *1812 rue Ste-Catherine Est, The Village* ☎ *514/598–8243* ⊕ *www.studbar.com* Ⓜ *Papineau.*

★ Sky

BARS/PUBS | This massive complex houses a bar, restaurant, and dance club popular with both gay men and women. The best time to come is during the summer, as the pièce de résistance is the beachlike roof deck with city views and a pool (possibly the hottest destination in the Village). ✉ *1478 rue Ste-Catherine Est, The Village* ☎ *514/529–6969* ⊕ *www.complexesky.com* Ⓜ *Beaudry.*

Stereo

DANCE CLUBS | Some of the most beautiful cross-dressers sashay on the huge dance floor of this converted theater. It's popular with both men and women, straight and gay, and often attracts hip-hop hordes near dawn on Friday and Saturday. Don't even bother arriving before 2 am. ✉ *858 rue Ste-Catherine Est, The Village* ☎ *514/658–2646* ⊕ *www.stereonightclub.net* Ⓜ *Beaudry or Berri-UQAM.*

🛍 Shopping

The Gay Village is known for its excellent furniture stores as much as it is for its vibrant nightlife. Rue Amherst (now rue Atateken) is nearly overflowing with antiques shops; plenty of unique treasures are just waiting to be discovered, most being midcentury modern. The Beaudry métro station is your best bet.

ANTIQUES

★ Antiquités Curiosités

ANTIQUES/COLLECTIBLES | A sea of chairs, lamps, and other 1930s to 1980s furnishings and accessories awaits you at Antiquités Curiosités, but it's the beautifully restored Mad Men–era teak pieces that are the biggest draws. Retro curiosities like rotary phones also tickle the fancy. ✉ *1769 rue Atateken, The Village* ☎ *514/525–8772* Ⓜ *Beaudry.*

★ Boutique Spoutnik

ANTIQUES/COLLECTIBLES | Mod, space-aged, kitsch—this boutique has it all. From Russell Spanner dressers to vintage needlepoint dog-portraits-turned-cushions to ceramic lamps in atomic designs circa 1950, Spoutnik is a veritable Aladdin's Cave of retro treasures. Owner Sylvie Rochon takes her work seriously, carefully curating her collection and adding her own artistic touches to vintage objects. Her boutique has been featured in several Québec publications. ✉ *2120 rue Atateken, The Village* ☎ *514/525–8478* ⊕ *www.boutiquespoutnik.com* ⊘ *Closed Sun. and Mon.* Ⓜ *Sherbrooke.*

The Plateau Mont-Royal and Mile End

Plateau Mont-Royal—or simply the **Plateau** as it's more commonly called these days—is still home to a strong Portuguese community, though gentrification of the Plateau has pushed up rents and driven many students, immigrant families, and single young graduates to neighborhoods farther north and east. As a result, much of the housing originally built for factory workers has been bought and renovated by professionals, artists, performers, and academics eager to find a place to live close to all the action. The Plateau is always bustling, even in the dead of winter, but on sunny summer weekends it's packed with Montrealers who come here to shop, dine, and people-watch.

Many of the older residences in the Plateau and the nearby neighborhoods have the graceful wrought-iron balconies and twisting staircases that are typical of Montréal. The stairs and balconies, treacherous in winter, are often full of families and couples gossiping, picnicking, and partying come summer. If Montrealers tell you they spend the summer in Balconville, they mean they don't have the money or the time to leave town and won't get any farther than their balconies.

Almost blending seamlessly with the Plateau is **Mile End,** one of the hippest neighborhoods in town, the world's second "coolest" after Brooklyn's Williamsburg, according to HuffPo. This funky area starts buzzing the moment restaurants open for brunch. Historically home to Montréal's working-class Jewish community, it is now full of inexpensive, often excellent restaurants and shops selling handicrafts, design furniture, and secondhand clothes. Head east from Parc off streets like Bernard, St. Viateur, and Fairmount. By day it's a great place to take a stroll or sit on a café's *terrasse* (patio) to watch the passers-by—from artsy bohemians to Hasidic Jews.

GETTING HERE AND AROUND
The Plateau's most convenient métro station is Mont-Royal on the Orange Line. It's a large district, but relatively flat and easy to walk around. If you want to cover more ground without resorting to a taxi, there are several Bixi bicycle stands in the area, and plenty of bike lanes.

Mile End borders the Plateau and Outremont. To reach Mile End by public transit, take the métro's Orange Line to Laurier or Bus 55 from Place d'Armes métro station; get off at Fairmount or St. Viateur and walk west from there.

◉ Sights

Boulevard St-Laurent
NEIGHBORHOOD | A walk here is like a walk through Montréal's cultural history. The shops and restaurants, synagogues and churches that line the 10-block stretch north of rue Sherbrooke reflect the various waves of immigrants that have called it home. Keep your eyes open and you'll see Jewish delis, Hungarian sausage shops, Chinese grocery stores, Italian coffee bars, Greek restaurants, Vietnamese sandwich shops, and Peruvian snack bars. You'll also spot some of the city's trendiest restaurants, cafés and galleries, as well as the dernier cri in skateboard fashion. The first immigrants to move into the area in the 1880s were Jews

Montréal's Markets 🍽

Marché Jean-Talon in the north end of the city has an Italian flavor; the surrounding streets are home to some of the finest pizza and caffe lattes anywhere. **Marché Atwater** has an indoor hall, packed with eateries, butchers, bakeries, and fine food emporiums.

The markets are a great place to pick up nonperishables such as jam from Île d'Orléans or cranberries harvested late September to mid-October; or maple syrup and butter, year-round.

escaping pogroms in Eastern Europe. It was they who called the street "the Main," as in Main Street—a nickname that endures to this day. Even Francophone Montrealers sometimes call it "Le Main." ⊠ *The Plateau* Ⓜ *St-Laurent, Sherbrooke, or Mont-Royal.*

Musée des Hospitalières de l'Hôtel-Dieu
MUSEUM | The nuns of the Religieuses Hospitalières de St-Joseph ran Montréal's Hôpital Hôtel-Dieu for more than 300 years, until the province and the Université de Montréal took it over in the 1970s. The first sisters—girls of good families caught up in the religious fervor of the age—came to New France with Jeanne Mance in the mid-1600s to look after the poor, the sick, and the dying. The order's museum—tucked away in a corner of the hospital the nuns built but no longer run—captures the spirit of that age with a series of meticulously bilingual exhibits. Just reading the excerpts from the letters and diaries of those young women helps you to understand the zeal that drove them to abandon the comforts of home for the hardships of the colonies. The museum

also traces the history of medicine and nursing in Montréal. *Guided tours are available for groups of 10 or more by reservation. Hours vary depending on the season.* ⊠ *201 av. des Pins Ouest, The Plateau* ☎ *514/849–2919* ⊕ *www. museedeshospitalieres.qc.ca* ⊠ *C$10 (cash only)* Ⓜ *Sherbrooke, then Bus 144; or Place-des-Arts, then Bus 129 or 80.*

Parc Lafontaine

CITY PARK | You could say that Parc Lafontaine is a microcosm of Montréal: the eastern half is French, with paths, gardens, and lawns laid out in geometric shapes; the western half is English, with meandering paths and irregularly shaped ponds that follow the natural contours of the land. In summer you can take advantage of bowling greens, tennis courts, an open-air theater (Théâtre de Verdure), where there are free events, and two artificial lakes with paddleboats. In winter one lake becomes a large skating rink. The park is named for Sir Louis-Hippolyte Lafontaine (1807–64), a pioneer of responsible government in Canada. His statue graces a plot on the park's southwestern edge. ⊠ *3933 av. Parc Lafontaine, The Plateau* ☎ *514/872–6381* Ⓜ *Sherbrooke or Mont-Royal.*

Rue Prince-Arthur

NEIGHBORHOOD | In the 1960s rue Prince-Arthur was the Haight-Ashbury of Montréal, full of shops selling leather vests, tie-dyed T-shirts, recycled clothes, and drug paraphernalia. It then became fashionable again in the 1980s, when the blocks between avenue Laval and boulevard St-Laurent were transformed into a pedestrian mall, abuzz with happy patrons dining and clinking glasses on the outdoor terraces of the inexpensive, BYOB Greek, Vietnamese, Italian, Polish, and Chinese restaurants. These days Prince-Arthur has been struggling to get its groove back after major roadworks a few years ago forced many businesses to shutter. The street isn't what it once was, but there are still a few restos and

it's a pleasant strip for a stroll, with long benches for sitting while listening to buskers and licking an ice cream from Gelateria Pagliacci (125 rue Prince-Arthur E.). ⊠ *The Plateau* Ⓜ *Sherbrooke.*

🍴 Restaurants

Dotted with bistros and cafés, the Plateau has a bohemian edge that can't be found anywhere else in the city. Chef-owned eateries favor market cuisine served in a decor of brick walls and hardwood floors. Noisy French-style bistros, like L'Express, are local institutions, as are cafés populated by poets and academics with laptops. There's vegetarian cooking, and Thai, along with sushi and stubborn little bakeries that refuse to mechanize.

As Montréal's equivalent of Brooklyn and Shoreditch, Mile End caters mostly to hip creatives. Between hipster-run cafés and locally sourced revisited British gastropubs, this neighborhood sets the trends and constantly pushes the limits of culinary experimentation.

★ Au Pied de Cochon

$$$ | **BISTRO** | Not for the timid, the menu at this famous bistro—one of the late Anthony Bourdain's favorites—is an ode to gluttony and nose-to-tail cooking. Wild restaurateur and chef Martin Picard serves pickled bison tongue, guinea hen liver mousse, a whole pig's head for two, and pork hocks braised in maple syrup. **Known for:** foie gras poutine; Au Pied de Cochon food truck; local celebrity chef. ⑤ *Average main: C$28* ⊠ *536 av. Duluth Est, The Plateau* ☎ *514/281–1114* ⊕ *www. aupieddecochon.ca* ⊙ *Closed Mon. and Tues.* Ⓜ *Mont-Royal.*

Aux Vivres

$$ | **VEGETARIAN** | **FAMILY** | A favorite among vegans, celiacs, and vegetarians—and even omnivores—Aux Vivres serves dishes and beverages that are creative, inspiring, and delicious—not to mention packed with vitamins. A large chalkboard

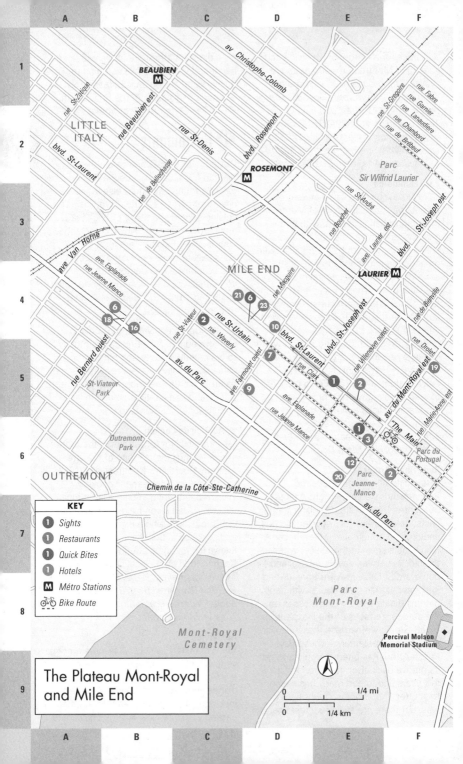

The Plateau Mont-Royal
and Mile End

3

Sights ▼

1	Boulevard St-Laurent **E5**
2	Musée des Hospitalières de l'Hotel Dieu **G7**
3	Parc Lafontaine **I4**
4	Rue Prince-Arthur **H7**

Restaurants ▼

1	Au Pied de Cochon **H5**
2	Aux Vivres **E5**
3	Beautys Luncheonette **E6**
4	Chez Victoire **H3**
5	ChuChai **G5**
6	Helm Microbrasserie **B4**
7	Kem CoBa **D5**
8	La Banquise **H4**
9	La Tamalera **D5**
10	Lawrence **D4**
11	Le Bowhead **H7**
12	Le Filet **E6**
13	Le Majestique **G6**
14	L'Express **H6**
15	Maison Publique **G2**
16	Melina Phyllo Bar **B4**
17	Moishe's **G6**
18	Nouveau Palais **B4**
19	Patisserie Au Kouign Amann **F5**
20	Restaurant Hà **E6**
21	Restaurant Maïs **C4**
22	Schwartz's Delicatessen **G7**
23	Sparrow **D4**
24	Yokato Yokabai **G5**

Quick Bites ▼

1	Boulangerie Hof Kelsten **E5**
2	Café Olimpico **C4**
3	Café Replika **G6**
4	Pâtisserie Rhubarbe **F2**
5	St-Viateur Bagel & Café **G3**
6	Salon de thé Cardinal **D4**

Hotels ▼

1	Auberge de la Fontaine **H4**
2	Casa Bianca Bed & Breakfast **F6**

Art in the Métro

Montréal was ahead of the curve in requiring all construction in the métro system to include an art component, resulting in such dramatic works as Frédéric Back's mural of the history of music in Place des Arts and the swirling stained-glass windows by Marcelle Ferron in Champs-de-Mars. The art nouveau entrance to the Square-Victoria station, a gift from the city of Paris, is the only original piece of Hector Guimard's architectural-design work outside the City of Light.

Operating since 1966, the métro is among the most architecturally

distinctive subway systems in the world, with each of its 65 stations individually designed and decorated.

The newer stations along the Blue Line are all worth a visit as well, particularly Outremont, with a glass-block design from 1988. Even Place-d'Armes, one of the least visually remarkable stations in the system, includes a treasure: look for the small exhibit of archaeological artifacts representing each of Montréal's four historical eras (aboriginal, French, English, and multicultural).

holds specials of the day. **Known for:** Dragon bowl; vegan cheesecake (gâteau fauxmage); vegan- and celiac-friendly. ⑤ *Average main: C$14* ⊠ *4631 boul. St-Laurent, The Plateau* ☎ *514/842–3479* ⊕ *www.auxvivres.com* Ⓜ *Mont-Royal.*

★ Beautys Luncheonette
$$ | DINER | FAMILY | The Schkolnick family has been serving brunch at this Montréal landmark since 1942 and very little has changed since, both in decor and classic menu. The Beautys Special—bagel, lox, and cream cheese—is the ultimate classic. **Known for:** historic venue; bagel with lox; long lines on the weekend. ⑤ *Average main: C$12* ⊠ *93 av. du Mont-Royal Ouest, The Plateau* ☎ *514/849–8883* ⊕ *www.beautys.ca* Ⓜ *Mont-Royal.*

Chez Victoire
$$$ | MODERN FRENCH | A beacon of the French cultural diaspora in Montréal, Chez Victoire is the epitome of Plateau-Mont-Royal's joie de vivre and warmth. Fittingly, the creative menu features French-inspired seasonal market cuisine. **Known for:** organic wines; homemade charcuterie; smoked-meat burger. ⑤ *Average main: C$22* ⊠ *1453 av. du Mont-Royal Est, The Plateau*

☎ *514/521–6789* ⊕ *chezvictoire.com* Ⓜ *Mont-Royal.*

ChuChai
$$$ | THAI | Vegetarians and meat eaters alike love this casual Thai restaurant where no meat is served. The chefs prepare meatless versions of such classics as calamari with basil, crispy duck with spinach, chicken with green beans, fish with three hot sauces, and beef with yellow curry and coconut milk—substituting the real thing for soy and seitan. **Known for:** vegan and vegetarian Thai fare; mock duck; "Thaïpas" (Thai tapas). ⑤ *Average main: C$21* ⊠ *4088 rue St-Denis, The Plateau* ☎ *514/843–4194* ⊕ *www. chuchaimontmontreal.ca* ☉ *Closed Sun. and Mon. No lunch Tues. and Wed.* Ⓜ *Mont-Royal.*

Helm Microbrasserie
$$ | CANADIAN | FAMILY | Few places in Montréal are more Quebecois than this lively microbrewery/gastropub, where the atmosphere is electrifying on hockey night if the local team, the Canadiens, is playing. With its own set of brews named after iconic Mile End streets and a terroir-inspired, locally sourced menu, HELM

(which stands for barley, water, yeast, and malt in French) is in and of itself a vibrant homage to the city's dynamic beer culture. **Known for:** Montréal-inspired micro brews; locally sourced meals; great place to watch hockey. $ *Average main: C$14* ⊠ *273 rue Bernard Ouest, Mile End* ☎ *514/276–0473* ⊕ *www.helmmicrobrasserie.ca* Ⓜ *Rosemont.*

★ **Kem CoBa**

$ | CAFÉ | FAMILY | Only one word accurately describes the all-natural goodness at this ice cream and sorbet stand: *yum.*Flavors change frequently based on what chefs find at the market, but the lightly salted butter ice cream is a staple; partner it with the apple sorbet and you'll have yourself an apple pie on a cone. Or better yet give the "soft serve of the week" a taste; oddly satisfying combinations like blueberry and honey as well as rosewater, raspberry, and lychee are to be expected. **Known for:** cash only; eccentric soft-serve flavors; local favorite. $ *Average main: C$5* ⊠ *60 av. Fairmount Ouest, Mile End* ☎ *514/419–1699* ⊕ *www.kemcoba.com* ▭ *No credit cards* ⊘ *Closed Oct.–Apr.* Ⓜ *Laurier.*

★ **La Banquise**

$ | CANADIAN | FAMILY | Québec is notorious for poutine—French fries topped with cheese curds and gravy—and La Banquise has been the place for an authentic experience since 1968 with an extensive menu featuring 28 varieties. Neophytes might want to stick with La Classique, but mouthwatering novelties like La Taquise (guacamole, sour cream, tomatoes), the Obélix (smoked meat), and the Véganomane (vegan sauce and cheese) are quite alluring. **Known for:** open 24 hours; cash only; smoked-meat poutine. $ *Average main: C$11* ⊠ *994 rue Rachel Est, The Plateau* ☎ *514/525–2415* ⊕ *www.labanquise.com* ▭ *No credit cards* Ⓜ *Mont-Royal.*

La Tamalera

$ | MEXICAN | FAMILY | The kitschy-cool décor includes a display of religious icons as well as vibrantly colorful furniture, while the menu is Mexican street cuisine at its best. The food here is simple and the menu small, but everything is fresh and delicious. **Known for:** corn-based homemade tacos; Mexican-inspired brunch; vibrant decor. $ *Average main: C$11* ⊠ *226 av. Fairmount Ouest, Mile End* ☎ *438/381–5034* ⊕ *www.latamaleramontreal.com* ▭ *No credit cards* ⊘ *Closed Mon. No dinner Sat. and Sun.* Ⓜ *Laurier.*

★ **Lawrence**

$$$ | CANADIAN | There are lines outside this hip and trendy establishment before the restaurant even opens for Sunday brunch. The chef's British background means that the homemade scones and clotted cream here are required eating. **Known for:** British-inspired fare; arctic char and sea urchin; Sunday brunch. $ *Average main: C$22* ⊠ *5201 boul. St-Laurent, Mile End* ☎ *514/503–1070* ⊕ *www.lawrencerestaurant.com* ⊘ *Closed Mon.* Ⓜ *Laurier.*

Le Bowhead

$$ | VEGETARIAN | Opened in June 2019, this is Montréal's first meat-free pub restaurant. In addition to plant-based comfort foods, Le Bowhead sources beers, wines, and spirits that are 100% vegan, meaning that no animal-based fining agents have been used in the filtration process. **Known for:** vegan sliders; ANML fries (a plant-based variation on poutine); vegan wine and spirits. $ *Average main: C$12* ⊠ *3723 boul. St-Laurent, The Plateau* ☎ *514/977–0838* Ⓜ *St-Laurent.*

Le Filet

$$$$ | MODERN CANADIAN | A study in contrasts, Le Filet has a discreet blink-and-you'll-miss-it facade with a glitzy black-and-gold interior and a hot-spot buzz. Though it's been around a while, there is no mixed messaging when it comes

to the exacting presentation and superb food and wine. **Known for:** beef onglet; expert sommeliers; maple oysters. ⑤ *Average main: C$35* ✉ *219 av. Mont-Royal Ouest, The Plateau* ☎ *514/360-6060* ⊕ *lefilet.ca* ◷ *Closed Sun. and Mon.* Ⓜ *Mont-Royal.*

★ Le Majestique

$$ | MODERN CANADIAN | With its bric-à-brac décor, retro knickknacks, and sceney vibes, Majestique is a quirky wine bar that's open until the wee hours with an excellent selection of small plates. The snazzy surroundings only add to the charm of this fine-dining-meets-casual-savoir-faire; the salmon confit, the quinoa croquette, and rotating choice of fresh oysters are musts. **Known for:** buzzy oyster house; quirky wine bar; foot-long piglet hotdog. ⑤ *Average main: C$13.50* ✉ *4105 boul. St-Laurent, The Plateau* ☎ *514/439-1850* ⊕ *www.restobarmajestique.com* ◷ *Brunch on Sun. only.* Ⓜ *Mont-Royal.*

★ L'Express

$$$ | FRENCH | FAMILY | This iconic Montréal bistro hasn't changed much since its opening in 1980 and it's just as well—regulars would throw a fit if it did. Quintessential French fare is fairly priced and appetizing, outstanding even, with dishes like steak tartare with fries, salmon with sorrel, and calf's liver with tarragon. **Known for:** steak tartare; lively atmosphere; late-night dining. ⑤ *Average main: C$23* ✉ *3927 rue St-Denis, The Plateau* ☎ *514/845-5333* ⊕ *www.restaurantlexpress.com/en* Ⓜ *Sherbrooke.*

Maison Publique

$$$$ | MODERN BRITISH | Local celebrity chef Derek Dammann teamed up with famed British chef Jamie Oliver to open this pub-style restaurant that perfectly blends Canadian and British traditions. The interior is dark and cozy; the handwritten menu changes frequently based on what's in season. **Known for:** Welsh rarebit; dishes intended for sharing; celebrity chef owners. ⑤ *Average main:*

C$35 ✉ *4720 rue Marquette, The Plateau* ☎ *514/507-0555* ⊕ *www.maisonpublique.com* ◷ *Closed Mon. and Tues.* Ⓜ *Laurier.*

Melina Phyllo Bar

$ | GREEK | FAMILY | It may be in the heart of trendy Mile End, but this "phyllo bar" looks like it was transported directly from Athens, with food arriving on checkered cobalt-blue wax paper. The spanakopita, with a perfect crunchy exterior, makes for an excellent lunch on the go, as does the Melina sandwich, with its spicy feta spread, kalamata hummus, cucumbers, tomatoes, and graviera. **Known for:** bougatsa pastry; vegan and vegetarian eats; takeout Greek. ⑤ *Average main: C$7* ✉ *5733 av. du Parc, Mile End* ☎ *514/270-1675* ▱ *No credit cards* Ⓜ *Parc.*

★ Moishe's

$$$$ | STEAKHOUSE | Elegant and old-school, Montréal's premier steak house has been in the Lighter family since 1938 and family members have consistently been hands-on when it comes to selecting and aging their own antibiotics-and-hormone-free steaks, sourced from local farmers. Fresh oysters are a terrific starter, and fresh fish preparations are available, but make no mistake: this is a steak house. **Known for:** Monte Carlo potato; quality, aged steaks; coleslaw and pickles starter. ⑤ *Average main: C$43* ✉ *3961 boul. St-Laurent, The Plateau* ☎ *514/845-3509* ⊕ *www.moishes.ca* Ⓜ *St-Laurent.*

Nouveau Palais

$$ | AMERICAN | FAMILY | Hipsters head to this laid-back '70s diner for one thing: delicious, classic greasy spoon dishes with a modern twist (a close second is the décor; think wood paneling and vinyl seats). The Palace Hamburger (Palais Burger) is gaining a reputation among Montrealers as one of the best in the city, and the sweet-potato pie also has fans. **Known for:** open late; house burger; 1970s vibe. ⑤ *Average main: C$18* ✉ *281 rue Bernard Ouest, Mile End*

☎ 514/273–1180 ⊕ www.nouveaupalais. com Ⓜ Rosemont.

Patisserie Au Kouign Amann

$ | BAKERY | FAMILY | The compact bakery serves some of the best croissants in Montréal, but the specialty here is the eponymous "kouign amann," a multi-layered butter and sugar cake originally from Brittany. The aroma of freshly baked bread is alluring to say the least and the passion for pastries is evident and some-times demonstrated by perfectionist owner Breton Nicolas Henri. **Known for:** kouign amman; perfect croissants; tiny gem. Ⓢ Average main: C$6 ⊠ 316 av. du Mont Royal Est, The Plateau ☎ 514/845–8813 ⊟ No credit cards ◐ Closed for part of the summer Ⓜ Mont-Royal.

Restaurant Hà

$$$ | MODERN ASIAN | Located at the foot of Mount Royal, this unassuming but contemporary local hot spot serves some of the best Vietnamese fare in the city on one of the most enjoyable patios in Montréal. Simple yet edgy are the oper-ative words to describe the menu here. Steamed buns attractively blackened with squid ink, ginger-carrot crispy tofu, and grilled chicken à la citronelle with nappa cabbage are among the surprising novelties. **Known for:** authentic Vietnam-ese food; stunning terrace; squid ink steamed buns. Ⓢ Average main: C$21 ⊠ 243 av. du Mont-Royal Ouest, The Pla-teau ☎ 514/848-0336 ⊕ www.restauran-tha.com ◐ Closed Mon. Ⓜ Mont-Royal.

Restaurant Maïs

$$ | LATIN AMERICAN | A beautiful young crowd, tasty cocktails, and delicious tacos are what this dynamic restaurant and bar is all about. The menu is a mix of some of the best Latin fare in Montréal—with toppings like marinated chilis, home-made jalapeño crema, and cumin-roasted walnuts, or the more carnivore-friendly veal tongue with red peanut salsa—as well as other great "Latin-inspired fare." For something festive, order a Paloma (a savvy mix of tequila, lime, hibiscus

syrup, and fresh grapefruit juice). **Known for:** Latin and Latin-inspired cuisine; vegan-friendly and gluten-free; Paloma cocktail. Ⓢ Average main: C$20 ⊠ 5439 boul. St-Laurent, Mile End ☎ 514/507–7740 ⊕ restaurantmais.com ◐ Closed Sun. and Mon. No lunch Sat.

★ Schwartz's Delicatessen

$$ | DELI | FAMILY | You simply haven't really eaten in Montréal if you haven't eaten at Schwartz's, Canada's oldest deli. This Montréal classic has zero frills decor-wise, yet crowds have been coming since 1928 for a thick and legendary smoked-meat sandwich on rye with mustard. **Known for:** local institution; sandwiches with smoked meat marinated in herbs and spices; long wait for a table. Ⓢ Average main: C$16 ⊠ 3895 boul. St-Laurent, The Plateau ☎ 514/842–4813 ⊕ www.schwartzsdeli. com Ⓜ Sherbrooke.

Sparrow

$$ | MODERN BRITISH | Part cocktail bar, part British restaurant, this en vogue spot has welcoming aviary decor motifs. Diners can get a traditional English breakfast in the morning, followed by a Sunday roast and a good old-fashioned basil gimlet. **Known for:** organic, hormone-free burgers; brunch; great cocktails. Ⓢ Average main: C$13 ⊠ 5322 boul. St-Laurent, Mile End ☎ 514/507–1642 ⊕ www.lesparrowbar. com Ⓜ Laurier.

Yokato Yokabai

$$ | JAPANESE | Frequently cited as the best ramen house in Montréal bar none, Yokato Yokabai is indeed a discreet restaurant that deserves to be visited by all noodle lovers—especially when temperatures drop below freezing point here. The décor features dark-wood paneling and minimal knickknacks and immediately transports diners to a Japa-nese hole-in-the-wall. **Known for:** Tonkotsu ramen; atmospheric décor; long waits. Ⓢ Average main: C$14 ⊠ 4185 Drolet, The Plateau ☎ 514/282–9991 ⊕ www. yoka.ca Ⓜ Mont-Royal.

☕ Coffee and Quick Bites

Boulangerie Hof Kelsten

$ | **BAKERY** | The mastermind behind this photogenic bakery had been making bread for Montréal's best restaurants for years before he decided to open up his own place. His own shop is a favorite with locals, who line up every weekend for fresh baguettes. **Known for:** chocolate babka; Jewish cuisine; panettone. Ⓢ *Average main: C$8.50* ✉ *4524 boul. St-Laurent, The Plateau* ☎ *514/649–7991* ⊕ *hofkelsten.com* ⊘ *Closed Mon. and Tues.* Ⓜ *Mont-Royal.*

Café Olimpico

$ | **CAFÉ** | **FAMILY** | Open daily from 7 am to midnight, this Mile End staple is a popular spot for great Italian coffee in Montréal's most fashionable neighborhood. It's is a great place to get a real feel of authentic Montréal. **Known for:** gourmet coffee; sunny patio; local spot. Ⓢ *Average main: C$3.50* ✉ *124 rue St-Viateur Ouest, Mile End* ☎ *514/495–0746* ⊕ *www.cafeolimpico.com* ⊟ *No credit cards* Ⓜ *Rosemont.*

Café Replika

$ | **TURKISH** | **FAMILY** | College students, freelancers, and local hipsters flock to this understated Turkish café for two reasons: the gourmet coffee and the food. Between the Nutella and sea salt cookie, and the feta and sausage omelet and the boreks (a traditional flaky pastry sprinkled with sesame seeds), it's hard to pick just one thing off Replika's menu. **Known for:** latte art; Turkish fare; friendly owners. Ⓢ *Average main: C$7* ✉ *252 rue Rachel Est, The Plateau* ☎ *514/903–4384* ⊕ *www.cafereplika.com* Ⓜ *Mont-Royal.*

★ Patisserie Rhubarbe

$ | **BAKERY** | **FAMILY** | This small and tastefully decorated bakery is, simply put, a Montréal treasure. Locals come from all over the city to pick up delicious desserts like lemon tarts and Paris-Brest that taste as good as they look. **Known for:** afternoon tea; Paris-Brest; long wait

for a table. Ⓢ *Average main: C$7* ✉ *1479 av. Laurier Est, The Plateau* ☎ *514/316–2935* ⊕ *www.patisserierhubarbe.com* ⊘ *Closed Mon. and Tues.* Ⓜ *Laurier.*

Salon de thé Cardinal

$ | **BRITISH** | If it wasn't for the trendy young clientele, you'd think that time had stood still at Salon de thé Cardinal, where you can find a good old-fashioned afternoon tea served with dainty mismatched tableware in a Victorian-style space filled with antiques, thick runner rugs, and carved wood. Food-wise, the menu varies between sweet (blueberry scones, bourbon cookies, various English cakes) and savory (ploughman's plate, cucumber sandwiches), both complemented by a plethora of fragrant teas. **Known for:** Victorian tearoom; freshly baked scones; delicious teas. Ⓢ *Average main: C$11* ✉ *5326 boul. St-Laurent, Mile End* ☎ *514/903–2877* ⊕ *www.thecardinaltea. com* ⊘ *Closed Mon.–Wed.* Ⓜ *Laurier.*

★ St-Viateur Bagel & Café

$ | **CAFÉ** | **FAMILY** | Even New Yorkers have been known to (collective gasp!) prefer Montréal's light and crispy bagel to its bulkier Manhattan cousin, due to the dough of the Quebecois version being boiled in honey-sweetened water before baking in a wood-burning oven. St-Viateur Bagel & Café is a great place to get them, espcially with smoked salmon. **Known for:** delicious bagels; classic and creative options; local favorite. Ⓢ *Average main: C$8* ✉ *1127 av. Mont-Royal Est, The Plateau* ☎ *514/528–6361* ⊕ *www. stviateurbagel.com* Ⓜ *Laurier.*

🛏 Hotels

Full of artists and academics, the Plateau and Mile End are bustling neighborhoods with a high density of bistros, brewpubs, martini bars, cupcake emporiums, designer boutiques, and parks. This is no place for quiet contemplation. In summer, join the crowds at outdoor markets and street fairs. There aren't many places to stay, but they include some lovely auberges and B&Bs.

Auberge de la Fontaine

$$ | **B&B/INN** | **FAMILY** | Built out of two adjoining houses with a signature yellow front door, laquered-barn-board facade, and welcoming flower boxes, this turn-of-the-20th-century residence overlooks Parc Lafontaine and one of the city's major bicycle trails. **Pros:** near bars and restaurants; most rooms have whirlpool baths; some rooms have private balconies with park views. **Cons:** lobby is serviceable but lacking glamour; some rooms are unrenovated and quite small; parking can be difficult. $ *Rooms from: C$235* ✉ *1301 rue Rachel Est, The Plateau* ☎ *514/597–0166, 800/597–0597* ⊕ *www.aubergedelafontaine.com* ⇌ *21 rooms* ⚞⚟ *Free breakfast* Ⓜ *Mont-Royal.*

Casa Bianca Bed & Breakfast

$ | **B&B/INN** | Popular with love-struck couples visiting friends on the Plateau, this renovated mansion is an ode to French Renaissance Revival architecture while also promoting an organic and vegetarian ethic, from all offerings at breakfast to all bedding and cleaning products. **Pros:** facing Mont-Royal; claw-foot tubs; private terrace with flowers. **Cons:** IKEA college student decor; creaky hardwood floors; no soundproofing in bedrooms. $ *Rooms from: C$150* ✉ *4351 av. de l'Esplanade, The Plateau* ☎ *514/312–3837* ⊕ *www. casabianca.ca* ⇌ *5 rooms* ⚞⚟ *Free breakfast* Ⓜ *Mont-Royal.*

▼ Nightlife

The restaurants and bars along St-Denis and Mont-Royal are popular with everyone from rambunctious students to serious food-lovers. Boulevard St-Laurent ("The Main"), especially between rue Sherbrooke and avenue des Pins, is home to the see-and-be-seen crowd, with merrymakers spilling out at all hours of the night.

Mile End has become well-known for inspired cuisine, affordable lounges, and relaxed bars, and is slowly becoming a second village to the hipster gay crowd, who tend to forgo the main Village.

BARS AND LOUNGES

Bar Waverly

BARS/PUBS | Named for the street that epitomizes the Mile End, this neighborhood bar has a warm staff, friendly atmosphere, and a great selection of scotch. Owners Richard Holder and Olivier Farley have been in the business for years, and it shows. Nightly DJs provide an edgier vibe, while huge floor-to-ceiling windows make it perfect for people-watching. ✉ *5550 boul. St-Laurent, Mile End* ☎ *514/903–1121* ⊕ *www. barwaverly.com* Ⓜ *Laurier.*

★ Bily Kun

BARS/PUBS | This Czech-themed bar is a favorite hangout of Plateau locals. There's live jazz during the cocktail hour and a DJ or classical performances later in the evening. Try an absinthe-laced apple cocktail from the extensive alcohol menu as you nibble on a few tapas. Bily Kun gets packed, though the high ceilings help alleviate the feeling of claustrophobia. ✉ *354 av. du Mont-Royal Est, The Plateau* ☎ *514/845–5392* ⊕ *www.bilykun. com* Ⓜ *Mont-Royal.*

La Buvette chez Simone

BARS/PUBS | Lively but not obnoxious, this easygoing wine bar is a great place to visit with friends. Arrive early (it opens at 4 pm but the kitchen only gets going at 5 pm), because it's always busy and it doesn't take reservations. Many wines are available by the glass, in 2- and 4-ounce pours, with an emphasis on French varietals. Dress is casual, though the after-work crowd ups the glam factor. ✉ *4869 av. du Parc, Mile End* ☎ *514/750–6577* ⊕ *www.buvettechezsimone.com* Ⓜ *Laurier or Mont-Royal.*

★ Reservoir

BARS/PUBS | It's all about the beer at this friendly restaurant and bar, where it's all brewed right on the premises. Packed almost every night of the week, this bar has everything from India pale ales to German-inspired wheat beers. The upstairs patio is the ideal spot for watching locals stroll along the quaint cobblestone avenue. ⌂ *9 av. Duluth Est, The Plateau* ☎ *514/849–7779* ⊕ *www. brasseriereservoir.ca* Ⓜ *Sherbrooke.*

Suwu

BARS/PUBS | This self-described "hip-hop eatery" and neighborhood bar invites you to relax and pull up a chair or cozy couch. Simple but intense dishes like truffle-oil popcorn and a grilled cheese mac-and-cheese sandwich (yes, you read that right) are paired with powerful cocktails (try the signature Wu-Tang) to help make this one of the hottest destinations on The Main—without any of the usual pretension. Open nightly from 5 to 3. ⌂ *3581 boul. St-Laurent, The Plateau* ☎ *514/564–5074* ⊕ *www.suwumontreal. com* Ⓜ *St-Laurent.*

Whisky Café

BARS/PUBS | Known for its happy hour, this bar, café, and cigar lounge is elegant but unpretentious—it's the perfect spot for a romantic rendezvous. The selection of more than 150 varieties of scotch, plus an impressive choice of wines, champagnes, and ports, leaves most everyone's thirst quenched. ⌂ *5800 boul. St-Laurent, Mile End* ☎ *514/278–2646* ⊕ *www.whiskycafe.com* Ⓜ *Rosemont.*

DANCE CLUBS
Tokyo Bar

DANCE CLUBS | A Montréal mainstay that's been going strong since 1997, Tokyo Bar caters to a young professional crowd. The DJs primarily spin hip-hop and house, but the best thing here, for sure, is the heated rooftop terrace and bar, which has a fantastic view of The Main (boulevard St-Laurent). ⌂ *3709 boul. St-Laurent, The Plateau* ☎ *514/842–6838* ⊕ *www.*

tokyobar.com ◔ *Closed Mon.–Wed.* Ⓜ *St-Laurent.*

LIVE MUSIC
Barfly

MUSIC CLUBS | Fans of blues, punk, country, and bluegrass jam into this tiny hole-in-the-wall, which has some of the cheapest drink prices on St-Laurent. A very popular hangout for locals, Barfly is arguably the premier dive bar in the city. ⌂ *4062 boul. St-Laurent, The Plateau* ☎ *514/284–6665* Ⓜ *Sherbrooke or St-Laurent.*

Casa del Popolo

MUSIC CLUBS | One of the city's treasured venues for indie rock, jazz, reggae, blues, folk, and hip-hop, this neighborhood bar is ideal for discovering up-and-coming local acts or forgotten international giants still touring. While you enjoy the music, take a look at the original art and sample some of the tasty vegetarian food. ⌂ *4873 boul. St-Laurent, The Plateau* ☎ *514/284–3804* ⊕ *www.casadelpopolo. com* Ⓜ *Mont-Royal.*

🎭 Performing Arts

THEATER
Mainline Theatre

THEATER | Operated by the same people who present the Montréal Fringe Festival every summer, the Mainline opened in 2006 to serve the city's burgeoning Anglo theater community and has been going strong ever since. ⌂ *3997 boul. St-Laurent, The Plateau* ☎ *514/849–3378* ⊕ *www.mainlinetheatre.ca* Ⓜ *St-Laurent or Mont-Royal.*

Théâtre du Rideau Vert

THEATER | The oldest professional French theater company in North America, Théâtre du Rideau Vert has been winning over audiences with its contemporary productions since 1948. Many popular francophone actors got their big break here. ⌂ *4664 rue St-Denis, The Plateau* ☎ *514/844–1793* ⊕ *www.rideauvert.qc.ca* Ⓜ *Mont-Royal.*

🛍 Shopping

The Plateau has long been recognized as one of North America's hippest neighborhoods, and though trends typically come and go, its cachet endures. Rue St-Denis is home to both independent boutiques and chain stores selling local and international fashion, as well as numerous jewelry stores, all at prices for every budget. Boulevard St-Laurent and avenue Mont-Royal both offer opportunities for vintage shopping, with St-Laurent also known for contemporary furniture and decor stores.

Just north of the Plateau, the Mile End offers an eclectic mix of artsy boutiques and shops stocked with up-and-coming Montréal designers.

CLOTHING

Bodybag by Jude
CLOTHING | When Nicole Kidman wore one of this designer's zip denim dresses, Judith Desjardins's star was set. The designer has a penchant for all things British, so look for cheeky checks and plaids. ⊠ *17 rue Bernard Ouest, Mile End* ☎ *514/274–5242* ⊕ *www.bodybagbyjude. com* Ⓜ *Rosemont.*

★ Boutique 1861
CLOTHING | This boutique stocks romantic, lacy, and affordable finds from local and international designers, including Arti Gogna and Champagne & Strawbery. With everything white—hardwood floors, couches, and armoires—the boudoir vibe is irresistible. Just look for the pink-and-black cameo signage. The name comes from the smaller branch at 1861 rue Ste-Catherine. ⊠ *3670 boul. St-Laurent, The Plateau* ☎ *514/670–6110* ⊕ *www.1861.ca.*

Citizen Vintage
CLOTHING | If you're a slave to all things vintage, then this Mile End boutique has your name on it. Bright, spacious, and carefully curated by the owners (who scour North America for their finds),

this store makes shopping easy, as everything is arranged by color. The stock changes almost daily, so don't feel you can only visit once. *There's a second location in the Plateau at 4059 boul. Saint-Laurent.* ⊠ *5330 boul. St-Laurent, Mile End* ☎ *514/439–2774* ⊕ *www. citizenvintage.com* Ⓜ *Laurier.*

★ Deuxième Peau
CLOTHING | Tucked away in a basement, the tiny "Second Skin" sells a fine assortment of French lingerie. It's hard to miss the curvy mannequins in their ground-floor window, adorned in the likes of Aubade, Chantelle, and Prima Donna. While you're feeling brave and beautiful, kill two birds with one stone and try on a bathing suit from the shop's tasteful collection of fine French, Spanish, and Australian designers. ⊠ *4457 rue St-Denis, The Plateau* ☎ *514/842–0811* ⊕ *www. deuxiemepeau.com* Ⓜ *Mont-Royal.*

★ Éditions de Robes
CLOTHING | Owner Julie Pesant has stocked her boutique with top-quality Montréal-made-and-designed dresses in a multitude of styles that can easily be dressed up or down with a simple change of accessories. From peplums to lace, satin to jersey, long and short, they're all here. *There's also an outpost at 2122 rue Crescent near the Montréal Museum of Fine Arts.* ⊠ *5334 boul. Saint-Laurent, Mile End* ☎ *514/271–7676* ⊕ *www.editionsderobes.com* ⊙ *Closed Mon.* Ⓜ *St-Laurent, then bus 55.*

General 54
CLOTHING | The neighborhood Mile End earned its reputation for all things cool with funky shops like this one. The natural-hue clothes—most by local designers—are feminine and elegant, and owner Jennifer Glasgow sells her eponymous clothing line here. The location on The Main is warm and welcoming, with exposed brick and intricately patterned floors. ⊠ *5145 boul. St-Laurent, Mile End* ☎ *514/271–2129* ⊕ *www.general54.com* Ⓜ *Laurier.*

Kanuk

CLOTHING | This company's snowy owl trademark has become something of a status symbol among the shivering urban masses. The Québec-made coats and parkas sold here are built to keep an Arctic explorer warm and dry. Try on coats in a variety of styles and lengths, with optional fur hoodies. Rain gear is also available. ✉ *485 rue Rachel Est, The Plateau* ☎ *514/284–4494, 877/284–4494* ⊕ *www.kanuk.com* ☾ *Closed late Mar.– early Sept. Closed Sun.* Ⓜ *Mont-Royal.*

★ M0851

CLOTHING | Sleek, supple leather clothing and bags from the Québec designer Frédéric Mamarbachi have a cult following from Antwerp to Tokyo. The rough-hewn wood floors and concrete walls of this branch give it an industrial-chic vibe. ✉ *3526 boul. St-Laurent, The Plateau* ☎ *514/849–9759* ⊕ *www.m0851.com* Ⓜ *St-Laurent or Sherbrooke.*

Mousseline

CLOTHING | With sizes running from 2 to 22, this place makes finding the perfect fit a snap. Choosing from among the casual wear by fashion labels like James Perse, Pas de Calais, and Odd Mooly might be a bit more difficult. Be sure to pick up a comforting sweater from Autumn Cashmere. ✉ *220 av. Laurier Ouest, Mile End* ☎ *514/878–0661* ⊕ *www.boutiquemousseline.com* Ⓜ *Laurier.*

Muse

CLOTHING | Designer Christian Chenail's contemporary take on fashion always has a French twist, and his daring black gowns are showstoppers. His flirty skirts and dresses usually come in cheerful shades of red and blue and call to mind the styles of the '50s. ✉ *4467 rue St-Denis, The Plateau* ☎ *514/848– 9493* ⊕ *www.muse-cchenail.com* Ⓜ *Mont-Royal.*

Unicorn

CLOTHING | Young Quebecois designers like Barilà, Valérie Dumaine, and Mélissa Nepton are the stars of this beautiful Mile End boutique, which also stocks unique national and international labels. All the black and white in the window display hints at the minimalist aesthetic within. ✉ *5135 boul. St-Laurent, Mile End* ☎ *514/544–2828* ⊕ *www.boutiqueunicorn.com* Ⓜ *Laurier.*

★ Vestibule

CLOTHING | This cheerful boutique is a dream-come-true for owner Audrey Morissette, who adores all things whimsical and feminine. Uniting her love of fashion and decor, the shop is filled with pretty items ranging from jewelry to clothing to candles, as well as ceramics and other household items. ✉ *5170 boul. St-Laurent, Mile End* ☎ *514/543–1618* ⊕ *www.boutiquevestibule.com* Ⓜ *Laurier.*

FOOD

★ La Vieille Europe

FOOD/CANDY | For a taste of the old Main, where generations of immigrants came to shop, look no farther than this deli packed with sausages, cheeses, European chocolates, jams, and atmosphere. Pick up a rich shot of espresso on your way out. *Call ahead as hours vary seasonally.* ✉ *3855 boul. St-Laurent, The Plateau* ☎ *514/842–5773* Ⓜ *St-Laurent or Sherbrooke.*

SHOES

John Fluevog

SHOES/LUGGAGE/LEATHER GOODS | Unusually curved lines, from the heels of his shoes to the interior design of his funky boutique, have cultivated a devout following for the Canadian shoe designer. Belts and bags are also available, letting you create a quirky yet coordinated outfit. Look to the soles for curious and inspiring messages. ■ TIP➔ **There's a second location in Old Montréal.** ✉ *3857 rue St-Denis, The Plateau* ☎ *514/509–1627* ⊕ *www.fluevog.com* Ⓜ *Sherbrooke.*

Outremont

Above the Plateau and next to Parc du Mont-Royal, **Outremont** has long been Montréal's residential francophone enclave (as opposed to Westmount, always stubbornly English right down to its neo-Gothic churches and lawn-bowling club). It has grand homes, tree-shaded streets, perfectly groomed parks, and two upscale shopping and dining strips along rue Laurier and avenue Bernard. The latter, with wide sidewalks and shady trees, is particularly attractive. The eastern fringes of Outremont are home to Montréal's thriving Hasidic community.

GETTING HERE AND AROUND

By métro, take the Blue Line to Outremont station. You can also get to Outremont from Downtown on Bus 55, which goes along St. Laurent Boulevard, or Bus 80, which goes through Mont-Royal Park along avenue du Parc. Both bus routes can be picked up outside the Place-des-Arts métro, and you need to get off at rue Laurier and walk west from there. (Outremont begins on the west side of Parc; the east side of Parc is Mile End.)

Alternately, you could stay on Bus 80 for a few more stops until you come to Bernard and then walk west. Both Laurier and Bernard avenues are Outremont's primary hubs for commercial activity. The Outremont métro stop lets you off on avenue Van Horne, another commercial hub but without the fun, interesting boutiques and restaurants of Laurier and Bernard. If you're coming from Downtown and feeling fit you could walk to Outremont in roughly 30–45 minutes, or, for that matter, just hop on a Bixi bicycle, taking the same route as Bus 80 and getting there in half the time.

◉ Sights

★ Avenue Bernard

NEIGHBORHOOD | If your taste runs to the chic and fashionable, then there is simply no better street than rue Bernard, west of Avenue Querbes, for people-watching. Its wide sidewalks and shady trees make it ideal for the kind of outdoor cafés and restaurants that attract the bright and the beautiful. ✉ *Outremont* Ⓜ *Outremont.*

⑪ Restaurants

Outremont caters to affluent French-speaking professionals with restaurants that look as good as the food being served. There are plenty of charming outdoor terraces in the warm months.

Brasserie Les Enfants Terribles

$$$ | CANADIAN | With its cavernous corner spot on Outremont's trendy avenue Bernard, sophisticated yet playful decor, and artfully prepared comfort food, this brasserie is always a good bet for quality food and excellent people-watching. The menu at Les Enfants Terribles is a mix of high-class cuisine and comfort food favorites, from salmon tartare, grilled oyster mushroom salad, and spaghetti bolognese to fish-and-chips and mac 'n' cheese. **Known for:** pouding chômeur cake; after-theater crowd; elevated comfort food. Ⓢ *Average main: C$25* ✉ *1257 av. Bernard Ouest, Outremont* ☎ *514/759–9918* ⊕ *www. jesuisunenfantterrible.com* Ⓜ *Outremont.*

Damas

$$$ | MIDDLE EASTERN | Colorful and cozy, with dishes that are perfect for sharing, Damas is a treat. Try *fatta* (yogurt, tahini, pita, pistachios, pine nuts, and herbs), hummus with lamb, or the *moujaddaraa* (braised lentils with bulgur and caramelized onions, tomato salsa and yogurt mint sauce). **Known for:** authentic Syrian cuisine; hummus with lamb; Mediterranean

Sights ▼

1 Avenue
  Bernard..... **B6**
2 Chiesa della
  Madonna della
  Difesa **B3**
3 Marché
  Jean-Talon . **A2**

Restaurants ▼

1 Beaufort
  Bistro........ **C2**
2 Bottega
  Pizzeria...... **B3**
3 Brasserie
  Harricana... **A3**
4 Brasserie
  Les Enfants
  Terribles..... **B6**
5 Damas....... **A6**
6 Dinette Triple
  Crown **B4**
7 Impasto **B3**
8 Kitchen
  Galerie **A3**
9 La
  Chronique... **D6**
10 La
  Cornetteria . **B4**
11 La Croissanterie
  Figaro **D7**
12 La Récolte .. **B2**
13 Le Glacier
  Bilboquet ... **B7**
14 Le Petit
  Alep **A2**
15 Leméac **D7**
16 Manitoba ... **A4**
17 Montréal
  Plaza **D3**
18 Pastaga **B4**
19 Pizzeria
  900........... **B7**
20 Tapeo........ **A1**

Quick Bites ▼

1 Caffe San
  Simeon...... **B3**
2 Toi Moi
  et Café **D6**

Outrement
and Little Italy

KEY

1 Sights
1 Restaurants
1 Quick Bites
M Métro Stations

wines. $ *Average main: C$30* ✉ *1201 av. Van Horne, Outremont* ☎ *514/439–5435* ⊕ *www.restaurant-damas.com* ⊙ *No lunch* Ⓜ *Outremont.*

La Chronique

$$$$ | **FRENCH** | Although La Chronique is indeed an elegant place with white walls and high ceilings flooded with light, people don't come here for the setting; they come for the excellent food. Without fuss or fanfare, La Chronique has remained one of the best French restaurants in town since it opened in 1995. **Known for:** tasting menu; seared foie gras; excellent French cuisine. $ *Average main: C$45* ✉ *104 av. Laurier Ouest, Outremont* ☎ *514/271–3095* ⊕ *www.lachronique. qc.ca* ⊙ *No lunch Sat.–Mon.* Ⓜ *Laurier.*

★ La Croissanterie Figaro

$$ | **BISTRO** | **FAMILY** | The self-proclaimed "un coin perdu de Paris" is famous for its wraparound patio, Parisian vibe, and 100-year-old corner building featuring stained glass and woodwork, an art deco chandelier, and an art nouveau bar. Although this is a full bistro serving three meals every day of the week, it shines brightest in the morning. **Known for:** charming setting; croissant with almond paste; opens early and closes late. $ *Average main: C$12* ✉ *5200 rue Hutchison, Outremont* ☎ *514/278–6567* ⊕ *www. lacroissanteriefigaro.com* Ⓜ *Outremont.*

Le Glacier Bilboquet

$ | **CANADIAN** | **FAMILY** | Families and couples with dogs congregate here on warm summer nights, where the artisanal ice-cream recipes are prepared by hand. Real cream and real milk are the star ingredients, while the sorbets are 80% fruit puree. **Known for:** cranberry sorbet; maple taffy ice cream; late hours in summer. $ *Average main: C$8* ✉ *1311 rue Bernard Ouest, Outremont* ☎ *514/276–0414* ⊕ *www.bilboquet.ca* ▭ *No credit cards* Ⓜ *Outremont.*

★ Leméac

$$$$ | **BISTRO** | This sophisticated French bistro pleases Montrealers with its flawless classics and its heated wraparound outdoor terrace—not to mention the late-night two-course table d'hôte menu at just C$30. Regulars gravitate toward dishes such as the beef or salmon tartare, grilled Cornish hen, asparagus and wild mushroom risotto, mushroom ravioli, and hanger steak—all served with ceremonial aplomb on white linen tablecloths. **Known for:** being busy; salmon tartare; late-night special. $ *Average main: C$40* ✉ *1045 av. Laurier Ouest, Outremont* ☎ *514/270–0999* ⊕ *www. restaurantlemeac.com* Ⓜ *Outremont.*

★ Pizzeria 900

$$ | **MODERN ITALIAN** | No one does pizza quite like these pizzaiolos; they are, after all, legally certified by the *Associazione Vera Pizza Napolitana* in Italy. Using all-natural and nonprocessed ingredients, and adhering to traditional pizza-making methods (like using a 900-degree oven), Pizzeria 900 is one of the most sought-after pizza spots in town with one of the most sought-after patios. **Known for:** prix-fixe lunch; Neapolitan-style pizza; stylish space. $ *Average main: C$15* ✉ *1248 rue Bernard Ouest, Outremont* ☎ *438/386–0900* ⊕ *no900.com* Ⓜ *Outremont.*

☕ Coffee and Quick Bites

Toi Moi et Café

$$ | **BISTRO** | Film producers and poets congregate at this corner café-bistro, sitting on the terrace to sip award-winning espresso. Although there's a hearty lunch and dinner menu of salads, tofu salads, and grilled meat, brunch is the big draw. **Known for:** single-origin specialty coffees; student and artist crowd; exclusive blends like baklava coffee. $ *Average main: C$12* ✉ *244 av. Laurier Ouest, Outremont* ☎ *514/279–9599* ⊕ *www. toimoicafe.com* Ⓜ *Laurier.*

🎭 Performing Arts

CLASSICAL MUSIC

Salle Claude-Champagne

MUSIC | This beautiful concert hall hosts more than 150 symphonic and operatic performances every year by the music faculty of the Université de Montréal. The repertoire includes both classic and contemporary works. ✉ 220 av. Vincent-d'Indy, Outremont ☎ 514/343–6427 ⊕ www.musique.umontreal.ca Ⓜ Édouard-Monpetit.

THEATER

Théâtre Outremont

CONCERTS | Inaugurated in 1929, this gorgeous art deco theater rapidly became a local favorite and had its heyday in the '70s before it fell into disarray. After reopening its doors in the early '90s, the theater has regained much of its steam with mostly theater and live music acts. ✉ 1248 av. Bernard O., Outremont ☎ 514/495–9944 ⊕ www.theatreoutremont.ca Ⓜ Outremont.

🛍 Shopping

Avenue Laurier in Outremont is a good destination for those in pursuit of a little luxury.

CLOTHING

Billie

CLOTHING | One of Montréal's favorite boutiques, Billie has rows of bookcases, drawers, and shelves that give the feeling of raiding your best friend's closet. Look for chic dresses and blouses from Alice + Olivia, cozy sweaters from 360 Sweater, and eclectic shoes by Cynthia Vincent. If you are shopping for kid sizes, visit Billie le Kid at 1001 avenue Laurier Ouest. ✉ 1012 av. Laurier Ouest, Outremont ☎ 514/270–5415 ⊕ www.billieboutique.com Ⓜ Laurier.

★ Lyla

CLOTHING | Some of the finest lingerie in the city—including brands like Eres and La Perla—is stocked at this lovely little shop. The staff is extremely helpful in finding what fits and flatters. Two other reasons to stop and shop: exquisite fashions from Europe and a great selection of swimsuits and darling cover-ups. ✉ 400 av. Laurier Ouest, Outremont ☎ 514/271–0763 ⊕ www.lyla.ca Ⓜ Laurier.

Mimi & Coco

CLOTHING | You'll want to snap up several of the locally designed T-shirts at Mimi & Coco, perhaps pairing them with luxe knitwear from Italy. Beautiful floor-to-ceiling windows create a bright, inviting interior, even on cloudy days. The shop also sells dog collars and leashes, with profits going to a nonprofit foundation that works to promote animal rescue and adoption. Come at lunchtime and sample one of Mandy's gourmet salads from the in-store counter. ✉ 201 av. Laurier Ouest, Outremont ☎ 514/906–0349 ⊕ www.mimicoco.com Ⓜ Laurier.

★ Très Chic Styling

CLOTHING | Stylish Hervé Léger dresses at two for C$500? Style-savvy cofounders Maryam Rafa and Angelica Koinis believe that women should look good and dress well without having to spend a small fortune. Designer denim and fabulous cocktail dresses and evening gowns for half off (or more) have built their reputation. ✉ 1060 av. Laurier Ouest, Outremont ☎ 514/274–3078 ⊕ www.tcstyling.com Ⓜ Laurier.

FOOD

Gourmet Laurier

FOOD/CANDY | Acres of chocolate and candy and the best coffee beans in town draw well-heeled shoppers to this Outremont shop. The colossal assortment of fine cheeses, charcuterie , and other local and imported goodies add to the appeal. ✉ 1042 av. Laurier Ouest,

Outremont ☎ 514/274–5601 ⊕ www.
gourmetlaurier.ca Ⓜ Laurier.

Yannick Fromagerie
FOOD/CANDY | This cheese shop is the
go-to destination for the city's top chefs
and cheese aficionados. Yannick Achim
carries 400 varieties, buying from local
dairies and stocking an astonishing
international selection. You'll find Pikauba
cheese from Québec beside pecorino
made with raw sheep's milk and laced
with black truffles. Cheese lovers here
eagerly trade advice on building the
perfect after-dinner cheese plate. ⊠ *1218
rue Bernard O., Outremont* ☎ 514/279–
9376 ⊕ www.yannickfromagerie.ca
Ⓜ Outremont.

Little Italy

Farther north is **Little Italy,** which is still
home base to Montréal's sizable Italian
community of nearly a quarter of a million
people. While families of Italian descent
now live all over the greater Montréal
area, many come back here every week
or so to shop, eat out, or visit family and
friends, and the 30-odd blocks bounded
by rues Jean-Talon, St-Zotique, Marconi,
and Drolet remain its heart and soul.
You'll know you've reached Little Italy
when the gardens have tomato plants
and grapevines, there are sausages and
cans of olive oil in store windows, and
the heady smell of espresso emanates
from cafés.

GETTING HERE AND AROUND
You can take both the Orange and Blue
lines to get to Little Italy: get off at
Jean-Talon station and walk six short
blocks to get to boulevard St-Laurent.
Bus 55, which runs north along St-Laurent, will also get you here fairly quickly
from Downtown, or you could just take
a Bixi bike and get here in roughly 20
minutes. Once here, you can stop for
produce and cheese at the Marché
Jean-Talon, and you might just see a

wedding party outside the Madonna della
Difesa church.

⊙ Sights

Chiesa della Madonna della Difesa
RELIGIOUS SITE | If you look up at the
cupola behind the main altar of Little
Italy's most famous church, you'll spot
Montréal's most infamous piece of
ecclesiastical portraiture. Yes, indeed,
that lantern-jaw fellow on horseback who
looks so pleased with himself is Benito
Mussolini, the dictator who led Italy into
World War II—on the wrong side. The
mural, by Guido Nincheri (1885–1973),
was completed long before the war
and commemorates the signing of the
Lateran Pact with Pope Pius XI, one of
Il Duce's few lasting achievements. The
controversy shouldn't distract you from
the beauties of the rest of the richly
decorated church. ⊠ *6800 av. Henri-Julien, Little Italy* ☎ 514/277–6522 ☜ *Free*
⊙ *Closed Sat. and Sun.* Ⓜ *Beaubien or
Jean-Talon.*

★ Marché Jean-Talon
MARKET | The smells of grilling sausages,
roasting chestnuts, and fresh pastries
at this market will surely excite your
olfactory system. To further delight your
senses there are dozens of tiny shops
full of Québec cheeses, Lebanese
sweets, country pâtés, local wines, and
handmade chocolates. Less threatening
to the waistline but a feast for the eyes
are the huge mounds of peas, beans,
apples, carrots, pears, garlic, and other
produce on sale at the open-air stands.
Visit on weekends during the warm summer months, and it will feel as if all of
Montréal has come out to shop. ⊠ *7070
rue Henri-Julien, Little Italy* ☎ 514/277–
1588 ⊕ www.marchespublics-mtl.com
Ⓜ *Jean-Talon.*

🍴 Restaurants

Little Italy offers a nostalgic look back at what La Bella Italia used to be 30 or 40 years ago, as old men congregate in front of their favorite café and chat about politics and last night's soccer game. With its location just steps away from Jean-Talon Market, it's only fitting that historic Piccola Italia would go on to become the sought-after dining destination that it is today. It's now neighbored by the trendsetting Mile-Ex and Rosemont area, where chefs, moving away from Old Montréal and Downtown's expensive rents, benefit from splendid spaces and eager locals, which include young professionals and diners hungry for new experiences.

Beaufort Bistro

$$ | **SCANDINAVIAN** | **FAMILY** | The only Norwegian-inspired eatery in Montréal, Beaufort Bistro has admittedly been getting a lot of attention. Part-time restaurant, part-time busy café (complete with freelancers and students on a deadline), this white-washed cozy space serves the only authentic open-faced sandwiches—smørrebrød—this side of the pond, as well as a variety of mains, like rostis (potato galettes), tartares, and, of course, blinis and gravlax (this is a Scandi café, after all). **Known for:** Norwegian brunch; several vegan and vegetarian options; great coffee. ⓢ *Average main: C$18* ✉ *414 rue St-Zotique Est, Rosemont* ☎ *514/274–6969* ⊕ *www.beaufortbistro. ca* ⊗ *No lunch* Ⓜ *Beaubien.*

Bottega Pizzeria

$$ | **PIZZA** | **FAMILY** | Nobody questions the authenticity of the Neapolitan-style pizza here, seeing as there's a nearly 4-ton wood-burning pizza oven made from Vesuvian rock in the kitchen which cooks pizza in 90 seconds flat, at 500 degrees Celsius (932 °F). There are just a few toppings available, but all are fabulously flavorsome, like fresh tomatoes, vegetables, and top-quality salumi. **Known for:**

excellent gelato to-go; authentic Neapolitan-style pizza; panozzi, calzoni, and tronchetti. ⓢ *Average main: C$16* ✉ *65 rue St-Zotique Est, Little Italy* ☎ *514/277–8104* ⊕ *www.bottega.ca* ⊗ *Closed Mon. No lunch Sat.–Wed.* Ⓜ *Beaubien.*

★ Brasserie Harricana

$$ | **MODERN CANADIAN** | **FAMILY** | Instagram-famous for its dusty pink chairs and pleasing, contemporary space, this seriously cool brasserie is home to 41 home-brews—sold by the bottle at the boutique upstairs—and a solid menu that includes monkfish burgers, beer-can roast chicken, and a hearty rib eye. Waiters are masters at their craft; don't hesitate to ask for beer pairings with your meal. **Known for:** some vegan and vegetarian options; architectural space; beer-can roast chicken. ⓢ *Average main: C$20* ✉ *95 rue Jean-Talon Ouest, Little Italy* ☎ *514/303–3039* ⊕ *www.brasserie-harricana.com* Ⓜ *De Castelnau.*

★ Dinette Triple Crown

$$ | **SOUTHERN** | Dinette Triple Crown is relatively small (a counter with just eight stools), but the real draw here is not indoor dining but taking the comfort food to go. Locals know to ask for a picnic basket (fully equipped with cutlery, dishes, and a tablecloth) that will be enjoyed in Little Italy Park across the street. **Known for:** large selection of bourbon; fried chicken; Southern fare. ⓢ *Average main: C$17* ✉ *6704 rue Clark, Little Italy* ☎ *514/272–2617* ⊕ *www.dinettetriplecrown.com* ⊗ *Closed Tues. and Wed.* Ⓜ *Beaubien.*

★ Impasto

$$$ | **MODERN ITALIAN** | This unpretentious, industrial-chic Little Italy restaurant has garnered a great reputation, thanks in part to its celebrity-chef owners, Stefano Faita and Michele Forgione. Start by sharing the artisanal salumi platter, move on to a primi of some of the best fresh pasta dishes in town, like the mafalde all'amatriciana, the melt-in-your-mouth ricotta gnocchi or the *Porchetta del nonno*

(grandpa's pork roast), a must-order if it's on the menu. **Known for:** modern Italian fare; stylish decor; Grandpa's pork roast. ⑤ *Average main: C$30* ✉ *48 rue Dante, Little Italy* ☎ *514/508–6508* ⊕ *www. impastomtl.ca* ⊘ *Closed Sun. and Mon. No lunch Sat.–Wed.* Ⓜ *Jean-Talon.*

Kitchen Galerie

$$$$ | **BISTRO** | With its small ingredient-based menu, this homey bistro is an example of excellence through simplicity. The chefs do everything—the shopping, the chopping, the cooking, the greeting, and the serving, and the focus is on meats, fish, and vegetable dishes all inspired by what local farmers bring to the adjacent Jean-Talon market that morning. **Known for:** gnocchi with lobster, garlic cream confit, mozzarella, and cherry tomatoes; market cuisine; communal seating. ⑤ *Average main: C$35* ✉ *Marché Jean-Talon, 60 rue Jean-Talon Est, Little Italy* ☎ *514/315–8994* ⊕ *www.kitchen-galerie.com* ⊘ *Closed Sun. and Mon.* Ⓜ *Jean-Talon.*

La Cornetteria

$ | **BAKERY** | This lovely little bakery, which magically transports its patrons (or at least, their tastebuds) to Italy, specializes in the cornetto, the Italian version of the croissant. Freshly baked every morning, these delightful pastries are available plain or filled with Nutella, ricotta cream, or almond paste. **Known for:** nutella cornetto; traditional cannolis; stracchino sandwiches. ⑤ *Average main: C$4* ✉ *6528 boul. St-Laurent, Little Italy* ☎ *514/277–8030* ⊕ *www.lacornetteria. com* 🚫 *No credit cards* Ⓜ *Beaubien.*

La Récolte

$$$ | **ECLECTIC** | One could visit La Récolte (literally, "the harvest") every week and never eat the same meal twice, for the blackboard menu is entirely based on locally sourced market finds. In fact, resourceful La Récolte prides itself on serving organic, eco-friendly brunches on Sunday without compromising its creativity. **Known for:** long lines; butternut

squash mille-feuille; leek-and-mushroom Benedictine. ⑤ *Average main: C$30* ✉ *764 rue Bélanger, Rosemont* ☎ *514/508-5450* ⊕ *la-recolte.ca* ⊘ *Closed Mon. and Tue.* Ⓜ *Jean-Talon.*

Le Petit Alep

$$ | **MIDDLE EASTERN** | **FAMILY** | This casual Middle Eastern spot is comfortable and homey but still has style, with music, ivy, exposed-stone walls and a lovely terrasse come summer. The menu is perfect for grazing, and excellent sharing options include the *mouhamara* (pomegranate-and-walnut spread), *sabanegh* (spinach, coriander, and onion pies), *fattouche* (a salad with pita chips and mint), and *yalandji* (vine leaves stuffed with rice, chickpeas, walnuts, and tomatoes). **Known for:** Syrian and Armenian cuisine; atmospheric decor; daily specials. ⑤ *Average main: C$13* ✉ *191 rue Jean-Talon Est, Rosemont* ☎ *514/270–9361* ⊕ *www.petitalep.com* ⊘ *Closed Sun. and Mon. and a few weeks in summer.* Ⓜ *Jean-Talon.*

Manitoba

$$$ | **MODERN CANADIAN** | Bringing a taste of the forest to adoring local foodies, food writers, and adventurous eaters, Manitoba was one of the most percussive restaurant openings of recent years and remains one of the city's top food spots. Serving perhaps the most distinctive fare in the city, with a boreal hunter-gatherer premise, dishes may include rabbit liver pâté and cedar jelly, deer steak, and fried lichen. **Known for:** boreal cuisine; deer steak; foraged foods. ⑤ *Average main: C$30* ✉ *271 rue St-Zotique Ouest, Little Italy* ☎ *514/270–8000* ⊕ *restaurantmanitoba.com* ⊘ *Closed Sun. No lunch Sat.–Wed.* Ⓜ *Parc.*

Montréal Plaza

$$$ | **MODERN CANADIAN** | You won't see anything too familiar on the menu at this fresh, light-filled restaurant with its high ceilings, clean white walls and tablecloths, and modern mix of wood, glass, and sliding industrial windows that open

to outdoor seating in summer. You *will* find whimsical yet unpretentious dishes that surprise and delight—just be sure to order a side of deep-fried Brussels sprouts no matter your main dish. **Known for:** affordable wines; creative menu; desserts. $ *Average main: C$24* ✉ *6230 rue St-Hubert, Rosemont* ☎ *514/903-6230* Ⓜ *Beaubien.*

Pastaga

$$ | CANADIAN | Don't be fooled by the name: Pastaga is not a pasta joint; the name is a slang term for alcoholic drinks composed of anis, specifically pastis. Although famous for its signature dish of crispy pork belly marinated in brown sugar (or maple when in season) and inventive chopped liver "à la juive" (creamy chopped liver, hard-boiled egg, crunchy bagel chips, and tart-marinated onions), Pastaga is best known for its all-natural wine list, which is certain to yield uncommon finds. **Known for:** local celebrity chef; maple crispy pork belly; natural wines. $ *Average main: C$20* ✉ *6389 boul. St-Laurent, Rosemont* ☎ *438/381-6389* ⊕ *www.pastaga.ca* Ⓜ *Beaubien.*

Tapeo

$$ | SPANISH | Bringing tapas uptown, this Spanish-inspired eatery is a chic yet casual place to drink imported wines and share a few small plates. The Tapeo version of the classic *patatas bravas* served with a spicy tomato sauce and aioli is always a good choice, as are the roasted vine tomatoes and the grilled chorizo. **Known for:** patatas bravas; chef's table; house churros. $ *Average main: C$15* ✉ *511 rue Villeray, Villeray* ☎ *514/495-1999* ⊕ *www.restotapeo.com* ⊘ *Closed Mon. No lunch Sat. and Sun.* Ⓜ *Jarry.*

☕ Coffee and Quick Bites

Caffè San Simeon

$ | CAFÉ | In the heart of Little Italy, this historic coffee shop filled with regulars chatting away in Italian, is one of the city's best nonhipster places to get some

excellent brew, be it an espresso, latte, or cappuccino. There also are a few pastries available. **Known for:** old-school Italian café; Malibu coffee; open late and early. $ *Average main: C$5* ✉ *39 rue Dante, Little Italy* ☎ *514/272-7386* ▭ *No credit cards* Ⓜ *Jean-Talon.*

🛍 Shopping

Little Italy is a gourmet shopper's paradise.

FOOD

★ Marché Milano

FOOD/CANDY | A huge expansion in 2013 made this local favorite, in business since 1954, even more popular with customers, who form long lines for prepared foods at the takeout counter. There's a vast selection of cheeses, oils, vinegars, and baked goods. For some elbow room, go during the week. ✉ *6862 boul. St-Laurent, Little Italy* ☎ *514/273-8558* ⊕ *www.milanofruiterie.com* Ⓜ *De Castelnau or Jean-Talon.*

Parc du Mont-Royal

In geological terms, Mont-Royal is just a bump of basaltlike rock worn down by several ice ages to a mere 760 feet. But in the affections of Montrealers it's a Matterhorn. Without a trace of irony, they call it simply *la Montagne* or "the Mountain," and it's easy to see why it's so well loved.

For Montrealers it's a refuge, a semitamed wilderness within the city. It's where you go to get away from it all. And even when you can't get away, you can see the mountain glimmering beyond the skyscrapers and the high-rises—green in summer, gray and white in winter, and gold and crimson in fall.

The nearly 500 acres of forests and meadows were laid out by Frederick Law Olmsted (1822–1903), the man responsible for New York City's Central

It's well worth the métro ride up to Little Italy's busy Marché Jean-Talon to see French Canadian farmers sell their local produce and prepared food.

Park. Olmsted believed that communion with nature could cure body and soul, so much of the park has been left as wild as possible, with narrow paths meandering through tall stands of maples and red oaks. In summer it's full of picnicking families; in winter cross-country skiers and snowshoers take over, while families skate at Lac aux Castors and ride sleds and inner tubes down groomed slopes. The nonprofit organization Les amis de la montagne (🌐 www.lemontroyal.qc.ca/en) offers year-round outdoor and educational activities for locals and visitors, like rowboat rentals, mountain clean-ups, and guided walks in summer and guided snowshoeing excursions followed by a bone-warming hot chocolate or mulled wine in winter.

GETTING HERE AND AROUND

If you're in good shape, you can walk, uphill all the way, from Downtown. Climb rue Peel to the entrance to Parc du Mont-Royal and then up the steep stairway to the top of the mountain. Or you can simply take the métro to the Mont-Royal station and catch Bus 11. If you have a car, there's good parking in Parc du Mont-Royal and at the Oratoire St-Joseph (the latter asks for a contribution of $5 per vehicle Monday to Saturday for anyone not attending a service or coming to pray). Biking up the mountain will test your endurance, but the park has an extensive network of scenic trails.

TIMING

Depending on your interest, you could spend anywhere from a few hours—if you simply just want to see the view—to the entire day here. If you're here for the afternoon, there's a cafeteria in the park for lunch, or you can pick up picnic provisions before you set out.

👁 Sights

Chalet du Mont-Royal

VIEWPOINT | No trip to Montréal is complete without a visit to the terrace in front of the Chalet du Mont-Royal. It's not the only place to get an overview of the city, the river, and the countryside beyond,

but it's the most spectacular. On clear days you can see not only the Downtown skyscrapers, but also Mont-Royal's sister mountains—Monts St-Bruno, St-Hilaire, and St-Grégoire. These isolated peaks, called the Montérégies, or Mountains of the King, rise dramatically from the flat countryside. Be sure to take a look inside the chalet, especially at the murals depicting scenes from Canadian history. There's a snack bar in the back. ⊠ *Off voie Camillien-Houde, Parc du Mont-Royal* ☎ *514/843–8240, ext. 0 for Les amis de la montagnes* ⊕ *www.lemontroyal. qc.ca/en* ✉ *Free* Ⓜ *Mont-Royal, then Bus 11 westbound.*

★ **Croix sur la Montagne** (*Cross atop Mont-Royal*)
RELIGIOUS SITE | Visible from up to 50 miles away on a clear day, the 98-foot-high steel cross at the top of Mont-Royal has been a city landmark since it was erected in 1924, largely with money raised through the efforts of 85,000 high-school students. Once upon a time, it took four hours and the labor of three to replace the 249 electric bulbs used to light the cross; today, the iconic cross is illuminated via a high-tech remote-control LED system. ⊠ *Parc du Mont-Royal* ⊕ *www.lemontroyal.qc.ca.*

Lac aux Castors (*Beaver Lake*)
CITY PARK | FAMILY | Mont-Royal's single body of water, actually a reclaimed bog, is a great place for kids (and parents) to float model boats or rent a rowboat in the summertime. In winter, the lake's frozen surface attracts whole families of skaters, and nearby there's a groomed slope where kids of all ages can ride inner tubes. The glass-fronted Beaver Lake Pavilion is a pleasant bistro that serves lunch and dinner. Skate and cross-country-ski rentals are available downstairs. ⊠ *Off chemin Remembrance, Parc du Mont-Royal* ⊕ *www.lemontroyal.qc.ca* Ⓜ *Mont-Royal, then Bus 11 westbound.*

Maison Smith
MUSEUM | If you need a map of Mont-Royal's extensive hiking trails or want to know about the more than 180 kinds of birds here, the former park keeper's residence is the place to go. It's also a good spot for getting a snack, drink, or souvenir. The pretty little stone house—built in 1858—is the headquarters of Les amis de la montagne (The Friends of the Mountain), a non-profit organization that offers various guided walks—including moonlight snowshoe excursions and cross-country ski lessons in winter around the mountain and in nearby areas. ⊠ *1260 chemin Remembrance, Parc du Mont-Royal* ☎ *514/843–8240* ⊕ *www. lemontroyal.qc.ca* Ⓜ *Mont-Royal, then bus 11 westbound.*

Observatoire de l'Est
VIEWPOINT | If you're just driving across Mont-Royal, be sure to stop for a few moments at its eastern lookout for a view of the Stade Olympique and the east end of the city. Tourists enjoy the location as it's a great photo spot. ⊠ *Voie Camillien-Houde, Parc du Mont-Royal* Ⓜ *Mont-Royal.*

Côte-des-Neiges

Not too many tourists venture north and east of Parc du Mont-Royal, but the primarily residential neighborhood of Côte-des-Neiges has much to offer.

One of Montréal's most-visited sites—the Oratoire St-Joseph (St. Joseph's Oratory)—sits atop the northern slope of Mont-Royal, dominating the surrounding neighborhood of Côte-des-Neiges. More than 2 million people of all faiths visit the shrine every year. The most devout pilgrims climb the staircase leading to the main door on their knees, pausing on each of its 99 steps to pray.

Even without the Oratoire (as well as the Cimetière de Notre-Dame-des-Neiges, another site worth seeing),

Parc du Mont-Royal, Westmount, and Côte-des-Neiges

KEY

- 🔵 Sights
- 🔴 Restaurants
- 🟠 Quick Bites
- Ⓜ Métro Station
- 🚌 Bus 11 Route
- 🚲 Bike Route

Côte-des-Neiges is a district worth visiting. It's also an area where the dominant languages are neither English nor French.

It's largely working-class immigrants who live here—Filipino, Latin American, Southeast Asian, West Indian, Arab, Jewish, Chinese, and most recently people from Eastern Europe and Africa. It's also home to a sizable number of students, many of whom attend the Université de Montréal, as well as other smaller surrounding colleges and universities.

GETTING HERE AND AROUND
Côte-des-Neiges is bordered by avenue Decelles to the north and the Cimetière de Notre-Dame-des-Neiges to the south. It's easy to get here by public transit, either the métro to the Côte-des-Neiges station or the 166 Bus from the Guy-Concordia métro station to chemin Queen-Mary. If you take a car—which is not a bad idea if you plan to visit the Parc du Mont-Royal as well—it's usually easy to get a parking space at the Oratoire St-Joseph (a contribution of $5 per vehicle is requested Monday to Saturday, except for those attending services or coming to the Oratoire to pray).

WHEN TO GO
Côte-des-Neiges bustles during the day, but is a little quieter at night.

⊙ Sights

Cimetière de Notre-Dame-des-Neiges (*Our Lady of the Snows Cemetery*)
CEMETERY | At 343 acres, Canada's largest cemetery is not much smaller than the neighboring **Parc du Mont-Royal**, and, as long as you just count the living, it's usually a lot less crowded. You don't have to be morbid to wander the graveyard's 55 km (34 miles) of tree-shaded paths and roadways past the tombs of hundreds of prominent artists, poets, intellectuals, politicians, and clerics. Among them is Calixa Lavallée (1842–91), who wrote "O Canada," the country's national anthem.
■ TIP→ The cemetery offers some guided tours in summer. Phone ahead for details. ⊠ *4601 chemin de la Côte-des-Neiges, Côte-des-Neiges* ☎ *514/735–1361* ⊕ *www.cimetierenotredamedesneiges.ca* Ⓜ *Côte-des-Neiges, then Bus 165 southbound.*

★ Cimetière Mont-Royal
CEMETERY | If you find yourself humming "Getting to Know You" as you explore Mont-Royal Cemetery's 165 acres, blame it on the graveyard's most famous permanent guest, Anna Leonowens (1834–1915). She was the real-life model for the heroine of the Rodgers and Hammerstein musical *The King and I*. The cemetery—established in 1852 by the Anglican, Presbyterian, Unitarian, and Baptist churches—is laid out like a terraced garden, with footpaths that meander between crab-apple trees and past Japanese lilacs. If you're lucky, you may spot a fox sunbathing on one of the tombstones in winter. ⊠ *1297 chemin de la Forêt, Côte-des-Neiges* ☎ *514/279–7358* ⊕ *www.mountroyalcem.com* Ⓜ *Mont-Royal, then Bus 11 westbound.*

★ Oratoire St-Joseph (*St. Joseph's Oratory*)
RELIGIOUS SITE | Each year some 2 million people from all over North America and beyond visit St. Joseph's Oratory. The most devout Catholics climb the 99 steps to its front door on their knees. It is the world's largest and most popular shrine dedicated to the earthly father of Jesus (Canada's patron saint), and it's all the work of a man named Brother André Besette (1845–1937).

By worldly standards Brother André didn't have much going for him, but he had a deep devotion to St. Joseph and an iron will. In 1870 he joined the Holy Cross religious order and was assigned to work as a doorkeeper at the college the order operated just north of Mont-Royal. In 1904 he began building a chapel on the mountainside across the road to honor his favorite saint, and the rest is history. Thanks to reports

3

Montréal CÔTE-DES-NEIGES

Saint Joseph's Oratory is Canada's largest church and claims to have one of the largest domes in the world.

of miraculous cures attributed to St. Joseph's intercession, donations started to pour in, and Brother André was able to start work replacing his modest shrine with something more substantial. The result, which wasn't completed until after his death, is one of the most triumphal pieces of church architecture in North America.

The oratory and its gardens dominate Mont-Royal's northwestern slope. Its copper dome—one of the largest in the world—can be seen from miles away. The interior of the main church is equally grand, although it's also quite austere. The best time to visit it is on Sunday for the 11am solemn mass, when the sanctuary is brightly lit and the sweet voices of Les Petits Chanteurs de Mont-Royal—the city's best boys' choir—fill the nave with music.

The crypt is shabbier than its big brother upstairs but more welcoming. In a long, narrow room behind the crypt, 10,000 votive candles glitter before a dozen carved murals extolling the virtues of St.

Joseph; the walls are hung with crutches discarded by those said to have been cured. Just beyond is the simple tomb of Brother André, who was canonized a saint in 2010. His preserved heart is displayed in a glass case in one of several galleries between the crypt and the main church.

High on the mountain, east of the main church, is a garden commemorating the Passion of Christ, with life-size representations of the 14 stations of the cross. On the west side of the church is Brother André's original chapel, with pressed-tin ceilings and plaster saints that is, in many ways, more moving than the church that overshadows it. Note: the oratoire operates a shuttle bus for visitors who aren't up to the steep climb from the main parking lot to the entrance of the crypt church. The main church is several stories above that, but escalators and two elevators ease the ascent. *Renovations are underway, so expect some potential disruption during your visit.* ✉ *3800 chemin Queen Mary,*

Côte-des-Neiges ☎ 514/733–8211, 877/672–8647 ⊕ www.saint-joseph.org ✉ Free. Parking: $5 contribution of $C5 per vehicle requested (except for those attending services or coming to pray). C$4 for museum. Ⓜ Côte-des-Neiges.

🍴 Restaurants

Duc de Lorraine
$$ | CAFÉ | A light croissant or rich pastry from the city's oldest patisserie makes for a nice break after visiting the Parc Mont-Royal or Oratoire St-Joseph. For lunch, try one of the quiches, a sandwich on a fresh, chewy baguette, or the soup du jour followed by a scoop of homemade ice cream or a *tartelette poire et amande* (pear and almond tart). **Known for:** Parisian-style pastry shop; ample patio; almond paste croissant. Ⓢ *Average main: C$15 ✉ 5002 Côte-des-Neiges, Côte-des-Neiges* ☎ *514/731–4128* ⊕ *www.ducdelorraine. ca* Ⓜ *Côte-des-Neiges.*

🎭 Performing Arts

Segal Centre for the Performing Arts
THEATER | English-language favorites like *Harvey, Inherit the Wind* and *Joseph and the Amazing Technicolor Dreamcoat* get frequent billing at this Côte-des-Neiges venue, along with locally written works. The center is best known, however, as the home to the **Dora Wasserman Yiddish Theatre,** which presents such musical works as *The Jazz Singer* and *The Pirates of Penzance* in Yiddish. ✉ *5170 chemin de la Côte-Ste-Catherine, Côte-des-Neiges* ☎ *514/739–2301, 514/739–7944* ⊕ *www. segalcentre.org* Ⓜ *Côte-Ste-Catherine.*

Hochelaga-Maisonneuve

The neighborhood of Hochelaga-Maisonneuve, aka **HoMa,** is one of the best spots to go if you're craving green space, plus it has one of Montréal's best markets.

Free Church Tours 👁

Nearly all of Montréal's numerous historic churches offer free admission, and some, like St. Joseph's Oratory, one of the world's most visited shrines, offer guided tours. The cost for a guided tour of St. Joseph's Oratory, held at 1:30 and 3 in summer; by appointment only in winter) is $6 per person.

In fact, it's worth the trip on the métro's Green Line just to see the four institutions that make up Montréal's Space for Life, an innovative natural science museum complex—the first in the world to link humans with nature. It includes the Jardin Botanique (Botanical Garden); the Insectarium, which houses the world's largest collection of bugs (closed for renovations until likely well into 2021); the Biodôme, a great place to experience different ecosystems under one roof; and the stunning Rio Tinto Alcan Planetarium.

Parc Maisonneuve is a lovely green area, and an ideal place for a stroll or a picnic. The leaning tower that supports the roof of the Stade Olympique (Olympic Stadium), which played host to the 1976 Summer Olympics, dominates the skyline here. The area is largely working-class residential, but it's becoming a *quartier branché*, or hip 'hood, with some good restaurants and little shops along rue Ontario Est.

Until 1918, when it was annexed by Montréal, the east-end district of Maisonneuve was a city unto itself, a booming, prosperous industrial center full of factories making everything from shoes to cheese. The neighborhood was also packed with houses for the almost entirely French-Canadian workforce, who kept the whole machine humming.

KEY

1 Sights
M Métro Stations
🚲 Bike Route

Hochelaga-Maisonneuve

Maisonneuve was also the site of one of Canada's earliest experiments in urban planning. The Dufresne brothers, a pair of prosperous shoe manufacturers, built a series of grand civic buildings along rue Morgan—many of which still stand—including a theater, public baths, and a bustling market, as well as Parc Maisonneuve. All this was supposed to make working-class life more bearable, but World War I put an end to the brothers' plans and Maisonneuve became part of Montréal, twinned with the east-end district of Hochelaga.

GETTING HERE AND AROUND

It's not necessary to drive to the area, as the Pie-IX and Viau métro stops on the Green Line provide easy access to all the sites, including the Insectarium and the Jardin Botanique. For bikers, it's a straight shot across the path on rue Rachel.

TIMING

If traveling with kids, you'll probably want to dedicate more time to exploring the area to see the sites. One of the city's major markets—Marché Maisonneuve—is on the corner of rue Ontario and avenue Bennett, and is well worth a stop.

⊙ Sights

Biodôme

NATURE PRESERVE | FAMILY | Not everyone thought it was a great idea to transform an Olympic velodrome into a natural-history exhibit, but the result is one of the city's most popular attractions, part of the Space for Life complex. Four ecosystems—a boreal forest, a tropical forest, a polar landscape, and the St. Lawrence

River—are under one climate-controlled dome. You follow pathways through each environment, observing indigenous flora and fauna. *The tropical forest is as hot and humid as the real thing, and the Québec and Arctic exhibits can be frigid. If you want to stay comfortable, dress in layers.* ⊠ *4777 av. Pierre-de-Coubertin, Hochelaga-Maisonneuve* ☎ *514/868–3000* ⊕ *espacepourlavie.ca* ⊠ *C$20.50* Ⓜ *Viau or Pie-IX.*

Château Dufresne

HOUSE | The adjoining homes of a pair of shoe manufacturers, Oscar and Marius Dufresne, provide a glimpse into the lives of Montréal's francophone bourgeoisie in the early 20th century. The brothers built their beaux arts palace in 1916 along the lines of the Petit-Trianon in Paris, and lived in it with their families—Oscar in the eastern half and Marius in the western half.

Worth searching out are the domestic scenes on the walls of the Petit Salon, where Oscar's wife entertained friends. Her brother-in-law relaxed with his friends in a smoking room decked out like a Turkish lounge. During the house's incarnation as a boys' school in the 1950s, the Eudist priests who ran it covered the room's frieze of nymphs and satyrs with a modest curtain that their charges lifted at every opportunity. ■ TIP→ **A digital tour by tablet is available.** ⊠ *2929 rue Jeanne-d'Arc, Hochelaga-Maisonneuve* ☎ *514/259–9201* ⊕ *www.chateaudufresne.com* ⊠ *C$14* ⊗ *Closed Mon. and Tues.* Ⓜ *Pie-IX.*

★ Jardin Botanique (*Botanical Garden*)

GARDEN | **FAMILY** | Creating one of the world's great botanical gardens in a city with a winter as harsh as Montréal's was no mean feat, and the result is that no matter how brutal it gets in January there's one corner of the city where it's always summer. With 181 acres of plantings in summer and 10 greenhouses open all year, Space for Life Montréal's Jardin Botanique is the second-largest

attraction of its kind in the world (after England's Kew Gardens). It grows more than 26,000 species of plants, and among its 30 thematic gardens are a rose garden, an alpine garden, and—a favorite with the kids—a poisonous-plant garden.

You can attend traditional tea ceremonies in the Japanese Garden, which has one of the best bonsai collections in the West, or wander among the native birches and maples of the Jardin des Premières-Nations (First Nations Garden). The Jardin de Chine (Chinese Garden), with its pagoda and waterfall, will transport you back to the Ming dynasty. In the fall, all three cultural gardens host magical mixes of light, color, plant life and sculpture during the annual Gardens of Light spectacle. ⊠ *4101 rue Sherbrooke Est, Hochelaga-Maisonneuve* ☎ *514/872–1400* ⊕ *www.espacepourlavie.ca* ⊠ *C$20.50* ⊗ *Closed Mon. Nov.–mid-May* Ⓜ *Pie-IX or Viau.*

Maisonneuve

NEIGHBORHOOD | World War I and the Depression killed early 20th-century plans to turn this industrial center into a model city with broad boulevards, grand public buildings, and fine homes, but just three blocks south of the Olympic site a few fragments of that dream have survived the passage of time.

A magnificent beaux arts building, site of the old public market, which has a 20-foot-tall bronze statue of a farm woman, stands at the northern end of tree-lined avenue Morgan. Farmers and butchers have moved into the modern building next door that houses the **Marché Maisonneuve**, which has become one of the city's major markets, along with Marché Jean-Talon and Marché Atwater. The old market is now a community center and the site of summer shows and concerts.

Monumental staircases and a heroic rooftop sculpture embellish the public baths

across the street. The **Théâtre Denise Pelletier,** at the corner of rues Ste-Catherine Est and Morgan, has a lavish Italianate interior; **Fire Station No. 1,** at 4300 rue Notre-Dame Est, was inspired by Frank Lloyd Wright's Unity Temple in suburban Chicago; and the sumptuously decorated **Église Très-Saint-Nom-de-Jésus,** has one of the most powerful organs in North America. The 198-acre **Parc Maisonneuve,** stretching north of the botanical garden, is a lovely place for a stroll. ⊠ *Hochelaga-Maisonneuve* Ⓜ *Pie-IX or Viau.*

Rio Tinto Alcan Planetarium

OBSERVATORY | FAMILY | In early 2013, Montréal got a new, ultramodern, C$48 million planetarium, one of only a handful of planetariums worldwide to have two circular theaters—one for astronomy exhibits and the other a high-tech multimedia venue. Part of the Space for Life complex, this state-of-the-art facility delivers a futuristic experience unlike any other. The permanent exhibit, EXO: Our Search for Life in the Universe, lets the whole family have fun exploring life on Earth and (perhaps) in the universe through interactive and hands-on stations. *Hours vary seasonally.* ⊠ *4801 av. Pierre-de-Coubertin, Hochelaga-Maisonneuve* ☎ *514/868–3000* ⊕ *www.espacepourlavie.ca/en/planetarium* ☎ *C$20.50* ☽ *Closed Mon. Sept.–June* Ⓜ *Viau.*

🎭 Performing Arts

Théâtre Denise Pelletier

THEATER | With an objective to introduce younger audiences to theater, the Pelletier, which celebrated its 50th year in 2014, puts on French-language productions in a beautifully restored Italianate hall. It's a 15-minute walk from the métro station. ⊠ *4353 rue Ste-Catherine Est, Hochelaga-Maisonneuve* ☎ *514/253–8974* ⊕ *www.denise-pelletier.qc.ca* Ⓜ *Joliette or Pie-IX.*

🛍 Shopping

TOYS

Franc Jeu

TOYS | FAMILY | The antithesis of the bigbox toy store, this shop carries Corolle dolls from France, as well as educational toys from Québec's Jouets Boom and Gladius lines. ⊠ *Place Versailles, 7275 rue Sherbrooke Est, Hochelaga-Maisonneuve* ☎ *514/352–1771* ⊕ *www.francjeumontreal.com* Ⓜ *Radisson.*

The Islands

The two islands just east of the city in the St. Lawrence River—Île Ste-Hélène, formed by nature, and Île Notre-Dame, created with the stone rubble excavated from the construction of Montréal's métro—are now used for Montréal's indoor-outdoor playground, Parc Jean-Drapeau.

Expo '67, which the World's Fair staged to celebrate the centennial of the Canadian federation, was brought here by the city's then-mayor, Jean Drapeau. It was the biggest party in Montréal's history, and it marked a defining moment in its evolution as a modern metropolis.

The spirit of coming here for excitement and thrills lives on. La Ronde, a major amusement park that has the world's highest double wooden roller coaster, is on Île Ste-Hélène. On Île Notre-Dame, there's Casino de Montréal, which includes gaming tables and more than 3,200 slot machines. The casino might be the only vestige of nightlife on the islands.

For a completely different kind of fun, however, there's much to learn about the Islands' history. At the Stewart Museum at the Old Fort, kids will love watching soldiers in colonial uniforms hold flag-raising ceremonies twice a day, rehearse maneuvers, and even practice drills and fire muskets.

Golfing in Montréal

Teeing up in Montréal

Montréal golf enthusiasts have several excellent golf courses available to them, many less than a half-hour drive from Downtown. If you're willing to trek a bit farther (about 45 minutes), you'll find some of the best golfing in the province. For a complete listing of the many golf courses in the area, Tourisme Québec (⊕ www.bonjourquebec.com) is the best place to start.

Club de Golf Métropolitain Anjou *(Anjou Metropolitan Golf Club).* One of the longest courses in the province, the Championship course features an undulating landscape with five lakes and some tricky bunkers, all calling for accurate shots. Beginners and improvers can hone their skills on the short Executive course, where more accomplished players will also enjoy a quick round. A clubhouse featuring a restaurant, several banquet halls, a pro shop with an indoor practice range (winter only), and an outdoor driving range all serve to make this a top-notch facility. A dress code is in effect. The club is in Anjou, a 20-minute drive from Downtown Montréal. ⊠ *9555 boul. du Golf* ☎ *514/353–5353* ⊕ *www.golfmetropolitainanjou.com* ✉ *Championship Course, C$29–C$53; Executive Course, C$15* ⵌ *Championship Course: 18 holes, 7005 yards, par 3, 4, and 5; Executive Course: 6 holes, 1022 yards, par 3* ✆ *Facilities: Driving range, golf carts, restaurant* Ⓜ *Honoré-Beaugrand.*

The Falcon. Designed by Graham Cooke, this course winds through a verdant, well-wooded landscape dotted with water hazards and sand traps, and offers an exciting challenge. Five sets of tees accommodate different skill levels. It's 25 minutes west of Downtown in the picturesque and largely Anglophone village of Hudson (which is worth a visit in itself). ⊠ *59 rue Cambridge, Hudson* ☎ *450/458–1997* ⊕ *www.falcongolf.ca* ✉ *C$40–C$58 weekdays, C$20–C$72 weekends and holidays* ⵌ *18 holes, 7096 yards, par 72* ✆ *Facilities: Driving range, putting green, golf carts, rental clubs, lessons, restaurant, clubhouse, practice facilities.*

Golf Dorval. The two original courses here, designed by Graham Cooke, were combined into a single challenging par-72 golf course with a rolling parkland setting. There are four levels of difficulty, finishing with a long, narrow par-4 18th hole with a slope up to the green. A lighted driving range with 50 stations and two putting greens are also available. ⊠ *2000 av. Reverchon, Dorval* ☎ *514/631–4653* ⊕ *www.golfdorval.com* ✉ *C$33–C$53* ⵌ *18 holes, 6643 yards, par 72* ✆ *Facilities: Driving range, putting green, golf carts, rental clubs, lessons, snack bar.*

Golf Ste-Rose. With lovely views of the Rivière des Mille-Îles, hardwood forests, and myriad ponds, this course may be the most beautiful in Québec. It's a short hop over the bridge to the island of Laval. The course features four sets of tees to accommodate different skill levels. Recently renovated to improve the pace of play, the 18-hole course was designed by John Watson, one of the great names of Canadian golf course architecture. ⊠ *1400 boul. Mattawa, Ste-Rose* ☎ *450/628–6072, 450/628–3573* ⊕ *www.golfsterose.com/en* ✉ *C$27–C$55* ⵌ *18 holes, 6134 yards, par 70* ✆ *Facilities: Driving range, golf carts, rental clubs, restaurant, bar.*

GETTING HERE AND AROUND

Both Île Ste-Hélène and Île Notre-Dame are very accessible. You can drive to them via the Pont de la Concorde or the Pont Jacques-Cartier, take the ferry from the Old Port to Île Ste-Hélène (seasonal), or take the métro from the Berri-UQAM station to Jean-Drapeau.

TIMING

If you're traveling with kids, there's enough here to keep them occupied for a full day, especially in nice weather. Because the Islands are so easy to get to with the ferry, visiting can be tacked on to time spent in Old Montréal.

Sights

Biosphère

BUILDING | FAMILY | Nothing captures the exuberance of Expo '67 better than the geodesic dome designed by Buckminster Fuller (1895–1983) as the American Pavilion. It's only a skeleton now—the polymer panels that protected the U.S. exhibits from the elements were burned out in a fire long ago—but it's still an eye-catching sight, like something plucked from a science-fiction movie.

Science of a nonfictional kind, however, is explored in the special environmental center the federal government has built in the middle of the dome. It focuses on the challenges of preserving the Great Lakes and St. Lawrence River system, but it has lively and interactive exhibits on climate change, sustainable energy, and air pollution. Kids and others can use games and interactive displays arranged around a large model of the waterway to explore how shipping, tourism, water supplies, and hydroelectric power are affected. ⊠ *Île Ste-Hélène, 160 chemin Tour-de-l'Îsle, The Islands* ☎ *514/496–8435* ⊕ *www.parcjeandrapeau.com/en/biosphere-environment-museum-montreal* ⊠ *C$15* ⊗ *Closed Mon. and Tues. Jan.–May; Closed mid-Dec.–mid-Jan.* Ⓜ *Jean-Drapeau.*

Casino de Montréal

CASINO—SIGHT | You have to be at least 18 to visit Montréal's government-owned casino, but you don't have to be a gambler. The 24-hour-a-day, fully renovated casino now houses four bars and five restaurants, ranging from deli style to gourmet, including l'Atelier de Joël Robuchon, a French celebrity chef with fine dining outposts around the globe. You can even come just to look at the architecture—the main building was the French pavilion at Expo '67. But if you do want to risk the family fortune, there are more than 3,000 slot machines, a keno lounge, a high-stakes gaming area, and 120 tables for playing blackjack, baccarat, roulette, craps, and various types of poker. There is also music, including cabaret. ⊠ *1 av. du Casino, Île Notre-Dame, The Islands* ☎ *514/392–2746, 800/665–2274* ⊕ *www.casino-de-montreal.com* ⊠ *Free* Ⓜ *Jean-Drapeau, then Bus 167.*

La Ronde

AMUSEMENT PARK/WATER PARK | FAMILY | Every year, it seems, this amusement park, at the eastern end of Île Ste-Hélène, adds some new and monstrous way to scare the living daylights (and maybe even your lunch) out of you. The most recent additions include Chaos, a single loop that takes you forward, backward, and upside down while sitting face-to-face with other riders; the Titan, a giant swaying pendulum that will have you—or the kids—soaring and spinning 148 feet above the park, traveling at speeds up to 70 miles per hour; and the Maison Rouge, a haunted house and "labyrinth of terror." Demon, an extreme ride, will—at high speed (of course)—twist you, twirl you, and turn you upside down, then douse you with water jets. The park also aims to terrify you with such stomach-turning champions as the Endor, the Goliath, the Vampire, Monstre, and Vol Ultime. For the less daring, there are Ferris wheels, boat rides, and kiddie rides. The popular **International Fireworks Competition** is held here on Saturday

162

The Islands

and Wednesday in late June and July. ✉ *22 chemin Macdonald, Île Ste-Hélène* ☎ *514/397–2000* ⊕ *www.sixflags.com/ larondeen* 🎟 *C$72, or from C$52 when purchased online at least one day before your visit* ⊙ *Hours vary seasonally* Ⓜ *Jean-Drapeau.*

★ Parc Jean-Drapeau
BEACH—SIGHT | FAMILY | Île Ste-Hélène and Île Notre-Dame now constitute a single park named, fittingly enough, for Jean Drapeau (1916–99), the visionary (and spendthrift) mayor who built the métro and brought the city both the 1967 World's Fair and the 1976 Olympics. The park includes La Ronde (a major amusement park), acres of flower gardens, a beach with filtered water, the Formula 1 Grand Prix Circuit Gilles Villeneuve, performance spaces, and the Casino de Montréal. There's history, too, at the Old Fort, where soldiers in colonial uniforms display the military methods used in ancient wars. In winter you can skate on the old Olympic rowing basin or slide down iced trails on an inner tube. ✉ *The Islands* ☎ *514/872–6120* ⊕ *www.parcje-andrapeau.com* Ⓜ *Jean-Drapeau.*

Stewart Museum
MUSEUM | Housed in the arsenal of Île Ste-Hélène's 1820s Old Fort, the Stewart Museum encompasses two floors full of interesting historical objects. The permanent collection has close to 27,000 artifacts consisting of military objects, images, rare books, maps, and pieces of weaponry, all of which document the history of Montréal, l'Île Ste-Hélène, and the surrounding area, from the early First Nations to today. Open year-round, the Stewart Museum is definitely worth a visit for those interested in the history of New France. ✉ *20 chemin du Tour-de-l'Île, Île Ste-Hélène, The Islands* ☎ *514/861–6701* ⊕ *www.stewart-mu-seum.org* 🎟 *C$15* ⊙ *Closed Mon.* Ⓜ *Jean-Drapeau.*

🏃 Activities

RACING
Grand Prix
AUTO RACING | In early June you can join the glitterati of Europe and North America in the grandstand to watch million-dollar Formula One cars shriek around the the Gilles Villeneuve Circuit, a 4.3-km (2.7-mile) track—if you're lucky enough and rich enough to get a ticket, that is. This is the kind of crowd that uses Perrier to mop up caviar stains from the refreshment tables. During the off season, the track is accessible to everyone. Locals spend sunny summer weekends cycling, rollerblading, and taking walks around this world-famous circuit.

Tickets start at C$90 for general admission (one day) and from C$200 for grandstand tickets (three days). Be sure to book your room early for that entire week, as hotels operate at maximum capacity (and maximum cost). ✉ *Parc Jean Drapeau, 222 Circuit Gilles Villeneuve, The Islands* ☎ *514/350–0000, 855/790–1245 toll-free* ⊕ *www.circuit-gillesvilleneuve.ca.*

SWIMMING
Parc-Plage l'Île Notre-Dame (*Plage Jean-Doré*)
SWIMMING | The city's man-made beach on the west side of Île Notre-Dame probably has the cleanest water (tested and monitored) in Montréal. The dress code at the neighboring casino might ban camisoles and strapless tops, but here anything seems to go on hot summer days, when the beach is a sea of oiled bodies. You get the distinct impression that swimming is not uppermost on the minds of many of the scantily clad hordes. If you do want to go in, however, the water is filtered and closely monitored for contamination, and there are lifeguards on duty. A shop rents swimming and boating paraphernalia, and there's a restaurant and picnic areas. ✉ *The Islands* ☎ *514/872–6120* ⊕ *www.*

Did You Know?

A relic of Canada's World's Fair Exposition in 1967, the massive Biosphère has withstood fire and ice storms to become a museum devoted to the environment.

parcjeandrapeau.com ⌖ *C\$9, C\$5.50 after 4pm* Ⓜ *Jean-Drapeau, then Bus 167.*

Sud-Ouest and Lachine

Low rent and proximity to Downtown make the Sud-Ouesta an historically industrial and poor, working-class area. It consists of Verdun, Saint-Henri, Griffintown, and La petite Bourgogne (aka Little Burgundy). The latter three form what has officially become known as Les Quartiers du Canal, or the Canal Neighborhoods, a gentrifying area lining the Lachine Canal that was once home to factory workers, railway workers, and jazz musicians. These days, this area is better known for its small chef-owned restaurants, design boutiques, antique shops, and condos populated by young professionals and creatives. Take the time to explore the Griffintown Design District, spanning rues Peel, Ann, Wellington, William, and Notre-Dame O., to get a taste of its 50 or so creative furniture design stores, art galleries, architects' ateliers, and trendy cafés and restos. The bilingual Design District booklet can be uploaded from ⊕ *lesquartiersducanal.com/en/griffintowndesigndistrict.*

If you want to work up an appetite for lunch—or just get some exercise—rent a bike on rue de la Commune, in Old Montréal, and ride west along the 14-km (9-mile) Lachine Canal through what used to be Montréal's industrial heartland to the shores of Lac St-Louis. You could stop at the Marché Atwater to buy some cheese, bread, wine and fruit for a picnic in the lakefront park at the end of the trail. If pedaling sounds too energetic, hop aboard an excursion boat and dine more formally in one of the century-old homes that line the waterfront in Lachine, the historic city borough at the western end of the canal that was once the staging point for the lucrative fur trade.

◉ Sights

Fur Trade at Lachine National Historic Site
MUSEUM | Located in the waterfront park at the end of the Lachine Canal, on the shores of Lac St. Louis, this 1803 stone warehouse has been converted into a museum that commemorates the industry that dominated Canada's early history. ✉ *1255 boul. St-Joseph, Lachine* ☎ *888/773–8888, 514/637–7433* ⊕ *www.pc.gc.ca* ⌖ *C\$4.*

Lachine Canal National Historic Site
TRAIL | FAMILY | The canal is all about leisure—biking, rollerblading, strolls along the water and picnicking—but it wasn't always so. Built in 1825 to get boats and cargo around the treacherous Lachine Rapids, it quickly became a magnet for all sorts of industries. But when the St. Lawrence Seaway opened in 1959, allowing large cargo ships to sail straight from the Atlantic to the Great Lakes without stopping in Montréal, the canal closed to navigation and became an illicit dumping ground for old cars and the bodies of victims of underworld killings. The area around it degenerated into an industrial slum.

A federal agency rescued the site in 1978, planting lawns and trees along the old canal, transforming it into a long, narrow park, or *parc linéaire*. Some of the the abandoned canneries, sugar refineries, and steelworks have since been converted into desirable residential and commercial condominiums. The bicycle path is the first link in the more than 97 km (60 miles) of bike trails that make up the **Pôle des Rapides** (*514/364–4490* ⊕ *www.mtl.org/en/what-to-do/heritage-and-architecture/pole-des-rapides-montreal*).

Two permanent exhibits at the **Lachine Canal Visitor Services Centre**, at the western end of the canal, explain its history and construction. The center also has a shop and lookout terrace. ✉ *Lachine*

166

Sud-Ouest and Lachine

GRIFFINTOWN

LITTLE BURGUNDY

Vinet Park

Éclusiers Park

LIONEL-GROULX

CHARLEVOIX METRO

Marguerite Bourgeoys Park

LACHINE

TO LACHINE CANAL NATIONAL HISTORIC SITE (approx 11km)

Parc Aqueduc de Montréal

Canal de l'Aqueduc

Lachine Canal

St. Lawrence River

DE L'ÉGLISE

VERDUN

LACHINE

Port De Plaisance ◆
Rene Levesque Park ◆

St. Lawrence River

KEY

1 Exploring Sights
1 Restaurants
1 Quick Bites
1 Hotels
M Métro Stations

☎ 514/283–6054 ⊕ www.pc.gc.ca ✉ Free
Ⓜ Angrignon, then bus 195.

🍴 Restaurants

Blackstrap BBQ

$$ | SOUTHERN | FAMILY | Memphis-style barbecue is the name of the game at this popular, self-serve spot owned and operated by a champion pit master honing his skill behind the smoker and Missouri-imported barbecue pits. Pork, brisket, chicken, and ribs all get a secret-rub treatment and are then cooked slowly for up to 16 hours. **Known for:** "burnt ends" poutine; Memphis-style barbecue; locally sourced meat. ⑤ Average main: C$15 ✉ 4436 rue Wellington, Verdun ☎ 514/507–6772 ⊕ www.blackstrapbbq.ca Ⓜ De l'Église.

⭐ Joe Beef

$$$$ | MODERN CANADIAN | Eating out at this establishment in the St. Henri/Little Burgundy neighborhood is a little like being invited to a dinner party by a couple of friends who just happen to be top-notch chefs. Everything written on the chalkboard menu is simple, hearty, and just delicious, from the fresh oysters to the organic rib steak and the now famous lobster spaghetti. **Known for:** lobster spaghetti; leafy patio; celebrity chef. ⑤ Average main: C$38 ✉ 2491 rue Notre-Dame Ouest, Verdun ☎ 514/935–6504 ⊕ www.joebeef.ca Ⓢ Closed Sun. and Mon. No lunch Ⓜ Lionel-Groulx.

Restaurant le H4C

$$$$ | CANADIAN | Housed inside a stately former bank topped by a clock tower, this well-worth-the-trek restaurant uses the bank's old vault as a walk-in cellar, while the dining room features stone walls and elegant leather chairs. Main dishes are hard to predict because of the product-driven cuisine but regularly features local and seasonal ingredients such as snow crab, Québec halibut, asparagus, and fiddleheads—but one thing that indeed does not change is the dedication and resourcefulness of the chef. **Known**

for: seasonal tasting menus only (C$85); old bank building; delicious brunch menu (C$45). ⑤ Average main: C$85 ✉ 538 pl. St-Henri, Verdun ☎ 514/316–7234 ⊕ www.leh4c.com Ⓢ Closed Mon. and Tues. No dinner Sun. Ⓜ Place St-Henri.

⭐ Le Vin Papillon

$$ | MODERN ITALIAN | First and foremost a wine bar, this tiny, atmospheric 30-seat spot also dishes out delicious vegetable-centric, market-based cuisine. The cuisine features local and seasonal ingredients, and the flavors are simple enough to go well with the stars of the show: the many wines on offer. **Known for:** Italian tapas; Brussels sprouts la plancha; extensive wine list. ⑤ Average main: C$15 ✉ 2519 rue Notre-Dame Ouest, Verdun ⊕ vinpapillon.com Ⓢ Closed Sun. and Mon. Ⓜ Lionel-Groulx.

Nora Gray

$$$ | MODERN ITALIAN | The crowd that fills this casual and lively spot nightly is hip, and the simple, modern Southern Italian comfort food and impeccable service keeps them coming back. Start your meal with the roasted cauliflower frittata or the Dungeness crab salad with confit Meyer lemon and deer carpaccio. **Known for:** Southern Italian cuisine; celery root Marsala, mixed mushrooms and hazelnuts; classic old-world wine list. ⑤ Average main: C$30 ✉ 1391 rue St-Jacques, Verdun ☎ 514/419–6672 ⊕ noragray.com Ⓢ Closed Sun. and Mon. Ⓜ Lucien L'Allier.

Satay Brothers

$ | ASIAN | Bringing southeast Asia to southwest Montréal, Satay Brothers is operated by two brothers obsessed with the street food found in Singapore, Malaysia, Thailand, and Cambodia. The eclectic and oddly charming space— think red walls, illuminated Chinese lanterns, a mishmash of Asian patterns and decor—features communal seating and a long bar facing the kitchen, which fires out steamed pork buns, laksa soup, papaya salad and, of course, satays to keep the constant and lively crowd fed.

Under the Big Tent

Montréal's reinvention of the ancient art of the circus began in the 1980s, when two street performers, Guy Laliberté and Daniel Gauthier, founded the now world-famous Cirque du Soleil. But it didn't stop there. The city is also home to a huge complex, out beyond Mont-Royal in the St-Michel district, housing Canada's National Circus School, En Piste (Circus Arts National Network), and Cirque du Soleil's head office. The school attracts budding acrobats and clowns from all over the world, as well as several other smaller schools, and puts on several performances throughout the year at the complex's performance venue, TOHU Cité des Arts du Cirque (⊕ *www.tohu.ca*). Montréal has become so synonymous with the circus arts that for 10 days each July since 2010, the city plays host to Montréal Complètement Cirque, a circus festival that transforms theaters, city streets, parks, and sidewalks into stages showcasing high-flying acrobatic performances by talented artists from around the world.

Cirque du Soleil. This amazing circus is one of Montréal's great success stories. The company—founded in 1984 by a pair of street performers—has completely changed people's idea of what a circus can do. Its shows, now an international phenomenon, use no animals. Instead, colorful acrobatics flirt with the absurd through the use of music, humor, dance, and glorious (and often risqué) costumes. The Cirque has companies in Las Vegas and one each in Orlando and Los Angeles—but none in Montréal (though its HQ and a circus school are located in the northern part of the city). Nevertheless, every couple of years one of its international touring companies returns to where it all began, the Old Port, and sets up the familiar blue-and-yellow tent for a summer of sold-out shows. ⊠ *Montréal* ☎ *514/790–1245, 800/361–4595* ⊕ *www. cirquedusoleil.com.*

Cirque Éloize. This award-winning troupe has been touring the globe since 1993, and with well over 4,000 performances under its belt, shows no signs of slowing down. Constantly evolving, Cirque Éloize uses artistic mediums like video and music to bring the circus arts to the masses. ⊠ *Montréal* ☎ *514/596–3838* ⊕ *www. cirque-eloize.com.*

Les 7 doigts de la main. Literally translated as "the seven fingers of the hand," the name is a play on a French expression about working collectively toward a common goal, and these seven fingers—the seven founding partners of the circus—have done just that, building up a world-renowned circus troop over the past decade or so. Combining acrobatics, theater, and dance, they've performed at special events across the globe, including a Royal Variety Performance for Queen Elizabeth II and at the Olympics in Turin and Vancouver. They even made an appearance on *America's Got Talent.* ⊠ *Montréal* ☎ *514/521–4477* ⊕ *www.7doigts.com.*

Cirque du Soleil is Montréal's hometown circus, founded here in 1984. Today there are several troupes across several countries that perform hundreds of shows per year.

Known for: festive ambience; papaya salad; long lines. [$] *Average main: C$10* ✉ *3721 Notre-Dame rue Ouest, Verdun* ☎ *514/933–3507* ⊕ *www.sataybrothers. com* ⊗ *Closed Mon. and Tues. No lunch mid-May–mid-Oct.* Ⓜ *Lionel-Groulx.*

☕ Coffee and Quick Bites

Patrice Pâtissier

$ | BAKERY | FAMILY | Pick up a pastry to go at the counter or choose one of the plated desserts to enjoy on-site at Patrice Pâtissier, a beautifully designed pastry shop and lunch spot, overseen by one of Québec's most renowned pastry chefs. The almond cream with seasonal fruits is luscious and will certainly please those following a gluten-free and/or vegan diet. **Known for:** Sunday brunch; kouign amann; celebrity chef. [$] *Average main: C$4.50* ✉ *2360 rue Notre-Dame Ouest, Local 104, Verdun* ☎ *514/439–5434* ⊕ *patrice-patissier.ca* ⊗ *Closed Mon. and Tues.* Ⓜ *Lionel-Groulx.*

Hotels

ALT Montréal Griffintown

$ | HOTEL | FAMILY | This stylish, tech-savvy Griffintown hotel appeals for its affordable set rates, modular loft-style rooms, partially open 7th floor terrace, light ecofootprint, and the ultimate luxury of no set checkout time. **Pros:** no set checkout time; close to Downtown; underground parking with Tesla charging stations available. **Cons:** minimalist service may not suit those who want more pampering; no restaurant; a bit of a walk to the métro. [$] *Rooms from: C$199* ✉ *120 rue Peel, Verdun* ☎ *514/375–0220, 855/823–8120* ⊕ *www.althotels.com/en/montreal* 🛏 *154 rooms* ⦿ *No meals* Ⓜ *Bonaventure, then bus 107.*

🎬 Performing Arts

Théâtre Corona

CONCERTS | Built in 1912, this exquisite former cinema and vaudeville theater in the heart of St-Henri has proudly preserved its small stage for the maneuvering of scenery, the artists' lodges under the stage, and the orchestra pit in the foreground. It is the only vintage movie theater in Montréal whose exterior facade and interior have remained almost unchanged. Today the Corona serves as a concert venue for artists like Milk & Bone, Bobby Bazini, Tom Odell, and Rumours of Fleetwood Mac. ✉ *2490 rue Notre Dame Ouest, Westmount* ☎ *855/310–2525* ⊕ *www.theatrecorona. ca/en* Ⓜ *Lionel-Groulx.*

Chapter 4

SIDE TRIPS FROM MONTRÉAL

4

Updated by
Chris Barry

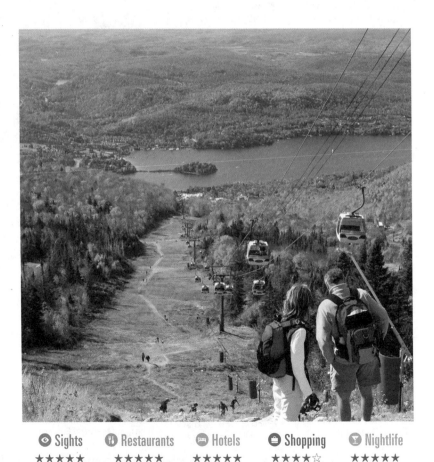

👁 Sights   🍴 Restaurants   🛏 Hotels   🛍 Shopping   🍸 Nightlife

★★★★★   ★★★★★   ★★★★★   ★★★★☆   ★★★★★

WELCOME TO SIDE TRIPS FROM MONTRÉAL

TOP REASONS TO GO

★ **Ski at Mont-Tremblant:** Heading 150 km (90 miles) north of Montréal takes you to some of the best skiing east of the Rockies, as well as fine hotels and restaurants, a lively ski village, and great golf courses.

★ **Take a driving tour of Eastern Townships wineries:** The vineyards here resemble those in the Niagara Region and Okanagan Valley.

★ **Visit Abbaye St-Benoit-du-Lac:** The Benedictine monks built this splendid church—with its fairy-tale castle bell tower—on the shores of Lake Memphrémagog.

★ **Spend a night among wolves in Parc Omega:** Go with an experienced guide to explore the lives of these great predators in their natural habitat—the magnificent Outaouais region.

★ **Go leaf-peeping ... anywhere:** From mid-September through mid-October the entire Laurentians, Eastern Townships, and Outaouais are ablaze with spectacular fall foliage.

1 Oka. Oka is most famous for its abbey and provincial park, which also features one of Montreal's only nearby nude beaches.

2 St-Sauveur-des-Monts. The unofficial gateway to the Laurentiens.

3 Morin Heights. A small, primarily Anglo-phone hamlet that's home to the popular Ski Morin Heights recreational center.

4 Ste-Adèle. With numerous nearby ski hills and dozens of restaurants and hotels, this is the largest village in the Laurentiens.

5 Val-David. Home to the largest farmers' market in the Laurentiens and the hugely successful 1001 Pots ceramics exhibit/workshop.

6 Ste-Agathe-des-Monts. Best known for its ski hills and winter activities, Ste-Agathe also plays home to some of the best beaches in the Laurentiens.

7 Mont-Tremblant. Consistently ranked one of the top ski centers in eastern North America.

8 Montebello. Best known for its historic Le Château Montebello, a spectacular hotel that's also the largest log cabin in the world.

9 Gatineau. Directly across the water from Ottawa, the nation's capital, Gatineau is a large town that's home to the Canadian Museum of History.

10 Bromont. An all-season recreational center and the only night skiing in the Townships.

11 Knowlton (Lac Brome). The quintessential Eastern Townships resort town.

12 Abbaye St-Benoît-du-Lac. An impressive abbey located on spectacular grounds bordering Lac Memphrémagog, you can purchase sparkling apple wine and some of the best cheese in Québec here.

13 Parc du Mont-Orford. One of the top ski centers in the Townships, in addition to being a nature reserve.

14 Magog. A bustling little town located on the banks of Lac Memphrémagog, Magog has one of the nicest beaches in the Townships.

15 North Hatley. One of eastern Québec's prettiest villages.

16 Sherbrooke. This is the Townships premier city, with trendy restaurants and boutiques lining Wellington street in the downtown core.

17 Notre-Dame-des-Bois. In the shadow of Mont-Mégantic with a world-renowned observatory.

In the minds of many who live here, one of Montréal's greatest attributes is its proximity to the sheer physical beauty of the surrounding countryside. From Downtown Montréal you can head in pretty well any direction and within an hour or so, you'll be, if not in the wilderness, then at least in the thick of cottage country. The three most popular side-trip destinations from Montréal are the Laurentians, the Eastern Townships, and the Outaouais—each possessing its own distinct characteristics and flavor.

Most people traveling to this region do so by car, making it easy to spend as much or as little time in any given area as desired. Nevertheless, Québec has created the Route Verte (Green Route), a 5,000-km (3,100-mile) network of bike trails in the southern part of the province. Many of the trails are currently open for access.

MAJOR REGIONS

The Laurentians (les Laurentides) range is a delightful year-round destination for getting outdoors, whether it's for golf and white-water rafting in the summer or skiing and dog sledding in the winter. Along with its stunning natural beauty, it's also known for its authentic Québec food—all of this to be found in little towns like **Oka**, less than an hour's drive from Downtown Montréal, traffic allowing. The main tourist region, which actually encompasses only a small part of the Laurentian mountain range, is divided into two major regions: the Lower Laurentians (les Basses Laurentides) and the Upper Laurentians (les Hautes Laurentides). But don't be fooled by the designations; they don't signify great driving distances. The rocky hills here are relatively low, but many are eminently skiable, with a few peaks above 2,500 feet. Mont-Tremblant, at 3,150 feet, is the region's highest. The resort area begins at **St-Sauveur-des-Monts** (Exit 60 on Autoroute 15) and extends north to **Mont-Tremblant**. Beyond, the region turns into a wilderness of lakes and forests best visited with an outfitter. Fishing guides are concentrated around Parc du Mont-Tremblant. To the first-time visitor, the hilly areas around St-Sauveur, **Ste-Adèle**, **Morin Heights**, Val-Morin, and **Val-David** up to **Ste-Agathe-des-Monts** form a pleasant hodgepodge of villages, hotels, and inns that seem to blend one into another. Tourisme Lauren-tides in Mirabel provides information and offers a daily lodging-booking service. Its main information center is at the Porte du Nord complex at Exit 51 on Autoroute 15.

The Outaouais. First settled in the mid-19th century and long known for its logging, the Outaouais (pronounced: ewt–away) region is now a nature lover's paradise as well, with 20,000 lakes, countless rivers, 400 km (249 miles) of hiking trails, and 2,730 km (1,696 miles) of snowmobile trails. To fully experience the majesty of the Outaouais wilderness you could spend close to a week here, but simply driving to any of the region's major provincial parks is a good one-day journey. **Montebello**, a little country village on the banks of the Ottawa River, is only a 1½-hour drive from Montréal, and is where you'll find Le Château Montebello, the largest log structure ever built. From there you can find excursions to take you to the surrounding countryside, or if you'd prefer, you can simply take in nearby Omega Park, a safari adventure where you'll bear witness to many of the region's creatures interacting within their natural environment. It encompasses an enormous body of land located in the southwest corner of the province. **Gatineau**, just about two hours outside Montréal, is in another quaint area of Outaouais. Bordering Ontario, and just across the river from Ottawa, this region contains the vast and gorgeous Gatineau Park.

The Eastern Townships (also known as les Cantons de l'Est, and formerly as l'Estrie) refers to the southeast corner of the province of Québec, which borders Vermont, New Hampshire, and Maine, and is known for its mountains, spas, lush forests, and many vineyards. In winter, the Townships are the place to be for serious ski and snowboard enthusi-asts, boasting many of the province's highest peaks and most challenging

trails. In summer, boating, swimming, sailing, golfing, in-line skating, hiking, and bicycling take over. And every fall the inns are booked solid with visitors eager to take in the brilliant foliage. Fall is also a good time to visit the wineries (although most are open all year). Because of its mild microclimate, the Townships area has become one of the more prominent wine regions in Canada, with a dozen of Québec's 33 commercial wineries.

Planning

When to Go

The Laurentians are a big skiing destina-tion in winter, but the other seasons all have their own charms: you can drive up from Montréal to enjoy the fall foliage; to hike, bike, play golf, camp, or fish; or to engage in spring skiing—and still get back to the city before dark. The only slow periods are early November (aka "mud season"), when there isn't much to do, and June, when the area has plenty to offer but is plagued by black flies. Control programs have improved the situation somewhat.

The Outaouais region is beautiful at any time of year, but unless you're looking to spend several days there it's best to go in summer and stay in the lower region, around Montebello. Making your way up to the provincial parks in the north is a lengthy journey at best, but in winter, potentially hazardous road conditions could well add several more hours to your trip.

The Eastern Townships are best in fall, when the foliage is at its peak; the region borders Vermont and has the same dramatic colors. It's possible to visit wineries at this time, but you should call ahead, since harvest is a busy time.

Getting Here and Around

The Laurentians: Autoroute 15 is the fastest and most direct route from Montréal to the most in-demand spots in the Laurentians. This limited access highway peters out at Ste-Agathe and morphs into Autoroute 117, which runs all the way to Rouyn-Noranda. Exit numbers on Autoroute 15 reflect the distance from Montréal. Autoroute 15 starts at the New York–Québec border where it connects to Interstate 87, so it's also the most direct route for most visitors from the United States. The highway crosses into Montréal on the Champlain Bridge and follows the Décarie and Metropolitan expressways across the island. Visitors arriving from Boston and points east on Interstate 91 can follow Autoroute 55 from the border north to Autoroute 10 (the Autoroute des Cantons de l'Est) and then drive west until it merges with Autoroute 15 at the Champlain Bridge.

The Outaouais: To get to the Outaouais take Autoroute 15 North roughly 40 km (25 miles) until you get to Autoroute 50 West heading toward Lachute. Drive another 70 km (43 miles) past Lachute and you'll soon be in Montebello. Continue on another 15 km (9 miles) to reach Gatineau.

The Eastern Townships: For the Eastern Townships, take Autoroute 10 Est (the Autoroute des Cantons de l'Est) from Montréal, or U.S. 91 from New England, which becomes Autoroute 55 as it crosses the border into the Eastern Townships.

Visitor Information

THE LAURENTIANS Tourisme Laurentides (Porte du Nord). ✉ 1000 Hwy. 15 N, St-Jérôme ✛ Exit 51, Autoroute 15N ☎ 450/224–7007 from Montréal area, 800/561–6673 from rest of North America ⊕ www.laurentides.com.

THE OUTAOUAIS Tourisme Outaouais. ✉ 103 rue Laurier, Gatineau ☎ 819/778–2222 ⊕ www.tourismeoutaouais.com.

THE EASTERN TOWNSHIPS Tourisme Cantons-de-l'Est. ✉ 20 rue Don-Bosco Sud, Sherbrooke ☎ 819/820–2020, 800/355–5755 ⊕ www.easterntownships.org.

Oka

40 km (25 miles) west of Montréal.

If you like apples and delicious cheese, Oka is sure to be a highlight of your trip. It was once the home of Cistercian monks, but the urban sprawl has driven them from their abbey, on the shores of Lac des Deux-Montagnes, to seek solace farther north in St-Jean-de-Matha in the Lanaudière region, but the cheese they made famous is still produced by a private firm here and is available in local shops. The rolling hills around the little town of Oka are where you'll find many of the apple orchards. If you love cider, follow the *Route des Vergers*, stopping at various properties along this "Orchard Route" to sample the local wares. There's also a winery on the route: La Bullerie, whose whites and reds include the port-like *L'été Indien* (Indian Summer).

GETTING HERE AND AROUND
To get from Montréal to Oka, take Autoroute 15 North to Autoroute 640 West.

TOURS
★ **La Bullerie**
SELF-GUIDED | Formerly La Roche Des Brises, La Bullerie is located on delightfully bucolic grounds where visitors are invited to tour the facilities and sample this celebrated winery's wares. Guests are even encouraged to picnic on-site, with baskets stocked with various local cheeses, cold meats and, of course, La Bullerie wine, on offer at the gift shop. Wine tastings are also available at $10 for three and $18 for six samplings

respectively. ✉ *The Bullerie, 2007 Main Road, St-Joseph-du-Lac* ☎ *450/ 472–2722* ⊕ *labullerie.com.*

 ## Sights

Hudson

TOWN | A quick detour on the ferry (*C$11 one-way;* ⊕ *traverseoka.ca*) across Lac des Deux-Montagnes brings you to this small town with old houses now used for art galleries, boutiques, and Christmas shops. In winter there's an "ice bridge": basically a plowed path across a well-frozen lake. Taking a walk across the bridge is a singular experience. If you happen to visit on a Saturday from May to October, make a stop at the popular **Finnegan's Market** (⊕ *www.finnegansmarket.com*). Open from 9 to 4, the flea market sells antiques, jewelry, crafts, and preserves, among other goods. ✉ *Hudson* ⊕ *hudson.quebec/en.*

Parc d'Oka (*Oka National Park*)
NATIONAL/STATE PARK | Beautifully surrounded by low hills, this park has a lake fringed by a sandy beach and plenty of opportunities for outdoor sports, including hiking and biking trails, kayaking, canoeing, fishing, and, in winter, snowshoeing and cross-country skiing. Locals also consider it to be one of the top camping destinations. Administered by the province along environmentally conscious lines—they implemented the Ecological Integrity Monitoring Program (EIMO) in 2004—it has nearly 900 campsites, and you can rent bicycles, cross-country skis, snowshoes, canoes, and kayaks from the office. Note that the strip at the far eastern end of the beach is "clothing optional," or, in effect,

"clothing nonexistent." ✉ *2020 chemin Oka* ☎ *450/479–8365, 800/665–6527 activities* ⊕ *www.sepaq.com* 🖃 *C$8.75.*

🛍 Shopping

★ Magasin de l'Abbaye d'Oka

LOCAL SPECIALTIES | This shop offers a wide variety of local products, not the least being the abbey's famous Oka cheese. They also have a small dining area where you can dine on Oka cheese poutine and other tasty sundries. ✉ *Magasin de l'Abbaye d'Oka, 1600 Oka Road, Oka* ☎ *450/479–6170* ⊕ *www.abbayeoka.ca.*

St-Sauveur-des-Monts

85 km (53 miles) north of Oka, 63 km (39 miles) north of Montréal.

Just a 45-minute drive from Montréal (or 90 minutes when the traffic's heavy, as it frequently is), St-Sauveur is probably the busiest little town in Québec, especially on weekends. Its rue Principale bristles with bars and restaurants that serve everything from lamb brochettes and spicy Thai stir-fries to steaks and burgers. On summer weekends, the street is so jammed with cars and the sidewalks so packed with visitors that it's sometimes called Crescent Street North after the action-filled street in Montréal. Despite the glitz and the sea of condos that surround it, however, the town has managed to retain a bit of rural charm in its fine old church and veranda-fronted clapboard homes.

St-Sauveur in winter is no less busy. The "mountains" surrounding the town hardly qualify as Alpine—none has a vertical drop of more than 700 feet—but they're close to Montréal, well serviced by lifts, and lit at night, so the winter sports scene here is very lively. Whether you ski or not, the après-ski scene in St-Sauveur is worth sampling.

GETTING HERE AND AROUND

Take Highway 15 north from Montréal and get off at Exit 60. The best way to explore the main street is to find a parking lot and walk around. Driving through town is difficult in winter, impossible in summer.

VISITOR INFORMATION

CONTACT Tourist Welcome Bureau of Pays-d'en-Haut. ✉ *1014 rue Valiquette, Ste-Adèle* ☎ *450/229–6637* ⊕ *www. lespaysdenhaut.com.*

👁 Sights

Mont-St-Sauveur Water Park

AMUSEMENT PARK/WATER PARK | **FAMILY** | Slides, a giant wave pool, a wading pool, and snack bars will all keep the kids occupied here. The river rafting attracts an older, braver crowd; the nine-minute ride follows the natural contours of steep hills. On the tandem slides, plumes of water flow through figure-eight tubes and make for a great time. But if you'd rather stay dry, take an adventure through the trees on their zipline or enjoy a fast ride with the Viking Alpine Coaster. ✉ *350 rue St-Denis* ☎ *450/227–4671* ⊕ *www. sommets.com/en* 🖃 *C$42.*

Musée du ski des Laurentides

MUSEUM | The Laurentians are one of the oldest ski regions in North America, and ski buffs will enjoy this little museum tracing the long history of this area with great photos, artifacts, and some interesting models of early ski lifts. It also houses the Temple de la Renomée du ski (the Ski Hall of Fame). ✉ *30 rue Filion* ☎ *450/227–2564* ⊕ *www.museeduskideslaurentides.com* 🖃 *Free, though donation of $3 suggested.*

🛏 Hotels

Relais St-Denis

$ | **B&B/INN** | Once a wartime refuge for well-heeled English children and their governesses, this inn and spa now offers

One of the most popular times to visit the region is in fall, when the mountains are splashed with a spectrum of warm yellows, oranges, and reds.

everyone a refuge from everyday stress, with a fireplace and a whirlpool bath in every room and a year-round outdoor heated pool and steam room. **Pros:** variety of spa services and in-room massage packages; kitchenette in all rooms and suites; walking distance to restaurants, outlet shopping, and activities. **Cons:** no restaurant on-site; decor is basic and could use updating; Wi-Fi can be slow. $ *Rooms from: C$159* ✉ *61 rue St-Denis* ☎ *450/227–4766, 888/997–4766* ⊕ *www. relaisstdenis.com* ↩ *42 rooms* ⊘ *No meals.*

🛍 Shopping

SHOPPING CENTERS
Rue Principale
SHOPPING NEIGHBORHOODS | Small fashion boutiques, restaurant terraces, and cute gift shops in old French-Canadian and Victorian homes adorned with bright awnings and flowers line this popular tree-lined shopping street. ✉ *St-Sauveur-des-Monts.*

🏃 Activities

SKIING
Sommet St-Sauveur
SKIING/SNOWBOARDING | The hills surrounding St-Sauveur might be relatively low, but this vibrant ski resort is long-established and perennially popular for good reason. It has an extensive skiable area, good snow-making and lift capacity, and many trails that are lit at night, making it possible for energetic Montrealers to drive up after work for a couple of hours of skiing. There are several other hills in the area, but Mont-St-Sauveur is the largest, with a 700-foot vertical drop and 142 acres of skiable terrain. Seventeen of its 38 trails are for beginners and intermediates, 16 are for experts, and 5 are rated extreme. Mont-Avila has 13 trails (2 beginner, 3 intermediate, 5 difficult, 3 extremely difficult), a snow park, a fun tubing park, and the Viking, a toboggan-style ride in a cart that twists and turns on a track through the forest. ✉ *350 av. St-Denis, St-Sauveur* ☎ *450/227–4671* ⊕ *www.sommets.com.*

Station de Ski Mont-Habitant

SKIING/SNOWBOARDING | More than 60 years in operation, Mont-Habitant is one of the last of the independent ski operations in St-Sauveur. This mountain has always been a favorite with families and with beginner and intermediate skiers because the vertical drop is just 600 feet and the 10 trails are relatively gentle. Mont-Habitant also has St-Sauveur's only beach, which makes it very popular in summer. ⊠ *12 chemin des Skieurs* ☎ *450/227–2637, 866/887-2637* ⊕ *www.monthabitant.com* ⌗ *C$43 day pass.*

Morin Heights

10 km (6 miles) west of St-Sauveur-des-Monts, 73 km (45 miles) northwest of Montréal.

If St-Sauveur is too busy and overdeveloped for your liking, Morin Heights is a great alternative, with plenty of restaurants, bookstores, boutiques, and craft shops to explore free from the crowds. The town's British architecture and population reflect its settlers' heritage; most residents here speak English.

In summer, windsurfing, swimming, and canoeing on the area's two lakes—Claude and Lafontaine—are popular. In fall and winter, come for the foliage and the Alpine and Nordic skiing.

GETTING HERE AND AROUND

From Montréal to Morin Heights, take Autoroute 15 North, then take Exit 60.

🛏 Hotels

Morin Heights is true cottage country, and thus options for accommodation are slim. Your best bet might be to rent a cottage, or as they're known by French-speaking locals, a *chalet* ⊕ *www.chaletsauquebec.com.* The Montréal pages for ⊕ *craigslist.com* and ⊕ *kijiji.ca* are full of posts advertising private chalet rentals in the Laurentians. If you'd prefer to go through a third party, most area real estate agents broker short- and long-term cottage and chalet rentals as well; try Remax Laurentides (☎ *450/227–8411*).

Hotel Alila

$ | B&B/INN | This auberge by the main road is one of the best-equipped spa destinations in the area, and its outdoor terrace is a pleasant place to relax. **Pros:** some rooms have beautiful views of the Rivière du Nord; whirlpool baths and fireplaces in some units; garden has cold-water pools. **Cons:** isolated from village; close to highway; breakfast not included. $ *Rooms from: C$108* ⊠ *500 Rte. 364, Morin-Heights* ☎ *450/644–0168* ⊕ *www.alila.ca* ⇆ *29 rooms* ⊖ *No meals.*

🛍 Shopping

CRAFTS

Créations d'Aujourd'hui

CRAFTS | Specializing in decorative accessories, unique jewelry, candles, soaps, and natural perfumes, most created by local artists and artisans, many of the items on sale here have been transformed and repurposed by the shop's owner to give them a distinctive second life. ⊠ *Créations d'Aujourd'hui, 910, chemin du Village, Morin Heights* ☎ *450/644–0089* ⊕ *creationsdaujourdhui.weebly.com.*

SPAS

Amerispa Spa Nordique

SPA/BEAUTY | Only 45 minutes outside Montréal, this is a great place to escape and unwind. Hidden in a Laurentian forest of maples, firs, and birches is a beautifully rustic pavilion housing a spa with hot tubs and cold pools, eucalyptus-scented steam baths, and thermal and Nordic waterfalls. The Elixir Ice Cider Massage with companion body wrap is a must. ⊠ *160 rue Watchorn, Morin-Heights* ☎ *450/226-7722, 866/263-7477* ⊕ *www.amerispa.ca.*

⚡ Activities

Ski Morin Heights

SKIING/SNOWBOARDING | FAMILY | This small, family-oriented ski center with 32 trails (for all levels) offers a warm and friendly place to enjoy winter sports. Downhill and cross-country skiing, snowboarding, and snowshoeing are available and free daycare is offered to skiers. ✉ 231 rue Bennett, Morin-Heights ☎ 450/227–2020 ⊕ www.sommets.com/en/ski-mountains/sommet-morin-heights/ ⚒ C$50 ski pass for the day.

Ste-Adèle

12 km (7 miles) north of Morin Heights, 85 km (53 miles) north of Montréal.

Although Ste-Adèle is not as pretty as St-Sauveur, this town has a lot to offer, with attractions and activities to please families, outdoors enthusiasts, and visitors who want to experience something of the local culture. With a permanent population of more than 10,000, it's the largest community in the lower part of the Laurentians, and has good boutiques, restaurants, summer theater (performed in French), and art galleries. Active types can find horseback riding, golf, and lengthy bike trails in summer and skiing in winter.

GETTING HERE AND AROUND
From Montréal to Ste-Adèle, take Autoroute 15 North and then take Exit 67.

VISITOR INFORMATION
CONTACT Tourist Welcome Bureau of Pays-d'en-Haut. ✉ 1014, rue Valiquette ☎ 450/229–6637 ⊕ www.lespaysdenhaut.com.

◉ Sights

Au Pays des Merveilles

AMUSEMENT PARK/WATER PARK | FAMILY | Fairy-tale characters such as Snow White, Little Red Riding Hood, and Alice in Wonderland wander the grounds, playing games with children. Small fry may also enjoy the petting zoo, amusement rides, wading pool, and puppet show. A ride called Le Petit Train des Merveilles (the Little Train of Wonders) is a nod to the historic train that launched the tourism industry in the Laurentians. There are 45 activities, enough to occupy those aged two to eight for about half a day. Check the website for discount coupons. The theme park is completely accessible to strollers and wheelchairs. ✉ 3795 Chemin de la Savane ☎ 450/229–3141 ⊕ www.paysmerveilles.com ⚒ C$20.

🍴 Restaurants

Nickels

$$ | DELI | FAMILY | One of the last surviving franchises of Celine Dion's formerly ubiquitous Nickels chain, large portions of reasonably priced smoked meat, barbecued chicken, and other classic deli fare are on the menu at this family restaurant. **Known for:** smoked meat; affordable; classic deli. ⑤ Average main: C$15 ✉ 480, boul. Sainte-Adèle, St-Adèle ☎ 450/229-9553 ⊕ nickelsdeli.com.

🛏 Hotels

Auberge & Spa Beaux Rêves

$ | B&B/INN | With a year-round Nordic spa and outdoor hot tub, hammocks hung all around the property, and a waterfall, relaxation is the order of the day at this rustic riverside retreat. **Pros:** personalized packages tailored to meet specific needs; all rooms overlook the river and have balconies or walk-out terraces; all about "unplugging". **Cons:** can be noisy due to close proximity to the road; no phone or television in rooms; no pool. ⑤ Rooms from: C$158 ✉ 2310 boul. Ste-Adèle ☎ 450/229–9226, 800/279–7679, 514/316-7808 From Montreal ⊕ www.beauxreves.com ⥌ 9 rooms, 1 loft ⑩ Some meals.

Hôtel Mont-Gabriel

$ | HOTEL | FAMILY | At this 1,200-acre resort you can relax in a contemporary room with a valley view or commune with nature in a rustic-style cabin with a fireplace, and there are activities aplenty. **Pros:** beautiful grounds; ski-out from many rooms; reasonable packages on offer. **Cons:** rooms are on the small side; can be noisy; some complaints of poor service. $ *Rooms from: C$159* ✉ *1699 chemin du Mont-Gabriel* ☎ *450/229–3547, 800/668–5253* ⊕ *www.montgabriel.com* ↪ *132 rooms* ▮◎▮ *No meals.*

Le Chantecler

$ | HOTEL | FAMILY | A longtime favorite with Montrealers, this hotel has seen better days, but it remains a good choice for active types wanting to expend some energy. **Pros:** friendly, helpful staff; lakeside rooms; year-round activities. **Cons:** can be hard to get a reservation; rooms in need of renovation; restaurant sometimes closed. $ *Rooms from: C$165* ✉ *1474 chemin Chantecler* ☎ *450/229–3555, 888/839–9681* ⊕ *www.lechantecler.com* ↪ *137 rooms* ▮◎▮ *No meals.*

🏃 Activities

GOLF

Club de Golf Chantecler

GOLF | Every hole here will provide panoramic views of the surrounding Laurentian scenery. Opened in 1950, this semiprivate club offers a mountainside course with long and narrow fairways and three sets of tees for different skill levels. Just one hour from Montréal, it's easy and convenient for a day trip. ✉ *2520 chemin du Club* ☎ *450/476–1339, 450/229–3742* ⊕ *www.groupebeaudet.com* ▰ *C$29–C$35* ⚑ *18 holes, 6120 yards, par 72* ☞ *Facilities: Putting green, golf carts, pull carts, rental clubs, pro shop, restaurant, bar.*

SKIING

Ski Mont-Gabriel

SKIING/SNOWBOARDING | Part of Les Sommets chain of ski resorts, Mont Gabriel has five lifts, 18 superb downhill trails, which are primarily for intermediate and advanced skiers, and a vertical drop of 656 feet. It's about 19 km (12 miles) northeast of Ste-Adèle. ✉ *1501 chemin du Mont-Gabriel* ⊕ *www.sommets. com/en/ski-mountains/sommet-gabriel/* ▰ *C$40 day ski pass.*

Val-David

33 km (20 miles) west of Ste-Adèle, 82 km (51 miles) north of Montréal.

Val-David is a major destination for mountain climbers, hikers, and campers. It's also a place that many Québec artists and artisans call home, a fact suggested by the several galleries and marvelous art shops in town.

GETTING HERE AND AROUND

The village is just a couple of kilometers east of Exit N6 on Autoroute 15, making it easy to get to by car, but it's also accessible by bicycle: Le P'tit Train du Nord cycling trail runs right through town.

VISITOR INFORMATION

CONTACT Tourist Bureau of Val-David. ✉ *2525 rue de l'Église, Val-David* ☎ *888/322–7030, 819/324–5678* ⊕ *www. valdavid.com.*

👁 Sights

Village du Père Noël (*Santa Claus Village*) **AMUSEMENT PARK/WATER PARK | FAMILY |** Santa is not just for Christmas here. In his summer residence kids can sit on his knee and speak to him in French or English, then have fun in the grounds, which contain bumper boats, a petting zoo with goats, sheep, horses, and colorful birds; games; and a large outdoor pool in the summer. There is a snack bar, but visitors are encouraged to bring their own food (there are numerous picnic tables). During the cold winter months, the park transforms into a winter wonderland with skating rinks and tubing fun for the kids. ⊠ *987 rue Morin, Val-David* ☎ *819/322–2146, 800/287–6635* ⊕ *www. noel.qc.ca* ✉ *C$20.*

🍴 Restaurants

★ Au Petit Poucet
$$ | CANADIAN | FAMILY | For a true Quebecois treat, stop by this rustic cabin for breakfast or lunch. Founded in 1945, it's a big draw with tourists and locals alike. **Known for:** generous portions; good variety of breakfast options; fresh baked country bread. ⑤ *Average main: C$20* ⊠ *1030 Rte. 117, Val-David* ☎ *819/322–2246, 888/334–2246* ⊕ *www.aupetitpoucet.com* ⊗ *No dinner.*

🛏 Hotels

★ La Maison de Bavière
$ | B&B/INN | Walking into this charming B&B is like being transported to a cozy Bavarian mountain inn. **Pros:** directly across from the P'tit Train du Nord cycling and cross-country ski trail; two-minute walk to the village of Val-David; lovely backyard facing the rushing Rivière du Nord. **Cons:** only four rooms; common area is small and right off the bedrooms, so guests need to keep voices down; the bedroom of the efficiency/studio apartment is only accessible by a short ladder. ⑤ *Rooms from: C$140* ⊠ *1470 chemin de la Rivière, Val-David* ☎ *819/322–3528, 866/322–3528* ⊕ *www.maisondebaviere. com* ⇆ *6 rooms* ◎ *Some meals.*

🎭 Performing Arts

★ Le Centre d'exposition de Val-David
ART GALLERIES—ARTS | Showcasing the work of regional and international artists, the nonprofit Le Centre d'exposition de Val-David is the largest art gallery and

exhibition hall in the area. Admission is free. ⊠ *Le Centre d'exposition de Val-David, 2495 de l'Église, Val-David* ☎ *819/322-7474* ⊕ *centreexpositionvaldavid.com.*

🛍 Shopping

CERAMICS
1001 Pots
CERAMICS/GLASSWARE | One of the most interesting events in Val-David is this ceramic exhibition, held from July through mid-August, which started in 1988. On view is the Japanese-style pottery of 1001 Pots' founder Kinya Ishikawa—as well as pieces by up to 100 other ceramists. Ishikawa's studio also displays work by his wife, Marie-Andrée Benoît, who makes fish-shaped bowls with a texture derived from pressing canvas on the clay. There are workshops for adults and children throughout the exhibition, and there is always at least one artisan on-site. While you're there, take the time to enjoy tea in one of the three beautiful gardens and learn the art of the Japanese tea ceremony. ⊠ *2435 rue de l'Église, Val-David* ☎ *819/322–6868* ⊕ *www.1001pots.com* ✉ *C$2 for exhibition* ☞ *C$2 admission.*

HOUSEHOLD
Atelier Bernard Chaudron, Inc.
CERAMICS/GLASSWARE | If you're looking for an interesting conversation piece to bring back home with you, check out master craftsman Bernard Chaudron's hand-forged, lead-free pewter household objects that include oil lamps, hammered-silver beer mugs, pitchers, candleholders, and animal-themed knife rests. ⊠ *2347 rue de l'Église, Val-David* ☎ *819/322–3944, 888/322–3944* ⊕ *www. chaudron.ca.*

Activities

SKIING

Centre de Ski Vallée-Bleue

SKIING/SNOWBOARDING | Family-run and family-focused, this ski hill suits everyone, from beginners to advanced level skiers and snowboarders, with 19 trails, 3 lifts, and a vertical drop of 365 feet. ⊠ *1418 chemin Vallée-Bleue, Val-David* ☎ *819/322–3427, 866/322–3427* ⊕ *www.vallee-bleue.com* ⛷ *C$33 ski pass.*

Ste-Agathe-des-Monts

5 km (3 miles) north of Val-David, 96 km (60 miles) northwest of Montréal.

The wide, sandy beaches of Lac des Sables are the most surprising feature of Ste-Agathe-des-Monts, a tourist town best known for its ski hills. Water activities include canoeing, kayaking, swimming, and fishing. Ste-Agathe is also a stopover point on the Linear Park, the bike trail between St-Jérôme and Mont-Laurier.

GETTING HERE AND AROUND

From Montréal to Ste-Agathe-des-Monts, take Autoroute 15 North. Take Exit 89 to reach QC–329 South, and then take QC–117.

VISITOR INFORMATION

CONTACT Tourist Bureau of Ste-Agathe-des-Monts. ⊠ *24 rue St-Paul est* ☎ *819/326–3731, 888/326–0457* ⊕ *www.sainte-agathe.org/en.*

Beaches

Major Beach

SWIMMING | FAMILY | The biggest, most popular municipal beach in Ste-Agathe. Full-day admission is $10. **Amenities:** lifeguards; parking (free); showers; water sports. **Best for:** swimming ⊠ *Major Beach, 1 Chemin du Lac des Sables* ☎ *819/326-3731, 888/ 326-0457* ⊕ *ville.*

Camping

In the woods near a lively resort area, Au Parc des Campeurs has activities for all age groups, from sport competitions to outings for the kids. There's a sandy beach where you can rent canoes and kayaks and launch your boat from the town's marina. Reservations for this campground (open mid-May through September) are recommended. ⊠ *2 chemin du Lac-des-Sables, Ste-Agathe-des-Monts* ☎ *819/324–0482 or 800/561–7360* ⊕ *www.campingsteagathe.com.*

sainte-agathe-des-monts.qc.ca/citoyens/activites/plages-municipales.

Hotels

Hôtel Spa Watel

$ | HOTEL | If you're looking for a room with a double-size Jacuzzi, a fireplace, and a balcony with a superb view of Lac des Sables, try this white-painted, lodge-style hotel, which is also convenient for the boutiques and cultural activities in Ste-Agathe. **Pros:** adjacent to three beaches; indoor and outdoor pools and Jacuzzis; year-round outdoor spas. **Cons:** not all rooms have a Jacuzzi, fireplace, and lake view; some lake-view rooms are off an enclosed glass balcony, motel style, so they don't receive direct air from outside; the facilities could stand to benefit from a little updating. $ *Rooms from: C$120* ⊠ *250 rue St-Venant* ☎ *819/326–7016, 800/363–6478* ⊕ *www.hotelspawatel.com* ⇆ *31 rooms* ⏹ *Some meals.*

Activities

BOAT TOURS

***Alouette V* and VI**

TOUR—SPORTS | These sightseeing boats offer guided 50-minute tours of Lac des

Sables. They run at least seven times a day from mid-June to mid-August and five times a day from mid-August to mid-October. The first boat leaves the dock at 11:30 am. ✉ *Municipal Dock, rue Principale* ☎ *819/326–3656, 866/326–3656* ⊕ *www.croisierealouette.com* 🎫 *C$21,75 for 50-minute cruise.*

Mont-Tremblant

25 km (16 miles) north of Ste-Agathe-des-Monts, 100 km (62 miles) north of Montréal.

At more than 3,000 feet, Mont-Tremblant is one of the highest peaks in the Laurentians and a major draw for skiers. The resort area at the foot of the mountain (called simply Tremblant) is spread around 14-km (9-mile)-long Lac Tremblant and is consistently—and justifiably—ranked among the top ski resorts in eastern North America.

The hub of the resort is a pedestrians-only village that gives an architectural nod to the style of New France, with dormer windows and colorful steep roofs on buildings that house pubs, restaurants, boutiques, sports shops, a movie theater, self-catering condominiums, and hotels. A historical town this is not: built for the resort, it may strike you as a bit of Disney in the mountains.

GETTING HERE AND AROUND

The easiest way to get here is by car. Drive north on Autoroute 15 until it ends just beyond Ste-Agathe-des-Monts and then continue on Route 117 (a four-lane highway) for another 30 km (18 miles) to the Mont-Tremblant exit (Exit 119). The resort's parking lots are vast, but they fill up quickly. A shuttle bus links them to the main resort and ski area. Mont-Tremblant has two tourist offices, one in the village and one in the downtown area.

VISITOR INFORMATION
CONTACT Tourisme Mont-Tremblant.
✉ *5080 Montée Ryan* ☎ *877/425–2434, 819/425–2434* ⊕ *www.mont-tremblant. ca.*

◉ Sights

La Diable Vistors' Centre
INFO CENTER | The park entrance closest to Mont-Tremblant is at La Diable Vistors' Centre, just beyond the village of Lac-Supérieur and about a half-hour drive from the resort. ✉ *3824 chemin du Lac Supérieur, Lac Supérieur* ☎ *819/688–2281 visitor center, 800/665–6527 Sépaq (government national park agency)* ⊕ *www.sepaq.com/pq/mot.*

★ Parc National du Mont-Tremblant
NATIONAL/STATE PARK | **FAMILY** | This vast wildlife sanctuary has more than 400 lakes and rivers and is home to nearly 200 species of birds and animals, so it's great for wildlife watching. Cross-country skiers, snowshoers, and snowmobilers enjoy the park's trails in winter and camping, fishing, canoeing, and hiking are the popular summer activities. The park was once the home of the Algonquins, who called this area Manitonga Soutana, meaning "mountain of the spirits." ✉ *Mont-Tremblant* ☎ *800/665–6527* ⊕ *www.sepaq.com* 🎫 *C$9 per day.*

🍴 Restaurants

Auberge du Coq de Montagne
$$ | **ITALIAN** | Five minutes from the ski slopes and right on Lac Moore, this rustic restaurant, which opens onto a terrace during the summer months, looks a bit shabby from the outside but has garnered much praise for its Italian dishes. These include tried-and-true favorites such as veal marsala and veal *fiorentina* (cooked with spinach and cheese). **Known for:** Italian dishes like veal marsala; homemade pasta. ⑤ *Average main: C$20* ✉ *2151 chemin du Village* ☎ *819/425–3380* ⊕ *auberge-du-coq-de-montagne.*

Renting a Ski Chalet in Mont-Tremblant

If you think you'd like to spend more than a few days in the Laurentians you might want to consider renting a chalet from a private owner. There are generally plenty to choose from, and not only is a private rental often less expensive than staying at a hotel, it's a lot homier as well, especially if you are traveling with children. And even with the many restaurants in Mont-Tremblant, every once in a while it's nice to buy groceries and come home to cook your own dinner.

Options range from cozy little cottages for four to multibedroom properties where you could have a real house party with family and friends. If you fill a place to capacity the cost can be very competitive, particularly if you don't mind being outside the main hub of the resort or out of the peak season. Some places offer weekend rates as well as renting by the week. Very good sources for chalet rentals in this part of the province are the websites ⊕ www.chalets-mont-tremblant.com and ⊕ www.chaletsauquebec.com, and the Montréal pages for ⊕ craigslist.com and ⊕ kijiji.ca are full of posts advertising private chalet rentals in the Laurentians. If you'd prefer to go through a third party, most area real estate agents broker short- and long-term cottage and chalet rentals as well. Try Remax Laurentides at 286 Principal in St-Sauveur (☎ 450/227–8411) for starters.

ibooked.ca ☯ Closed Easter Mon.–late May; early Oct.–mid-Dec.

🛏 Hotels

★ Fairmont Tremblant

$$$ | HOTEL | FAMILY | The centerpiece of the Tremblant resort area takes its cues from the grand 19th-century railroad "castle hotels" scattered throughout Canada. **Pros:** poolside barbecue during the summer; dogs (under 50 lbs.) allowed; easy access to ski hills and the village. **Cons:** it's in the fairly busy village rather than more scenic grounds; valet parking $25 plus tax; public parking (fees may apply) is a 10-minute walk away. ⑤ Rooms from: C$320 ✉ 3045 chemin de la Chapelle ☎ 819/681–7000, 800/257–7544 ⊕ www.fairmont.com/tremblant ⌲ 314 rooms ⑩ Free breakfast.

Le Grand Lodge

$ | HOTEL | FAMILY | At this Scandinavian-style log-cabin hotel, on 13½ acres on the shore of Lac Ouimet, you'll find great year-round amenities and activities for families and sports lovers and a resorty feel that survives its busy conference trade schedule. **Pros:** peaceful environment amid woods and walking trails; ice rink and ice path in winter; private beach. **Cons:** rooms and suites not very stylish; narrow swimming pool; fireplaces are gas, not wood-burning. ⑤ Rooms from: C$156 ✉ 2396 rue Labelle ☎ 819/425–2734, 800/567–6763 ⊕ www.legrandlodge.com ⌲ 112 rooms ⑩ Free breakfast.

Quintessence

$$$$ | HOTEL | There are spectacular views of Lac Tremblant from every room of this quiet, chic, boutique hotel near the ski slopes. **Pros:** very large, elegant rooms ranging from 700 to 1,200 square feet; massages in your suite; concierge can provide firewood; lovely garden. **Cons:** very expensive; furnishings could be of better quality; offer of babysitting service for guests but not all sitters satisfactory. ⑤ Rooms from: C$510 ✉ 3004 chemin de la Chapelle ☎ 819/425–3400,

866/425–3400 ⊕ www.hotelquin-
tessence.com ⌔ 31 suites ⏏ Free
breakfast.

Performing Arts

Festi Jazz

FESTIVALS | Tons of fun and complete-
ly free, the very popular five-day jazz
festival in early August draws in at least
15,000 tourists and locals to Mont-Tremblant. The concerts take place under the
stars on two outdoor stages and in at
least 10 restaurants, bars, and hotels in
the Village or St-Jovite (downtown area).
⊠ Mont-Tremblant ⊕ www.jazzmttrem-
blant.com.

Festival International du Blues de Tremblant

(Tremblant International Blues Festival)
CONCERTS | People don't just flock to
Mont-Tremblant for outdoor fun. This
place is becoming a music lovers' paradise, especially for 10 days in July when
the Blues Festival takes place with more
than 130 shows. Artists such as Otis
Taylor, JJ Grey & Mofro, and Thornetta
Davis entertain fans on outdoor stages
and in intimate clubs right in the village.
⊠ Mont-Tremblant ☎ 819/681–3000
⊕ blues.tremblant.ca/en/.

Activities

GOLF

Mont-Tremblant

GOLF | The same company that operates
the ski resort also runs two of the most
challenging and popular championship golf courses in Québec. **Le Géant**
(the Giant) was designed by Thomas
McBroom to take full advantage of
the fantastic scenery. **Le Diable** (the
Devil), with long narrow fairways and
strategically placed red sand bunkers,
was designed by Michael Hurdzan and
Dana Fry. Also at Le Diable, you can find
the reputable Tremblant Golf Academy.
⊠ Mont-Tremblant ☎ 866/356–2233,
866/783–5634 ⊕ www.tremblant.ca
⌔ C$119 ⛳ Le Diable, 18 holes, 7056

yards, par 71; Le Géant, 18 holes, 6836
yards, par 72 ☞ Facilities: Le Diable:
Driving range, putting green, golf carts,
caddies (digital/GPS), rental clubs, pro
shop, golf academy/lessons, restaurant,
bar; Le Géant: Driving range, putting
green, golf carts, rental clubs, pro shop,
gold academy/lessons, restaurant, bar.

SKIING

Mont-Tremblant

SKIING/SNOWBOARDING | With a 2,116-foot
vertical drop, 654 acres of skiable terrain,
95 trails, 18 acres of ramps and jumps for
snowboarders, and enough state-of-the-
art snowmaking equipment to blanket a
small city, Mont-Tremblant is truly one of
the great ski resorts of North America,
arguably the best east of the Rockies. Its
14 lifts—including two heated gondolas
and five high-speed, four-passenger chairlifts—can handle 27,230 skiers an hour. It
has some of the toughest expert runs on
the continent, but it also has long, gentle
runs like the 6-km (3.7-mile) Nansen and
dozens of exciting trails for intermedi-
ate skiers. Its altitude and location, as
well as all that snowmaking equipment,
gives it some of eastern Canada's most
reliable ski conditions, especially now
that winters are getting warmer. All this
doesn't come cheap, mind you. A day lift
ticket costs C$99, or C$93 if purchased
48 hours in advance, but for serious
skiers there is no better mountain in
Québec. ⊠ 1000 chemin des Voyageurs
☎ 866/356–2233, 819/681–3000 ⊕ www.
tremblant.ca ⌔ One-day lift ticket C$99.

Montebello

130 km (80 miles) west of Montréal.

Located on the banks of the Ottawa
River, this little village is best known for
the Fairmont Le Château Montebello, a
spectacular hotel touted as the largest
log cabin in the world. Given the town's
relative proximity to Ottawa, the nation's
capital, more than a few world leaders

and dignitaries have visited Montebello for one of the many international summits hosted by the Château since it was built in 1930. The Outaouais in general is well-known for the rugged beauty of its wilderness, and even in this more populated southern section of the region there's still excellent fishing, hunting, canoeing, hiking, and wildlife-spotting, with a series of hiking paths starting right beside the Château Montebello. Even if an expedition into the bush isn't quite your thing, you can still get up close to the local wildlife in a more controlled environment at Parc Omega, home to a wide variety of indigenous species and domestic animals.

GETTING HERE AND AROUND

From Montréal, take Autoroute 50 West for 130 km (80 miles); it's about a 90-minute trip.

VISITOR INFORMATION

CONTACT Montebello Tourist Information Office. ⊠ *Gare de Montebello, 502-A rue Notre-Dame* ☎ *819/423–5602* ⊕ *www. tourismeoutaouais.com.*

Sights

Parc Omega

NATURE PRESERVE | FAMILY | In the 1,800 acres of hills, valleys, rivers, and streams that make up the park, visitors drive along designated trails to view wild animals roaming free in their beautiful natural environment. These include bear, Alpine ibexes, buffalo, wolves, elk, and more. There are also walking trails among nonaggressive species like white-tailed deer, with caged golf-cart rental available in summer to save the legwork. Also in summer, you can visit farm animals in the restored 19th-century Léopold's Farm and see a birds of prey show. ⊠ *399 Rte. 323 N* ☎ *819/423–5487* ⊕ *www. parc-omega.com* ⊠ *C$27–C$31, depending on season* ⊙ *Last admission 2 hrs before closing.*

Restaurants

La Belle Bédaine Casse-Croûte

$ | CANADIAN | If you're looking for elegant dining keep on going, but if you're after a bit of local color, a cold beer, a good burger, a steamie (hot dog), or maybe a sample of Québec's famed poutine, then La Belle Bédaine (which translates as "the happy belly") is just the place. Its good and basic menu comes with a terrace overlooking the river. **Known for:** breakfast menu; steamies; poutine. ⑤ *Average main: C$8* ⊠ *664 rue Notre-Dame* ☎ *819/423–5053* ⊟ *No credit cards.*

Le Napoleon

$$$ | ITALIAN | In what is basically a one-street town, this restaurant's reputation for serving outstanding food at affordable prices stands out, and the knowledgeable, personable waitstaff does, too. Though the cuisine is primarily Italian, some Mediterranean, French, and Quebecois influences are also in evidence, backed up by a fairly extensive and reasonably priced wine list. **Known for:** great wine list; good food at good prices; beautiful quiet area. ⑤ *Average main: C$23* ⊠ *489 rue Notre-Dame* ☎ *819/423–5555* ⊕ *www.le-napoleon.com* ⊟ *No credit cards* ⊙ *No lunch.*

Hotels

★ Fairmont Le Château Montebello

$$$ | HOTEL | FAMILY | On a bank of the Ottawa River, with its own marina, this grand log-built hotel provides rustic luxury, local flavor, beautiful grounds, great views, and heaps of activities—no wonder it's an annual family destination for many well-heeled Canadians. **Pros:** great place to bring children; indoor tennis; magnificent fireplace in lobby; state-of-the-art conference facility; beautiful pool and spa. **Cons:** small bathrooms; 90-minute drive from Montréal; no nearby restaurants of note; pricey, and a C$25 per-room, per-night resort fee is added to your bill at checkout; carpeting in some rooms looks a bit worn as does some of the furniture in the lounge. ⑤ *Rooms from: C$377* ⊠ *392 rue Notre-Dame* ☎ *819/423–6341, 866/540–4462* ⊕ *www. fairmont.com/montebello* ⇨ *211 rooms* ⦿ *No meals.*

Gatineau

205 km (127 miles) west of Montréal.

This town on the northern edge of the Ottawa River is best known for the nearby Gatineau Park and the many outdoor activities that can be done here. For more history, visit the Canadian Museum of History, which emphasizes the changes the country has undergone, from the prehistoric past to the present day. From Gatineau, it's a short walk over the Alexandra Bridge to visit Ottawa, the nation's capital. The view from either side of the river is stunning.

GETTING HERE AND AROUND
From Montréal, take Autoroute 50 west for 205 km (127 miles); it's about a two-hour trip.

VISITOR INFORMATION
CONTACT Gatineau Tourist Information Office. ⊠ *103 rue Laurier* ☎ *819/778–2222, 800/265–7822* ⊕ *www.tourisme-outaouais.com.*

◉ Sights

Canadian Museum of History
MUSEUM | FAMILY | Formerly known as the Canadian Museum of Civilization, this superb institution officially changed its name in 2013 when it received C$25 million in funding from the Canadian government in order to renovate and expand. More than 50,000 square feet of the existing museum has been reno-vated, and a new Canadian History Hall showcasing the people and events that have shaped Canada over the last 15,000 years was added in 2017. Other highlights include the First Peoples Hall, which has

some 2,000 objects on display, and the Children's Museum. ⊠ *100 rue Laurier* ☎ *819/776–7000 n/a, 800/555–5621 n/a* ⊕ *www.historymuseum.ca* ⊠ *C$20.*

Gatineau Park
BICYCLING | FAMILY | This massive park—nearly 364 square km (140 square miles)—brings nature lovers from all over throughout the year. You can hike up King Mountain on a challenging trail that takes you 300 meters (980 feet) above the Ottawa Valley, explore Lusk Cave, go camping, view the Luskville Falls, or swim at one of the six beaches here (there are also 50 lakes). In winter the cross-country skiing trails cover approximately 200 km (125 miles) of the park. From June to mid-October, you can use the park's south entrance on Taché Boulevard; stop at the reception center for visitor information. ⊠ *Gatineau* ☎ *819/827–2020* ⊕ *www.ncc-ccn/gc/ca/places/gatineau-park* ⊠ *C$12 per vehicle.*

Restaurants

★ Edgar
$$ | CANADIAN | Wonderful homemade pastries such as pear-and-almond tarts, lemon-curd doughnuts, and chai scones have brought renown to this little place (only 11 seats), but there's more to it than that. Breakfast and lunch are always busy, and weekend brunch, served until 2 pm, brings a line out the door. **Known for:** weekend brunch; homemade pastries; cute terrace. ⑤ *Average main: C$20* ⊠ *60 rue Bégin* ☎ *819/205–1110* ⊕ *www. chezedgar.ca* ⊙ *No dinner. Closed Mon.*

Hotels

Moulin Wakefield Mill Hotel and Spa
$$ | HOTEL | Part heritage mill with original features, part modern environmentally friendly building, this waterside hotel and spa on the edge of Gatineau Park has lots of character, wonderful views of the MacLaren Falls, and plenty of pamper-ing on offer. **Pros:** walking distance to

Gatineau Park; great views; pets allowed.
Cons: hotel caters mostly to adults;
expensive; hardwood floors in rooms in
the main building are in need of refinish-
ing. [$] *Rooms from: C$235* ✉ *60 chemin
Mill* ☎ *888/567–1838, 819/459–1838*
⊕ *www.wakefieldmill.com* ⤷ *42 rooms*
|◎| *Free breakfast.*

Bromont

78 km (48 miles) east of Montréal.

The boating, camping, golf, horseback riding, swimming, tennis, biking,
canoeing, fishing, hiking, cross-country
and downhill skiing, and snowshoeing
available here make this a place for all
seasons. Bromont has the only night
skiing in the Eastern Townships—and
there's even a slope-side disco, Le Bro-
montais. The town also has more than
100 km (62 miles) of maintained trails for
mountain bikers.

GETTING HERE AND AROUND
Bromont is about one hour from Montréal on Autoroute 10. Get off at Exit 78.

VISITOR INFORMATION
CONTACT Bromont Tourism Office. ✉ *15
boul. de Bromont* ☎ *877/276–6668,
450/534–2006* ⊕ *www.tourismebromont.
com.*

◉ Sights

★ **Route des Vins** (*Wine Route*)
WINERY/DISTILLERY | Make sure you bring
along a designated driver for this Wine
Route, which includes 22 wineries. Map
out your chosen stops then travel from
one to the next to learn about their history, local products and, best of all, sample
the wine. Most wineries have an area
outdoors where you can enjoy a picnic.
■ TIP→ **Call for hours as they may change
from one season to the next.** ✉ *Bromont*
☎ *888/811–4928* ⊕ *www.laroutedesvins.
ca/en.*

Vignoble de l'Orpailleur
WINERY/DISTILLERY | Established in 1982,
this vineyard produces 11 wines, including its Double Gold medal-winning ice
wine at the Finger Lakes International
competition. Guided tours (in French)
cost C$10 and are given three times a
day during the summer. You can also
stop by the museum, where you'll learn
about the history and production of wine,
from the cultivation of the vines to the
bottling process. Guided tours given in
Enlglish need to be reserved two weeks
in advance. The patio restaurant is a nice
place to take a break. ✉ *1086 rue Bruce
(Rte. 202), Dunham* ☎ *450/295–2763*
⊕ *www.orpailleur.ca.*

Vignoble Domaine Côtes d'Ardoise
WINERY/DISTILLERY | This winery, opened
in 1980, was one of the first to set up
shop in the area, and is considered to
be the oldest vineyard still in operation in Québec. On nearly 30 acres of
land, 50,000 vines go to produce some
award-winning reds, whites, rosés, and
ice wines. Visit for a tasting and enjoy a
picnic on the grounds. From July through
October, a sculpture garden showcases the works of more than 80 artists,
primarily from the area. ✉ *879 rue Bruce
(Rte. 202), Dunham* ☎ *450/295–2020*
⊕ *www.cotesdardoise.com.*

Vignoble Les Trois Clochers
WINERY/DISTILLERY | This lovely winery
is another great stop along the wine
route. It produces a dry, fruity white from
Seyval grapes as well as several other
white, red, and ice wines. In addition to
the tastings, you can take a tour of the
grounds (reservations required), stroll
along the trails, and stop for a picnic
before you move on to the next stop.
✉ *341 chemin Bruce (Rte. 202), Dunham*
☎ *450/295–2034* ⊕ *www.3clochers.com.*

The Eastern Townships

MONTREAL

MONTÉRÉGIE

EASTERN TOWNSHIPS

MAINE

NEW HAMPSHIRE

VERMONT

NEW YORK

CANADA
U.S.A.

Lac Mégantic

Lac Saint-François

Thetford Mines

Arthabaska

Victoriaville

Drummondville

Valcourt

Granby

Chambly

Bromont
Station de Ski Bromont

Knowlton (Lac Brome)

Dunham
Route des Vins

Sutton

Mansonville

Eastman

Parc du Mont-Orford

Magog

Abbaye St-Benoît-du-Lac

Owl's Head Ski Area

Sherbrooke

Lennoxville

North Hatley

Cookshire

Notre-Dame-des-Bois

Coaticook

Ayer's Cliff

Lac Massawippi

Lac Memphrémagog

Lac Brome

Lake Champlain

Lac Saint-Pierre

R. Saint-François

R. Richelieu

Fleuve Saint-Laurent

TO POINTE-DU-LAC

30 mi
30 km

112
161
112
20
55
143
139
222
222
222
243
216
253
147
245
10
202
112
55
133
35
40
87
133
10
91
10
25
640
20
20
15

🛏 Hotels

Auberge Château Bromont

$ | HOTEL | Among the rolling hills of the Townships and with great views of the local countryside from every room, this modern hotel is part of the Domaine Château-Bromont complex, and well priced, considering all the amenities available. **Pros:** outstanding views from each room; friendly staff; close to ski hill and golf course. **Cons:** lack of an elevator makes it difficult for guests on the upper floors, especially those with ski equipment; the decor is somewhat dated; some rooms still need to be renovated. ⑤ *Rooms from: C$129* ⊠ *95 rue de Montmorency* ☎ *888/276–6668* ⊕ *www.chateaubromont.com* ⌁ *40 rooms* ☷ *No meals.*

Hôtel Château Bromont

$ | HOTEL | Massages, algae wraps, and aromatherapy are just a few of the services at this European-style resort, which also includes a large, Turkish-style *hammam* (steam room) and the Château Bromont Golf Course. **Pros:** outdoor hot tubs; Turkish-style hammam; scenic mountain views. **Cons:** some rooms are small; windows facing the interior courtyard/indoor swimming pool do not open; some rooms are dated. ⑤ *Rooms from: C$180* ⊠ *90 rue Stanstead* ☎ *450/534–3433, 888/276–6668* ⊕ *www.chateaubromont.com* ⌁ *166 rooms* ☷ *No meals.*

🛍 Shopping

MARKETS

★ Bromont Five-Star Flea Market

OUTDOOR/FLEA/GREEN MARKETS | The gigantic sign on Autoroute 10 is hard to miss. More than 1,000 vendors at this indoor flea market sell T-shirts, household gadgets, and much more, on weekends (9–5) from April to the end of October. Shoppers come from as far away as Vermont. ⊠ *16 rue Lafontaine* ☎ *888/689–1255, 450/534–0440* ⊕ *www.mapbromont.com.*

🏃 Activities

GOLF

Royal Bromont

GOLF | Designed by Graham Cooke, one of the most reputable golf course architects, the Royal Bromont was built in 1992 and is located in the center of Bromont. All 18 holes provide wonderful views of the surrounding mountains and, from novice to expert, this golf course is considered to be one of the top places to play. In 1994 the Royal Bromont hosted the Canadian PGA Championships. ⊠ *400 chemin Compton* ☎ *450/534–4653, 888/281–0017* ⊕ *www.royalbromont.com* ⊠ *C$42–C$54* ⚡ *18 holes, 7036 yards, par 72* ⌕ *Facilities: driving range, putting green, golf carts, pull carts, rental clubs, pro shop, golf lessons, restaurant, bar.*

SHOW JUMPING

Parc Équestre Olympique Bromont

SPORTS VENUE | If you love horses and competitions, the Bromont Equestrian Center is the place to visit. Once an Olympic site, it hosts show jumping, dressage, and pony club events, and, in late July, the annual International Bromont Equestrian competition. ⊠ *450 chemin de Gaspé* ☎ *450/534–0787* ⊕ *www.parcequestrebromont.org.*

SKIING

★ Station de Ski Bromont

SKIING/SNOWBOARDING | FAMILY | Not many metropolises in eastern North America can boast a 1,300-foot ski mountain within an hour's drive of Downtown. That height and proximity has made Bromont very popular with Montréal day-trippers and weekenders. But Bromont's 156 trails (102 of them lighted at night) and nine lifts can handle the crowds quite comfortably. Like many other ski hills, Bromont operates as a year-round resort. In summer and early fall, you can take a mountain bike to the summit aboard a chairlift and test your nerves on one of 19 downhill trails, two of which are labeled "easy"—the rest are "hard" to "extreme." Part of the ski hill is converted into the **Bromont Aquatic Park** in summer, with a 24,000-square-foot wave pool and 25 rides and slides. ⊠ *150 rue Champlain* ☎ *450/534–2200, 866/276–6668* ⊕ *www. skibromont.com* ⤢ *Skiing C$37–C$42; aquatic park C$42; mountain biking C$49 per day.*

SPAS

★ Balnea Réserve Thermale

SPA/BEAUTY | Tucked away in a forest and overlooking a lake, this strikingly contemporary spa takes advantage of its location with air beds that float among lily pads, and tiers of sundecks with gorgeous views. In addition to steam rooms, saunas, and baths, Balnea also has 30 body treatments: you can bliss out with the gotu kola and green-tea wrap, a chocolate and grape-seed massage, or yoga by the lake. Full- and half-day spa packages are available. During the summer, Balnea plays host to Summer of Chefs, a gourmet cooking competition that takes places over 10 Sundays and features 10 of Québec's best chefs who take over the kitchen and create their own menu inspired by ingredients available at the nature reserve. ⊠ *319 chemin du Lac Gale* ☎ *866/734–2110, 450/534–0604* ⊕ *www.balnea.ca.*

Knowlton (Lac Brome)

49 km (29 miles) northeast of Bromont, 101 km (63 miles) southeast of Montréal.

Knowlton is the quintessential Eastern Townships resort town, with Loyalist-era buildings, old inns, great antiques shops, and enticing pastry shops. Fortunately, it's managed to retain its particular identity, with a main street full of stores selling antiques, art, clothes, and gifts. Interesting little restaurants have taken residence in renovated clapboard houses painted every color of the rainbow. A frequent feature on most menus here is Brome Lake duck, served in many

different ways. These internationally renowned birds are raised at a farm on the shores of Brome Lake just a few miles outside town. The main regional tourist office is in Foster, one of the other old villages that constitute Lac Brome, but walking maps of Knowlton are available from many local businesses.

GETTING HERE AND AROUND

To get from Montréal to Knowlton, take Autoroute 10 Est, head toward Autoroute 15 Sud, and take Exit 90 for QC–243.

VISITOR INFORMATION

CONTACT Lac Brome Tourism Officem. ⊠ *696 rue Lakeside, Lac Brome* ☎ *450/243–1221* ⊕ *www.touris-melacbrome.com/en/.*

◉ Sights

★ Musée Historique du Comté de Brome

MUSEUM | Here's a wonderful opportunity to learn about the Loyalists who settled the area after fleeing the American Revolution. Several buildings, including the former county courthouse dating back to 1859, the old firehall (fire station), and a former school, house an eclectic collection that include 19th-century farm tools, Native Canadian arrowheads, and a military collection that includes uniforms and a World War 1 Fokker aircraft. The museum also maintains the Tibbits Hill Pioneer School, a stone schoolhouse built in 1834 to serve rural families—kids can find out what education was like in the mid-19th century. ⊠ *130 chemin Lakeside, Knowlton* ☎ *450/243–6782* ⊕ *www.bromemuseum.com* ⤢ *C$8.*

🍴 Restaurants

Knowlton Pub

$$ | CANADIAN | Serving traditional pub fare, the Knowlton Pub has been around since time immemorial and is one of the best-known establishments in the Eastern Townships. The service is friendly but diners have been known to wait a little longer than they'd like for their food to be served, particularly on dinner theater nights. **Known for:** hearty burgers; unrushed service; local institution. $ *Average main: C$15* ✉ *267 Chemin Knowlton, Knowlton* ☎ *450/242-6862* ⊕ *n/a.*

🛏 Hotels

★ Auberge Knowlton

$ | **B&B/INN** | A local landmark since 1849, when it was first a stagecoach stop, and later a railway stop, this rustic inn is a special-occasion venue for locals and a delightful option for visitors who relish period style and good regional cuisine. **Pros:** within walking distance of Knowlton's main attractions; dog-friendly; storage, repair kits, and so on, for bicycles; atmospheric restaurant serving good food. **Cons:** on the main road through town, so not the most scenic location; no elevator; dark, natural light blocked via veranda roof on second floor. $ *Rooms from: C$130* ✉ *286 chemin Knowlton, Lac Brome, Knowlton* ☎ *450/242–6886* ⊕ *www.aubergeknowlton.ca* ⤳ *12 rooms* ⦿| *No meals.*

🎭 Performing Arts

Théâtre Lac Brome

THEATER | This local theater company stages plays, musicals, and productions of classic Broadway and West End hits from mid-June to Labor Day. It hosts professional and amateur English-language productions, but has also dabbled in bilingual productions as well as contemporary works by Canadian playwrights. The 175-seat, air-conditioned theater is behind the Knowlton Pub. ✉ *9 Mount Echo Rd., Knowlton* ☎ *450/242–2270* tickets ⊕ *www.theatrelacbrome.ca.*

👜 Shopping

ANTIQUES

Camlen

ANTIQUES/COLLECTIBLES | Cameron and Helen Brown (get it? Cam + len) import gorgeous antiques from China and eastern Europe, create reproductions using old wood and sell antique Canadian pieces. Their passion for, and dedication to, the art of furniture making are reflected in the high standard of workmanship. ✉ *110 Lakeside Rd., Knowlton* ☎ *450/243–5785* ⊕ *www.camlenfurniture.com.*

CLOTHING

Rococo

CLOTHING | Owners Carla Hadlock and Anita Laurent—the latter a former model—know fashion and style, and have many contacts in the business, so their collection of clothing and accessories includes many items obtained straight from manufacturers. You'll love the prices, too, which are a fraction of what you'd pay in a large retail store. ✉ *293 Knowlton Rd., Knowlton* ☎ *450/243–6948.*

🏃 Activities

Golf Inverness

GOLF | This is a lovely scenic course with far-reaching views to the distant mountains. It was designed by the great John Watson to take full advantage of the gently rolling natural landscape and has three sets of tees for different skill levels. Each green presents an interesting set of challenges, all have a well-placed bunker or two and three holes involve a water feature. Go for the blue tees if you want to test your skill at championship level. The elegant clubhouse dates back to 1915. ✉ *511 chemin Bondville, Knowlton* ☎ *450/242–1595, 800/468–1595* ⊕ *www.golf-inverness.com* ⛳ *C$35 weekdays, C$40 weekends* ⅄ *18 holes, 6326 yards, par 71* ☞ *Facilities: practice green, putting green, golf carts, pull carts, caddies, rental clubs, pro shop, lessons, restaurant, bar.*

Abbaye St-Benoît-du-Lac

132 km (82 miles) southeast of Montréal.

At this impressive abbey, a bell juts above the trees like a fairy-tale castle. Combine its calm and peaceful surroundings with the chance to pick up some of the products sold here, including sparkling apple wine and some of the best cheese in Québec, and you have an expedition that makes for a very memorable experience.

GETTING HERE AND AROUND
To get to the abbey from Magog, take Route 112 and follow the signs for the side road (Rural Route 2, or rue des Pères) to the abbey.

◉ Sights

★ Abbaye St-Benoît-du-Lac
RELIGIOUS SITE | Built by the Benedictines in 1912 on a wooded peninsula on Lac Memphrémagog, the abbey is home to upward of 50 monks. They sell apples and sparkling apple wine from their orchards, as well as cheeses: Ermite (which means "hermit"), St-Benoît, and ricotta. Gregorian prayers are sung daily, and some masses are open to the public; call for the schedule. Dress modestly if you plan to attend vespers or other rituals, and avoid shorts. If you wish to experience a few days of retreat, there are guesthouses for both men and women. Reserve well in advance. Overnight visits cost C$65–C$70 per night, which includes meals. Guided tours of the abbey cost C$12. ✉ *1 rue Main, St-Benoît-du-Lac* ☎ *819/843–4080, 819/843–2861 store* ⊕ *www.abbaye.ca* ⊗ *Closed major holidays. On July 11th, aka the Feast of Saint Benedict, there are no guided tours, and on August 3rd and 17th, there are no guided tours during the afternoon.*

Parc du Mont-Orford

19 km (12 miles) north of Abbaye St-Benoît-du-Lac, 115 km (72 miles) east of Montréal.

In addition to a multitude of year-round outdoor activities, such as hiking, camping, fishing, and snowmobiling, the provincial park here also serves as a nature reserve.

The annual music performances that make up the Festival Orford always draw crowds to the foot of Mont-Orford.

GETTING HERE AND AROUND
From Montréal, go east on Highway 10 (Autoroute des Cantons de l'Est), take Exit 115 onto QC–112 and go north onto QC–141 (chemin du Mont-Orford). Coming from the east, leave Highway 10 at Exit 118 and go north on QC–141.

◉ Sights

Festival Orford
FESTIVAL | Every summer, from the end of June to mid-August, a celebration of music and art brings classical music, jazz, and chamber orchestra concerts to Parc du Mont-Orford. It's organized by the Orford Arts Centre, which has been teaching students the art of classical music and performance since 1951. ✉ *3165 chemin du Parc, Orford* ☎ *819/843–3981 tickets, 800/567–6155 in Canada* ⊕ *www.orford.mu/en.*

Parc du Mont-Orford
NATIONAL/STATE PARK | **FAMILY** | The amount of activities seems almost endless at this 58-square-km (22-square-mile) park. Summertime sees hikers, campers, beach lovers, and canoers enjoying the grounds and in winter, showshoers and cross-country skiers take over. White-tailed deer and blue herons share the park with tourists. The scenery in the fall is spectacular, with vibrant orange, yellow, and red hues spreading across the landscape. ✉ *3321 chemin du Parc,*

Orford ☎ 819/843–9855, 800/665–6527 ⊕ www.sepaq.com/pq/mor ⊞ C\$9 a day.

🛏 Hotels

Estrimont Suites & Spa

\$ | HOTEL | With a Nordic waterfall, Scandinavian baths, and relaxation yurt, plus nearby golf courses, riding stables, and ski hills, this attractive complex fits the bill for an active or relaxing break. **Pros:** very reasonably priced spa packages; excellent place for conferences or business retreats; two outdoor hot tubs in scenic surroundings. **Cons:** only one suite is wheelchair accessible; rooms appear dated; children not allowed in spa yet children were there and noisy. ⓢ *Rooms from: C\$151 ⊠ 44 av. de l'Auberge (Rte. 141 Nord), Orford ☎ 800/567–7320, 819/843–1616 ⊕ www.estrimont.ca ⌐ 95 suites ⍾ Free breakfast.*

Magog

11 km (6 miles) south of Parc du Mont-Orford, 118 km (74 miles) east of Montréal.

This bustling town is at the northern tip of Lac Memphrémagog, a large body of water that reaches into northern Vermont. Its sandy beaches are a draw, and it's also a good place for boating, bird-watching, sailboarding, horseback riding, dog sledding, in-line skating, golfing, bass fishing, and snowmobiling. You might even see Memphré, the lake's sea dragon, on one of the many lake cruises—there have been more than 100 sightings since 1816.

In recent years this formerly depressed textile town has enjoyed something of an economic and cultural rebirth, partially due to the substantial number of artists who have chosen to relocate to this welcoming, and relatively inexpensive, region of the province. The streets downtown are lined with century-old houses

that have been converted into boutiques, stores, and eateries.

GETTING HERE AND AROUND

From Montréal to Magog, take Autoroute 10 Est, keep left toward Autoroute 15 Sud, and then take Exit 118 for QC–141.

VISITOR INFORMATION

CONTACT Memphrémagog Tourism Office. ⊠ *2911 chemin Miletta ☎ 819/843–2744, 800/267–2744 ⊕ www.tourisme-memphremagog.com.*

👁 Sights

Le Cep d'Argent

WINERY/DISTILLERY | The wines from this vineyard have won many awards, including four at a recent Finger Lakes International Wine Competition. The whites are very good, and the dessert wine—similar to a port and flavored with a little maple syrup—goes well with the local cheese. You can take a guided tour of the vineyard and winery, with a tasting of six different wines that have been paired with local foods, for C\$25, or participate in a discovery visit for families, in which adult family members can taste five different products for C\$15. In the new Interpretation Centre you can learn about the traditional ways of making champagne. ⊠ *1257 chemin de la Rivière ☎ 819/864–4441, 877/864–4441 ⊕ www.cepdargent.com.*

🛏 Hotels

Auberge l'Étoile Sur-le-Lac

\$ | B&B/INN | The majority of rooms at this popular inn on Magog's waterfront have lake views, including some with fireplaces. **Pros:** right on Lac Memphrémagog; various packages available; direct access to the popular cycling route Verte; Magog attractions all within comfortable walking distance. **Cons:** not recommended for guests who are looking for isolated, peaceful surroundings; if weather is not accommodating, the hotel does not have alternative activities on offer; heated pool water reported to be colder than lake. $ *Rooms from: C$189* ✉ *1200 rue Principale Ouest* ☎ *819/843–6521, 800/567–2727* ⊕ *www.etoile-sur-le-lac. com* ⇨ *60 rooms* ⊙ *Some meals.*

Spa Eastman
$$ | HOTEL | The oldest spa in Québec, once a simple health center, has evolved into a bucolic haven for anyone seeking rest and therapeutic treatments, including lifestyle and weight-management counseling. **Pros:** dinner included in room rate; a totally relaxing and peaceful respite; wheelchair-accessible rooms. **Cons:** no phone or TV might prove too isolating for some; limited dining selection; reports that not all staff are bilingual. $ *Rooms from: C$215* ✉ *895 chemin des Diligences, Eastman* ☎ *450/297–3009, 800/665–5272* ⊕ *www.spa-eastman.com* ⇨ *44 rooms* ⊙ *All meals.*

Nightlife

Auberge Orford
BARS/PUBS | Come by boat and you can moor right alongside this patio bar that overlooks the Magog River. Sometimes there's live entertainment, but when musicians aren't around, the flocks of ducks lining up alongside the café to beg crumbs from patrons' plates keep patrons entertained. ✉ *20 rue Merry Sud* ☎ *819/843–9361, 877/843–9361* ⊕ *www. auberge-orford.com.*

Café St-Michel
BARS/PUBS | In a century-old building, this pub, outfitted in shades of charcoal and ebony, serves Tex-Mex food, pasta, fish-and-chips and local beers. Its patio bar, at Magog's main intersection, may not be peaceful, but it's a great spot to watch the world go by. *Chansonniers* (singers) belt out popular hits for a full house on Friday and Saturday evening starting at 6 pm. ✉ *503 rue Principale Ouest* ☎ *819/868–1062* ⊕ *www.cafestmichel. com.*

Microbrasserie La Memphré
BREWPUBS/BEER GARDENS | Named after the monster said to lurk in Lake Memphrémagog, La Memphré dates back to the 1800s, when it belonged to Magog's first mayor. Now a microbrewery, it serves Swiss-cheese fondue, sausages with beer mustard, onion soup, and panini—all good accompaniments for a cold one. Hope for a train to go by when you're in the restaurant: if you hear the horns, a pitcher of house beer is only C$15! ✉ *12 rue Merry Sud* ☎ *819/843–3405* ⊕ *www.lamic.ca.*

🎭 Performing Arts

Le Vieux Clocher de Magog
MUSIC | Originally built in 1881 as a Methodist church, and converted into a theater by local impresario Bernard Caza 100 years later, this theater headlines well-known francophone comedians and singers such as Claude Dubois and Gilles Vigneault. Most, if not all, performances are in French. ✉ *64 rue Merry Nord* ☎ *819/847–0470* ⊕ *www.vieuxclocher. com.*

🏃 Activities

GOLF
Golf Owl's Head
GOLF | This course, close to the Vermont border, has some spectacular views. Laid out with undulating fairways, bent-grass greens, and 64 sand bunkers, the course, designed by Graham Cooke, is surrounded by mountain scenery. The clubhouse, a stunning timber-and-fieldstone structure with five fireplaces and 45-foot-high ceilings, is a popular watering hole. ✉ *187 chemin Owl's Head, Mansonville* ☎ *450/292–3342, 800/363–3342* ⊕ *www. owlshead.com* 💲 *C$44 weekdays, C$54 weekends* 🏌 *18 holes, 6710 yards, par 72* ☞ *Facilities: driving range, putting green, pitching area, golf carts, pull carts, rental clubs, pro shop, golf lessons, restaurant, bar.*

Manoir des Sables golf course

GOLF | Between Mount Orford and Lake Memphrémagog, this resort course comes with some of the best scenery in the Eastern Townships and has been voted a favorite course in Québec. The best views are from the second, third, and fourth holes. Several water hazards are dotted around the course, with streams cutting across more than half the fairways and ponds calling for accurate shots onto some greens. ✉ *90 av. des Jardins, Orford* ☎ *819/847–4299, 866/656–4747* ⊕ *www.hotelsvillegia. com* ✉ *Weekdays C$36, weekends C$40* 🏌 *18 holes, 6352 yards, par 71.*

Mont-Orford Golf Club

GOLF | This venerable course in the heart of the national park winds through forested land, with the peak of Mont-Orford visible from many of its greens. There are some tricky holes—look out for the pond to the right of the fairway and an uphill putt on the 5th, the two streams cutting across the 8th, and the sharp dog-leg on the 13th. All in all, it's a satisfying challenge and an exceptionally scenic course to play. ✉ *3074 chemin du Parc* ☎ *819/843–5688, 866/673–6731* ⊕ *www. orford.com* ✉ *C$40 weekdays, C$43 weekends* 🏌 *18 holes, 6095 yards, par 72* ☞ *Facilities: golf carts, rental clubs, pro shop, lessons, restaurant.*

SKIING

★ Owl's Head Ski Area

SKIING/SNOWBOARDING | On the Knowlton Landing side of Lake Memphrémagog, Owl's Head is great for skiers seeking sparser crowds—and the views from its peak are truly exceptional. It has eight lifts, a 1,772-foot vertical drop, and 50 trails, including a 4-km (2½-mile) intermediate run, the longest such run in the Eastern Townships. It's also one of the least expensive hills in the Townships. Under new management since 2017, the facility has been privy to many recent upgrades, and there are millions more pledged to further modernize the facility throughout 2020. ✉ *40 chemin du Mont-Owl's Head* ☎ *450/292–3342, 800/363–3342* ⊕ *www.owlshead.com* ✉ *C$58 day ski pass.*

North Hatley

10 km (6 miles) east of Magog, 133 km (83 miles) east of Montréal.

Along with Frelighsburg and Knowlton, North Hatley is undoubtedly one of Québec's prettiest villages. The small resort town on the tip of Lac Massawippi has a theater as well as some excellent inns and restaurants. Set among hills and farms, it was discovered by rich vacationers in the early 1900s, and has been drawing visitors ever since. It was particularly popular with magnates from the American South who were looking for a cool summer refuge that wasn't controlled by the Yankees. The result is that some of the village's most majestic buildings are more reminiscent of Georgia than Vermont.

GETTING HERE AND AROUND

From Montréal to North Hatley, take Autoroute 10 Est to Autoroute 15 Sud, and then take Exit 121 to get onto Autoroute 55 Sud. Take Exit 29 for QC–108.

 Restaurants

Pilsen Pub

$$$ | **AMERICAN** | Massawippi pale and brown ales and a vast selection of microbrews and imports are all on tap here. Pub food is served both in the upstairs dining room and in the tavern. **Known for:** a vast selection of microbrews and imports on tap; burgers and homemade soups; lively, welcoming atmosphere. ⑤ *Average main: C$21* ✉ *55 rue Principale* ☎ *819/842–2971* ⊕ *www.pilsen.ca.*

For just a few nights a year, during the Festival d'astronomie Populaire du Mont-Mégantic, the Astrolab du Mont-Mégantic's large telescope is accessible to the public.

🛏 Hotels

★ Manoir Hovey

$$$$ | HOTELHOTEL | Overlooking Lac Massawippi, with a private beach, this elegant retreat feels rather like a private estate, with many activities, such as tennis, boating, and bicycling, included in the room rate. **Pros:** lakeside setting; secluded; historic buildings; wheelchair accessible. **Cons:** main restaurant overpriced; grounds often taken over by weddings on weekends; 10% tax added to Saturday-night room rate. ⑤ *Rooms from: C$460* ⊠ *575 chemin Hovey* ☎ *819/842–2421, 800/661–2421* ⊕ *www. manoirhovey.com* ⇨ *36 rooms* ⊙ *Some meals.*

🎭 Performing Arts

★ Piggery

THEATER | Enriching the Townships' cultural landscape since 1965, this theater, in a former pig barn in the mountains, is known for showcasing English-language plays, with a focus on Canadian playwrights. Concerts, magic shows, and comedy acts also feature in a season that runs mid-May through October. ⊠ *215 chemin Simard* ☎ *819/842–2431* ⊕ *www. piggery.com.*

Sherbrooke

21 km (12 miles) northeast of North Hatley, 130 km (81 miles) east of Montréal.

Sherbrooke bills itself as the *Reine des Cantons de l'Est* (Queen of the Eastern Townships), and with a population of more than 150,000, it's far and away the region's largest and most important city. The Loyalists who founded the city in the 1790s and who named it for Sir John Coape Sherbrooke, one of Canada's pre-Confederation governors-general, used the power of the Rivière St-François to build a strong industrial base. Though the city's economic importance has waned, it still has significant manufacturing and textile plants, and Wellington Street, in the downtown area, is experiencing a significant face-lift, with trendy restaurants, bars, and clubs now occupying once-vacant lots.

GETTING HERE AND AROUND

Sherbrooke is easy to get to by car via Autoroute 10. From the United States, it's an easy stop on the way to Montréal if you cross the border via Interstate 91 and take Autoroute 55. There are also frequent bus connections between Montréal and Sherbrooke. The city is large and quite hilly, so getting around on foot can be difficult. But there's a well-developed bus system.

VISITOR INFORMATION

CONTACT Sherbrooke Tourism Office.
✉ 785 rue King Ouest ☎ 819/821–1919, 800/561–8331 ⊕ www.destinationsherbrooke.com.

Sights

Musée de la Nature et des Sciences

MUSEUM | FAMILY | Fun and educational for the whole family, this natural history museum utilizes imaginative multisensory displays with state-of-the-art light and sound effects—the buzzing of mosquitoes may be *too* lifelike—and hands-on displays to enhance the experience. Long-running temporary exhibits include Terra Mutantes, a geological experience portraying the birth of the Appalachian Mountains, and AlterAnima, exploring animal life in a mythical forest. Both will be available until May or June 2020. ✉ 225 rue Frontenac ☎ 819/564–3200, 877/434–3200 ⊕ mns2.ca/ 🎫 C$13.

Musée des Beaux-Arts de Sherbrooke

MUSEUM | This fine-arts museum has a permanent exhibit on the history of art in the region from 1800 to the present. More than 10 exhibits per year are staged in its three galleries, with an emphasis on artists from the Eastern Townships. ✉ 241 rue Dufferin ☎ 819/821–2115 ⊕ www.mbas.qc.ca 🎫 C$10 ☉ Closed Mon.

🍴 Restaurants

Auguste

$$$$ | BISTRO | FAMILY | Auguste placed Sherbrooke on the foodie map when it opened in 2008, and it continues to impress. Local ingredients take pride of place in this minimalist bistro-style restaurant, which features dishes like mushroom risotto or sweet potato ravioli. **Known for:** pouding chômeur (poor man's pudding) drenched in maple syrup; free children's dinner menu Sun.–Wed.; providing a true gastronomic experience. 🛈 *Average main: C$34* ✉ *82 rue Wellington N* ☎ *819/565–9559* ⊕ *www.auguste-restaurant.com* ☉ *No brunch weekdays.*

🎭 Performing Arts

Centennial Theatre

THEATER | On the campus of Bishop's University, this 600-seat theater presents a roster of jazz, classical, and rock concerts, as well as opera, dance, mime, and children's theater. ✉ 2600 rue College ☎ 819/822–9692 ⊕ www.centennialtheatre.ca.

Le Vieux Clocher de l'Université de Sherbrooke

MUSIC | Le Vieux Clocher de l'Université de Sherbrooke presents music, from classical to jazz, and a variety of theater and comedy shows. ✉ 2500, boul. de l'Université ☎ 819/820–1000 ⊕ www.centreculturueludes.ca.

🛍 Shopping

Boutique des Métiers d'Art

CLOTHING | Stop in this charming little shop filled with crafts, jewelry, kitchenware, and clothing made by artists from the Eastern Townships. ✉ 121 rue Frontenac ☎ 819/823–0221 ⊕ www.metiersdartestrie.com ☉ Closed Mon. and Tues.

Notre-Dame-des-Bois

72 km (43 miles) east of Sherbrooke, 204 km (127 miles) east of Montréal.

Notre-Dame-des-Bois is a sleepy little one-street village just north of the Maine border. It sits in the shadow of one of the region's tallest and steepest mountains—Mont-Mégantic, which soars 576 meters (1,890 feet) above the surrounding plain, with a height of 3,601 feet above sea level. In 2007, the Mont-Mégantic Observatory area was declared the first International Dark Sky Reserve, in recognition of the lack of light pollution that provides some of the clearest night skies in Québec, a quality that attracts stargazers, both professional and amateur.

GETTING HERE AND AROUND

Count on a three-hour journey from Montréal, some of it over paved but bumpy secondary roads. To get here, follow Autoroute 10 east past Sherbrooke to its end near Ascot Corner, then follow Route 112 to East Angus, then Route 253 to Cookshire, and finally Route 212 through L'Avenir to Notre-Dame-des-Bois. If you want to make the journey comfortably, plan to stay overnight somewhere rather than just coming for the day.

◉ Sights

Astrolab du Mont-Mégantic (*Mont-Mégantic's Observatory*)

OBSERVATORY | Both amateur stargazers and serious astronomers head to this observatory, located in a beautifully wild and mountainous area that in 2007 became the first-ever International Dark Sky Reserve. The observatory is at the summit of the Townships' second-highest mountain (3,601 feet above sea level and 1,890 feet above the surrounding landscape), whose northern face records annual snowfalls rivaling any in North America. A joint venture of the University of Montréal and Laval University, the observatory has a powerful telescope,

the largest on the East Coast. In the Astrolab's welcome center at the mountain's base, there is an exhibition and multimedia display to provide visitors with information about the night sky. ■ TIP→ **Hours vary depending on the season, so check website for updated information.** ⊠ *Parc Mégantic, 189 Rte. du Parc* ☎ *819/888–2941, 888/665–6527* ⊕ *www.astrolab-parc-national-mont-megantic.org* ✉ *Observatory and Astrolab: C$19 daytime, C$21–C$25 at night. Additional fee of C$9 charged to enter Parc Mégantic* ⚓ *Reservations essential.*

Parc du Mont-Méganti

NATIONAL/STATE PARK | If you're short on time or don't feel like a hike you can take a shuttle bus to the top of Mont-Mégantic for spectacular views of Québec, Maine, New Hampshire, and on really clear days, Vermont. But if you want the full experience, walk up. The park has 50 km (31 miles) of hiking trails that are also open in winter to snowshoers and cross-country skiers. For a real adventure, you can stay overnight in one of the park's rustic shelters. ⊠ *189 Rte. du Parc* ☎ *819/888–2941, 800/665–6527* ⊕ *www.sepaq.com/pq/mme* ✉ *C$9.*

🍽 Restaurants

★ Aux Berges de l'Aurore

$ | B&B/INN | From its lofty perch, this delightful century-old inn has spectacular views day and night—it's within the International Dark Sky Reserve—and is less than a minute's drive from Mont Mégantic National Park and the Astrolab. **Pros:** great scenery; close to area activities; delicious breakfasts; hiking trails on the property. **Cons:** minimum two-night stay holiday weekends and some other times; threadbare towels; no shampoo or conditioner provided; some bathrooms have musty odor. ⑤ *Rooms from: C$130* ⊠ *139 Rte. du Parc* ☎ *819/888–2715* ⊕ *www.auberge-aurore.qc.ca* ⤴ *5 rooms* ⦿ *Free breakfast.*

Chapter 5

QUÉBEC CITY

Updated by
Marie-Eve Vallieres

⊙ Sights	🍴 Restaurants	🛏 Hotels	🛍 Shopping	🍸 Nightlife
★★★★★	★★★★☆	★★★★★	★★★☆☆	★★★★☆

WELCOME TO QUÉBEC CITY

TOP REASONS TO GO

★ **See the Château Frontenac:** Even if you're not staying at Québec City's most famous landmark, make sure to pop into one of the world's legendary hotels.

★ **Dine at world-class restaurants:** High-end bistros; hip, hole-in-the-wall cafés; amazing breweries and wine bars: Québec City has it all.

★ **Explore La Citadelle:** Québec City's pièce de résistance is the largest fortified base in North America and site of the daily Changing of the Guard in summer.

★ **Play on the Plains of Abraham:** This huge park is a popular place for outdoor fun, from cross-country skiing and sledding in winter to picnicking, concerts, and in-line skating in summer.

★ **Get Festive:** For three weekends in January and February, the city hosts one of the biggest winter festivals in the world. In July, up to 80,000 people cheer some of the biggest rock and pop stars at the open-air Summer Festival.

The central portions of Upper Town (Haute-Ville) and Lower Town (Basse-Ville) make up the Old City or Old Québec (Vieux-Québec). You can walk downhill (or uphill, as the case may be) from one to the other, or ride the funicular that runs between them. Beyond the walls of Old City, approaching it from the west, is the Grande-Allée.

1 Upper Town. Crowning Cap Diamant and partially surrounded by the Fortifications, Upper Town hosts the city's main attractions, including the majestic Château Frontenac and La Citadelle, a star-shaped fortress. The sweeping views of the St. Lawrence River, the Laurentian Mountains to the north, and the Appalachians to the south are all enchanting.

2 Lower Town. A maze of cobblestone streets with tucked-away cafés, boutique hotels, artisan shops, and art galleries characterizes Lower Town.

3 Outside the Old City. Rue St-Jean, avenue Cartier, the Grande-Allée, and the St-Roch district all have restaurants, shops, and nightlife worth checking out.

Québec City's alluring setting atop Cape Diamond (Cap Diamant) evokes a past of high adventure, military history, and exploration. This French-speaking capital city is the only walled city north of Mexico. Visitors come for the delicious and inventive cuisine, the remarkable historical continuity, and to share in the seasonal exuberance of one of the largest francophone populations outside France.

The historic heart of this community is the Old City (Vieux-Québec), comprising the part of Upper Town (Haute-Ville) surrounded by walls and Lower Town (Basse-Ville), which spreads out at the base of the hill from Place Royale. Many sets of staircases and the popular funicular link the top of the hill with the bottom. Cobblestone streets, horse-drawn carriages, and elaborate cathedrals here are charming in all seasons. The Old City earned recognition as an official UNESCO World Heritage site in 1985, thanks largely to city planners who managed to update and preserve the 400-year-old buildings and attractions without destroying what made them worth preserving. The most familiar icon of the city, Fairmont Château Frontenac, is set on the highest point in Upper Town, where it holds court over the entire city.

Sitting proudly above the confluence of the St. Lawrence and St. Charles rivers, the city's famous military fortification, La Citadelle, built in the early 19th century, remains the largest of its kind in North America. In summer, visitors should try to catch the Changing of the Guard, held every morning at 10 am; you can get much closer to the guards here than at Buckingham Palace in London.

Enchanting as it is, the Old City is just a small part of the true Québec City experience. Think outside the walls and explore St-Roch, a Downtown hot spot, which has artsy galleries, foodie haunts, and a bustling square. Meander down the Grande-Allée and avenue Cartier to find a livelier part of town dotted with nightclubs and fun eateries. Or while away the hours in St-Jean-Baptiste, a neighborhood with trendy shops and hipster hangouts.

Planning

When to Go

Winter can be formidable, but the city stays alive—especially during the popular Winter Carnival. Spring is short and sweet with the *cabanes à sucre* (sugar shacks) bringing fresh maple goodies. In summer, the city's terraces and courtyards open and everyone comes out to enjoy the sunshine. In late September and early October, the region's foliage blazes with color.

Getting Here and Around

The Funiculaire du Vieux-Québec, a small elevator up the side of the steep embankment, travels between Upper and Lower towns. Another option, and a good workout, is to take one of the sets of stairs that start in Upper Town and end at the Quartier du Petit Champlain in Lower Town. Renting a car isn't recommended (parking can be a real issue) unless you're taking day trips outside the city.

AIR TRAVEL
If you're flying in, Jean-Lesage International Airport is about 19 km (12 miles) northwest of Downtown. Driving into town, take Route 540 (Autoroute Duplessis) to Route 175 (boulevard Laurier). The ride takes about 30 minutes. Taxis are available immediately outside the airport exit near the baggage-claim area. A ride into the city costs C$35.10.

BUS TRAVEL
Bus service in Québec City is an effective way to go from the Vieux-Québec to other parts of the city, particularly using the Metrobus lines (those with an 800 number). C$8.75 for a one-day ticket, C$3.50 for a one-way trip.

CAR TRAVEL
Montréal and Québec City are linked by Autoroute 20 on the south shore of the St. Lawrence River and by Autoroute 40 on the north shore. On both highways, the ride between the two cities is about 240 km (150 miles) and takes about three hours. U.S. I–87 in New York, U.S. I–89 in Vermont, and U.S. I–91 in New Hampshire connect with Autoroute 20, as does Highway 401 from Toronto. Driving northeast out of Montréal on Autoroute 20, follow signs for Pont Pierre-Laporte (Pierre Laporte Bridge) as you approach

Québec City. After you've crossed the bridge, take the exit to boulevard Laurier (Route 175), which becomes the Grande-Allée.

CRUISE SHIP TRAVEL
Charming shops and cobblestone streets greet visitors arriving to Québec City by boat. The cruise port, located on rue Dalhousie in Petite Champlain, is on the same street as the Musée de la Civilisation and just a few streets away from Place Royale. Take the (C$3.50) funicular on Petit-Champlain to get close to the Chateau Frontenac and stroll along Terrasse Dufferin.

TRAIN TRAVEL
VIA Rail, Canada's passenger rail service, has service between Montréal and Québec City. The trip takes less than three hours. One-way tickets cost C$89, but early reservation rates can be as low as C$29. A taxi from the Gare du Palais train station to the Fairmont Le Château Frontenac is about C$8.

Restaurants

Bistros, sidewalk cafés, and chic, cutting-edge restaurants make up the dining scene in Québec City. "Grab and go" is more the exception than the rule; be prepared to eat at a leisurely pace. Québec's culinary scene offers variety, including modern international cuisine and inventive farm-to-table bistros, traditional French dishes like foie gras and escargot; distinctly French-Canadian specialties such as *tourtière* (meat pie); and local fare such as ice cider, poutine, and maple sugar pie.

With so many options, choosing where to go can be difficult. Many establishments post their *menu du jour* outside, so you can stroll along and let your cravings guide the way. But bear in mind that reservations are a must at most restaurants during holidays, Winter Carnival, and in the summer months, when the coveted outdoor terraces open. When ordering, remember that in this French-speaking province, an *entrée* is an appetizer and the *plat principal* is the main course. Plan to tip at least 15% of the bill. *Restaurant reviews have been shortened. For full information, visit Fodors.com.*

What it Costs in Canadian Dollars			
$	$$	$$$	$$$$
RESTAURANTS			
under C$12	C$12– C$20	C$21– C$30	over C$30

Hotels

More than 35 hotels are located in Old Québec, and there's also an abundance of family-run bed-and-breakfasts. Landmark hotels are as prominent as the city's most historic sights, while modern high-rises outside the ramparts have spectacular views of the Old City. Another option is to immerse yourself in the city's historic charm by staying in an old-fashioned inn, where no two rooms are alike.

Be sure to make a reservation if you visit during peak season (May through September) or during the Winter Carnival, in late January and early February.

During especially busy times, hotel rates usually rise 30%. From November through April, many lodgings offer weekend discounts and other promotions. *Hotel reviews have been shortened. For full information, visit Fodors.com.*

What it Costs in Canadian Dollars			
$	$$	$$$	$$$$
HOTELS			
under C$160	C$160– C$200	C$201– C$250	over C$250

Nightlife

In winter, nightlife activity grows livelier as the week nears its end, beginning on Wednesday. As warmer temperatures set in, the café-terrace crowd emerges, and bars are active just about every night. Most bars and clubs stay open until 3 am.

Performing Arts

Québec City has a good variety of cultural institutions for a town of its size, from its renowned symphony orchestra to several small theater companies. To sample its nightlife, you'll probably find yourself heading to the clubs and cafés of rue St-Jean, avenue Cartier, and Grande-Allée, and to a lesser extent Lower Town.

Billetech. ⊠ *Centre Vidéotron, Parc de l'Expocité, 250 boul. Wilfrid-Hamel, Limoilou* ☎ *418/643–8131* ⊕ *www. billetech.com.*

Shopping

On the fashionable streets of Vieux-Québec, shopping has a European tinge. The boutiques and specialty shops clustered along narrow streets such as rue du Petit-Champlain and rues de Buade and St-Jean are especially traditional.

Stores are generally open Monday–Wednesday 9:30–5:30, Thursday and Friday until 9, Saturday until 5, and Sunday noon–5. In summer most shops have later evening hours.

Visitor Information

Québec City Tourist Information. ⊠ *12 rue Sainte-Anne, Upper Town* ☎ *418/641–6290, 877/266–5687* ⊕ *www.que-bec-cite.com/en.*

Upper Town

No other place in Canada has so much history squeezed into such a small spot. Upper Town was a barren, windswept cape when Samuel de Champlain decided to build a fort here nearly 400 years ago. Now it's a major tourist destination surrounded by cannon-studded stone ramparts.

Home to the city's most famous sites, Upper Town's Old City offers a dramatic view of the St. Lawrence River and the countryside, especially from a ride on the funicular (C$2) or while walking along the Terrasse Dufferin, in front of the Château Frontenac. Historic buildings that house bars, cafés, and shops and hotels line the neighborhood's winding streets. A 3-mile-long wall neatly splices off this section of the city with entrances on rues St-Jean and St-Louis, Vieux-Québec's two main thoroughfares. The wall itself is a national historic monument. It began as a series of earthworks and wooden palisades built by French military engineers to protect the Upper Town from an inland attack following the siege of the city by Admiral Phipps in 1690. Over the next century, the French expended much time, energy, and money to strengthen the city's fortifications. After the fall of New France, the British were equally concerned about strengthening the city's defenses and built an earth-and-wood citadel atop Cap Diamant. Slowly, the British replaced the palisades that surrounded the city with the massive cut-stone wall that has become the city's trademark attraction. The crowning touch came after the War of 1812, with the construction of the cut-stone, star-shaped citadel, perched high on Cap Diamant.

Like La Citadelle, most of the homes that line the narrow streets in Upper Town are made of granite cut from nearby quarries in the 1800s. The stone walls, copper roofs, and heavy wooden doors on the government buildings and high-steepled churches in the area also reflect the Upper Town's place as the political, educational, and religious nerve center of both the province and the country during much of the past four centuries.

GETTING HERE AND AROUND

Many people begin their tours in Upper Town, taking in the spectacular hilltop views as well as the Château Frontenac, which is probably Québec City's top site. The Fortifications border this section of the city. Walk along rue d'Auteuil, between rues St-Louis and St-Jean, to get a good sense of where the wall divides the Old City.

If you're coming from Lower Town, take the funicular, or brave one of the many staircases that connect the top of the hill to the bottom and bypass the funicular line, which gets long in the summer. Shops and restaurants provide an opportunity for a quick rest along the way uphill.

TIMING

Plan to spend a whole day visiting the many sights and shops clustered around the Château Frontenac. Rue St-Jean offers many lunch options, or do as the locals do and grab a sandwich and head to a bench in one of the area's parks.

Allot at least a half day for walking the walls of La Citadelle. Set out early in the morning to catch the Changing of the Guard (10 am in summer). Afterward, picnic on the Plains, or one of the terraces on the Grande Allée and avenue Cartier.

⊙ Sights

Basilique Cathédrale Notre-Dame de Québec (*Our Lady of Québec Basilica Cathedral*)
RELIGIOUS SITE | François de Laval, the first bishop of New France, once ruled a diocese that stretched to the Gulf of Mexico. Laval's original cathedral burned down and has been rebuilt several times, but the current basilica still has a

A castle in the clouds, the Fairmont Le Château Frontenac is dramatically positioned atop Cap Diamant overlooking the St. Lawrence River and Quebec City.

chancel lamp that was a gift from Louis XIV, the Sun King.

The church's interior includes a canopy dais over the Episcopal throne, a ceiling of painted clouds decorated with gold leaf, and richly colored stained-glass windows. The large crypt was Québec City's first cemetery; more than 900 bodies are interred here, including 20 bishops and four governors of New France. Samuel de Champlain may be buried near the basilica; archaeologists have been searching for his tomb since 1950. There are panels that allow you to read about the history of this church. If you prefer, guided tours of the cathedral and crypt (by appointment only) are also available. The Centre d'animation François-de-Laval uses videos and pictures to illustrate the life of Québec's first bishop and founder of Canada's Catholic Church. A "holy door" was added to the church in 2014. ✉ *16 rue de Buade, Upper Town* ☎ *418/692–2533* ⊕ *www.notre-dame-de-quebec.org/home* 🎫 *C$5.*

Cathedral of the Holy Trinity

RELIGIOUS SITE | The first Anglican cathedral outside the British Isles was erected in the heart of Québec City's Upper Town between 1800 and 1804. Its simple, dignified facade is reminiscent of London's St. Martin-in-the-Fields, and the pediment, archway, and Ionic pilasters introduced Palladian architecture to Canada. The land on which the cathedral was built was originally given to the Récollets (Franciscan monks from France) in 1681 by the king of France for a church and monastery. When Québec came under British rule, the Récollets made the church available to the Anglicans for services. Later, King George III ordered construction of the present cathedral, with an area set aside for members of the royal family. A portion of the north balcony is still reserved for the use of the reigning sovereign or his or her representative. The church houses precious objects donated by George III, and numerous plaques honor distinguished members of the local English community. The cathedral's impressive rear organ has 3,058 pipes. Even more impressive is the smaller English chamber organ, built in 1790, which was donated to the cathedral for the bicentenial celebrations in 2004. ⊠ *31 rue des Jardins, Upper Town* ☎ *418/692–2193* ⊕ *www.cathedral. ca* ⊠ *Free.*

Chapelle des Ursulines (*Ursuline Chapel*)
RELIGIOUS SITE | Founded in 1639, the Couvent des Ursulines is the oldest institution of learning for women in North America. Its chapel is where French general Louis-Joseph Montcalm was buried after he died in the 1759 battle that decided the fate of New France. It also houses the finest examples of wood carving anywhere in Québec, gilded by the nuns themselves. In 2001, Montcalm's remains were transferred to rest with those of his soldiers at the Hôpital Général de Québec's cemetery, at 260 boulevard Langelier. The exterior of the Ursuline Chapel was rebuilt in 1902, but the interior contains the original chapel, which took sculptor Pierre-Noël Levasseur from 1726 to 1736 to complete. The Ursulines is still an active elementary school today. ⊠ *2 rue du Parloir, Upper Town* ☎ *418/694–0694* ⊕ *www.ursulines-uc.com/en/visiting* ⊠ *Free* ⊙ *Closed Mon. and Nov.–Apr.*

Édifice Price
BUILDING | Styled after the Empire State Building, this 17-story, art deco structure was the city's first skyscraper when it was built in 1929. It served as headquarters of the Price Brothers Company, a lumber firm founded by Sir William Price, and today is an official residence of the premier of Québec, who uses the top two floors. ⊠ *65 rue Ste-Anne, Upper Town.*

⭐ **Fairmont Le Château Frontenac**
HOTEL—SIGHT | The most photographed landmark in Québec City, this imposing turreted castle with a copper roof owes its name to the Comte de Frontenac, governor of the French colony between 1672 and 1698. Samuel de Champlain

was responsible for Château St-Louis, the first structure to appear on the site of the Frontenac; it was built between 1620 and 1624 as a residence for colonial governors. In 1784 Château Haldimand was constructed here, but it was demolished in 1892. The original portions of the hotel opened the following year, one in a series of château-style hotels built across Canada to attract wealthy railroad travelers. It was remarkably luxurious for the time: guest rooms contained fireplaces, bathrooms, and marble fixtures, and a special commissioner purchased antiques for the establishment. The hotel was designed by New York architect Bruce Price, who also worked on Québec City's train station, Gare du Palais. The addition of a 20-story central tower in 1924 completed the hotel. Since then the Château, as it's called by locals, has accumulated a star-studded guest roster, including Prince William and Kate Middleton, Queen Elizabeth II, Princess Grace of Monaco, Alfred Hitchcock and Ronald Reagan, as well as Franklin Roosevelt and Winston Churchill, who met here in 1943 and 1944 for two wartime conferences. ⊠ *1 rue des Carrières, Upper Town* ☎ *418/692–3861* ⊕ *www.fairmont. com/frontenac.*

Fortifications of Québec National Historic Site
HISTORIC SITE | In the early 19th century this was just a clear space surrounded by a picket fence and poplar trees. The French began building ramparts along the city's cliffs as early as 1690 to protect themselves from British invaders. But the colonists had trouble convincing the French government to take the threat of invasion seriously, and when the British invaded in 1759 the walls were still incomplete. The British, despite attacks by the Americans during the American Revolution and the War of 1812, took a century to finish them—and they never saw armed conflict. From June to early October, the park is the starting point for walking the city's 5 km (3 miles) of

5

Upper Town (Haute-Ville)

Marché du Vieux-Port

Bassin Louise

rue Abraham Martin

quai St-André

rue St-Paul

des Remparts

côte Dambourges

rue Mar-de

rue Hébert

rue Laval

rue de la Vieille-Université

Port-Dauphin

r. du Sault-au-Matelot

rue St-Pierre

rue St-Paul

rue Bell

quai St-André

r. de Quercy

Musée de la Civilisation

rue St-Antoine

rue Dalhousie

rue de la Barricade

rue Prince-de-Galles

VIEUX-PORT

Le Terminal-Port of Québec

la Montagne

r. du Porche

OLD PORT

LOWER TOWN

Promenade de la Pointe-à-Carcy

St. Lawrence River

TO GROSSE ÎLE → NATIONAL PARK

TO LÉVIS

KEY

- 🔴 *Sights*
- 🔴 *Restaurants*
- 🔴 *Hotels*
- 🚢 *Ferry*
- ⊢—⊢ *Rail Line*
- —— *Ramparts*
- 🛈 *Tourist Information*

Sights ▼

1 Basilique Cathédrale Notre-Dame de Québec................ **F5**
2 Cathedral of the Holy Trinity **E6**
3 Chapelle des Ursulines................. **D5**
4 Édifice Price............. **D5**
5 Fairmont Le Château Frontenac................. **E6**
6 Fortifications of Québec National Historic Site.... **C3**
7 Henry Stuart House **A5**
8 Jardin des Gouverneurs **D7**
9 La Citadelle.............. **B7**
10 Louis S. St. Laurent Heritage House **A5**
11 Maison de la Littérature **D4**
12 Le Monastère des Augustins **F4**
13 Morrin Cultural Centre.......... **D4**
14 Musée de l'Amérique Francophone............. **F5**
15 Musée National des Beaux-Arts du Québec............... **A5**
16 Parc de l'Artillerie **C3**
17 Parc Jeanne d'Arc **A5**
18 Plains of Abraham **A5**
19 Séminaire de Québec................... **F5**
20 St-Louis Forts and Châteaux National Historic Site **F7**
21 Terrasse Dufferin........ **E7**
22 Wolfe-Montcalm Monument.............. **D7**

Restaurants ▼

1 Aux Anciens Canadiens **D6**
2 Café-Boulangerie Paillard.................. **D4**
3 Casse-Crêpe Breton..... **E4**
4 Chez Boulay Bistro Boréal............ **D4**
5 Le Champlain - Fairmont Château Frontenac **E6**
6 Le Chic Shack............ **F6**
7 Le Continental............ **E6**
8 L'Entrecôte Saint-Jean............... **D4**
9 Le Saint-Amour **C5**
10 Sapristi.................... **C4**

Hotels ▼

1 Auberge Place d'Armes **E5**
2 Fairmont Le Château Frontenac Hotel.......... **E6**
3 Hilton Quebec **B4**
4 Hôtel Cap Diamant...... **C7**
5 Hôtel Champlain **D5**
6 Hôtel Château Bellevue **D7**
7 Hôtel du Vieux-Québec............. **E4**
8 Hôtel Le Clos St-Louis **C6**
9 Hôtel Manoir Victoria ... **E3**
10 Hôtel Marie-Rollet....... **D5**
11 Le Monastère des Augustines **F4**
12 Manoir d'Auteuil.........**C5**
13 Quebec City Marriott Downtown **B3**

The History of Québec City

Québec City was founded by French explorer Samuel de Champlain in 1608 and is the oldest municipality in the province. In the 17th century, the first French explorers, fur trappers, and missionaries arrived to establish a colony.

French explorer Jacques Cartier arrived in 1535, and although he did attempt to set up a (short-lived) colony, it was Champlain who founded "New France" some 70 years later and built a fort (called Place Royale today) on the banks of the St. Lawrence.

The British were persistent in their efforts to dislodge the French from North America, but the colonists of New France built forts and other military structures, such as a wooden palisade (defensive fence) that reinforced their position on top of the cliff. It was Britain's naval supremacy that ultimately led to New France's demise. After capturing all French forts east of Québec, General James Wolfe led his army to Québec City in the summer of 1759.

After a monthslong siege, thousands of British soldiers scaled the heights along a narrow cow path on a moonless night. Surprised to see British soldiers massed on a farmer's field so near the city, French general Louis-Joseph Montcalm rushed out to meet them in what became known as the Battle of the Plains of Abraham.

The French were routed in the 20-minute skirmish, which claimed the lives of both Wolfe and Montcalm. The battle symbolically marks the death of New France and the birth of British Canada.

British rule was a boon for Québec City. Thanks to more robust trade and large capital investments, the fishing, fur-trading, shipbuilding, and timber industries expanded rapidly.

Wary of new invasions from its former American colonies, the British also expanded the city's fortifications. They replaced the wooden palisades with a massive stone wall and built a star-shaped fortress. Both structures still stand.

The constitution of 1791 established Québec City as the capital of Lower Canada, a position it held until 1840, when the Act of Union united Upper and Lower Canada and made Montréal the capital. When Canada was created in 1867 by the Act of Confederation, which united four colonial provinces (Québec, Ontario, New Brunswick, and Nova Scotia), Québec City was named the province's capital city, a role it continues to play. In Québec, however, the city is known officially as *la capitale nationale*, a reflection of the nationalist sentiments that have marked Québec society and politics since the 1960s.

walls. There are two guided tours (adults C$9.80); one starts at the interpretation center and the other begins at Terrasse Dufferin. ✉ *2 rue d'Auteuil, Upper Town* ⊕ *www.pc.gc.ca/fortifications.*

Henry Stuart House

HOUSE | If you want to get a firsthand look at how the well-to-do English residents of Québec City lived in a bygone era, this is the place. Built in 1849 by the wife of wealthy businessman William Henry, the Regency-style cottage was bought in 1918 by the sisters Adèle and Mary

Kids will love watching the Royal 22nd Regiment's Changing of the Guard every summer day at 10 am, from June 24 until the first Monday in September.

Stuart. Active in such philanthropic organizations as the Red Cross and the Historical and Literary Society, the sisters were pillars of Québec City's English-speaking community. They also maintained an English-style garden behind the house. Soon after Adèle's death in 1987 at the age of 98, the home was classified a historic site for its immaculate physical condition and the museum-like quality of its furnishings, almost all of them Victorian. Guided tours of the house and garden start on the hour and include a cup of tea and piece of lemon cake. ⊠ *82 Grande Allée Ouest, Upper Town* ☎ *418/647–4347* ⊕ *www.maisonhenrystuart.qc.ca* 🖭 *C$8* ⊘ *Closed Mon. and Sun. Closed Sept–late June.*

Jardin des Gouverneurs (*Governors' Park*)
CITY PARK | In this small park just south of the Château Frontenac stands the **Wolfe-Montcalm Monument,** a 50-foot-tall obelisk that pays tribute to both a winning (English) and a losing (French) general. The monument recalls the 1759 battle on the Plains of Abraham, which

essentially ended French rule here. British general James Wolfe lived only long enough to hear of his victory; French general Louis-Joseph Montcalm died shortly after Wolfe, with the knowledge that the city was lost. On the south side of the park is **avenue Ste-Geneviève,** lined with well-preserved Victorian houses dating from 1850 to 1900. Many have been converted to inns, B&Bs, and hotels. ⊠ *Upper Town.*

★ **La Citadelle**
MILITARY SITE | Built at the city's highest point, on Cap Diamant, the Citadelle is the largest fortified base in North America still occupied by troops. The 25-building fortress was intended to protect the port, prevent the enemy from taking up a position on the Plains of Abraham, and provide a refuge in case of an attack. Having inherited incomplete fortifications, the British completed the Citadelle as protection against French and, eventually, American attacks. Nevertheless, by the time it was finished in 1832, the attacks against Québec City had ended.

Since 1920 the Citadelle has served as a base for Canada's most storied French-speaking military formation, the Royal 22e Régiment (Royal 22nd Regiment), known across Canada as the Van Doos, from the French "vingt-deux" (22). Firearms, uniforms, and decorations from as far back as the 17th century are displayed in the **Musée du Royal 22e Régiment** (Royal 22nd Regiment Museum) in the former powder magazine, built in 1750. If weather permits, you can watch the Changing of the Guard, a ceremony in which troops parade before the Citadelle in red coats and black fur hats while a band plays. The regiment's mascot, a well-behaved goat, watches along. The queen's representative in Canada, the governor-general, has a residence in the Citadelle, and it's open for tours in summer. Québec City's oldest military building, the Cape Diamond Redoubt, was constructed in 1693 under the supervision of the engineer Josué Boisberthelot de Beaucours and is now included in the guided tours. You must take a tour to access the Citadelle, since it's a military base. ■ TIP→ **The location— set high above the St. Lawrence river with stunning views of the city and surrounding countryside—is worth a visit even if you don't want to pay (or wait) to take a tour.** ✉ *Côte de la Citadelle, Upper Town* ☎ *418/694–2815* ⊕ *www.lacitadelle.qc.ca* 💲 *C$16* ↻ *Changing of the Guard at 10 am in summer.*

Louis S. St. Laurent Heritage House

HOUSE | A costumed maid or chauffeur greets you when you visit this elegant Grande Allée house, the former home of Louis S. St. Laurent, prime minister of Canada from 1948 to 1957. Within the house, which is now part of the federally owned Plains of Abraham properties, period furnishings and multimedia touches tell St. Laurent's story and illustrate the lifestyle of upper-crust families in 1950s Québec City. ✉ *201 Grande Allée Est, Montcalm* ☎ *418/648–4071* 💲 *C$10, including house, nearby Martello Towers,*

and minibus tour of Plains of Abraham ⊙ *Closed Oct.–June.*

★ Maison de la Littérature

BUILDING | Well worth a stop for design, architecture, and book lovers alike, this stunning library houses permanent exhibitions on French Canadian literature. Set in a former 19th century Methodist church, the now white-washed, design-heavy building was completely revamped a few years ago, winning international acclaim and architecture awards in the process. ✉ *40 rue Saint-Stanislas, Upper Town* ☎ *418/641–6797* ⊕ *www.maison-delalitterature.qc.ca* ⊙ *Closed Mon.*

★ Le Monastère des Augustines (*Augustinian Monastery and Museum*)

HOTEL—SIGHT | Augustinian nuns arrived from Dieppe, France, in 1639 with a mission to care for the sick in the new colony. They established the first hospital north of Mexico, the **Hôtel-Dieu,** the large building west of the monastery. The monastery underwent a complete renovation and expansion, in 2015, and now includes a quiet, health-conscious restaurant (with silent breakfast!), as well as accommodations—both contemporary rooms and more basic but comfortable "cell" rooms with antique furniture—for those looking for a quiet retreat (electronics must be shut off on premises). The museum houses an extensive collection of liturgical and medical artifacts of all kinds, and it's also worth visiting the richly decorated chapel designed by artist Thomas Baillairgé (1829–1932), as well as the vaults, which date to 1659 and were used by the nuns as shelter from British bombardments. There is still a small order of nuns living in a section of the monastery. ✉ *32 rue Charlevoix, Upper Town* ☎ *418/692–2492* ⊕ *www.monastere.ca* 💲 *C$10 admission, C$15 for guided tours* ⊙ *Closed Mon. and statutory holidays.*

Morrin Cultural Centre

LIBRARY | FAMILY | This stately gray-stone building has served many purposes, from imprisoning and executing criminals

The Fortifications

UPPER TOWN

LOWER TOWN

Convention Center

MONTCALM

Parc des Champs-de-Bataille

Plains of Abraham

La Citadelle

St. Lawrence River

Discovery Pavilion of the Plains of Abraham

Fairmont Le Château Frontenac

0 — 1/4 mile
0 — 400 meters

KEY

Symbol	Meaning
●	Sights
—	Ramparts
🛈	Tourist Information

Sights

1 Henry Stuart House **C1**
2 La Citadelle **G3**
3 Montcalm Monument **D2**
4 Musée National des Beaux-Arts du Québec **B2**
5 Parc des Champs-de-Bataille **D2**
6 Parc Jeanne d'Arc **D2**
7 Plains of Abraham **E2**
8 St-Louis Forts and Chateaux National Historic Site **H2**
9 Tours Martello **C2**
10 Wolfe Monument **B2**

to storing the national archives. Built between 1808 and 1813, it was the first modern prison in Canada and was converted into Morrin College, one of the city's first private schools, in 1868. That was also when the **Literary and Historical Society of Québec**, forerunner of Canada's National Archives, moved in. The college is no longer in operation, but historical and cultural talks are held in English, and tours of the building, including two blocks of prison cells, the Victorian-era library, and College Hall, are available. ⊠ *44 rue Chaussée des Ecossais, Upper Town* ☎ *418/694–9147* ⊕ *www.morrin. org* 🖼 *Library free; guided tours C$12* 🕙 *Closed Sat. and Sun.*

Musée de l'Amérique Francophone
MUSEUM | FAMILY | A former student residence of the Séminaire de Québec houses this museum, which focuses on the history of the French in North America. Among other things, you can view about 20 of the museum's 400 landscape and still-life paintings, some from as early as the 15th century, along with French colonial money and scientific instruments drawn from collections created by the priests for the education of their students, starting in 1806. The attached former chapel is used for exhibits, conferences, and cultural activities. An exhibit called The Rediscovered Colony shows artifacts from the first French attempt at colonization of the area in 1540. ⊠ *2 côte de la Fabrique, Upper Town* ☎ *418/692–2843* ⊕ *www.mcq.org* 🖼 *C$17* 🕙 *Closed Mon. Sept.–June.*

★ Musée National des Beaux-Arts du Québec (*National Museum of Fine Arts of Québec*)
MUSEUM | FAMILY | Situated on the city's liveliest avenue, the Grand Allée, this neoclassical museum in the park with a slick and modern wing is a remarkable steel-and-glass setting for its collection of 22,000 traditional and contemporary pieces of Québec art. Designed by starchitects Rem Koolhaas and Shohei

Shigematsu, the Lassonde Pavilion, added in 2016, features three stacked, cascading galleries; a grand stairwell that spirals dramatically from the top floor to the basement, where a rising almost-mile-long tunnel connects to the museum's three other wings; and views of the neighboring neo-Gothic church from both the rooftop terrace and courtyard. MNBAQ houses works by local legends Jean-Paul Riopelle, Jean-Paul Lemieux, Alfred Pellan, Fernand Leduc, and Horatio Walker that are particularly notable, as well as temporary exhibits by international artists such as Miro and Giacometti. The original museum building in Parc des Champs-de-Bataille is part of an abandoned prison dating from 1867; a hallway of cells, with the iron bars and courtyard, has been preserved as part of a permanent exhibition on the prison's history. ⊠ *Parc des Champs-de-Bataille, Upper Town* ☎ *418/643–2150* ⊕ *www. mnbaq.org* 🖼 *C$22, half-price Wed. evenings* 🕙 *Closed Mon. Sept.–May.*

Parc de l'Artillerie (*Artillery Park*)
MILITARY SITE | The strategic importance of Artillery Park, part of the Fortifications of Quebec, lies in its prime location overlooking both the plateau to the west of the city, from which an army could lay siege to it, and St. Charles River, where boats could land soldiers. Under French rule, all the lines of defense that were proposed or built passed through this territory. By the end of the 17th century, the park was already recognized as a strategic site and both French and English military engineers erected various fortifications here over the years. The lavish **Quartier des Officiers,** built in 1712, was used as officers' quarters of the Royal Artillery until the late 19th century, when the Canadian government converted the barracks into a cartridge factory following the departure of the troops. It would go on to play a predominant effort in both of Canada's world-war efforts; several thousand men and women of Quebec worked there. ⊠ *2 rue d'Auteuil, Upper*

Town ☎ 888/773–8888, 418/648–7016
⊕ www.pc.gc.ca/en/lhn-nhs/qc/fortifica-
tions/decouvrir-discover/natcul2/natcul2a
🖼 C$7.80 for guided tours ⊙ No guided
tours Oct.–May.

★ Parc Jeanne d'Arc

CITY PARK | Bright with colorful flowers
in summer, this urban park is lined with
stunning 19th-century mansions and is
often adorned with seasonal decorations. It makes for a lovely place to rest
between museums. The focus of the
park is an equestrian statue of Joan of
Arc. A symbol of military courage and
of France itself, the statue stands in
tribute to the heroes of 1759 near the
place where New France was lost to the
British. The park also commemorates the
Canadian national anthem, "O Canada";
it was played here for the first time on
June 24, 1880. ✉ Ave. Wilfrid-Laurier,
Upper Town.

★ Plains of Abraham

HISTORIC SITE | FAMILY | This park, named
after Abraham Martin, who used the
plains as a pasture for his cows, is the
site of the famous battle on September
13, 1759, that decided New France's
fate as part of the acrimonious Seven
Years' War. On that date, British soldiers
under the command of General Wolfe
climbed the steep cliff under the cover of
darkness, ultimately defeating the French
through a single deadly volley of musket
fire, causing the battle to be over within
30 minutes. Today, people cross-country ski here in winter and in-line skate
in summer. At the **Museum of the Plains
of Abraham**, check out the multimedia
display, which depicts Canada's history.
✉ Museum of the Plains of Abraham,
835 av. Wilfrid-Laurier, Level 0 (next to
Drill Hall), Upper Town ☎ 418/649–6157
⊕ www.ccbn-nbc.gc.ca 🖼 Discovery
Pavilion C$14 for 1-day pass (summer
only), bus tour and Odyssey exhibition
included.

Séminaire de Québec

HISTORIC SITE | Behind iron gates, next to
the Notre-Dame-de-Québec cathedral,
lies a tranquil courtyard surrounded
by austere stone buildings with rising
steeples, structures that have housed
classrooms and student residences since
1663. François de Montmorency Laval,
the first bishop of New France, founded
the Québec Seminary to train priests in
the new colony. In 1852 the seminary
gave birth to Université Laval, the first
francophone university in North America.

Today priests still live on the premises,
and Québec City's architecture school
occupies part of the building. The on-site
Musée de l'Amérique francophone gives
tours of the seminary grounds and the
interior in summer. The small Second
Empire–style **Chapelle Extérieure**, at the
west entrance of the seminary, was built
in 1888 after fire destroyed the 1750 original. Joseph-Ferdinand Peachy designed
the chapel; its interior is patterned after
that of the Église de la Trinité in Paris.
✉ 1 côte de la Fabrique, Upper Town
☎ 418/692–2843, 866/710–8031 🖼 C$16.

St-Louis Forts and Châteaux National Historic Site

ARCHAEOLOGICAL SITE | Venture under the
Terrasse Dufferin to see archaeological
treasures from the official residence
and power base of the French and
British governors. Massive excavations unearthed artifacts from the first
château, built under the direction of
Governor Montmagny, to the time the
Château St-Louis burned in 1834. Wine
bottles, kitchenware—even remains of
walls and door frames—give clues to the
luxurious life of the governors, who were
among the most powerful men in the
nation. Don't miss the guided tours and
activities. History buffs might consider
attending one of the in-depth archaeol-
ogy conferences held here. ✉ Terrasse
Dufferin, Upper Town ☎ 418/648–7016
⊕ www.pc.gc.ca 🖼 C$7.80 for guided
tours ⊙ Closed Nov.–mid-May.

Québec City's Best Walking Tours 👁

Ghost Tours of Québec. Costumed actors lead ghoulish 90-minute evening tours of Québec City murders, executions, and ghost sightings. The tours (C$22) are available in English or French, from May through October. After the walk, you can buy a copy of *Ghost Stories of Québec*, which has stories not told on the tours. ✉ *34 boul. Champlain, Lower Town* ☎ *855/692–9770* ⊕ *www.ghosttoursofquebec.com.*

Tours Voir Québec. This tour company offers English- and French-language (and Spanish from June to September) walking tours of the Old City, starting at C$23. Other tours include a "Bury Your Dead" murder mystery tour based on the novels of Louise Penny, as well as a popular food tour with tastings at various establishments for C$55. ✉ *12 rue St-Anne, Upper Town* ☎ *418/694–2001, 866/694–2001* ⊕ *www. toursvoirquebec.com.*

Terrasse Dufferin
VIEWPOINT | This wide boardwalk with an intricate wrought-iron guardrail has a panoramic view of the St. Lawrence River, the town of Lévis on the opposite shore, Île d'Orléans, the Laurentian Mountains to the north, and the edge of the Appalachians to the south. It was named for Lord Dufferin, governor of Canada between 1872 and 1878, who had this walkway constructed in 1878. Château St-Louis, whose remains can be seen under the walkway, was home to every governor from 1626 to 1834, when it was destroyed by fire. There are 90-minute tours of the fortifications that leave from here. The **Promenade des Gouverneurs** begins at the boardwalk's western end; the path skirts the cliff and leads up to Québec's highest point, Cap Diamant, and also to the Citadelle. ✉ *Upper Town.*

Wolfe-Montcalm Monument
MEMORIAL | This tall obelisk marks the place where the British general James Wolfe and French marquis Louis-Joseph Montcalm died during the Battle of Québec in September 1759. Wolfe landed his troops about 3 km (2 miles) from the city's walls; 4,500 English soldiers scaled the cliff and began fighting on the Plains of Abraham. Wolfe was mortally wounded in battle and was carried behind the

lines to this spot. Montcalm, who had been famous for winning four major battles in North America, was also fatally injured; he was carried into the walled city, where he died the next morning. ✉ *Rue de Bernières and av. Wolfe-Montcalm, Montcalm.*

🍴 Restaurants

In addition to quick to-go *boulangeries* (bakeries), cafés, and diners, Upper Town also has its share of legendary, white-tablecloth restaurants (albeit more popular with tourists than locals) known for market-fresh ingredients and legions of creative chefs and sommeliers.

Aux Anciens Canadiens
$$$ | **CANADIAN** | Named for a 19th-century book by Philippe-Aubert de Gaspé, who once resided in the 1675 house, this establishment has a modern menu and a good wine list, but most people come for the authentic French-Canadian cooking. Servers are dressed in period costume and each of the five dining rooms has a different theme, such as the bright and cheerful *vaisselier* (dish room), featuring colorful antique dishes and a fireplace. **Known for:** Lac St.-Jean tourtière (meat pie); maple-syrup pie with fresh cream; historical setting. $ *Average main:*

C$29 ✉ 34 rue St-Louis, Upper Town
☎ 418/692–1627 ⊕ www.auxancienscan-
adiens.qc.ca.

★ Café-Boulangerie Paillard

$ | CAFÉ | FAMILY | Owned by Yves Simard
and his wife, Rebecca, this bakery,
pastry counter, sandwich bar, pizza shop
(summer only), and ice-cream parlor
is known for its selection of nouvelle
French pastries, whole grain breads,
gourmet sandwiches, and artisanal
gelato. Long wooden tables, designed
to get customers talking to each other,
create a convivial atmosphere. **Known for:**
efficient service; delicious sandwiches
and pastries; potential line at lunch. ⑤ *Average main: C$10* ✉ 1097 rue St-Jean,
Upper Town ☎ 418/692–1221 ⊕ www.
paillard.ca.

Casse-Crêpe Breton

$ | CAFÉ | This simple, busy café-style res-
taurant serves crepes in generous pro-
portions with a variety of options—from
a menu of more than 20 fillings, pick your
own chocolate or fruit combinations or
design a larger meal with cheese, ham,
and vegetables. Tables surround four
round griddles at which you watch your
creations being made. **Known for:** quick
service; inexpensive menu; Viennese
coffee topped with whipped cream.
⑤ *Average main: C$7* ✉ 1136 rue St-Jean,
Upper Town ☎ 418/692–0438 ⊕ www.
cassecrepebreton.com.

★ Chez Boulay Bistro Boréal

$$$$ | CANADIAN | Chefs Jean-Luc Boulay
and Arnaud Marchand, who are both
revered in this town, delight patrons
with elegant interpretations of cuisine
inspired by northern Québec and made
entirely from local ingredients, including
reinvented classic desserts, such as
iced nougat with cloudberries. A mix of
locals celebrating special occasions and
tourists fresh from shopping rue St-Jean
dine in this elegant dining room on bison
tartare, braised beef ravioli with candied
red cabbage, and salmon in a flavorful

Poutine Stop 🍴

As far as fast food goes, nothing is
more Quebecois than poutine, that
rough-and-ready dish made of fries,
cheese curds, and gravy. In Québec
City, regional chain Chez Ashton,
founded in 1969, is the local favorite
for hurried lunchers and late-night
snackers. Also well worth trying
here is a hot-dog du lac, a "steamie"
(steamed hot dog) with mayo,
cabbage, and a few fries on top. ✉ 54
Côte du Palais, Upper Town ⊕ *www.
chezashton.ca.*

cranberry glaze. **Known for:** distinctive
cuisine; excellent wine list; vegetarian
menu. ⑤ *Average main: C$35* ✉ 1110 rue
St-Jean, Upper Town ☎ 418/380–8166
⊕ www.chezboulay.com.

★ Le Champlain - Fairmont Château Frontenac

$$$$ | MODERN CANADIAN | Chef Stéphane
Modat has made this elegant, romantic
dining room one of the city's top gastro-
nomical tables, showcasing unexpected
combinations, delicious flavors, locally
sourced ingredients, and whimsical presentations (like digging through chocolate
"earth" in a flower pot for tasty sweet
bites). Although service can be a bit stiff,
the food is anything but, and the rewards
on the plate are definitely worth any
formality. *The Sunday brunch is a must,
with tons of delicious small bites and
more classic offerings.* **Known for:** creative
gastronomy such as red deer tartare
and Lapland-sourced reindeer; C$109
tasting menu; excellent Sunday brunch.
⑤ *Average main: C$45* ✉ Fairmont Le
Château Frontenac, 1 rue des Carrières,
Upper Town ☎ 418/692–3861 ⊕ www.
restaurantchamplain.com ⊙ Closed Mon.
No dinner Sun.

Le Chic Shack

$ | FAST FOOD | FAMILY | At this refreshing alternative to the Old City's ubiquitous white-linen bistros, you can get fast food that's also high quality. Burgers made from grass-fed cattle served on soft artisanal brioche buns make this a prime locale for lunch goers. **Known for:** great burgers; quality fast food; delicious milkshakes. $ Average main: C$11 ⊠ 15 rue du Fort, Upper Town ☎ 418/692–1485.

Le Continental

$$$$ | EUROPEAN | If Québec City had a dining hall of fame, Le Continental would be there among the best. Since 1956 this historic spot, steps from the Château Frontenac, has been serving solid, traditionally gourmet dishes, such as tableside-prepared orange duckling and filet mignon, which is flambéed in a cognac sauce and then luxuriously covered in a gravy seasoned with mustard and sage. **Known for:** classic gastronomy; tableside "guéridon" service; old-school excellence. $ Average main: C$60 ⊠ 26 rue St-Louis, Upper Town ☎ 418/694–9995 ⊕ www.restaurantlecontinental.com ⊗ No lunch weekends.

L'Entrecôte Saint-Jean

$$$ | FRENCH | Steak frites (steak with fries) is on menus everywhere in Québec City and in lots of other places throughout the world, but this popular and lively establishment has a 30-year reputation as the master of the dish—L'entrecôte is a particular sirloin cut, usually long and relatively thin. Diners at this red-and-blue-trimmed house choose between three steak sizes, and each comes smothered in the restaurant's signature peppery sauce with a heaping pile of crispy fries. **Known for:** steak frites and signature sauce; unpretentious, well-made food; great patio. $ Average main: C$27 ⊠ 1080 rue St-Jean, Upper Town ☎ 418/694–0234 ⊕ www.entrecotesaint-jean.com ⊗ No lunch Sun.

Le Saint-Amour

$$$$ | FRENCH | At one of the city's most romantic and treasured restaurants, chef Jean-Luc Boulay entices diners with such creations as red-deer steak grilled with a wild-berry and peppercorn sauce, and filet mignon with port wine and local blue cheese as well as inspired desserts. Paul McCartney and Sting have both eaten here. **Known for:** foie gras; curated wine list with more than 1,000 choices; romantic atmosphere. $ Average main: C$65 ⊠ 48 rue Ste-Ursule, Upper Town ☎ 418/694–0667 ⊕ www.saint-amour.com ⊗ No lunch on weekends.

Sapristi

$$ | ITALIAN | FAMILY | The menu at this Italian-leaning restaurant with an industrial-cool feel is satisfying, with a number of imaginative pizzas and pastas, salads and such. Try the fried mozzarella or the chef's risotto, which changes daily. **Known for:** creative pizzas; hip and popular; gluten-free options. $ Average main: C$17 ⊠ 1001 rue St-Jean, Upper Town ☎ 418/692–2030 ⊕ sapristi.ca ⊗ Closed Mon.

🛏 Hotels

Upper Town, inside the Old City's walls, is famous for its accommodations in historic buildings, decorated with antique furnishings and heavy fabrics. Few have restaurants, but there are lots of places to eat nearby.

Auberge Place d'Armes

$$$ | B&B/INN | Old Québec charm meets modern convenience at this property near the Château Frontenac, which attracts a mix of couples and businesspeople staying on expense accounts. **Pros:** central location; romantic; good restaurant on premises, Chez Jules. **Cons:** no elevator means working off breakfast on the stairs; no on-site parking; dated furniture. $ Rooms from: C$235 ⊠ 24 rue St-Anne, Upper Town ☎ 418/694–9485

⊕ www.aubergeplacedarmes.com ⟲ 21 rooms ⏐◉⏐ Free breakfast.

★ Fairmont Le Château Frontenac Hotel

$$$$ | HOTEL | In this landmark building, perked up with some sleek and well-integrated modern touches, the public rooms—from the cozy and elegant Bar 1608 to the 700-seat ballroom reminiscent of the Hall of Mirrors at Versailles—are all opulent; guest rooms are just as elegantly furnished, like minichâteaux, with gold and green touches. **Pros:** top historic attraction; great river views; le labo toiletries. **Cons:** it gets busy in public spaces; rooms are small for the price; some guest rooms inferior to Deluxe category are not renovated. ⑤ *Rooms from: C$259* ✉ *1 rue des Carrières, Upper Town* ☎ *418/692–3861, 800/441–1414* ⊕ *www. fairmont.com/frontenac* ⟲ *648 rooms* ⏐◉⏐ *No meals.*

Hilton Québec

$$ | HOTEL | Next to Parliament Hill, this hotel may be all business (as in, it caters primarily to a corporate clientele) but it has chic and contemporary rooms with views of Vieux-Québec or the Laurentian Mountains to the north. **Pros:** direct access to the convention center; amazing executive lounge; great city views. **Cons:** blocky exterior; can be businesslike; lacks Old Québec charm. ⑤ *Rooms from: C$199* ✉ *1100 boul. René-Lévesque Est, Upper Town* ☎ *418/647–2411, 800/447–2411 in Canada* ⊕ *www.hiltonquebec. com* ⟲ *571 rooms* ⏐◉⏐ *No meals.*

Hôtel Cap Diamant

$$ | B&B/INN | An eclectic collection of vintage furniture and ecclesiastical accents—stained glass from a church, a confessional door, an angel or two—complement the decorative marble fireplaces, stone walls, and hardwood floors at this hotel. **Pros:** Victorian style and charm; a four-season veranda; some rooms have private balconies. **Cons:** stairs to third-floor rooms are a bit steep; poor soundproofing; smaller rooms will hardly accommodate luggage. ⑤ *Rooms from:*

C$190 ✉ *39, av. Ste-Geneviève, Upper Town* ☎ *418/694–0313, 888/694–0313* ⊕ *www.hotelcapdiamant.com* ⟲ *12 rooms* ⏐◉⏐ *Free breakfast.*

Hôtel Champlain

$$ | HOTEL | FAMILY | Tucked away on a quiet street in Old Québec, with small but well-equipped rooms and a good breakfast buffet, the Champlain is a good fit for those after attentive service, boutique charm, and a central location. **Pros:** family packages available; on-site parking; wine bar with Quebecois wines. **Cons:** small bathrooms; no in-room coffee; decor is a bit eclectic. ⑤ *Rooms from: C$179* ✉ *115 rue Ste-Anne, Upper Town* ☎ *418/694–0106* ⊕ *hotelchamplain. hotelsduvieuxquebec.com* ⟲ *55 rooms* ⏐◉⏐ *Free breakfast.*

Hôtel Château Bellevue

$$ | HOTEL | Behind the Château Frontenac, facing a pleasant park, this 1898 hotel occupies four heritage houses with the same green roofing, and offers modern rooms with standard hotel furnishings in a good location, often with views of the St. Lawrence River. **Pros:** access to indoor pools and spa at hotel next door; good continental breakfast; river views. **Cons:** decor can be eclectic; lacks Old Québec charm; poor soundproofing. ⑤ *Rooms from: C$199* ✉ *16 rue de la Porte, Upper Town* ☎ *418/692–2573, 800/463–2617* ⊕ *hoteloldquebec.com* ⟲ *49 rooms* ⏐◉⏐ *Free breakfast.*

Hôtel du Vieux-Québec

$ | HOTEL | Nicely situated at the end of rue St-Jean, surrounded by stores and restaurants, this friendly spot has rooms spread over three floors, including a suite with a king bed and huge flat-screen television, and a "superior room" with two queen beds and an exposed brick wall. **Pros:** lively location; breakfast delivered to your door with a weather report; good restaurant. **Cons:** can be noisy; rooms can feel a little stuffy; breakfast only free when booked directly on hotel's website. ⑤ *Rooms from: C$159* ✉ *1190 rue*

St-Jean, *Upper Town* ☎ *418/692–1850,*
800/361–7787 ⊕ *www.hvq.com* ⇆ *45*
rooms ⦿| *Free breakfast.*

Hôtel Le Clos St-Louis

$$ | **B&B/INN** | Winding staircases, period
antiques, and crystal chandeliers add
to the Victorian elegance of this central
inn, made up of two updated 1845-era
houses. **Pros:** four-poster and sleigh beds;
cheery breakfast room; bar and mas-
sotherapy on premises. **Cons:** Victorian
ruffles not for everyone; no elevator;
guests must remove footwear upon
entry. $ *Rooms from: C$199* ✉ *69 rue*
St-Louis, Upper Town ☎ *418/694–1311,*
800/461–1311 ⊕ *www.clossaintlouis.com*
⇆ *18 rooms* ⦿| *Free breakfast.*

Hôtel Manoir Victoria

$$$ | **HOTEL** | The recent renovations at
this European-style hotel, with a discreet
entrance on Côte du Palais, include the
elegantly simple rooms with hardwood
furnishings and white bedding. **Pros:**
room service from Chez Boulay; heated
bathroom floors; indoor parking. **Cons:**
lobby can get busy with restaurant
or convention crowds; pool is on the
small side; not all rooms are renovated.
$ *Rooms from: C$215* ✉ *44 côte du*
Palais, Upper Town ☎ *418/692–1030,*
800/463–6283 ⊕ *www.manoir-victoria.*
com ⇆ *156 rooms* ⦿| *No meals.*

Hôtel Marie Rollet

$ | **B&B/INN** | Located on a charming street
corner at the heart of Vieux-Québec, this
intimate inn built in 1876 by the Ursuline
order has quaint decor and antiques and
sometimes small but warm rooms. **Pros:**
central location; rooftop terrace with
garden view; private bathroom in every
room. **Cons:** no elevator; steep stairs;
very small bathrooms. $ *Rooms from:*
C$129 ✉ *81 rue Ste-Anne, Upper Town*
☎ *418/694–9271, 800/275–0338* ⊕ *www.*
hotelmarierollet.com ⇆ *11 rooms* ⦿| *No*
meals.

★ Le Monastère des Augustines

$ | **B&B/INN** | Stay in a 17th-century mon-
astery—and the birthplace of the first
hospital in North America—that's been
transformed into a contemporary holistic
retreat. **Pros:** historical building; modern,
design-oriented rooms; free access
to museum. **Cons:** monastic-like stays
(including detoxing from your devices)
not for everyone; en-suite in contemporary rooms only; mum's the word at
this silent retreat. $ *Rooms from: C$95*
✉ *77 rue des Remparts, Upper Town*
☎ *844/694–1639* ⊕ *monastere.ca/en*
⇆ *65 rooms* ⦿| *Free breakfast.*

Manoir d'Auteuil

$$ | **HOTEL** | Art deco and art nouveau
meet in this hotel, where an ornately
sculpted iron banister wraps up through
four floors, leading to guest rooms with
varying styles and features. **Pros:** direct
view of the Parliament building; close to
the convention center; art deco charm.
Cons: midweek business clientele takes
over lobby; no elevator; not all rooms
are created equal. $ *Rooms from:*
C$179 ✉ *49 rue d'Auteuil, Upper Town*
☎ *418/694–1173, 866/662–6647* ⊕ *www.*
manoirdauteuil.com ⇆ *27 rooms* ⦿| *Free*
breakfast.

Quebec City Marriott Downtown

$$ | **HOTEL** | This former bank building
exudes a quiet elegance, with modern
guest rooms with wood furniture and
stained-glass windows, two fireplaces,
and a tiny wood-lined corner bar in the
lobby. **Pros:** the French food from Que
Sera Sera restaurant's open kitchen;
central location; laundry machines. **Cons:**
a bit starchy; lacks Old Québec charm;
street can be busy. $ *Rooms from:*
C$199 ✉ *850 pl. d'Youville, Upper Town*
☎ *418/694–4004, 866/694–4004* ⊕ *www.*
marriott.com ⇆ *111 rooms* ⦿| *No meals.*

North America's first ice hotel, rebuilt each winter, is only 15 minutes from Québec City by car, and worth a tour even if you don't spend the night.

🍸 Nightlife

BARS AND LOUNGES

Bar Les Voûtes Napoléon
BARS/PUBS | The brick walls and wine cellar–like atmosphere help make Les Voûtes a popular place to listen to Quebecois music. Much of the beer here is from local microbreweries. ⊠ *680 rue Grande-Allée Est, Upper Town* 🕾 *418/640–9388* ⊕ *www.voutesdenapoleon.com.*

★ Bar 1608
BARS/PUBS | One of the city's most romantic spots is the Château Frontenac's bar, which boasts one of the most interesting cocktail lists in town. You can also have some wine, a bit of charcuterie and cheese, and relax while looking at the St. Lawrence River or the two fireplaces. ⊠ *1 rue des Carrières, Upper Town* 🕾 *418/266–3906.*

L'Atelier
BARS/PUBS | Doubling up as a restaurant that notably serves all kinds of tartares, L'Atelier is a hot spot of Québec City mixology, as the chief mixologist is notorious for his creative and delicious cocktails; case in point, the Whisky Tiki. ⊠ *624 Grande-Allée Est, Upper Town* 🕾 *418/522–2225.*

Le Pub Saint-Alexandre
BARS/PUBS | This popular English-style pub offers dozens of single-malt scotch and more than 200 kinds of beer, 30 of which are on tap, and many of which are exclusive imports. ⊠ *1087 rue St-Jean, Upper Town* 🕾 *418/694–0015* ⊕ *www.pubstalexandre.com.*

L'Inox
BARS/PUBS | A popular Upper Town brew-pub, L'Inox serves beers that have been brewed on-site, like Trouble-Fête and Coulée-Douce, as well as a rotating list of limited-edition brews. Inside are billiard tables and excellent European-style hot dogs (featuring long, tasty sausages served on a baguette); outside there's a summer terrace. ⊠ *655 rue Grande-Allée Est, Upper Town* 🕾 *418/692–2877* ⊕ *www.brasserieinox.com.*

BREWPUBS
★ Bar Le Sacrilège
BREWPUBS/BEER GARDENS | Across the street from Église St-Jean-Baptiste, this place bears its name well, with a couple of church pews and religious icons. Le Sacrilège has local microbrews like Boréale and Trou du Diable in bottles and on tap, and the special changes daily. It also has the best terrace in the city, an enclosed garden that's constantly full in summer. Live music or DJs play on a regular basis. ⊠ 447 rue St-Jean, Upper Town ☎ 418/649–1985 ⊕ lesacrilege. com.

Performing Arts

Art is everywhere in Québec City—from theater and chic galleries to accordion-playing street performers and statue mimes in the parks. From September through May, a steady stream of concerts, plays, and performances is presented in theaters and halls. In summer, many indoor theaters close, and outdoor shows of all kinds abound, most of them free.

★ Orchestre Symphonique de Québec
(Québec Symphony Orchestra)
MUSIC | Canada's oldest symphony orchestra, directed by the dynamic French conductor Fabien Gabel, performs mainly at Louis-Fréchette Hall in the Grand Théâtre de Québec. ⊠ 269 boul. René-Lévesque Est, St-Jean-Baptiste ☎ 418/643–8486 ⊕ www.osq.org.

Théâtre Capitole
MUSIC | This cabaret-style theater schedules pop music and musical comedy shows. It also specializes in revival pieces with songs by singers like Elvis or Johnny Cash, or whole genres, like disco. ⊠ 972 rue St-Jean, Upper Town ☎ 418/694–4444 ⊕ www.lecapitole.com.

Shopping

ART GALLERIES
Galerie Art Inuit Brousseau et Brousseau
ART GALLERIES | Inuit art is the specialty of this large, well-known gallery. The gallery director, Jean-Francois Brousseau, selects works by artists represented by the North Canadian Inuit cooperatives, and the gallery receives much praise for improving life in the Canadian Arctic. ⊠ 35 rue St-Louis, Upper Town ☎ 418/694–1828 ⊕ www.artinuitbrousseau.ca.

Galerie Michel Guimont
ART GALLERIES | Located in the Old Port area, this is probably the most sought-after gallery for contemporary art in Québec City, with solid exhibits of paintings, drawings, and prints from emerging and well-established artists. ⊠ 273 rue St-Paul, Lower Town ☎ 418/692–1188 ⊕ galeriemichelguimont.com.

DEPARTMENT STORES
La Maison Simons
DEPARTMENT STORES | This growing Canadian chain store started here in Québec City in the 19th century, and is still owned by its founding family. The store carries designer clothing, linens, and other household items. There are two other locations at Place Sainte-Foy and Galeries de la Capitale shopping centers. ⊠ 20 côte de la Fabrique, Upper Town ☎ 418/692–3630 ⊕ www.simons.ca.

FOOD
Les Délices de l'Érable
FOOD/CANDY | Find a sweet souvenir at this maple syrup shop, which has everything from maple cookies to muffins and serves some of the best gelato in town. An exhibit space upstairs explains the process behind maple syrup and showcases artifacts from this Québec tradition. ⊠ 1044 rue St-Jean, Upper Town ☎ 418/692–3245 ⊕ www.deliceserableetcie.com.

A Québec City Cheese Primer

It used to be that all good cheese in Québec City was imported from France—not anymore. During the last several decades there's been an impressive and still-growing cheese movement in La Belle Province. Regional cheese makers long produced award-winning aged cheddar, but that's been joined by a wealth of specialty cheeses, including *lait cru* (unpasteurized) cheeses that you'll want to sample before going home. There are more than 400 original varieties made here.

Luckily, there are enough cheese shops to keep you cheese shop–hopping all afternoon.

Aux Petits Délices. In the market at Les Halles du Petit Quartier, Aux Petits Délices has a large selection of specialty cheeses, along with crackers, charcuterie, and condiments for a picnic on the Plains. Knowledgeable staff can help with selection. ✉ *1191 av. Cartier, Montcalm* ☎ *418/522–5154.*

Épicerie Européenne. Stop by the Épicerie Européenne in the St-Jean-Baptiste quarter, and let the knowledgeable consultants help you choose from their excellent selection of cheeses. ✉ *560 rue St-Jean, St-Jean-Baptiste* ☎ *418/529–4847.*

Épicerie J.A. Moisan. This is the oldest continuously operating grocery store in Québec City, stocked with a great selection of charcuterie, cheese, fruit and vegetables, local beers, specialty sodas, spices, and much more. ✉ *699 rue St-Jean, St-Jean-Baptiste* ☎ *418/522–0685.*

Some good cheeses to watch out for at local shops include Bleu Bénédictin from St-Benoît Abbey, Île aux-Grues four-year-old cheddar, Le Migneron de Charlevoix, and Le Louis d'Or, made in Central Québec. There's also a *chèvre noire*, a raw, goat "cheddar" by Fromagerie Tournevent—wrapped in black wax—that's not to be missed. If Gouda is your thing, try a piece from Fromagerie Bergeron.

JEWELRY

Zimmermann

JEWELRY/ACCESSORIES | Exclusive hand-made jewelry can be found at this city landmark. ✉ *46 côte de la Fabrique, Upper Town* ☎ *418/692–2672* ⊕ *www.zimmermann-quebec.com.*

🏃 Activities

ICE-SKATING

Ice-skating in Québec City is a popular pastime for locals and visitors alike.

★ Place d'Youville

ICE SKATING | This well-known outdoor rink, just outside St-Jean Gate, is open daily October through the end of March, from noon to 10 pm. Skate rental is C$8, and skating itself is free. A locker will run you C$1. ✉ *Upper Town* ☎ *418/641–6256.*

Plains of Abraham

ICE SKATING | The sports field at the western end of Battlefields park features a large skating rink. ✉ *Montcalm* 🛷 *Free. Skate rental C$8 for 2 hrs.*

SKIING

CROSS-COUNTRY

Parc des Champs-de-Bataille (*Battlefields Park*)

SKIING/SNOWBOARDING | You can reach this park from Place Montcalm. It has more than 10 km (6 miles) of scenic, marked, cross-country skiing trails. Skis and snow-shoes can be rented at the Musée des Plaines. ✉ *835 av. Wilfrid-Laurier, Montcalm.*

SNOW SLIDES

The snow slide from Dufferin Terrace is easily one of the most exciting winter activities in Québec.

Glissades de la Terrasse

SNOW SPORTS | FAMILY | A wooden toboggan takes you down a 270-foot-high snow slide that's adjacent to the Château Frontenac. Three rides cost C$10. ⊠ Québec City ☎ 418/829–9898.

SPAS

Strøm Spa Nordique

SPA—SIGHT | Designed by a local star-architect firm, this Nordic-oriented spa—a branch of the Montréal-based upscale spa company—has a panoramic view of the Lac des Nations. Enjoy outdoor whirlpools, thermal and Nordic baths, a Finnish sauna, a eucalyptus steam bath, and thermal and Nordic waterfalls. ⊠ 515 boul. Champlain, Upper Town ☎ 418/425-2772 ⊕ https://www.stromspa.com/en/.

Lower Town

Seeing all the bustle and upscale commerce here, it's hard to imagine that 40 years ago, this area was run-down and looking for a new lease on life. Today, after exploring Place Royale and its cobblestone streets, you can walk along the edge of the St. Lawrence River and watch the sailboats and ships go by, shop at the market, or kick back on a terrasse (patio) with a local craft beer. Rue Petit-Champlain also has charming places to stop and listen to street musicians, and the scene near the Old Port starts buzzing as soon as the sun goes down.

If there's a cradle of French civilization in North America, you're standing in it when you visit Lower Town. In 1608, Champlain chose this narrow, U-shaped spit of land sandwiched between the frigid waters of the St. Lawrence River and the craggy heights of Cap Diamant as the site for his settlement. Champlain later abandoned the fortified abitation (residence) at the foot of Cap Diamant and relocated to the more easily defendable Upper Town.

Nevertheless, the area continued to flourish as a bustling port and trading center for French merchants, fur traders, and coureurs des bois (woodsmen), and France's Native American allies. It was also the base from which dozens of military campaigns and fact-finding missions were launched into the heart of the continent. A bust of France's Sun King, Louis XIV, was erected in the main square, Place du Marché, which was renamed Place Royale in 1686. Destroyed by British cannons that were set up on the opposite shore during the siege of 1759, the port and buildings were rebuilt by the British, and the area quickly regained its role as Canada's leading commercial and business center.

Lower Town went into an economic tailspin in the late 1800s, becoming a slum whose narrow streets were lined with pawnshops, rough-and-tumble taverns, and smoky brothels that catered to sailors and lumberjacks. This lasted until the 1960s, when it received a multimillion-dollar face-lift that remade it into a sanitized version of its 1700s self. Today, once-dilapidated houses and warehouses contain busy boutique hotels, stylish boutiques, chic art galleries, and popular restaurants and bars. Lower Town, home to approximately 850 people, is bounded by the Dufferin-Montmorency Highway to the west, the St. Charles River to the north, the St. Lawrence River to the east, and Petit Champlain shopping area to the south.

GETTING HERE AND AROUND

Because Lower Town is the oldest part of the city, many prefer to see it first to get a sense of how the city developed chronologically. If coming from Upper Town, head down L'Escalier Casse-Cou, a stairway steep enough to earn that name, which means "Breakneck Stairs." Have your camera ready; you'll get that quintessential Petit-Champlain photo at the top of the staircase.

TIMING

You'll need one full day to see the area surrounding two of the city's most famous squares, Place Royale and Place de Paris. Pause for lunch before touring the Musée de la Civilisation and the antiques district.

Sights

★ **Église Notre-Dame-des-Victoires** (*Our Lady of Victory Church*)
RELIGIOUS SITE | The fortress shape of the altar is no accident; this small but beautiful stone church on Place Royale is linked to a bellicose past. Grateful French colonists named it in honor of the Virgin Mary, whom they credited with helping French forces defeat two British invasions: one in 1690 by Admiral William Phipps and the other by Sir Hovendon Walker in 1711. The church itself was built in 1688, making it the city's oldest—it has been restored twice since then. Several interesting paintings decorate the walls, and a model of *Le Brezé*, the boat that transported French soldiers to New France in 1664, hangs from the ceiling. The side chapel is dedicated to Ste. Geneviève, the patron saint of Paris. ⊠ *32 rue Sous-le-Fort, Lower Town* ☎ *418/692–1650* ⊕ *www.notre-dame-de-quebec.org* ⊑ *C$5 for guided tours.*

★ **L'Escalier Casse-Cou**
BUILDING | The steepness of the city's first iron stairway, an ambitious 1893 design by city architect and engineer Charles Baillairgé, is ample evidence of how it got its name: Breakneck Steps. Still, those 59 steps were quite an improvement on the original stairway, built in the 17th century, that linked the Upper Town and Lower Town. There are shops and restaurants at various levels. ⊠ *Lower Town.*

Maison Chevalier
HOUSE | This old stone house (which is actually three houses brought together) was built in 1752 for the shipowner Jean-Baptiste Chevalier. The architecture is quintessential New France, with its mansards and scarlet roof. The building is not open to visitors but well worth a look from the outside. ⊠ *50 rue du Marché-Champlain, Lower Town* ☎ *418/646–3167.*

Maison Louis-Jolliet
HOUSE | Louis Jolliet, the first European to see the Mississippi River, and his fellow explorers used this 1683 house as a base for westward journeys. Today it's the lower station of the funicular. A monument commemorating Jolliet's 1672 trip to the Mississippi stands in the small park next to the house, which is at the foot of the Escalier Casse-Cou (Breakneck Staircase). ⊠ *16 rue du Petit-Champlain, Lower Town* ⊕ *www.quebec-cite.com/en/businesses/transportation-sightseeing/local/funicular/funiculaire-du-vieux-quebec.*

★ **Musée de la Civilisation** (*Museum of Civilization*)
MUSEUM | FAMILY | Wedged between narrow streets at the foot of the cliff, this spacious museum with a striking limestone-and-glass facade was designed by architect Moshe Safdie to blend into the landscape. Its campanile (bell tower) echoes the shape of the city's church steeples. Two excellent permanent exhibits examine Québec's history. *People of Québec, Now and Then* engagingly synthesizes 400 years of social and political history—including the role of the Catholic church and the rise of the Québec nationalist movement—with artifacts, time lines, original films and interviews, and news clips. It's a great introduction to the issues that face the province today. *This Is Our Story* looks at the 11 aboriginal nations that inhabit Québec. The temporary exhibits here are

Lower Town (Basse-Ville)

TO SAINT-ROCH →

↑ TO VIA RAIL CANADA STATION

Marché du Vieux-Port

Bassin Louise

Lock

UPPER TOWN

Antiques District

Musée Naval de Québec

Couvent des Ursulines

Place de l'Hôtel-de-Ville

Séminaire du Québec

Notre-Dame de Québec Basilica-Cathedral

OLD PORT

Parc Montmorency

Musée de la Civilisation

Agora Port de Québec

Escalier Frontenac

L'Escalier du Casse-Cou

Le Terminal-Port of Québec

Fairmont Le Château Frontenac

Funicular

Place des Canotiers

Terrasse Dufferin

LOWER TOWN

QUARTIER PETIT-CHAMPLAIN

St. Lawrence River

KEY

1 Sights
1 Restaurants
1 Hotels
🚢 Ferry
├─┼─┤ Rail Line
── Ramparts
🛈 Tourist Information

0 ——— 1/8 mile
0 ——— 200 meters

TO LÉVIS

Sights ▼

1 Église Notre-Dame-des-Victoires **C6**
2 L'Escalier Casse-Cou **B6**
3 Maison Chevalier **B6**
4 Maison Louis-Jolliet.... **B5**
5 Musée de la Civilisation **D5**
6 Old Port **E5**
7 Place des Canotiers **C6**

8 Place Royale **C6**
9 Rue du Petit-Champlain......... **A6**

Restaurants ▼

1 Buffet de L'Antiquaire.. **D4**
2 Café La Maison Smith.. **B6**
3 Chez Muffy **C5**
4 Écho buvette **D5**

5 Laurie Raphaël Restaurant-Atelier-Boutique **C6**
6 Le Café du Monde **E5**
7 Le Cochon Dingue **B6**
8 L'Échaudé................ **D5**
9 Légende.................. **B2**
10 L'Orygine................ **D6**
11 Taverne Louise.......... **D4**

Hotels ▼

1 Auberge St-Antoine **C5**
2 Hayden's Wexford House **A7**
3 Hôtel des Coutellier.... **B2**
4 Hôtel Le Germain Québec................... **D5**
5 Hôtel Le Priori........... **C5**
6 Hôtel Le St-Paul.......... **C2**
7 Hôtel 71 .... **C5**

One of Lower Town's top sights is the Place Royale, also one of the oldest public squares in the country.

also worth a visit. ⊠ *85 rue Dalhousie, Lower Town* ☎ *418/643–2158, 866/710–8031* ⊕ *www.mcq.org* ✉ *C$22* ⊙ *Closed Mon. Sept.–June.*

Old Port (*Vieux Port*)

PROMENADE | On warm summer nights, the Old Port harbors an interesting and varied nightlife scene, but in the daytime it is just as fun. Restored for the city's 400th anniversary in 2008, the harbor dates from the 17th century, when ships brought supplies and settlers to the new colony. At one time this was among the busiest ports on the continent. ⊠ *Lower Town.*

Place des Canotiers

CITY PARK | What used to be a vast parking lot across from the Museum of Civilization has been replaced by an elegant and modern park that provides great views of Upper Town and improves access to the river for locals who now linger and stroll here and also for the cruise ships that often moor here. Even the new multistory parking garage has been dressed up in an elegant wooden facade that gives the area extra character. ⊠ *40 rue Dalhousie, Lower Town* ⊕ *www.capitale. gouv.qc.ca/parcs-et-places-publiques/ places-publiques/place-des-canotiers.*

★ Place Royale

PLAZA | The houses that encircle this cobblestone square, with steep Normandy-style roofs, dormer windows, and chimneys, were once the homes of wealthy merchants. Until 1686 the area was called Place du Marché, but its name changed when a bust of Louis XIV was placed at its center. During the late 1600s and early 1700s, when Place Royale was continually under threat of British attack, the colonists moved progressively higher to safer quarters atop the cliff in Upper Town. After the French colony fell to British rule in 1759, Place Royale flourished again with shipbuilding, logging, fishing, and fur trading. The *Fresque des Québécois*, a 4,665-square-foot trompe-l'oeil mural depicting 400 years of Québec's history, is to the east of the square, at the corner of rue Notre-Dame and côte de la Montagne. ⊠ *Lower Town.*

★ Rue du Petit-Champlain
NEIGHBORHOOD | The oldest street in the city was once the main thoroughfare of a harbor village, with trading posts and the homes of rich merchants. Today it has pleasant boutiques, art galleries, and cafés, and on summer days the street is packed with tourists. Natural-fiber weaving, Inuit carvings, hand-painted silks, local fashion design, and enameled copper crafts are among local specialties for sale here. If you're coming from Upper Town, take the *Escalier Casse-Cou* (Breakneck Steps) down, and the funicular back up (or round-trip): both deliver you to the start of this busy, unique street. ⊠ *Lower Town* ⊕ *www.quartier-petitchamplain.com.*

🍴 Restaurants

Lower Town has its fair share of renowned eateries, and you'll find some of the best terraces in town. Dine after the sun goes down under twinkling lights at L'Echaudé, rediscover the best of Quebecois savoir faire with Laurie Raphael's Nordic tasting menu. For impeccable upscale fare, go to L'Initiale.

Buffet de L'Antiquaire
$$ | CANADIAN | Hearty home cooking, generous portions, and rock-bottom prices have made this no-frills, diner-style eatery in the heart of the antiques district, a Lower Town institution. It's a good place to sample traditional Quebecois dishes such as pea soup and *cipaille* (a deep-dish layered pie using poultry, meat, or seafood), and the homemade and delicious sugar pie, crepes, and other desserts. **Known for:** traditional dishes; old-school diner; Québec City institution. ⑤ *Average main: C$12* ⊠ *95 rue St-Paul, Lower Town* ☎ *418/692–2661* ⊕ *lebuffet-delantiquaire.com.*

Café La Maison Smith
$ | CAFÉ | FAMILY | This casual and attractive café right on the corner of scenic Place Royale is a great place to stop for an afternoon pick-me-up, be it coffee or various indulgent sweets. For a light lunch, there are yummy sandwiches, quiches, and soups. **Known for:** outdoor seating; great sandwiches; coffee roasted on-site. ⑤ *Average main: C$9* ⊠ *23 rue Notre-Dame, Lower Town* ☎ *581/742–6777* ⊕ *lamaisonsmith.com.*

★ Chez Muffy
$$$$ | CANADIAN | At this restaurant, inside the museumlike Auberge Saint-Antoine, Chef Julien Ouellet creates menus that change with the seasons, but fresh, locally sourced ingredients are at the core of the classic, elegant menu. The space has stone walls and attractive wooden floors and exposed beams from the building's warehouse days. **Known for:** historic warehouse setting; seasonal tasting menu; extensive wine list. ⑤ *Average main: C$35* ⊠ *10 rue St-Antoine, Lower Town* ☎ *418/692–1022* ⊕ *www.saint-antoine.com/chez-muffy.*

Écho buvette
$$ | CANADIAN | L'Échaudé's youngest sister was born out of a desire to attract travelers and locals for 5 à 7 (happy hour) with good wines and good food. Their creative terroir tapas, like the Arctic char carpaccio and the bison hanger steak (or their gnocchi with herbs for something lighter) are wonderfully complemented by the baby-blue walls and bright space. **Known for:** vegetarian and gluten-free menu; large selection of wines by the glass. ⑤ *Average main: C$18* ⊠ *67 rue du Sault-au-Matelot, Lower Town* ☎ *418/914-4393* ⊕ *echobuvette.com.*

★ Laurie Raphaël Restaurant-Atelier-Boutique
$$$$ | FRENCH | Local and regional products are emphasized here, and the food is among the best gastronomical offerings in Québec. Among local celebrity chef Daniel Vézina's creations are crystallized foie gras with truffle snow, and venison tartare. **Known for:** smart, high-end gastronomy; elegant setting; tasting menus. ⑤ *Average main:*

Did You Know?

You'll find some of the best buys on Inuit carvings, hand-painted silks, and enameled copper crafts on touristy rue du Petit-Champlain.

C$155 ✉ 117 rue Dalhousie, Lower Town
☎ 418/692–4555 ⊕ www.laurieraphael.
com ⊗ Closed Sun.–Tues., and Jan. 1–15.

Le Café du Monde
$$$ | CAFÉ | Next to the cruise terminal in
the Old Port, this massive, Parisian-bis-
tro-style restaurant with etched-glass
dividers and palm trees has a spectacular
view to equal its food. The outdoor ter-
race in front overlooks the St. Lawrence
River, while the side verrière (glass atri-
um) looks onto l'Agora amphitheater and
the old stone Customs House. **Known
for:** lively scene; great views; delicious
seafood. ⑤ Average main: C$30 ✉ 84
rue Dalhousie, Suite 140, Lower Town
☎ 418/692–4455 ⊕ www.lecafedu-
monde.com.

L'Échaudé
$$$ | FRENCH | A mix of businesspeo-
ple and tourists frequents L'Échaudé
because of its location between the
nearby business and antiques districts.
For lunch, the flank steak with shallots is
a classic, and every day there's excellent
fish, tartares, and pasta on the menu.
Known for: French-inspired dishes; elegant
decor; three-course brunch. ⑤ Average
main: C$25 ✉ 73 rue Sault-au-Matelot,
Lower Town ☎ 418/692–1299 ⊕ www.
echaude.com.

Le Cochon Dingue
$$ | CAFÉ | FAMILY | The café dishes at this
cheerful chain, whose name translates
into the Crazy Pig, include delicious
tartares, steak with fries, hearty soups,
a selection of international dishes like
satays and "général Dingue" chicken, as
well as substantial desserts like sugar
pie with vanilla cream. At the boulevard
Champlain location, sidewalk tables
and indoor dining rooms artfully blend
the chic and the antique; black-and-
white checkerboard floors contrast with
ancient stone walls. **Known for:** often
long waits for a table; affordable bistro;
good people-watching. ⑤ Average main:
C$14 ✉ 46 boul. Champlain, Lower Town

A View From the Water ◉

Crossing the St. Lawrence River
on the Québec–Lévis Ferry will
reward you with a striking view of
the Québec City skyline, with the
Château Frontenac and the Québec
Seminary high atop the cliff. The
view is even more impressive at
night. Ferries generally run every
20 or 30 minutes from 6 am until 6
pm, and then every hour until 2:20
am; there are additional ferries
from April through November. ✉ 10
rue des Traversiers, 1 block south of
pl. de Paris ⊕ www.traversiers.gouv.
qc.ca

☎ 418/692–2013 ⊕ www.cochondingue.
com.

Légende
$$$ | CANADIAN | Set on the ground floor
of the Hôtel des Coutellier, in the Old
Port area, Légende is set in a large wood
and stone room with plush banquettes
and an elegant bar. There are a lot of
sharing plates—the smartly prepared
fish and seafood board (including things
like salmon rillettes and welk salad) is
particularly delightful. **Known for:** local
ingredients, served creatively; open
space; vast patio in summer. ⑤ Average
main: C$28 ✉ 255 rue St-Paul, Lower
Town ☎ 418/614–2555 ⊕ restaurantleg-
ende.com/restaurant-legende-quebec.

L'Orygine
$$$ | CANADIAN | One hundred percent
organic—that is the promise of L'Ory-
gine, a brand-new bistro in the heart of
the Lower Town. With an emphasis on
freshness and local flavors, the chef pre-
pares seasonal dishes that are (almost)
guilt-free, such as lobster cavatelli and a
creative mix of duck and eggplant. **Known
for:** vegetarian menu; seasonal cuisine;

good location. $ *Average main: C$25* ✉ *36 1/2 rue Saint-Pierre, Lower Town* ☎ *418/872-4386* ⊕ *lorygine.com* ⊗ *no lunch on weekdays except Fri.*

Taverne Louise

$$$ | CANADIAN | As a nod to Queen Victoria's slightly rebellious fourth daughter, who happened to adore Québec City, Taverne Louise aims to please with its two distinct areas: one that's more laid-back and casual, with local beers on tap, and the other slightly more upscale with a regiment of tapas and privately imported wines. The space, with exposed stone and large ancestral windows, is the perfect backdrop for the restaurant's now iconic *foie gras au torchon* and a glass of rosé Lambrusco. **Known for:** chef's table; outstanding wine list with private imports; charming space. $ *Average main: C$30* ✉ *48 rue Saint-Paul, Lower Town* ☎ *418/780–7255* ⊕ *louisetbv.ca.*

🛏 Hotels

Many visitors insist on staying near the water, among the quays, warehouses, and cobblestone squares—as well as many boutique hotels, inspired eateries, and impressive entertainment venues.

★ Auberge St-Antoine

$$$$ | HOTEL | This charming hotel incorporates the historic stone walls of a 19th-century warehouse along with artifacts dating to the 1600s, many of which were found during an expansion and are now in glass displays in the public areas and guest rooms. **Pros:** unique architectural accents and exhibits; some rooms have fireplaces and terraces; excellent restaurant. **Cons:** low vacancy means guests must plan well in advance; the eclectic decor doesn't always match the price; not all terraces have nice views. $ *Rooms from: C$349* ✉ *8 rue St-Antoine, Lower Town* ☎ *418/692–2211, 888/692–2211* ⊕ *www.saint-antoine.com* ⤶ *95 rooms* ⦿ *No meals.*

Hayden's Wexford House

$ | B&B/INN | The attentive hosts make budget travelers and young couples feel right at home at this charming B&B, comfortably removed from the torrent of tourists but only a scenic 15-minute walk from all the Lower Town sites. **Pros:** big breakfast; quiet location near the river; ample parking. **Cons:** no TVs or telephones; books up fast in the summer months; lack of on-site amenities. $ *Rooms from: C$140* ✉ *450 rue Champlain, Lower Town* ☎ *418/524–0524* ⊕ *www.haydenwexfordhouse.com* ▭ *No credit cards* ⤶ *3 rooms* ⦿ *Free breakfast.*

Hôtel des Coutellier

$$$ | HOTEL | Charming details like buttery croissants delivered to the room each morning, exposed brick walls, and lush linens make this boutique hotel a popular base for demanding travelers. **Pros:** an elevator (a rarity in this part of town); breakfast delivered each morning; old-world charm. **Cons:** small and open-plan bathrooms; in-room temperature controls aren't intuitive; a bit of a climb to Upper Town attractions. $ *Rooms from: C$205* ✉ *253 rue St. Paul, Lower Town* ☎ *418/692–9696, 888/523–9696* ⊕ *www.hoteldescoutellier.com* ⤶ *24 rooms* ⦿ *Free breakfast.*

★ Hôtel Le Germain Québec

$$$$ | HOTEL | Sophistication and attention to every detail prevails in the modern rooms of this chic boutique hotel—from the custom-designed swing-out night tables to the white goose-down duvets and custom umbrellas. **Pros:** deluxe continental breakfast; higher floors have views of the St. Lawrence River or the Old City; pets welcome. **Cons:** minimal interior is not for everyone; lacks Old Quebec spirit; not all rooms have separate bath and shower. $ *Rooms from: C$295* ✉ *126 rue St-Pierre, Lower Town* ☎ *418/692–2224, 888/833–5253* ⊕ *www.legermainhotels.com/en/quebec* ⤶ *60 rooms* ⦿ *Free breakfast.*

Québec Summer Festival

Festival d'Été International de Québec *(Québec City Summer Festival).* An annual highlight in the first half of July is this exuberant Summer Festival, 11 days of rock, folk, hip-hop, and world music. The main concerts take place each evening on three outdoor stages in or near the Old City, including one holding up to 80,000 people on the Plains of Abraham. A pass (C$115) grants admission to all events throughout the festival.

Some concerts at indoor theaters cost extra, but free music and activities, such as family concerts and street performers during the day, are also plentiful. At night rue St-Jean near the city gate turns into a free street theater, with drummers, dancers, and skits. Book accommodation several months in advance if you plan to attend. ✉ *Québec City* ☎ *418/523–4540, 888/992–5200* ⊕ *www.infofestival.com.*

Hôtel Le Priori

$$ | HOTEL | Housed in a 300-year-old building with stone and brick walls, this boutique hotel has a rigorously modern decor, with custom leather beds, stainless steel sinks, slate floors, and three-head shower jets. **Pros:** both hot and cold food at the buffet breakfast; modern but warm rooms; unbeatable Old Québec location. **Cons:** high-occupancy rates mean that you'll need to reserve some time ahead; some rooms are small (while some are also spacious); suites are in a separate building. ⑤ *Rooms from: C$199* ✉ *15 rue Sault-au-Matelot, Lower Town* ☎ *418/692–3992, 800/351–3992* ⊕ *www.hotellepriori.com* ⮐ *28 rooms* ❑| *Free breakfast.*

Hôtel Le St-Paul

$$$ | HOTEL | Perched at the edge of the antiques district, this basic four-story hotel inside what was once a 19th-century office building, is near art galleries and the train station, and features a good restaurant and wine bar on the ground floor. **Pros:** charming vintage details; modern bathrooms; convenient location. **Cons:** mostly no frills; not all rooms are renovated; ambient street noise. ⑤ *Rooms from: C$209* ✉ *229 rue St-Paul, Lower Town* ☎ *418/694–4414, 888/794–4414* ⊕ *www.lesaintpaul.qc.ca* ⮐ *27 rooms* ❑| *Free breakfast.*

★ Hôtel 71

$$$$ | HOTEL | Guest rooms at this luxury hotel, inside the city's first National Bank of Canada office, have 12-foot-high ceilings, excellent amenities, and stunning views of Old Québec. **Pros:** decadent and modern; luxurious packages; excellent on-site Italian restaurant. **Cons:** chic interiors not kid-friendly; valet service is steep; poor soundproofing. ⑤ *Rooms from: C$299* ✉ *71 rue St-Pierre, Lower Town* ☎ *418/692–1171, 888/692–1171* ⊕ *www.hotel71.ca* ⮐ *69 rooms* ❑| *Free breakfast.*

Performing Arts

Théâtre Petit-Champlain

MUSIC | The charming and intimate Théâtre Petit-Champlain is a fine spot to hear contemporary francophone music during the year and take in a play in summer. ✉ *68 rue du Petit-Champlain, Lower Town* ☎ *418/692–2631* ⊕ *www.theatrepetitchamplain.com.*

Shopping

ANTIQUES

French-Canadian, Victorian, and art deco furniture, clocks, silverware, and porcelain are some of the rare collectibles found here, mainly on quaint and historic rue St-Paul street. Authentic Québec pine furniture, characterized by simple forms and lines, is rare—and pricey.

Antiquités Bolduc

ANTIQUES/COLLECTIBLES | The largest antiques store on rue St-Paul sells furniture, household items, old paintings, and knickknacks from the 19th and 20th centuries. ⊠ *89 rue St-Paul, Lower Town* ☎ *418/694–9558* ⊕ *www.lesantiquites-bolduc.com.*

Gérard Bourguet Antiquaire

ANTIQUES/COLLECTIBLES | You're not likely to find any bargains here, but this shop has a very good selection of authentic 18th- and 19th-century Québec pine furniture. ⊠ *97 rue St-Paul, Lower Town* ☎ *418/694–0896.*

L'Héritage Antiquité

ANTIQUES/COLLECTIBLES | This is probably the best place in the antiques district to find good Quebecois furniture, clocks, oil lamps, porcelain, and ceramics. It's a very welcoming store as well. ⊠ *109 rue St-Paul, Lower Town* ☎ *418/692–1681.*

CLOTHING
Charlevoix Pure Laine

CLOTHING | Discover the beautiful Charlevoix sheep wool at this lovely boutique. Passionate craftswomen (and craftsmen, too!) work tirelessly to upcycle and recycle this regional wool, transforming it into stockings, toques, throws, and soles. ⊠ *61 1/2 rue du Petit-Champlain, Lower Town* ☎ *418/692–7272* ⊕ *charlevoixpurelaine.ca.*

★ Lowell

SHOES/LUGGAGE/LEATHER GOODS | The official Québec City outpost for a Montréal-based company (where goods are designed and made), this boutique offers distinctive, durable and well-designed leather goods, sleek computer bags, and colorful messenger bags with an old-school vibe. ⊠ *66 boul. Champlain, Lower Town* ☎ *418/614–0851* ⊕ *lowellmtl.ca.*

les ptits mosüs

TOYS | FAMILY | The name says it all: "les ptits mosüs" means "the naughty kids" in Quebecois, so it's only logical that this lovely boutique is dedicated to the little ones. Expect a highly curated selection of local designers with items ranging from clothing to toys, and from books to tableware. ⊠ *88 1/2 rue du Petit Champlain, Lower Town* ☎ *418/914–5838* ⊕ *lesptitsmosus.com.*

CRAFTS
Boutique des Métiers d'Art du Québec

CRAFTS | This boutique, run by the Conseil des métiers d'art, a coordinating body that oversees all kinds of arts and crafts disciplines and organizes annual fairs, features the best from Québec in glass art, porcelain, jewelry, woodworking, and much more, most with a stylish, contemporary feel. ⊠ *29 rue Notre-Dame, Lower Town* ☎ *418/694–0267* ⊕ *www.metiersdart.ca.*

Outside the Old City

Venture outside the walls for a glimpse of the real Québec City. Grande-Allée and avenue Cartier buzz with clubs and bars inside Queen Anne–style mansions. Cafés, galleries, and good restaurants are popping up regularly in St-Roch, the city's urban core. If you do have a car, it's a beautiful drive on boulevard Champlain, which runs from Lower Town all around the southern edge of Québec City, following the St. Lawrence River: you might want to take a stroll along the Promenade Samuel-de-Champlain, a stunning, modern linear park created in 2008 for the city's 400th anniversary. Above are the cliffs that lead to the Plains of Abraham, and farther on are the Sillery Coves. Any one of the steep hills will take you back toward the main roads that run east–west or the highways that cross north–south: Duplessis, the farthest west; Henri IV; Robert-Bourassa; and Dufferin-Montmorency.

GETTING HERE AND AROUND

It's a 15-minute walk from the Old City to avenue Cartier, but the bus system is excellent here and easy to use. There are many bus stops throughout Upper Town, and a number of lines run up and down boulevard René-Lévesque and Grande Allée. There are many options available from place d'Youville or on rue Hon-oré-Mercier. If you do choose to walk, take a detour to avenue Laurier or avenue Georges VI for a tour through leafy green streets with gorgeous homes.

St-Roch, on the other hand, is a little less convenient by bus from the Old City. Plan to catch cabs, which aren't hard to find, to take you there and back. But with the area's increasing attractiveness and atmosphere, it's a no-brainer.

TIMING

There's no need to dedicate more than half a day to see the area around Grande-Allée or the St-Roch neighborhood. Both are great destinations for lunch, an afternoon browsing in the shops, or an evening out at a restaurant or bar.

⊙ Sights

Aquarium du Québec

ZOO | FAMILY | Breakfast with the walrus-es, lunch (carefully) with the polar bears, and spend the afternoon watching the seals do their tricks at this clifftop aquar-ium overlooking the St. Lawrence and Québec City's two main bridges. When you tire of the mammals, check out the thousands of species of fresh- and saltwater·fish in the aquarium's massive, three-level aquatic gallery, or have some hands-on experiences with mollusks, starfish, and stingrays. Don't miss the jellyfish ballet or seahorse tanks. This is the only aquarium in North America with examples of all five species of cold-water seals. ⊠ 1675 av. des Hôtels, Ste-Foy, Outside the Old City ☎ 866/659–5264, 418/659–5264 ⊕ www.aquariumduque-bec.com ☒ C$20.50.

Avenue Cartier

NEIGHBORHOOD | The mix of reasonably priced restaurants and bars, groceries and specialty food shops, hair salons, and stores makes Cartier a favorite lunchtime and after-work stop for many Downtown office workers. After business hours the street hums with locals running errands or soaking up the sun on patios. When darkness falls, the avenue's patrons get noticeably younger. The attraction? A half-dozen nightclubs and pubs that offer everything from wine and quiet conver-sation to Latin music and earsplitting dance tunes. ⊠ Montcalm, Outside the Old City.

Grande-Allée

NEIGHBORHOOD | One of the city's oldest streets, the Grande Allée was the route people took from outlying areas to come sell their furs in town. In the 19th century the wealthy built neo-Gothic and Queen Anne–style mansions here, which now house trendy cafés, clubs, and restaurants. The street actually has four names: inside the city walls it's rue St-Louis; outside the walls, Grande Allée Est; farther west, Grande Allée Ouest; then finally, boulevard Laurier. ⊠ Outside the Old City.

Hôtel du Parlement

GOVERNMENT BUILDING | The only French-speaking legislature in continental North America, the 125-member Assem-blée Nationale du Québec meets behind the stately walls of this Second Empire-style building erected between 1877 and 1886. If the Assemblée is sitting, see if you can get into the visitors gallery to hear heated exchanges between the federalist-leaning Liberals and the seces-sionist Parti Quebecois. Failing that, the buildings themselves, designed by Québec architect Eugène-Étienne Taché, are worth a visit. The facade is decorated with statues of such important figures of Québec history as Cartier, Champ-lain, Frontenac, Wolfe, and Montcalm. A 30-minute tour (in English, French,

Sights ▼

1	Aquarium du Québec	H9
2	Avenue Cartier	A9
3	Grande-Allée	E8
4	Hôtel du Parlement	F6
5	Maison J. A. Moisan	D5
6	Observatoire de la Capitale	E6
7	Parc linéaire de la rivière Saint-Charles	A2
8	Promenade Samuel-de-Champlain	H9
9	Saint Matthew's Cemetery	E5
10	St-Roch	B2

Restaurants ▼

1	Albacore	E4
2	ARVI	C1
3	Battuto	A5
4	Bistro B	A9
5	Café Saint-Henri	E2
6	Chez Victor	B7
7	Ciel!	E8
8	Le Billig	C5
9	Le Bouchon du Pied Bleu	A3
10	Le Café du Clocher Penché	A3
11	Le Café Krieghoff	B9
12	Le Parlementaire	F6
13	Louis Hébert	E7
14	Nina Pizza Napolitaine	A3
15	Noctem Artisans Brasseurs	C3
16	Patente et Machin	A3

Hotels ▼

1	Château Bonne Entente	A7
2	Hôtel Château Laurier	F7
3	Hôtel Delta Québec	E5
4	Hôtel Le Concorde Québec	E8
5	Hôtel-Musée Premières Nations	A2
6	Hôtel Palace Royal	F4
7	Hotel Pur	B3
8	Hôtel Royal William	B3
9	Ice Hotel	F1

or Spanish) takes in the President's Gallery, the Parlementaire restaurant, the Legislative Council Chamber, and the National Assembly Chamber. Tours may be restricted during legislative sessions. Outdoor tours of the gardens and statues are also available during summer. ⊠ *1045 rue des Parlementaires, Outside the Old City* ☎ *418/643–7239, 866/337–8837* ⊕ *www.assnat.qc.ca* ⊠ *Free.*

★ Maison J. A. Moisan

STORE/MALL | Founded in 1871 by Jean-Alfred Moisan, this place claims the title of the oldest continuously operating grocery store in North America. The original display cases, woodwork, and tin ceilings preserve the old-time feel. The store sells hard-to-find products from various regions of Québec, including cheeses, charcuterie, and some outstanding local ales. The original owner's upstairs home has now been turned into a classic B&B with all the trimmings. ⊠ *699 rue St-Jean, Outside the Old City* ☎ *418/522–0685* ⊕ *www.jamoisan.com.*

★ Observatoire de la Capitale

VIEWPOINT | FAMILY | Located atop the Édifice Marie-Guyart, the city's tallest building, Observatoire de la Capitale offers a spectacular panorama of Québec City from 31 stories up. The site features an overview of the city's history with 3-D imagery, audiovisual displays in both French and English, and a time-travel theme with a 1960s twist. ⊠ *1037 rue de la Chevrotière, Outside the Old City* ☎ *418/644–9841* ⊕ *www.observatoire-capitale.org* ⊠ *C$14.75* ☉ *Closed on Mon. Oct–Feb.*

Parc linéaire de la rivière Saint-Charles (*St Charles River Linear Park*)

NATURE PRESERVE | This 32-kilometer (20-mile) stretch of trails and walkways follows the St. Charles River from its source at Lake St. Charles, to the northwest (which supplies a large part of Québec City's drinking water), all the way to the Bassin Louise Marina, in the Vieux-Port. Many sections are in quiet stretches of

Stop and Shop ❢❢

The Halles du Petit Quartier small but busy food and shopping mall on avenue Cartier has restaurants and shops that sell jewelry, fish, flowers, pastries, breads, vegetables, fresh coffee, candies, and some excellent local cheeses, as well as a few Italian and other European specialties. There's no fast food here, but if you're looking for picnic snacks for a day trip to the Plains of Abraham, plan to fill your basket here before you head to the park.

forests, or run along wetlands and meadows. The trails immediately west of the harbor offer a green oasis at the heart of the city. It's also possible to rent kayaks and paddle over 11 km (6.5 miles) of the northernmost part of the river. ⊠ *Outside the Old City* ☎ *418/691–4710* ⊕ *www. societerivierestcharles.qc.ca.*

Promenade Samuel-de-Champlain

PROMENADE | This 4-kilometer (2.5-mile) park along the St. Lawrence River is a local favorite, with an amazing view of the river and the two bridges that cross it to the west, as well as some smart, whimsical, and modern landscape design. On a sunny summer day, the place is busy with strollers, bikers, and in-line skaters, as well as kids playing in the fountains and on the lawns. You will find a café and observation tower toward the western end of the park. In summer, special buses will take you from Lower Town to the promenade. ⊠ *Boul. Champlain, Outside the Old City* ☎ *418/528–0773, 418/528–0773* ⊕ *www.capitale.gouv.qc.ca/realisations/ promenade-samuel-champlain.*

St. Matthew's Cemetery

CEMETERY | The burial place of many of the earliest English settlers in Canada was established in 1771 and is the oldest cemetery remaining in Québec City. Also buried here is Robert Wood, the disavowed half-brother of Queen Victoria. Closed in 1860, the cemetery has been turned into a park. Next door is **St. Matthew's Anglican Church,** now a recently renovated public library. It has a book listing most of the original tombstone inscriptions, including those on tombstones removed to make way for the city's modern convention center. ✉ *755 rue St-Jean, Outside the Old City.*

★ St-Roch

TOWN | Hip bars and trendy shops pepper St-Roch, once an industrial area and now a technology hub. With so little locals living in the old part of town, St-Roch is a great place to mingle with residents. New spots are popping up constantly. The "main drags" of the neighborhood are boulevard Charest and rue Saint-Joseph, which offer a mix of office buildings, lunch spots, and after-work hangouts. Jardins Saint-Roch, a large square, provides good people-watching.

Look for Église St-Roch, a massive stone church, and you'll quickly find rue St-Joseph, the district's other major thoroughfare, known for trendy shops and third-wave cafés. Shop for new duds here and walk west to go dine in one of the neighborhood's sleek new bistros. The popularity of the area has spawned many new restaurants. When it comes time for an after-dinner drink, there's a plethora of pubs and terraces.

Art abounds in the neighborhood, from the famed street-art-covered viaduct (right by rue Saint-Paul) and modern sculptures to outdoor theater and circus acts.

St-Roch is a long, but downhill jaunt from the Old City and walkable if you have the time. If you're not in the mood for exercise, the best way to reach this neighborhood is by cab. Plan to spend about C$9 each way. There are usually plenty of cabs available for the reverse trip. Taking

the bus (800 or 801) is also an option. ✉ *St-Roch, Outside the Old City.*

🍴 Restaurants

There are many cute cafés and fine eateries within the walls of the Old City, but don't miss the thriving culinary scene beyond them. Le Café du Clocher Penché is arguably the bistro with the best brunch, and it gives you an excuse to visit trendy St-Roch. Or if you're looking for a little more luxury, head to Louis Hébert to nibble on trendy dishes while playing "spot the politico."

Work up a good appetite by wandering through the streets—and climbing those steep stairs. For something to nibble on for a picnic in the park, pop into one of the city's little out-of-the-way patisseries for buttery croissants and heavenly brioches.

★ Albacore

$$$ | SEAFOOD | Seafood lovers, rejoice: Québec City now has its very own ocean-based restaurant, and a great one at that. Helmed by a team of seasoned chefs, this gourmet restaurant provides diners with flavorful, flawless, and generously sized dishes of anything from scallops to clams and marlin tatakis, all nicely complemented by delicate side dishes such as lentils, sorbet (yes, ice cream for dinner!), and edible flowers. **Known for:** mandatory reservations; imaginative seafood; beautiful decor. $ *Average main: C$25* ✉ *819 Côte d'Abraham, Outside the Walls* ☎ *418/914–6441* ⊕ *albacore. business.site* ⊗ *Closed Mon.*

ARVI

$$$ | CANADIAN | The trek to Limoilou is worth it, if it's to dine at ARVI. Local critics have deemed ARVI an unforgettable gourmet experience, and it was selected as one of Canada's 35 top restaurants by Air Canada's in-flight magazine. **Known for:** vegetarian menu; food-and-wine pairing; delicate, creative plates. $ *Average main: C$30* ✉ *519 3e avenue, Limoilou*

☎ *581/742–4202* ⊕ *restaurantarvi.ca* ⏰ *Closed Sun. and Mon.*

★ Battuto

$$ | **MODERN ITALIAN** | Chef Guillaume Saint-Pierre's love for authentic Italian cuisine led him to open this popular 25-seat restaurant, located off the main Saint-Roch thoroughfares, where he can fully concentrate on that passion with gusto and skill. Italian tradition (there's arancini and *vitello tonatto*) blend with local flair (fresh fettucini with local corn, bacon and local mushroom). **Known for:** perfect fresh pasta; dolci that blend local flair and Italian know-how; hard-to-get table. $ *Average main: C$18* ✉ *527 boul. Langelier, St-Roch* ☎ *418/614–4414* ⊕ *www.battuto. ca* ⏰ *Closed Sun. and Mon.*

Bistro B

$$$$ | **BISTRO** | Behind the success of city hot spot Chez Muffy (formerly Panache), Chef François Blais decided on a more casual approach, including having a simple interior, when he opened his own restaurant on avenue Cartier. The "market cuisine" is straight to the point and well executed, and the whole menu fits on a blackboard, with a handful of appetizers, main courses, and desserts that change daily. **Known for:** open kitchen; upmarket French; upbeat atmosphere. $ *Average main: C$35* ✉ *1144 av. Cartier, Montcalm* ☎ *418/614–5444* ⊕ *www.bistrob.ca* 🚫 *No credit cards.*

★ Café Saint-Henri

$ | **CAFÉ** | Expect the usual crowd of students, freelancers, and others toting laptops at this third-wave café that has thoughtfully selected beans roasted on-site. Even so, the contemporary, all-white café is a welcome respite from the cold in wintertime—and the doughnuts alone are worth a visit. **Known for:** delicious artisan doughnuts; architectural highlight; beans roasted on the premises. $ *Average main: C$5* ✉ *849 rue Saint-Joseph Est, St-Roch* ☎ *581/300–7211* ⊕ *sainthenri.ca.*

Chez Victor

$$ | **MODERN AMERICAN** | Attracting an artsy crowd, this cozy burger joint with brick-and-stone walls has a wide range of topping combinations and daily special burgers, and French fries are served with a dollop of homemade mayonnaise (there are five varieties available) and poppy seeds. Salads, sandwiches, and a daily dessert made fresh by the pastry chef are also available. *This original location was so successful that it spawned several other branches, notably in the Vieux-Port.* **Known for:** hearty burgers; good selection of local beers; poutine. $ *Average main: C$17* ✉ *145 rue St-Jean, St-Jean-Baptiste* ☎ *418/529–7702* ⊕ *www.chezvictorburger.com.*

Ciel!

$$$ | **CANADIAN** | Spectacular views of the whole city are not the only reason to climb up to this rotating restaurant with unobstructed, panoramic views. The service here is friendly and well-managed, and the food, under the direction of chef David Forbes, is unfussy, creative, and delicious—try the roasted Arctic char with lemon gnocchi and shiitakes or something from the solid brunch menu (on weekends). **Known for:** 360-degree view of the city; elegant dining yet cozy; tasty farm-to-table dishes. $ *Average main: C$30* ✉ *1225 cours du General Montcalm, Outside the Old City* ☎ *418/640–5802* ⊕ *www.cielbistrobar. com.*

Le Billig

$$ | **CANADIAN** | **FAMILY** | At this lovely crepe shop , buckwheat flour crepes are filled with simple ham and cheese, or fancier combos like duck confit with onion marmalade, while a wheat crepe with salted caramel and sweet Chantilly cream makes a good dessert. The large shop also has bistro items like cod beignets, charcuterie plates, and cassoulet, and there's a nice selection of ciders and beers. **Known for:** great crepes, often original; ciders; gluten-free items. $ *Average main: C$16* ✉ *481 rue St-Jean, St-Jean-Baptiste, Outside the Old City* ☎ *418/524–8341.*

★ Le Bouchon du Pied Bleu

$$$$ | BISTRO | It's worth heading to the outskirts of the St-Roch Downtown district for this unique dining experience, inspired by the French *bouchons* (as bistros are called in the city of Lyon). For starters, big salad bowls appear at your table and you can help yourself—don't overdo it, though, because the appetizers and entrées that follow come in rich and generous servings, featuring lots of pork and charcuterie and cream. **Known for:** prix-fixe tasting menu; artisan charcuterie; Lyon-style restaurant. $ *Average main: C$35* ✉ *179 St-Vallier Ouest, St-Roch* ☎ *418/914–3554* ⊕ *piedbleu.com* ⊗ *Closed Mon. and Tues.*

★ Le Café du Clocher Penché

$$$ | FRENCH | The high ceilings and imposing vault door give away the fact that this was once a bank, but an amiable staff and inventive bistro cuisine (without pretentious fluff) make this establishment a local favorite, especially during lunch, when the restaurant is packed with suits and skirts who munch on well-prepared salads, pasta, and daily specials. Dinner draws the date-night crowd and groups of friends out for a fun, casual meal. **Known for:** changing menu using fresh, regional ingredients; best weekend brunch in the city; lively lunch scene. $ *Average main: C$24* ✉ *203 rue St-Joseph Est, St-Roch, Outside the Old City* ☎ *418/640–0597* ⊕ *www.clocherpenche. ca* ⊗ *Closed Mon. No dinner Sun.*

Le Café Krieghoff

$$ | BISTRO | This busy, noisy Paris-like bistro featuring artwork by its namesake Canadian painter and patios in front and back has been around for more than 40 years and is a big local literary hangout, with great coffee, tea, and desserts. Open every day from early morning to late evening, Krieghoff serves specialties that include salmon, quiche, "la

Toulouse" (a big French sausage with sauerkraut), steak with French fries, boudin (pig-blood sausage), and "la Bavette" (hanger steak). *A new location recently opened on Maguire Street in the Sillery district.* **Known for:** big bowls of hot chocolate; simple, flavorful dishes; good place to work or study. $ *Average main: C$15* ✉ *1089 rue Cartier, Outside the Old City* ☎ *418/522–3711* ⊕ *www. cafekrieghoff.qc.ca.*

Le Parlementaire

$$$ | CANADIAN | Despite its magnificent beaux arts interior and its reasonable prices, the National Assembly's restaurant (featuring breakfast and sometimes Sunday brunch) remains one of the best-kept secrets in town. Chef Yves Légaré prepares contemporary cuisine with products from Québec's various regions, such as minifondues made with Charlevoix cheese to ravioli made from lobster caught in the Gaspé to pork from the Beauce region, trout from the Magdalen Islands, or candied-duck salad. **Known for:** elegant, historic decor; tasty regional dishes; breakfast. $ *Average main: C$24* ✉ *1045 rue des Parlementaires, Montcalm, Outside the Walls* ☎ *418/643–6640* ⊕ *www.assnat.qc.ca* ⊗ *Closed Sat. and Sun. July–Labor Day; closed Sat.–Mon. Labor Day–June. No dinner.*

Louis Hébert

$$$ | FRENCH | With its fine French cuisine and convenient location in a 95-year-old house on the bustling Grande Allée, this restaurant has long been popular with many of Québec's élite. Dining areas range from the very public summer terrace to discreet second-floor meeting rooms, a solarium with bamboo chairs, and a cozy dining room with exposed stone walls and warm wood accents. **Known for:** large wine selection; fine dining; seafood and pasta. $ *Average main: C$30* ✉ *668 Grande Allée Est, Montcalm, Outside the Old City* ☎ *418/525–7812* ⊕ *www.louishebert.com* ⊗ *Closed Oct.–Apr.*

★ Nina Pizza Napolitaine

$$ | **ITALIAN** | Specializing in Neapoli-tan-style pizza and antipasti, this stylish pizzeria has been on everyone's lips ever since it opened (thanks to crowdfund-ing!). Its beast of an oven weighs 2.5 tons and was imported straight from Italy—and it's worth it: the thin-crust pizzas are cooked in just 90 seconds at 900 degrees. **Known for:** wood-fired pizzas; charcuteries plate; Aperol spritz. $ *Average main: C$16* ⌧ *410 rue Saint-Anselme, St-Roch* ☎ *581/742–2012* ⊕ *ninapizzanapolitaine.ca* ⊗ *Closed Tues.*

★ Noctem Artisans Brasseurs

$$ | **ECLECTIC** | A great selection of beers, brewed on premises or coming from some of the best microbreweries in Québec, attract diners here, along with the smart menu of reinvented pub food (fish and waffle, blood sausage pie, braised pork belly with chimichurri sauce and parsley root chips, for example). The decor, with raw plywood and exposed structures, is modern and trendy. **Known for:** great beer selection; creative pub food; trendy decor. $ *Average main: C$18* ⌧ *438 rue du Parvis, St-Roch* ☎ *581/742–7979* ⊕ *www.noctem.ca.*

Patente et Machin

$$$ | **ECLECTIC** | This fun and friendly place has a menu with terrific meats, grilled cheese, and whimsical ideas, like the use of guinea fowl wings in lieu of chicken wings. The food here has personality, humor, and...lots of butter. **Known for:** playful dishes; pleasantly chaotic service; great wine selection. $ *Average main: C$25* ⌧ *82 rue St-Joseph Ouest, St-Roch, Outside the Old City* ☎ *581/981–3999* ▭ *No credit cards.*

🛏 Hotels

Booking a room outside the walled city puts you in a mixed area of student housing, convention hotels, and chains, although there are still numerous inns, hotels, and B&Bs to choose from here.

Many of the options are within easy proximity to the Plains of Abraham, Hôtel du Parlement, and museums such as the Musée des Beaux-Arts du Québec.

Château Bonne Entente

$$ | **HOTEL** | Twenty minutes from Downtown, the 11-acre Château Bonne Entente offers modern simplicity at its finest, with classic rooms featuring white duvets, marble bathrooms, and refin-ished wood furniture and design-maga-zine-ready rooms. **Pros:** country-club feel; chic, relaxing atmosphere; free shuttle to Old Québec and Downtown. **Cons:** a drive to main sights; shuttle not available fall through spring; golf is 20 minutes away. $ *Rooms from: C$199* ⌧ *3400 chemin Ste-Foy, Ste-Foy, Outside the Old City* ☎ *418/653–5221, 800/463–4390* ⊕ *www.chateaubonneentente.com* ⇆ *165 rooms* ▮⦿▮ *No meals.*

Hôtel Château Laurier

$$ | **HOTEL** | Brown leather sofas and wrought-iron chandeliers fill the spacious lobby of this former private house. **Pros:** some rooms for budget travelers; Saint-Hubert BBQ serves great rôtisserie chicken and a great breakfast; convenient to Grande-Allée. **Cons:** some ambient noise; hotel a bit of a maze; rooms in old-er section of hotel are smaller. $ *Rooms from: C$199* ⌧ *1220 pl. George V Ouest, Outside the Old City* ☎ *418/522–8108, 877/522–8108* ⊕ *www.hotelchateaulauri-er.com* ⇆ *289 rooms* ▮⦿▮ *No meals.*

Hôtel Delta Québec

$$$ | **HOTEL** | Opposite the Parliament buildings, this recently renovated hotel with large, functional rooms is an excel-lent and stylish option for business and design-minded travelers. **Pros:** kid-friendly environment; some rooms are adapted for people with limited mobility; four-sea-son outdoor pool. **Cons:** building is unin-spiring; attracts convention groups; drab lobby. $ *Rooms from: C$229* ⌧ *690 boul. René-Lévesque Est, Montcalm, Outside the Old City* ☎ *418/647–1717, 800/268–1133* ⊕ *www.marriott.com/hotels/travel/*

yqbdr-delta-hotels-quebec ⇨ *377 rooms* ⫿⊙⫾ *No meals.*

Hôtel Le Concorde Québec

$$ | **HOTEL** | Built in 1974, this 29-story concrete high-rise with an excellent location on Grande Allée offers larger-than-average rooms with Keurig coffeemakers, huge windows, and good views of Battlefields Park and the St. Lawrence River. **Pros:** central location; revolving rooftop restaurant; heated pool. **Cons:** high-traffic hotel; pool is open only in summer; some rooms have outdated fabrics and decor. ⑤ *Rooms from: C$185* ⊠ *1225 cours du Général-de Montcalm, Montcalm* ☎ *418/647–2222, 800/463–5256* ⊕ *www.loewshotels.com* ⇨ *425 rooms* ⫿⊙⫾ *No meals.*

Hôtel-Musée Premières Nations

$$ | **HOTEL** | **FAMILY** | A warm welcome, spacious rooms outfitted with real pelts, and river views await at this luxury rural hotel, restaurant, and museum complex in Wendake, a 15-minute drive north of the city. **Pros:** luxury rural escape; spa features Nordic pools, heated sidewalks, a fire pit, and yurt; excellent restaurant. **Cons:** rustic style might not appeal to animal lovers; uneven service. ⑤ *Rooms from: C$179* ⊠ *5 pl. de la Rencontre, Wendake* ☎ *418/847–2222* ⊕ *www.tourismewendake.ca/hotel* ⊟ *No credit cards* ⇨ *55 rooms* ⫿⊙⫾ *No meals.*

Hôtel Palace Royal

$ | **HOTEL** | A soaring indoor atrium with balconies overlooking a tropical garden, swimming pool, and hot tub lends a sense of drama to this family-friendly hotel. **Pros:** eclectic design; rooms have views; good packages. **Cons:** atrium can feel a bit hot and humid; modern-Victorian decor may not appeal to everyone; customer service can vary in quality. ⑤ *Rooms from: C$159* ⊠ *775 av. Honoré-Mercier, Outside the Old City* ☎ *418/694–2000, 800/567–5276* ⊕ *www.hotelsjaro.com/palaceroyal/index-en.aspx* ⇨ *234 rooms* ⫿⊙⫾ *No meals.*

★ Hotel PUR

$ | **HOTEL** | Travelers with a preference for minimal and modern design will appreciate this slick boutique hotel with its light-filled rooms, great views, and location in an interesting neighborhood. **Pros:** clean, modern design; great dining room doubles as a bar late evenings; in bustling St-Roch district. **Cons:** minimal design doesn't work for everyone; customer service can vary in quality; hotel is not within short walking distance from Old Québec sights. ⑤ *Rooms from: C$139* ⊠ *395 rue de la Couronne, St-Roch, Outside the Old City* ☎ *418/647–2611* ⊕ *www.hotelpur.com* ⇨ *242 rooms* ⫿⊙⫾ *No meals.*

Hôtel Royal William

$ | **HOTEL** | Like its namesake, the first Canadian steamship to cross the Atlantic (in 1833), the Royal William embodies the spirit of technology and innovation. **Pros:** friendly staff; convenient location in a hip area; spacious rooms with kitchenettes. **Cons:** the public areas are uninspired; business travelers aren't usually big minglers; comfortable and practical but nothing exceptional. ⑤ *Rooms from: C$150* ⊠ *360 boul. Charest Est, St-Roch, Outside the Old City* ☎ *418/521–4488, 888/541–0405* ⊕ *www.royalwilliam.com* ⇨ *44 rooms* ⫿⊙⫾ *Breakfast.*

★ Ice Hotel (*Hôtel de Glace*)

$$$ | **HOTEL** | The first of its kind in North America, this hotel, open from the first week in January to the end of March at Village Vacances Valcartier, is built entirely from ice and snow each year. **Pros:** unique experience; spectacular engineering feat and design; festive atmosphere. **Cons:** thick snow and ice walls make for very silent rooms, which can be eerie; limited availability; 30-minute drive from Downtown Québec City. ⑤ *Rooms from: C$219* ⊠ *Village Vacances Valcartier, 1860, boul. Valcartier, Outside the Old City* ☎ *418/623–2888, 877/505–0423* ⊕ *valcartier.com* ⇨ *44 rooms* ⫿⊙⫾ *No meals.*

The rue du Trésor in Upper Town is an alleyway lined with local artists selling paintings and sketches.

🅈 Nightlife

BARS AND LOUNGES

Korrigane Brasserie Artisanale
BARS/PUBS | A popular after-work spot with the locals, this brewery crafts high-quality beer and tapas-inspired pub fare. A friendly vibe and ample seating make Korrigane the ideal spot for a *cinq à sept* or a low-key night out. In addition to the house brews, there's a good selection of other local options. ⌧ *380 rue Dorchester, St-Roch* ☎ *418/614–0932* ⊕ *www.korrigane.ca.*

★ Nénuphar
WINE BARS—NIGHTLIFE | Québec City's only speakeasy is well worth the walk from the Old Town. French for "waterlily" (as in Monet's arkworks), Nénuphar is almost like traveling in time back to turn-of-the-century Paris, thanks to velvet-heavy decor, early-1900s' paintings, and soft pink hues—not to mention the absinth! Expect a cozy, dimly lit locale with interesting bites, a long list of natural wines, and creative cocktails. The exterior, as with any good speakeasy, is a bit non-descript; if it feels like you're not at the right place, in fact, you probably are. ⌧ *801 4e Rue, Limoilou* ⊕ *www.nenupharbar.com* ⊙ *Closed Sun.–Wed.*

🅿 Performing Arts

Centre Vidéotron
MUSIC | This state-of-the-art arena opened in the fall of 2015, with the hope of attracting a National Hockey League franchise. For now, the hockey is from a junior league, but there are world-class concerts and popular acts playing here regularly. ⌧ *Parc de l'Expocité, 250 boul. Wilfrid-Hamel, Limoilou* ☎ *855/790–1245* ⊕ *www.lecentrevideotron.ca.*

Carrefour international de théâtre de Québec
THEATER | This international theatrical festival takes over several spaces in late May and early June: the Salle Albert-Rousseau, the Grand Théâtre de Québec, the Théâtre Périscope (near avenue Cartier), and Complexe Méduse. There are usually

at least one or two productions in English or with English subtitles, and an outdoor show that takes over different parts of the Downtown area. ⊠ *Québec City* ☎ *418/692–3131* ⊕ *www.carrefourtheatre.qc.ca.*

Coopérative Méduse

ART GALLERIES—ARTS | This multidisciplinary arts center, built in a row of historic houses mixed with new structures, is a hub for local artists and presents edgy installations and live shows, including a modern dance series. ⊠ *541 rue de St-Vallier Est, St-Roch* ☎ *418/640–9218* ⊕ *www.meduse.org.*

École de Cirque

CIRCUSES | For two weeks every late May, students of this circus school and others take to the trapeze to promote their art form through the Circus Days festival. Throughout the year, students and teachers put on various shows, training camps, and workshops, including a Christmas Cabaret, in the former church that now houses their school. ⊠ *750 av. 2e, Limoilou* ☎ *418/525–0101* ⊕ *www.ecoledecirque.com.*

Grand Théâtre de Québec

ARTS CENTERS | Québec City's main theater has two stages for symphonic concerts, opera, plays, and touring companies of all sorts. The Grand Théâtre also presents a dance series with Canadian and international companies. Inside, a three-wall mural by the Québec sculptor Jordi Bonet depicts death, life, and liberty. Bonet wrote "La Liberté" on one wall to bring attention to the Quebecois struggle for freedom and cultural distinction. ⊠ *269 boul. René-Lévesque Est, St-Jean-Baptiste* ☎ *418/643–8131* ⊕ *www.grandtheatre.qc.ca.*

★ Orchestre Symphonique de Québec

(*Québec Symphony Orchestra*)
MUSIC | Canada's oldest symphony orchestra, directed by the dynamic French conductor Fabien Gabel, performs mainly at Louis-Fréchette Hall in the

Grand Théâtre de Québec. ⊠ *269 boul. René-Lévesque Est, St-Jean-Baptiste* ☎ *418/643–8486* ⊕ *www.osq.org.*

Salle Albert-Rousseau

THEATER | A diverse repertoire, from classical music to comedy, is staged here. ⊠ *2410 chemin Ste-Foy, Ste-Foy* ☎ *418/659–6710* ⊕ *www.sallealbertrousseau.com.*

Théâtre Périscope

THEATER | This multipurpose theater hosts about a dozen different productions a year, staged by several different theater companies. New creations and experimental productions are always a strong part of the mix. ⊠ *2 rue Crémazie Est, St-Jean-Baptiste* ☎ *418/529–2183* ⊕ *www.theatreperiscope.qc.ca.*

🛍 Shopping

FOOD

Camellia Sinensis Maison de Thé

FOOD/CANDY | This modern and elegant space stocks 150 different teas from China, Japan, Africa, and beyond, most of them imported by the owners themselves. You can sign up for a number of tea-tasting sessions and workshops, or just sip some tea on premises ⊠ *624 rue St-Joseph Est, St-Roch, Outside the Old City* ☎ *418/525–0247* ⊕ *www.camellia-sinensis.com.*

La Boîte à Pain

FOOD/CANDY | Baker Patrick Nisot offers a selection of baguettes, multigrain breads (pumpernickel, rye), special flavors (olive, tomato and pesto, Sicilian), and dessert breads. Even something as common as a date square has a special and delicious twist to it. Sandwiches and salads are also available for lunch. No credit cards are accepted. Two more locations are available in Sainte-Foy and in the quaint Limoilou neighborhood. ⊠ *289 rue St-Joseph Est, St-Roch, Outside the Old City* ☎ *418/647–3666* ⊕ *boiteapain.com.*

Le Grand Marché
FOOD/CANDY | Québec City's answer to Paris's Le Bon Marché, this shop is a must for gourmet-loving travelers. Expect tons of artisan-made goods, such as upscale jams, honeys, ciders, cheeses, chocolate, beers, and maple—all locally made. In summertime, there is a shuttle service that goes here from Place d'Armes. ✉ *250-M boul. Wilfrid-Hamel, Outside the Old City* ☎ *418/692–2517* ⊕ *www.legrandmarchedequebec.com.*

GIFTS
Zone
HOUSEHOLD ITEMS/FURNITURE | Design-oriented, whimsical yet practical objects abound in this popular store, which features tons of interesting gadgets, tools, and accessories for the home and office. From the latest cooking implement to lovely decorative objects and fancy clocks, there's something for just about everyone. ✉ *999 av. Cartier, Montcalm* ☎ *418/522–7373* ⊕ *www.zonemaison. com.*

SHOPPING MALLS
Galeries de la Capitale
SHOPPING CENTERS/MALLS | **FAMILY** | Thirty-five restaurants, some 280 shops, an IMAX theater, and an adjacent indoor amusement park make this recently and extensively renovated mall ideal for a whole day of family retail therapy. ✉ *5401 boul. des Galeries, Lebourgneuf, Outside the Old City* ☎ *418/627–5800* ⊕ *www. galeriesdelacapitale.com.*

Laurier Québec
SHOPPING CENTERS/MALLS | There are more than 300 stores in Québec City's busiest mall, with everything from fashion and electronics to children's toys and books. Easily accessible by bus or (from some Downtown hotels) shuttle, it's next door to Place de la Cité and Place Sainte-Foy. Together, the three malls form the largest stretch of shopping in the city. ✉ *2700 boul. Laurier, Ste-Foy* ☎ *418/651–5000* ⊕ *laurierquebec.com.*

TOYS/GAMES
Benjo
TOYS | **FAMILY** | Whimsy runs wild at Benjo. This store features games and toys, kids' clothes, a large café with thrones for little princes and princesses, an ample bookstore filled with French storybooks (and some English), and even an electric train you can ride around the store. ✉ *550 boul. Charest Est, St-Roch, Outside the Old City* ☎ *418/640–0001* ⊕ *www.benjo.ca.*

🏃 Activities

Scenic rivers and nearby mountains (no more than 30 minutes away by car) make Québec City a great place for exploring the outdoors.

Québec City Tourist Information
TOUR—SPORTS | Contact the tourist board for information about sports and fitness activities around the city. ✉ *399 rue St-Joseph Est., St-Roch* ☎ *418/641–6654, 877/783–1608* ⊕ *https://www.quebec-cite.com/en/what-to-do/activities-attractions/sports-tourism/.*

BIKING
There are more than 100 km (60 miles) of fairly flat, well-maintained bike paths on Québec City's side of the St. Lawrence River and a similar amount on the south shore. Detailed route maps are available through tourism offices. The two best and most scenic of the bike paths are the one that follows the old railway bed in Lévis, accessible near the Québec-Lévis ferry terminal, and the one that follows the St. Lawrence River on the north shore, all the way to Montmorency Falls. Many parts of the regional network are now part of the province-wide Route Verte, a government-funded, 4,000-km-long (2,500-mile-long) circuit of long-distance bicycle paths and road routes.

Corridor des Cheminots
BICYCLING | Ambitious cyclists can embark on the 22-km-long (14-mile-long) trail that

runs from Québec City near Old Québec to the town of Shannon. It's a slow uphill on the way out—with the reward of an easier ride back. ⊠ *Québec City.*

Côte-de-Beaupré

BICYCLING | Paths along the beginning of the Beaupré coast, at the confluence of the St. Charles and St. Lawrence rivers, are especially scenic. They begin northeast of the city, at rue de la Vérendrye and boulevard Montmorency or rue Abraham-Martin and Pont Samson (Samson Bridge), and continue 10 km (6 miles) along the coast to Montmorency Falls. ⊠ *Québec City.*

Mont-Ste-Anne

BICYCLING | The site of the 1998 world mountain-biking championship and races for the annual World Cup has around 150 km (93 miles) of mountain-bike trails and an extreme-mountain-biking park. ⊠ *Québec City* ☎ *800/463–1568* ⊕ *www. mont-sainte-anne.com* 🖾 *C$15 trails only; C$43 unlimited access to ski lift and trails.*

BOATING AND FISHING

Permits are needed for fishing in Québec. Most sporting-goods stores and all Walmart and Canadian Tire stores sell permits. A one-day fishing permit for a nonresident is C$13, a three-day permit is C$29, a seven-day permit is C$45, and a season permit is C$67 (and includes all sport fish except Atlantic salmon).

Gesti-faune

BOATING | A corporate fishing outfitter, Gesti-faune has two properties within easy driving distance of Québec City. From May to September, the company's nature guides organize trout-fishing trips that include food and lodging in private wilderness retreats. Three-day trips, organized from May to September for groups of 14, cost from C$900 per person, and include everything, including gourmet cuisine. There are also daily packages starting at C$146 per person. Reservations are required. ⊠ *Québec City* ☎ *418/848–5424* ⊕ *www.gestifaune. com.*

Latulippe

BOATING | This store, a few minutes' drive from Old Québec, sells permits and also stocks a large amount of fishing and outdoor equipment. ⊠ *637 rue St-Vallier Ouest, St-Roch* ☎ *418/529–0024, 877/529–0024.*

Parc Nautique de Cap-Rouge

BOATING | This park, at the western tip of Québec City on the St. Lawrence River, has canoes and pedal boats to rent. ⊠ *4155 chemin de la Plage Jacques-Cartier, Cap-Rouge* ☎ *418/641–6148.*

Réserve Faunique des Laurentides

BOATING | This wildlife reserve has good lakes for fishing. It's approximately 48 km (30 miles) north of Québec City via Route 73. Reserve a boat 48 hours in advance by phone. ☎ *418/528–6868, 800/665–6527 fishing reservations* ⊕ *www.sepaq. com/rf/lau.*

DOG SLEDDING

For centuries, dog sledding has been a part of the Canadian winter experience. Outfitters around Québec City generally offer excursions from January through March.

Aventures Nord-Bec Stoneham

LOCAL SPORTS | FAMILY | This outfitter will teach you how to mush in the forest. A half-day expedition, which includes a crash course, dog sledding, a guided tour of kennels, and a snack, costs C$145 per person. Overnight camping trips, snowshoeing, and ice fishing are also available. In summer, this location offers fishing, mountain biking, and kennel tours. Transportation between Stoneham (a 30-minute drive from the Old City) and your hotel costs $45 extra. ⊠ *4 chemin des Anémones, Stoneham* ☎ *418/848–3732* ⊕ *www.traineaux-chiens.com.*

GOLF

The Québec City region has 18 golf courses, and most are open to the public. Reservations are essential in summer.

Club de Golf Cap-Rouge

GOLF | Established in 1959, this is one of the closest courses to the city center, just 25 minutes by car from Vieux-Québec in a pleasant suburban area. Its 18-hole course is set up with variations for women, men, and advanced players. You're close to the St. Lawrence River, so be careful not to let the wind play tricks on you. ⊠ *4600 rue St-Felix, Cap-Rouge* ☏ *418/653–9381* ⊕ *www.golfcap-rouge. qc.ca* ⊠ *C\$35–C\$90 depending on tee time* ⸓. *18 holes, 6756 yards, par 72.*

Club de Golf de Mont Tourbillon

GOLF | The cooler air of the Laurentian Mountains is quite welcome on a hot summer day, as you play golf and enjoy views of the rolling hillside and Lac Beauport. Mont Tourbillon features three courses and the brand-new, modern clubhouse offers a bistro with a pleasant terrace. It's 25 minutes from the city by car via Route 73 North (take the Lac Beauport exit). In winter, golfing yields the way to long, fun slides. ⊠ *55 montée du Golf, Lac-Beauport* ☏ *418/849–4418* ⊕ *www.monttourbillon.com* ⊠ *C\$40–50 weekends, C\$35–40 weekdays* ⸓. *Blue Course: 18 holes, 6090 yards, par 70; White Course: 18 holes, 5590 yards, par 70; Red Course: 18 holes, 4625 yards, par 70.*

Le Saint-Ferréol

GOLF | Located within sight of the Mont-Sainte-Anne ski slopes, this club has one of the best and best-priced courses in the region—it's been fine-tuned by pro Denis Gagné. The course is a half-hour drive northeast of Québec City, and features a large driving range for practice. ⊠ *1700 boul. les Neiges, St-Ferréol-les-Neiges* ☏ *418/827–3778* ⊕ *www.golfstferreol.com* ⊠ *C\$32–48 depending on tee time* ⸓. *18 holes, 6445 yards, par 72.*

HIKING AND JOGGING

Runners and foot soldiers have a choice of routes in areas like Battlefields Park, Cartier-Brébeuf, and along the waterfront in the city itself.

Bois-de-Coulonge Park

HIKING/WALKING | Along with Battlefields Park, Bois-de-Coulonge is one of the most popular places for jogging, with forest trails and river views. ⊠ *1215 Grand Allée Ouest, Ste-Foy* ☏ *418/528–0773.*

Cartier-Brébeuf National Historic Site

HIKING/WALKING | North of the Old City, along the banks of the St. Charles River, you'll be able to keep going along about 13 km (8 mile) of hiking and biking trails. This historic site commemorates the first winter the French explorer Cartier spent with the First Nations people at their village of Stadacona, and has a small museum. ⊠ *175 rue de l'Espinay* ☏ *418/648–4038, 888/773–8888.*

ICE-SKATING

In addition to rinks in town, Village Vacances Valcartier (see Snow Slides), just outside Québec City, offers skating trails with lighting and sound systems.

RAFTING

Just outside the city, the Jacques-Cartier River (to the west) and Riviére Malbaie (to the east) both make for an easy white-water rafting day trip. Village Vacances Valcartier (see Snow Slides) also runs three-hour rafting excursions on the river from May through September.

Excursions Jacques-Cartier

WHITE-WATER RAFTING | This outfitter runs rafting trips on the Jacques-Cartier River, about 48 km (30 miles) northwest of Québec City, from May through October. Tours originate from Tewkesbury, a half-hour drive from Québec City. A half-day trip ranges from C\$84 per person, wet suits included. ⊠ *860 av. Jacques-Cartier Nord, Stoneham-et-Tewkesbury* ☏ *418/848–7238* ⊕ *www.excursionsj-cartier.com.*

Did You Know?

If you visit Québec City during the Carnaval de Québec, you'll have the opportunity to tour Bonhomme's Ice Palace.

SKIING

Skiing is very popular here, whether it's downhill on one of the mountains surrounding the city or cross-country in an urban park. A dynamic landscape, top-notch ski resorts, and lots of fresh powder have helped make this a major training area for some of Canada's top athletes.

⇨ *For more cross-country and downhill skiing options near Québec City, see the Side Trips from Québec City chapter.*

Québec City Tourism

SKIING/SNOWBOARDING | General information about ski centers in Québec is available from Québec City Tourism. ⊠ *Québec City.* ☎ *877/783–1608, 418/641–6290* ⊕ *www.quebec-cite.com/en/what-to-do/activities-attractions/ideas/ski.*

CROSS-COUNTRY

Regroupement des Stations de Ski de Fond

SKIING/SNOWBOARDING | Thirty-seven cross-country ski centers in the Québec area have 2,000 km (1,240 miles) of groomed trails and heated shelters between them; contact this group for more information. Many also offer snowshoeing trails. ⊠ *Québec City* ⊕ *www.skidefondraquette.com.*

SKI CENTERS

Le Centre Touristique Duchesnay

SKIING/SNOWBOARDING | Located west of Québec City, this center has 150 km (93 miles) of marked trails, which can be used for snowshoeing and cross-country skiing in the winter. There's a wonderful lakeside inn on-site. ⊠ *140 Montée de l'Auberge, Ste-Catherine-de-la-Jacques-Cartier* ☎ *418/875–2122.*

Les Sentiers du Moulin

SKIING/SNOWBOARDING | This center is 19 km (12 miles) north of the city and has more than 20 marked trails covering 48 km (28 miles), overall, with 28 km (17 miles) multitrack. ⊠ *99 chemin du Moulin, Lac-Beauport* ☎ *418/849–9652.*

DOWNHILL

Multiple downhill ski resorts are nearby, and some are barely 30 minutes away from Downtown Québec City. Most have night skiing. ⇨ *For information on Le Massif and Mont-Ste-Anne, see the Côte-de-Beaupré section in Chapter 6, Side Trips from Québec City.*

Le Relais

SKIING/SNOWBOARDING | There are 28 trails and a vertical drop of 734 feet at this relatively small, family-friendly ski center, where you can buy lift tickets by the hour. Le Relais is about 20 minutes from Downtown Québec City. ⊠ *1084 boul. du Lac, Lac-Beauport* ☎ *418/849–1851* ⊕ *www.skirelais.com.*

Station Touristique Stoneham

SKIING/SNOWBOARDING | Stoneham is 20 minutes north of Old Québec. The hill has a vertical drop of 1,380 feet, with a number of long, easy slopes and some more challenging runs. It has 42 downhill runs and seven lifts, plus three terrain parks and one super-half-pipe. ⊠ *1420 av. du Hibou, Stoneham* ☎ *418/848–2411, 800/463–6888* ⊕ *www.ski-stoneham.com.*

SNOWMOBILING

Québec is the birthplace of the snowmobile, and with 32,000 km (19,840 miles) of trails, it's one of the best places in the world for the sport. Two major trails, the 2,000-km (1,250-mile) Trans-Québec Snowmobile Trail and the 1,300-km (806-mile) Fur Traders Tour, run just north of Québec City. Trail maps are available at tourist offices.

SNOW SLIDES

Village Vacances Valcartier

SNOW SPORTS | FAMILY | Hop on an inner tube or carpet and shoot down one of more than 35 snow slides here. Or join 6 to 12 others for a snow-raft ride on one of three groomed trails. You can also take a dizzying ride on the Tornado, a giant inner tube that seats eight and spins down the slopes. Rafting and sliding cost C$42 per day for those taller than 52 inches, C$35 for those between 39 and 52 inches, and free for those under 39 inches. Trails open daily at 10 am; closing times vary. ✉ *1860 boul. Valcartier, St-Gabriel-de-Valcartier* ☎ *418/844–2200, 888/384–5524* ⊕ *www.valcartier.com.*

SPAS

Sibéria Spa

SPA/BEAUTY | A 20-minute drive from Vieux-Québec, Siberia Spa offers thermal and cold baths, a eucalyptus steam room, a relaxing yurt, an elegant café set inside a former chapel, and a quiet pavilion where you can sit by a fire and look out to the Jacques Cartier River. Admission is C$42 (C$29, evenings) for use of the spa, with massages and packages running from C$80 to C$254. It's normally adults only, but families are welcome on Sunday mornings (between 9 am and noon) and on regular hours during the holidays and spring break. ✉ *339 boul. du Lac, Lac-Beauport* ☎ *418/841–1325* ⊕ *www.siberiastationspa.com.*

Sky Spa

SPA/BEAUTY | Set on the 17th floor of a modern tower in the bustling Sainte-Foy district, near the city's main shopping centers, the spa features a terrace that is open all year, thermal care programs, and a full set of spa care packages. Massages start at C$60, with a full treatment package offered for C$210. There's also a bistro and lots of spots to enjoy the view. ✉ *2828 boul. Laurier, 17th fl., Ste-Foy* ☎ *866/656–9111* ⊕ *skyspa.ca/quebec.*

WATER PARKS

Village Vacances Valcartier

WATER SPORTS | **FAMILY** | The largest water park in Canada has a wave pool, a 1-km (½-mile) tropical-river adventure called the Amazon, more than 35 waterslides, and a 100-foot accelerating slide on which bathers reach a speed of up to 80 kph (50 mph). The interior Bora Parc, featuring 14 slides, a river and a wave pool, is open year-round. Admission is C$45 a day for those at least 52 inches tall, C$38 for those between 39 and 52 inches, and free for those under 39 inches. The park also offers a flurry of winter slides and activities, a hotel and rafting excursions. ✉ *1860 boul. Valcartier, St-Gabriel-de-Valcartier* ☎ *418/844–2200, 888/384–5524* ⊕ *www.valcartier.com.*

WINTER CARNIVAL

For three weekends in January and February, Québec City throws one of the biggest winter parties in the world. Each year, an Ice Palace is built as the center of the festivities, which include dog sled races, two parades, and events on several city streets. Ice bars are plentiful on the Grande Allée, and the streets fill with families and visitors singing songs and blowing into trumpets.

★ Carnaval de Québec

LOCAL SPORTS | **FAMILY** | A flurry of activity, mainly on the Plains of Abraham but also on several of the city's main drags, surrounds Carnaval de Québec, which occurs over three weekends every January and February. Snow and ice sculpture contests, dog sled relays, and canoe races on the icy St. Lawrence River chase away winter doldrums. Visitors brave the cold to get a glimpse of Bonhomme, the friendly Carnival Master, and tour his Ice Palace, which is rebuilt each year. Caribou, a strong mixture of red wine, hard liquor, and maple syrup, is a popular libation during the festivities. ✉ *Québec City* ⊕ *www.carnaval.qc.ca.*

Chapter 6

SIDE TRIPS FROM QUÉBEC CITY

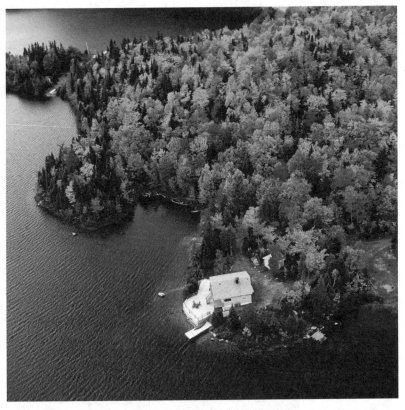

6

Updated by
Chris Barry

⊙ Sights	🍴 Restaurants	🛏 Hotels	🛍 Shopping	🍸 Nightlife
★★★★★	★★★★★	★★★★★	★★★★★	★★★★★

WELCOME TO
SIDE TRIPS FROM QUÉBEC CITY

TOP REASONS TO GO

★ **Ski at Le Massif:** This three-peak ski resort has the largest vertical drop in eastern Canada, at more than 2,500 feet.

★ **Whale-watch in Tadoussac:** About 220 km (137 miles) east of Québec City, you can see small white beluga whales—an endangered species—year-round in the Saguenay River.

★ **Farm-hop on Île d'Orléans:** The "Garden of Québec" is covered with farmland and bed-and-breakfasts, and makes for the perfect day or overnight trip from Québec City.

★ **Take the footbridge across Montmorency Falls:** These waterfalls on the Côte-de-Beaupré are double the height of Niagara Falls. The bridge and stairs, which go over and around them, make for a spectacular stroll.

★ **See Basilique Ste-Anne-de-Beaupré:** More than a million people a year make pilgrimages to this church, named after the patron saint of Québec.

1 Ste-Pétronille. Enjoy splendid views of Montmorency Falls and Cap Diamant.

2 St-Laurent de l'Île d'Orléans. Farm stands and strawberry fields.

3 St-Jean. Find preserved row houses from the 1800s and strawberry farms.

4 St-François. A rustic village with an observation tower.

5 Ste-Famille. The island's oldest parish.

6 St-Pierre. Shop for butters, jams, and ciders at the most populated part of the island.

7 Côte-de-Beaupré. Rich landscapes alongside the St. Lawrence River.

8 Baie-St-Paul. The cultural capital of the Charlevoix region.

9 St-Joseph-de-la-Rive. Board the ferry to the majestic L'Isle-aux-Coudres.

10 La Malbaie. Rich in history and natural beauty.

11 Tadoussac. One of the best whale-watching centers in Québec.

12 Port Saguenay. Famous for Lac Saint-Jean and home to the Saguenay Fjord.

13 Trois-Rivières. The second-oldest city in Québec.

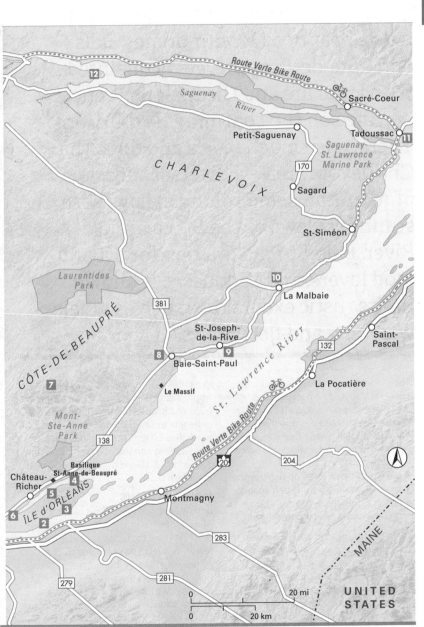

Experience a deeper understanding of this region's history and culture by venturing outside the city. In addition to the beauty of Montmorency Falls and Côte-de-Beaupré, get acquainted with rural life and the region's French heritage on the charming Île d'Orléans. There's also much to see and do in the Charlevoix area—a diverse landscape of mountains and rolling valleys with stunning views of the St. Lawrence River. Baie-St-Paul is a hub for art and food lovers, and Tadoussac is known for its rustic excursions, such as whale-watching and fjord tours.

Montmorency Falls is an excellent first stop on any adventure outside the city. From there, you can cruise up Québec's Côte-de-Beaupré and eventually make your way to Ste-Anne-de-Beaupré, where there's an immense neo-Roman basilica. Or take the bridge to Île d'Orléans, where you can pick fresh berries, sample ice cider fermented from frozen apples, and shop for antiques. A leisurely drive around the island can be done in a day.

Charlevoix, a couple of hours from Québec City, takes more planning and probably an overnight stay, but is well worth the drive. There are plenty of gorgeous villages and picnic spots along the way. Artists of all disciplines draw inspiration from this region, which is steeped in natural beauty and Algonquin history. Approaching Tadoussac, at the eastern edge of Charlevoix, the St. Lawrence River begins to seem like the open sea—it's more than 20 km (12 miles) wide at this point. Slicing into the land is the dramatic Saguenay Fjord, one of the largest fjords in the world.

MAJOR REGIONS

Île d'Orléans. The Algonquins called it Minigo, the "Bewitched Place," and over the years the island's tranquil rural beauty has inspired poets and painters. Île d'Orléans is only 15 minutes by car from Downtown Québec City, but a visit here is one of the best ways to get a feel for traditional life in rural Québec. Centuries-old homes and some of the oldest churches in the region dot the road that rings the island. About 8 km (5 miles) wide and 35 km (22 miles) long, Île d'Orléans is made up of six small villages that have sought over the years to retain their identities: **Ste-Pétronille, St-Laurent de l'Île d'Orléans, St-Jean, St-François, Ste-Famille,** and **St-Pierre.** The bridge to the mainland was built in 1935, and in 1970 the island was declared a historic area to protect it from most sorts of development.

To get to Île d'Orléans, take Route 440 (Autoroute Dufferin–Montmorency) northeast. After a drive of about 10 km (6 miles), take the bridge (Pont de l'Île d'Orléans) to the island. The main road, chemin Royal (Route 368), circles the island, extending 67 km (42 miles) through the island's six villages; the route turns into chemin du Bout de l'Île as it loops around the western tip of the island.

Côte-de-Beaupré. Driving along this coast offers views of Île d'Orléans, as well as Montmorency Falls and the famous pilgrimage site, Ste-Anne-de-Beaupré.

To get to the Côte-de-Beaupré, take Route 440 (Autoroute Dufferin–Montmorency) northeast from Québec City. It's approximately 9.5 km (6 miles) to the exit for the Chutes Montmorency and about 35 km (21 miles) to Ste-Anne-de-Beaupré.

Charlevoix. People refer to Charlevoix as the "Switzerland of Québec" due to its terrain of mountains, valleys, streams, and waterfalls. A couple of hours from Québec City, it takes more planning and probably an overnight stay, but is well worth the drive. Charlevoix's charming villages line the shore of the St. Lawrence River for about 200 km (125 miles). Artists of all disciplines draw inspiration from this region, which is steeped in natural beauty and Algonquin history. Approaching **Tadoussac,** at the eastern edge of Charlevoix, the St. Lawrence

River begins to seem like the open sea—it's more than 20 km (12 miles) wide at this point. Winter activities include downhill and cross-country skiing, snowmobiling, ice fishing, dog sledding, and snowshoeing. Charlevoix's many great local food products and restaurants are also a big draw for tourists. Slicing into the land is the dramatic Saguenay Fjord, one of the largest fjords in the world.

To get to Charlevoix from Québec City, take Route 440 (Autoroute Dufferin–Montmorency) northeast and then continue on Route 138 past Côte-de-Beaupré. From there you'll be able to branch out for destinations such as Petite-Rivière-St-François or Baie-St-Paul.

Planning

When to Go

Côte-de-Beaupré, Île d'Orléans, and Charlevoix are spectacular in the fall, when you can leaf-peep and go apple picking. Summer means roadside stands featuring fresh-from-the-farm produce on Île d'Orléans or Côte-de-Beaupré. Artists and art lovers flock to Baie-St-Paul in Charlevoix for festivals and gallery openings. It's also the perfect time to see beluga whales in Tadoussac. In winter, in all regions, there are plenty of cold-weather activities, including cross-country skiing, snowshoeing, and ice fishing. The area's best downhill skiing can be found in Charlevoix, but if you don't want to tackle driving on mountain roads, consider taking a shuttle. Spring has its own magic, when the snow melts and the maple syrup starts to flow.

Getting Here and Around

The best, and in some cases the only way to explore these regions is by car, and this makes it easy to spend as much or as little time as desired in any given area. Start by heading northeast out of Québec City on Route 440 (Autoroute Dufferin–Montmorency) and then Route 138 (Boulevard Ste-Anne).

Another way to explore the exceptional beauty of the region is to hop aboard Le Train du Massif Charlevoix, a train that runs mid-June through mid-October along the shoreline from Parc de la Chute-Montmorency station to Baie-St.-Paul or La Malbaie, with several excursion options. ⇨ *For further details, see under Baie-St.-Paul and La Malbaie.*

TRAIN INFORMATION Train de Charlevoix. ☎ *418/240–4124, 844/737–3282* ⊕ *www. traindecharlevoix.com.*

Québec continues to expand its Route Verte (Green Route), a 5,000-km (3,100-mile) network of bike trails in the southern part of the province.

⇨ *For more information on getting here and around, refer to Travel Smart.*

Restaurants

Some of the restaurants on the Côte-de-Beaupré and Île d'Orléans are open only during high season, May to October, so check ahead. But visitors who do arrive in season won't be disappointed. Fast-food or chain outlets are essentially absent from the island, and your best—and most widely available—option is to sample some of the regional cuisine on offer. And while fine dining is the order of the day on Île d'Orléans, those traveling on a budget won't go hungry, as there are some good pubs and family-style restaurants with fairly reasonable prices.

In Charlevoix, the same rules apply—call ahead if you're visiting from June to September or during the Christmas holidays. During summer, Charlevoix is a food lover's haven, with fresh berries and cheeses sold roadside and plenty of bistros in the towns. Pick up a map

(available at most hotels and restaurants) of *La Route des Saveurs*, a route through the region dotted with restaurants and farms, and taste your way to Tadoussac.

Hotels

Reservations at hotels are highly recommended, although off-season it's possible to book a room the same day. B&Bs are the most common lodging options on Île d'Orléans, although there is a handful of inns and one motel. Côte-de-Beaupré, on the other hand, not only has plenty of inns and B&Bs, but several hotels and motels as well.

Given its status as one of Québec's premier summer vacation destinations, the Charlevoix region has lots to offer travelers on almost any budget. Nevertheless, it's wise to book ahead in high season, especially if you're looking for one of the less expensive rooms here, which tend to fill up pretty quickly during the summer months.

Restaurant and hotel reviews have been shortened. For full information, visit Fodors.com.

What It Costs in Canadian Dollars			
$	$$	$$$	$$$$
RESTAURANTS			
under C$12	C$12–C$20	C$21–C$30	over C$30
HOTELS			
under C$160	C$160–C$200	C$201–C$250	over C$250

Visitor Information

CONTACTS Association Touristique Régionale de Charlevoix. ✉ *495 boul. de Comporté, C.P. 275, La Malbaie* ☎ *418/665–4454, 800/667–2276* ⊕ *www. tourisme-charlevoix.com.* **Bureau touristique de l'île d'Orléans.** (*Tourist*

Information Center Île d'Orléans) ✉ *490 Côte du Pont, St-Pierre-de-l'Île-d'Orléans* ☎ *418/828–9411, 866/941–9411.* **Centre d'Interpretation de la Côte-de-Beaupré.** (*Beaupré Coast Interpretation Center*) ✉ *7976 av. Royale, C.P. 40, Château-Richer* ☎ *418/824–3677, 877/824–3677* ⊕ *www.histoire-cotedebeaupre.org.*

Ste-Pétronille

17 km (10½ miles) northeast of Québec City.

The lovely village of Ste-Pétronille, the first to be settled on Île d'Orléans, is west of the bridge to the island. Founded in 1648, the community was chosen in 1759 by British general James Wolfe for his headquarters. With 40,000 soldiers and a hundred ships, the English bombarded French-occupied Québec City and the surrounding shorelines.

In the late 19th century, the English population of Québec developed Ste-Pétronille into a resort village. This area is considered to be the island's most beautiful, not only because of its spectacular views of Montmorency Falls and Québec City but also for its Regency-style English villas and exquisitely tended gardens.

GETTING HERE AND AROUND
Once across the bridge from the mainland, the Côte du Pont leads to Route 368. Turn right on chemin Royal and drive 4 km (2½ miles) to Ste-Pétronille.

◉ Sights

Maison Gourdeau de Beaulieu
HOUSE | The island's first home was built in 1648 for Jacques Gourdeau de Beaulieu, who was the first seigneur (a landholder who distributed lots to tenant farmers) of Ste-Pétronille. Remodeled over the years, this white house with blue shutters now incorporates both French and Québec styles. Its thick walls and dormer windows are characteristic

of Breton architecture, but its sloping, bell-shaped roof, designed to protect buildings from large amounts of snow, is typical Québec style. The house is not open to the public. ✉ *137 chemin du Bout de l'Île.*

Plante Family Farm
FARM/RANCH | Pick apples and strawberries (in season) or buy fresh fruits, vegetables, and apple cider at this family farm. In March/April, enjoy maple-sugar treats from the roadside shack. ✉ *20 chemin du Bout de l'Île* ☎ *418/828–9603.*

Rue Horatio-Walker
NEIGHBORHOOD | Art fans might want to explore this tiny street off chemin Royal, named after the early-19th-century painter known for his landscapes of the island. Horatio Walker lived on this street from 1904 until his death in 1938. At Nos. 11 and 13 rue Horatio-Walker are his home and workshop, but neither are open to the public. ✉ *Ste-Pétronille.*

Vignoble de Ste-Pétronille
WINERY/DISTILLERY | Since they bought it in 2003, Louis Denault and Nathalie Lane have turned this vineyard into one of the best wine producers in Québec. Most of the wine is produced from a hybrid variety called vandal-cliche, which was bred by a Laval University biologist to thrive in the area's climate, along with a growing proportion of vidal. The results are a range of fresh, crisp white wines (still and bubbly), as well as ice wine. The winery has also started producing small amounts of Riesling, and does some tasty reds. In summer, Panache Mobile, a food cart managed by Panache, one of Québec City's best restaurants, serves delicious lunches on a terrace with a stunning view of the St. Lawrence River and Montmorency Falls. ✉ *1A chemin du Bout de l'Île* ☎ *418/828–9554* ⊕ *www. vignobleorleans.com* ✉ *Wed.-Sat. only: 1 hour VIP tasting tour C$22.*

Montmorency Falls along the Côte-de-Beaupré might not be as wide, but it's nearly twice as tall as Niagara Falls.

🛏 Hotels

Auberge La Goéliche

$$$ | B&B/INN | This English-style country manor (rebuilt in 1996–97 following a fire) is steps away from the St. Lawrence River, and the small but elegant rooms, decorated with antiques, all have river views. **Pros:** spectacular location; great base for exploring the island; beautiful views of the river. **Cons:** riverfront but no access to the water; some rooms are quite small; restaurant has a limited menu. $ *Rooms from: C$238* ✉ *22 chemin du Quai* ☎ *418/828–2248, 888/511–2248* ⊕ *www. goeliche.ca* ➡ *16 rooms, 3 suites* ○ *Free breakfast.*

👜 Shopping

FOOD

Chocolaterie de l'Île d'Orléans

FOOD/CANDY | Belgian chocolate is combined with local ingredients to produce the handmade confections here: with a maple butter filling, for example, or *framboisette*, made from raspberries.

In summer try the 24 different kinds of ice creams and sherbets, or bring home some chocolate-infused jams. They've also opened a smaller counter in the presbytery of Saint-François, at the other end of the island. ✉ *150 chemin du Bout de l'Île* ☎ *418/828–2250* ⊕ *www.chocolaterieorleans.com.*

St-Laurent de l'Île d'Orléans

9 km (5½ miles) east of Ste-Pétronille.

Founded in 1679, St-Laurent is one of the island's maritime villages. Until as late as 1935, residents used boats as their main means of transportation. St-Laurent has a rich history in farming and fishing. Work is underway to help bring back to the island some of the species of fish that were once abundant here.

First Nations Village

Huron-Wendat Village. A 25-minute drive outside city limits takes you into another world, that of the Huron-Wendat Nation, one group of Canada's First Nations peoples. The Huron-Wendat are famous for their handcrafted clothing, decorations, and hunting tools, which are on display at the village. A "traditional site" offers a fascinating traditional village exhibition, complete with longhouse, dances, and storytelling. Visitors can take guided tours and discover some stunning crafts in the huge gift shop. Traditional meals are served in an on-site restaurant. The spectacular Kabir Kouba waterfall, carved into a deep and steep gorge, is definitely worth a stop as well. ⊠ *575 rue Stanislas-Kosca, Wendake* ☎ *418/842–4308* ⊕ *www.huron-wendat.qc.ca* ⊠ *Guided tour C$14.75.*

GETTING HERE AND AROUND

Continue along chemin Royal from Ste-Pétronille, looping around the western end of the island and driving east along the southern shore.

Sights

Église St-Laurent

RELIGIOUS SITE | The tall, inspiring church that stands next to the village marina on chemin Royal was built in 1860 on the site of an 18th-century church that had to be torn down. One of the church's procession chapels is a miniature stone reproduction of the original. ⊠ *1532 chemin Royal, St-Laurent* ☎ *418/828–2551* ⊠ *Free.*

La Forge à Pique-Assaut

STORE/MALL | This working forge belongs to the talented local artisan Guy Bel, who has done ironwork restoration for Québec City. He was born in Lyon, France, and studied there at the École des Beaux-Arts. You can watch him and his team at work; his stylish candlesticks, chandeliers, fireplace tools, and other ironwork are for sale. ⊠ *2200 chemin Royal, St-Laurent* ☎ *418/828–9300* ⊕ *www.forge-pique-assaut.com.*

Parc Maritime de St-Laurent

CITY PARK | This former boatyard includes the Chalouperie Godbout (Godbout Longboat), which holds a collection of tools used by specialist craftsmen during the golden era of boat-building. You can picnic here and watch fishermen at work, trapping eels in tall nets at low tide. ⊠ *120 chemin de la Chalouperie, St-Laurent* ☎ *418/828–9672* ⊕ *www.parcmaritime.ca* ⊠ *C$5.*

Restaurants

Moulin de St-Laurent

$$$ | **CAFÉ** | You can dine inside amid old stone walls or outside on the patios at the foot of a tiny, peaceful waterfall at this restaurant, which was converted from an early-18th-century stone mill. Scrumptious snacks, such as quiche and salads, are available on the terrace, and evening dishes include local pork tenderloin and venison stew. **Known for:** cozy atmosphere; hearty dishes; pleasant patio. ⑤ *Average main: C$26* ⊠ *754 chemin Royal, St-Laurent* ☎ *418/829–3888, 888/629–3888* ⊕ *www.moulin-stlaurent.qc.ca* ⊘ *Restaurant closed mid-Oct.–May.*

Tucked away on the far southeastern side of Île d'Orléans, St Jean is perhaps the most picturesque of all the small villages that pepper the island.

St-Jean

12 km (7 miles) northeast of St-Laurent.

The village of St-Jean used to be occupied by river pilots and navigators. At sea most of the time, the sailors didn't need the large homes and plots of land that the farmers did. Often richer than farmers, they displayed their affluence by building their houses with bricks brought back from Scotland as ballast. Most of St-Jean's small, homogeneous row houses were built between 1840 and 1860.

GETTING HERE AND AROUND

From St-Laurent, continue northeast along chemin Royal.

◉ Sights

Église St-Jean

RELIGIOUS SITE | At the eastern end of the village sits a massive granite structure built in 1749, with large red doors and a towering steeple. The church resembles a ship; it's big and round and appears to be sitting right on the river. Paintings of the patron saints of seamen line the interior walls. The church's cemetery is also intriguing, especially if you can read French. Back in the 1700s, piloting the St. Lawrence was a dangerous profession; the cemetery tombstones recall the many lives lost in these harsh waters. ✉ *2001 chemin Royal* ☎ *418/828–2551* 🏷 *Free.*

Manoir Mauvide-Genest

MUSEUM | St-Jean's beautiful Normandy-style manor was built in 1734 for Jean Mauvide, the surgeon to Louis XV, and his wife, Marie-Anne Genest. The most notable thing about this house, which still has its original thick walls, ceiling beams, and fireplaces, is the degree to which it has held up over the years. The house serves as an interpretation center of New France's seigneurial regime, with 18th-century furniture, a historic vegetable garden, a multimedia presentation, and tours with guides dressed in 18th-century costumes. ✉ *1451 chemin Royal* ☎ *418/829–2630* ⊕ *www.*

manoirmauvidegenest.com ✉ *C$9 with guided tour. Groups of 20 or more only.*

🍴 Restaurants

La Boulange

$$ | **BAKERY** | This excellent, friendly bakery is located in the village of St-Jean's historic rectory, across the street from the church and a promenade along the river. In addition to delicious fresh croissants, pastries, and breads, La Boulange also offers pizzas and other light lunches that you can enjoy on the large covered porch in the summer. **Known for:** great pastries; light lunches; covered patio. ⑤ *Average main: C$12* ✉ *2001 chemin Royal* ☎ *418/829–3162* ⊕ *laboulange.ca* 🚫 *No credit cards* ◷ *No dinner. Closed Jan.–Mar.; Mon.–Wed. May, June, Sept., and Oct.; Mon.–Thurs. Nov., Dec., and Apr.*

St-François

12 km (7 miles) northeast of St-Jean.

Sprawling open fields separate 17th-century farmhouses in St-François, the island's least-toured and most rustic village. At the eastern tip of the island, this community was settled mainly by farmers. St-François is the perfect place to visit one of the island's *cabanes à sucre* (maple-sugaring shacks), found along chemin Royal. Stop at a hut for a tasting tour; sap is gathered from the maple groves and boiled until it's reduced to syrup (it takes 40 gallons of sap to produce one gallon of syrup). Boiled a little more and poured over snow, it becomes a delicious toffee. Maple-syrup season is from mid-March through April.

GETTING HERE AND AROUND

From St-Jean, continue northeast along chemin Royal.

⊙ Sights

Église St-François

RELIGIOUS SITE | Built in 1734, St-François is one of eight extant churches in Québec dating from the French regime. At the time the English seized Québec City in 1759, General James Wolfe knew St-François to be a strategic point along the St. Lawrence. Consequently, he stationed British troops here and used the church as a military hospital. In 1988 a car crash set the church on fire, and most of the interior treasures were lost. A separate children's cemetery stands as a silent witness to the difficult life of early residents. ✉ *341 chemin Royal* ☎ *418/828–2551* 🚫 *Free.*

Observation Tower

VIEWPOINT | This 60-foot-high wooden tower within a picnic area is well sited for viewing the majestic St. Lawrence and the many small islands in the estuary. In spring and fall, wild Canada geese can be seen here. The area is about 2 km (1 mile) north of Eglise St-François on chemin Royal. ✉ *St-François.*

Ste-Famille

14 km (9 miles) west of St-François.

The village of Ste-Famille, founded in 1661, has exquisite scenery, including abundant apple orchards and strawberry fields with views of Côte-de-Beaupré and Mont-Ste-Anne in the distance. But it also has historic charm, with the area's highest concentration of stone houses dating from the French regime.

GETTING HERE AND AROUND

From St-François, chemin Royal cuts north across the eastern tip of the island and continues west along the northern shore.

👁 Sights

Église Ste-Famille

RELIGIOUS SITE | This impressive church, constructed in 1749, is the only one in Québec to have three bell towers at its front. The ceiling was redone in the mid-19th century with elaborate designs in wood and gold. The church also holds a famous painting, *L'Enfant Jésus Voyant la Croix* (Baby Jesus Looking at the Cross); it was done in 1670 by Frère Luc (Brother Luc), who had been sent from France to decorate churches in the area. ✉ *3915 chemin Royal* ☎ *418/828–2656* 🖥 *Free.*

🍴 Restaurants

Microbrasserie de l'île d'Orléans

$$ | CANADIAN | This is one of the most interesting microbreweries in the Québec City region, producing a colorful range of beers named after historical characters from Île d'Orléans. You can taste them all at the adjoining Pub Le Mitan, along with standard pub fare including burgers, pizzas, and fries. **Known for:** great beer; pub fare; river view. 💲 *Average main: C$17* ✉ *3885 chemin Royal* ☎ *418/203–0588* ∰ *www.microorleans.com* 🖥 *No credit cards* 🕒 *Closed Mon.–Thurs. mid-Oct.–May.*

St-Pierre

14 km (9 miles) southwest of Ste-Famille.

Established in 1679, this town is set on a plateau that has the island's most fertile land and has long been the center of traditional farming industries. The best products grown here are potatoes, asparagus, and corn. The Espace Félix-Leclerc—an exhibit by day and a *boîte à chansons* (combination coffeehouse and bar with live performances) by night—works to honor the late singer and songwriter, who made St-Pierre his home. The bridge back to the mainland and Route 440 is just west on chemin Royal.

GETTING HERE AND AROUND

From Ste-Famille, continue southwest along chemin Royal. After visiting St-Pierre, the same road will take you back to the bridge to return to the mainland.

👁 Sights

Cassis Monna et filles

STORE/MALL | This family farm has won international awards for its crème de cassis, a liqueur made from black currants. In its vast and attractive tasting room and shop, you can taste free samples of the strong, sweet cassis or black currant wines; the tour explains how they are made. In summer you can sample foods made with cassis at La Monnaguette, the house bistro featuring a terrace overlooking the river. ✉ *726 chemin Royal, St-Pierre-de-l'Île-d'Orléans* ☎ *418/828–1057* ∰ *www.cassismonna.com* 🖥 *Free; guided tours (upon reservation) for groups only.*

Église St-Pierre

RELIGIOUS SITE | The oldest church on the island dates from 1717. It's no longer used for worship, but it was restored during the 1960s and is open to visitors. Many original components are still intact, such as benches with compartments below where hot bricks and stones were placed to keep people warm in winter. Félix Leclerc, the first Quebecois singer-songwriter to make a mark in Europe, is buried in the cemetery nearby. ✉ *1249 chemin Royal, St-Pierre-de-l'Île-d'Orléans* ☎ *418/828–9824* 🖥 *Free.*

Côte-de-Beaupré

25 km (15 miles) east of Québec City.

As legend has it, when explorer Jacques Cartier first caught sight of the north shore of the St. Lawrence River in 1535, he exclaimed, "*Quel beau pré!*" ("What a lovely meadow!"), because the area was the first inviting piece of land he had spotted since leaving France. Today the Côte-de-Beaupré (Beaupré Coast), first settled by French farmers, stretches 40 km (25 miles) east from Québec City to the famous pilgrimage site of Ste-Anne-de-Beaupré. Historic Route 360, or avenue Royale, winds its way from Beauport to St-Joachim, east of Ste-Anne-de-Beaupré. The impressive Chute Montmorency (Montmorency Falls) lie between Québec City and Ste-Anne-de-Beaupré.

GETTING HERE AND AROUND

Route 440 (Autoroute Dufferin–Montmorency) heads northeast from Québec City along the Côte-de-Beaupré. It's approximately 9.5 km (6 miles) to the exit for the Chutes Montmorency and about 35 km (21 miles) to Ste-Anne-de-Beaupré.

◉ Sights

Atelier Paré (Economuseum of Wood Sculpture)
MUSEUM | Two centuries of wood sculpture tradition are showcased at this "economuseum," a combination workshop and store. Visitors can watch artisans at work, tour an outdoor museum, see a 13-minute video presentation (in English and French), and learn about key characters in Québec's history and culture through the Legend Theatre Workshop. ⊠ 9269 av. Royale, Ste-Anne-de-Beaupré 🕾 418/827–3992 ⊕ www.atelierpare.com 🗺 Free; guided tour C$4 ⊗ Closed Mon. and Tues. Oct.–May.

★ Basilique Ste-Anne-de-Beaupré
RELIGIOUS SITE | Named for Québec's patron saint (the mother of the Virgin Mary), this small town is on Route 138, east of Québec City. It attracts more than a million pilgrims each year who come to visit the region's most famous religious site.

The French brought their devotion to St. Anne (also the patron saint of shipwrecked sailors) when they sailed across the Atlantic to New France. According to

local legend, St. Anne was responsible for saving voyagers from shipwrecks in the harsh waters of the St. Lawrence. In 1650, Breton sailors caught in a storm vowed to erect a chapel in honor of this patron saint at the exact spot where they landed.

The present neo-Roman basilica, constructed in 1923, is the fifth to be built on the site where the sailors first touched ground. The original 17th-century wood chapel was built too close to the St. Lawrence and was swept away by river flooding.

The gigantic structure is in the shape of a Latin cross and has two imposing granite steeples. The interior has 22 chapels and 18 altars, as well as rounded arches and numerous ornaments in the Romanesque style. The 214 stained-glass windows, completed in 1949, are by Frenchmen Auguste Labouret and Pierre Chaudière.

Tributes to St. Anne can be seen in the shrine's mosaics, murals, altars, and ceilings. A bas-relief at the entrance depicts St. Anne welcoming her pilgrims, and ceiling mosaics represent her life. Numerous crutches and braces posted on the back pillars have been left by those who have felt the saint's healing powers. ⊠ 10018 av. Royale, Ste-Anne-de-Beaupré 🕾 418/827–3781 ⊕ www.ssadb.qc.ca 🗺 C$3.

Chapelle Commémorative (Memorial Chapel)
RELIGIOUS SITE | Across from Basilique Ste-Anne-de-Beaupré, this chapel was designed by Claude Bailiff and built in 1878. It was constructed on the transept of a church built in 1676, and Bailiff made use of the old stones and foundation. Among the remnants is a white-and-gold-trimmed pulpit designed by François Baillargé in 1807 and adorned with a sculpture depicting Moses and the Ten Commandments.

Côte-de-Beaupré
and île d'Orléans

Scala Santa, a smaller chapel next to this one, resembles a wedding cake. On bended knees, pilgrims climb its replica of the Holy Stairs, representing the steps Jesus climbed to meet Pontius Pilate. ⊠ *10018 av. Royale, Ste-Anne-de-Beaupré* ☎ *418/827–3781* ⊕ *www.sanctuaire-sainteanne.org.*

Chute Montmorency
BODY OF WATER | The river cascading over a cliff into the St. Lawrence is one of the most beautiful sights in the province—and at 27 stories high, the falls are almost double the height of Niagara's. The Montmorency River was named for Charles de Montmorency, viceroy of New France in the 1620s and explorer Samuel de Champlain's immediate commander. A cable car runs to the top of the falls in **Parc de la Chute-Montmorency** (Montmorency Falls Park) from late April to late October. During very cold weather the falls' heavy spray freezes and forms a giant loaf-shaped ice cone known to the Quebecois as the Pain du Sucre (Sugarloaf); this phenomenon attracts sledders and sliders from Québec City. Summer activities include three via ferrata trails built onto the cliff, as well as a zipline that shoots across the canyon, in front of the falls.

The park also has a history. The British general James Wolfe, on his way to conquer New France, camped here in 1759. In 1780 Sir Frederick Haldimand, then the governor of Canada, built a summer home atop the cliff. The structure burned down in 1993, however, and what stands today, Manoir Montmorency, is a re-creation. Offering a stunning view of the falls and river below, it's open year-round, with a restaurant and terrace open in summertime. ⊠ *2490 av. Royale, Beauport* ☎ *418/663–3330* ⊕ *www.sepaq.com/destinations/parc-chute-montmorency* ⊠ *C$6.96; Cable car C$14.57; parking C$3.48.*

La Halte Miel
ZOO | FAMILY | Things are buzzing at this workshop and store devoted to bees and honey. An exhibit explains every aspect of honey production, and you can taste honey and honey ice creams, chocolates, and snacks made by bees that have fed on different kinds of flowers, including clover and blueberry. It's a 10-minute drive east of Montmorency Falls. ⊠ *8862 boul. Ste-Anne, Château-Richer* ☎ *418/824–4411* ⊕ *www.naturoney.com/en/honey-place* ⊠ *Free.*

Réserve Faunique des Laurentides
NATURE PRESERVE | The Réserve Faunique des Laurentides wildlife reserve, which incorporates the Parc national de la Jacques-Cartier and hundreds of lakes, is approximately 60 km (37 miles) north of Québec City via Highway 73, which leads to the Saguenay region. It has great hiking trails and camping spots, and good lakes for canoeing and fishing (but you should phone 48 hours in advance to reserve a fishing time.) From July to September, you can join bilingual guides to observe black bears in their natural environment from the safety of the park's observation towers. In winter, the park is a popular venue for sledding, snowshoeing, and cross-country skiing. ☎ *418/528–6868, 418/890–6527 fishing reservations* ⊕ *www.sepaq.com/rf/lau.*

★ Réserve Faunique du Cap Tourmente
(*Cap Tourmente Wildlife Reserve*)
NATURE PRESERVE | FAMILY | Recognized as a Wetland of International Significance, this nature reserve protects a vital habitat for migrating greater snow geese, and sees more than a million fly through every October and May, with tens of thousands of birds present every day. The park harbors hundreds of other kinds of birds and mammals, and more than 700 plant species. This enclave also has 18 km (11 miles) of hiking trails; naturalists give guided tours. It's on the north shore of the St. Lawrence River, about 8 km (5 miles) east of Ste-Anne-de-Beaupré.

✉ *570 chemin du Cap Tourmente, St-Joachim* ☎ *418/827–4591* ⊕ *www.canada.ca/ en/environment-climate-change/services/ national-wildlife-areas/locations/cap-tourmente.html* 🖃 *C\$6.*

Restaurants

★ Auberge Baker

\$\$\$\$ | CANADIAN | The best of old and new blend at this restaurant in an 1840 French-Canadian farmhouse, built by the owners' ancestors, which lies east of Château-Richer toward Ste-Anne-de-Beaupré. Antiques and old-fashioned woodstoves decorate the dining rooms, where you can sample traditional Québec dishes, from *tourtière* (meat pie) and pork hocks to maple-sugar pie. **Known for:** French Canadian pea soup; tourtière; sugar pies. 🛈 *Average main: C\$40* ✉ *8790 av. Royale, Château-Richer* ☎ *418/824–4478, 866/824–4478* ⊕ *www. aubergebaker.com.*

🛍 Shopping

SPAS

Spa des neiges

SPA/BEAUTY | An *inukshuk* (Inuit stone marker) greets you at the entrance to this spa, set in elegant wood buildings right by the St. Lawrence River. Just the view, looking toward Île d'Orléans, is enough to relax anyone, but you can also enjoy the thermal baths (starting at C\$38) or get one of many treatments, including massages, body wraps, mani-pedis, exfoliation, and light therapy. ✉ *9480 boul. Ste-Anne, Ste-Anne-de-Beaupré* ☎ *418/702–0631* ⊕ *www.spadesneiges. com.*

🏃 Activities

Le Massif

SKIING/SNOWBOARDING | This three-peak ski resort has Canada's longest vertical drop east of the Rockies—2,526 feet. Owned by Daniel Gauthier, a cofounder of Cirque du Soleil, the resort has two multiservice chalets at the top and bottom. Six lifts and one gondola service the 53 trails, which are divided into runs for different levels; the longest run is 4.8 km (3 miles). There's also a section of expert glades. Nonskiers can go snowshoeing at the top of the mountain, and there is also an exciting, 7½-km (4¾-mile) sled trail. Equipment can be rented on-site, and the resort offers daycare for younger children and shuttles from Québec City, Beaupré, Baie-St-Paul, and the Montréal area. ✉ *1350 rue Principale, Petite-Rivière-St-François* ☎ *418/632–5876, 877/536–2774* ⊕ *www.lemassif.com.*

Mont-Ste-Anne

BICYCLING | Part of the World Cup downhill circuit, Mont-Ste-Anne is one of the largest resorts in eastern Canada, with a vertical drop of 2,050 feet, 71 downhill trails, two half-pipes for snowboarders, a terrain park, and 13 lifts, including a gondola. The mountain stays active even after the sun goes down, with 19 lighted downhill trails. Cross-country skiing is also a draw here, with 21 trails totaling 224 km (139 miles). When the weather warms, mountain biking becomes the sport of choice. Enthusiasts can choose from 150 km (93 miles) of mountain-bike trails and 14 downhill runs (and a gondola up to the top). Three bike runs are designated "extreme zones." ✉ *2000 boul. du Beau-Pré, Beaupré* ☎ *418/827–4561, 888/827–4579* ⊕ *www.mont-sainte-anne. com.*

Baie-St-Paul

120 km (72 miles) northeast of Québec City.

Baie-St-Paul, one of the oldest towns in the province, is popular with craftspeople, artists, and foodies. With its centuries-old mansard-roof houses, the village is on the banks of a winding river, on a wide plain encircled by high hills—the

Baie-St-Paul is a charming small town popular with writers and artists. Each August it hosts a modern art show.

crater of a large meteor that crashed to earth 350 million years ago. Boutiques and a handful of commercial galleries line the historic narrow streets in the town center; most have original artwork and crafts for sale. In addition, each August more than a dozen artists from across Canada take part in the Symposium of Modern Art.

GETTING HERE AND AROUND

By road, Baie-St-Paul is approximately 95 km (59 miles) northeast of Québec City via Route 440 and Route 138. Le Massif de Charlevoix train runs day trips from the Chutes Montmorency station mid-June–early July Thursday through Sunday, then Wednesday through Sunday until mid-October. Departing at 9:10 am and including breakfast en route, it arrives in Baie-St-Paul at 11:45 am; the return journey, including dinner, leaves at 3 pm and arrives back at Chutes Montmorency station at 4:45 pm. The fare is C$229 round-trip, plus C$60 for a guaranteed riverside seat.

◉ Sights

Maison d'affinage Maurice Dufour

FARM/RANCH | FAMILY | The Dufour family produces some of the best cheese in the region, made from the milk of the herds of sheep and cows that can be seen grazing around the property in the summer. A modern and elegant tasting room allows visitors to discover the various cheeses and find out more about production, and taste the fresh and fun wines that they make from local vines. They've even started distilling vodka and spirits from whey, a fun way to produce something delicious from cheese-making by-products. A restaurant called Les Faux Bergers, featuring lots of wood-fired dishes, is also on the premises. ⊠ *1339 boul. Mgr de Laval* ☎ *418/435–5692* ⊕ *www. famillemigneron.com.*

Maison René Richard

MUSEUM | Many of Québec's greatest landscape artists, including Jean-Paul Lemieux and Clarence Gagnon, have depicted the area, and a selection of these works is on show here (some are also for sale). The gallery was Gagnon's former studio and also the home of painter René Richard for the last 43 years of his life. Guided tours of the studio are available for groups. ✉ 58 rue St-Jean-Baptiste ☎ 418/435–5571 ⊕ www.grandquebec.com/charlevoix/maison-rene-richard ✍ Free; call for group tour rates.

Musée d'Art Contemporain de Baie-St-Paul
MUSEUM | This museum highlights modern and contemporary art created by Charlevoix artists from 1920 to 1970. It also has a robust collection from the province in general, with works from Georges D. Pepper, Kathleen Daly, René Richard, the Bolduc sisters, and others. For more than 30 years, the museum has been organizing a yearly modern art symposium, held in late July and early August. ✉ 23 rue Ambroise-Fafard ☎ 418/435–3681 ⊕ www.macbsp.com ✍ C$10.

 Hotels

Auberge à l'Ancrage
$$$ | B&B/INN | A restored 1920s redbrick home with antiques, a maritime theme, a wraparound porch, and a back garden that sits at the edge of the Gouffre River, Auberge à l'Ancrage is run by a charming couple who offer delicious, multicourse breakfasts and eagerly share information about activities and attractions in the area. **Pros:** quiet and privacy; only a few minutes' walk from downtown; riverside yard. **Cons:** rooms are on the smaller side; pricey. ⑤ Rooms from: C$213 ✉ 29 rue Ste-Anne ☎ 418/240–3264 ⊕ www.aubergeancrage.com ➦ 4 rooms ⏪ Free breakfast.

★ **Hotel Le Germain Charlevoix**
$$$$ | HOTEL | This stylish and modern hotel, owned by one of the best boutique hotel groups in Canada, consists of five distinct pavilions housing three eateries and rooms in various styles, including

lofts and dormitories, all with contemporary finishes and elegant design. **Pros:** convenient location on public square with train station; farm-to-table cuisine in three on-site eateries; contemporary design. **Cons:** layout with multiple pavilions is a bit complicated; inconsistent service. ⑤ Rooms from: C$265 ✉ 50 rue de la Ferme ☎ 418/240–4100, 877/536–2774 ⊕ www.legermainhotels.com/en/charlevoix ➦ 152 rooms ⏪ No meals.

St-Joseph-de-la-Rive

20 km (12½ miles) northeast of Baie-St-Paul.

A secondary road descends sharply into St-Joseph-de-la-Rive, with its line of old houses hugging the mountain base on a narrow shore route. Enjoyed for its warm microclimate, the town features peaceful inns and inviting restaurants. Drive through and see the traces of early town life and the beginning of local industry: an old firehouse and a hydroelectric building that houses a generator dating back to 1928.

GETTING HERE AND AROUND
From Baie-St-Paul, drive northeast on rue Leclerc (Route 362).

Sights

Île-aux-Coudres
ISLAND | A free, government-run ferry from the wharf in St-Joseph-de-la-Rive takes you on the 15-minute trip to the island where Jacques Cartier's men gathered *coudres* (hazelnuts) in 1535. Since then, the island has produced many a *goélette* (a type of sailing ship), and the families of former captains now run several small inns. You can bike around the island and see windmills and water mills, or stop at the stores selling paintings and crafts, such as traditional handwoven household linens. ✉ St-Joseph-de-la-Rive ☎ 877/787–7483 ferry schedules ⊕ www.

Charlevoix

172

170

Jonquière

Chicoutimi

172

← TO
LAC-ST-JEAN
AND VILLAGE HISTORIQUE
DE VAL-JALBERT

● **Port Saguenay**

La Baie

Saguenay

River

Saguenay
Fjord

172

Tadoussac

Lac Kénogami

170

170

381

175

170

○ Baie-Ste-
Catherine

138

Parc national des
Hautes-Gorges-
de-la-Rivière-Malbaie ◆

Poterie de Port-au-Persil ◆

Mont-Grand Fonds

○ Port-au-Persil

381

● **La Malbaie**

Lac
Malbaie

138

362

20

289

175

Lac
des
Neiges

Route 362 ◆

○ Ste-Irenée

St-Joseph-de-la-Rive ●

Baie-St-Paul

Île-aux-
Coudres ◆

287

○ La Pocatière

Le Massif

○ La-Petite-
Rivière

St. Lawrence River

138

132

Mont-Ste-Anne

○ Beaupré

362

QUÉBEC
CITY

○ Ste-Anne-de-Beaupré

Île
d'Orléans

132

Montmagny

QUÉBEC
MAINE

Beauport

20

283

● Trois-Rivières

281

277

216

283

73

0   20 mi

0   20 km

traversiers.com/en/our-ferries/lisle-aux-coudres-saint-joseph-de-la-rive-ferry/contact-information/.

Musée Maritime de Charlevoix (*Maritime Museum*)

MUSEUM | This museum, housed in an old shipyard, commemorates the days of the St. Lawrence goélettes, the feisty little wooden freighters that were the chief means of transporting goods along the north shore of the St. Lawrence River well into the 1960s. Very large families lived in cramped conditions aboard the boats, some of which are part of the exhibits. To modern eyes, it doesn't look like a comfortable existence, but the folklore of the goélettes, celebrated in poetry, paintings, and song, is part of the region's strong cultural identity. ✉ *305 rue de l'Église* ☎ *418/635–1131* ⊕ *www.museemaritime.com* ✉ *C$10.*

🛏 Hotels

Hôtel Cap-aux-Pierres

$ | **HOTEL** | New ownership invested in a substantial renovation of the Cap-aux-Pierres, and the rooms now have a modern and stylish decor and many have river views. **Pros:** indoor and outdoor pools; beautiful environment; good food. **Cons:** no air-conditioning; rooms are somewhat outdated; restaurant is a little pricey. ⑤ *Rooms from: C$139* ✉ *444 chemin la Baleine, Île-aux-Coudres* ☎ *888/554–6003, 418/438–2711* ⊕ *www.hotelcapauxpierres.com* ⊗ *Closed mid-Oct.–Apr.* ⇌ *98 rooms* ⦿ *Free breakfast.*

🛍 Shopping

BOOKS

Papeterie Saint-Gilles

BOOKS/STATIONERY | This paper factory produces handcrafted stationery using a 17th-century process. There's also a small museum, which explains through photographs and demonstrations how paper is manufactured the old-fashioned way. Slivers of wood and flower petals

The Scenic Route 👁

From Baie-St-Paul, instead of the faster Route 138 to La Malbaie, drivers can choose the open, scenic coastal drive on Route 362. This section of road has memorable views of charming villages and rolling hills—green, white, or ablaze with fiery hues, depending on the season—meeting the broad expanse of the "sea," as the locals like to call the St. Lawrence estuary.

are pressed into the paper sheets, which are as thick as the covers of a paperback book. The finished products—made into writing paper, greeting cards, and one-page poems or quotations—make beautiful, if pricey, gifts. Visitors can wander through the museum for free, and guided tours can be arranged for groups. ✉ *354 rue F.A. Savard* ☎ *418/635–2430, 866/635–2430* ⊕ *www.papeteriesaint-gilles.com.*

La Malbaie

35 km (22 miles) northeast of St-Joseph-de-la-Rive.

La Malbaie, one of the province's most elegant and historically interesting resort towns, was known as Murray Bay when wealthy Anglophones summered here. The area became popular with American and Canadian politicians in the late 1800s, when Ottawa Liberals and Washington Republicans partied decorously all summer with members of the Québec bourgeoisie. William Howard Taft built the "summer White House," the first of three summer residences, in 1894, when he was the American civil governor of the Philippines. He became the 27th president of the United States in 1908.

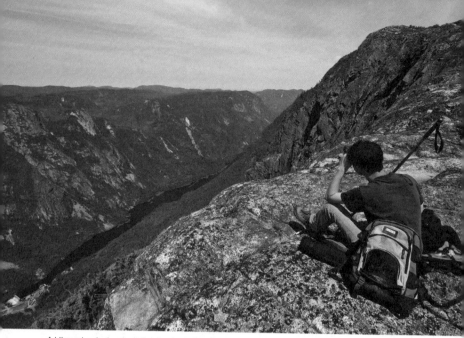

A hiker takes in the view of an ancient glacial valley.

Many Taft-era homes now serve as handsome inns, offering old-fashioned coddling with such extras as breakfast in bed, whirlpool baths, and free shuttles to the ski areas in winter. Many serve lunch and dinner to nonresidents, so you can tour the area going from one great French or Quebecois meal to the next.

GETTING HERE AND AROUND

Even if you don't want to visit St-Joseph-de-la-Rive, Route 362 between Baie-St-Paul and La Malbaie is much more scenic and well worth the extra half hour it adds to the trip from Québec City. Le Train de Charlevoix offers a day trip to La Malbaie Thursday through Sunday from mid-June to early July and Wednesday through Sunday until mid-October. It departs Chute Montmorency station at 9:10 am, with a stop en route at Baie-St-Paul; the round-trip takes 11 hours including time to get off and explore, and the fare, including breakfast and a four-course dinner, is C$369 (plus C$60 for a guaranteed riverside seat).

◉ Sights

Casino de Charlevoix

CASINO—SIGHT | The casino is one of four gaming halls in Québec (the others are in Montréal, Gatineau, and Mont-Tremblant) owned and operated by Loto-Québec. Charlevoix's, the smallest of the lot, still draws around 800,000 visitors a year—some of whom stay at the Fairmont Le Manoir Richelieu, which is connected to the casino by a tunnel. Largely renovated in 2016, it offers 21 gaming tables and more than 800 slot machines. The minimum gambling age is 18, and a photo ID is required to enter the casino. ✉ *183 rue Richelieu, Pointe-au-Pic* ☎ *418/665–5300, 800/665–2274* ⊕ *www.casinos.lotoquebec.com/en/charlevoix/home.*

Musée de Charlevoix

MUSEUM | The museum traces the region's history through a major permanent exhibit. Folk art, paintings, and artifacts help reveal the past, starting with the French, then the Scottish settlers, and the area's evolution into a vacation spot and artists' haven. Temporary exhibits change every season. ⊠ *10 chemin du Havre* ☎ *418/665–4411* ⊕ *www.musee-decharlevoix.qc.ca* ⊠ *C$8.*

Parc national des Hautes-Gorges-de-la-Rivière-Malbaie

BICYCLING | FAMILY | A 40-minute drive from La Malbaie will bring you to a stunning stretch of the Malbaie River, surrounded by impressive, steep slopes and rocky peaks. There are plenty of beautiful views to take in—whether it's from a kayak on the river or while hiking a network of trails—and lots of fresh air, in this central part of the Charlevoix Biosphere Preserve. ⊠ *25 boul. Notre-Dame* ☎ *418/439–1227* ⊕ *www.sepaq.com/pq/hgo* ⊠ *Park access, daily: C$9. Camping from C$24 per night.*

Restaurants

Pains d'exclamation

$ | BAKERY | FAMILY | This lively café-and-bakery offers a wide variety of classic and unique pastries and breads (hello, preserved-lemon bread!), sandwiches and quick breakfast and lunch options. It's a favorite with locals, who either eat in or take out after a quick chat with the friendly staff. **Known for:** great pastries; patio dining; quick, delicious lunches. ⑤ *Average main: C$10* ⊠ *398 rue Saint-Étienne, Pointe-au-Pic* ☎ *418/665–4000* ⊕ *www.painsdexclamation.com.*

Hotels

Auberge des Peupliers

$ | B&B/INN | About half the guest rooms at this hilltop inn overlook the St. Lawrence River, and the country-style accommodations are spread among three buildings, including a farmhouse more than two centuries old. **Pros:** lounge with fireplace and bar perfect for relaxing; excellent service; scenic location. **Cons:** need to drive to downtown La Malbaie; complaints of average food at a high price in the restaurant. ⑤ *Rooms*

Potter About ⬆

Visiting potters, many from France, study Canadian ceramic techniques at this pottery studio, about 25 km (15½ miles) east of La Malbaie. Classes for beginners are available from late June through August (by the hour or longer, starting at C$152). Half of the bright yellow barn housing the studio is a store, with ceramics and other crafts made by Québec artists. ⊠ *1001 rue St-Laurent (Rte. 138), St-Siméon, Québec* ⊕ *www.poteriedeportaupersil.com*

from: C$156 ⊠ *381 rue St-Raphaël* ☎ *418/665–4423, 888/282–3743* ⊕ *http://www.aubergedespeupliers.com/en/charlevoix-hotel/home/* ⇌ *22 rooms* ◎ *Free breakfast.*

Fairmont Le Manoir Richelieu

$$$ | RESORT | FAMILY | Linked to the Casino de Charlevoix by tunnel, this castlelike building and its sweeping grounds come with stunning views and some great sports and leisure facilities. **Pros:** good for families, with kids' club, kids' menu, and babysitting; scenic location; variety of dining options on-site. **Cons:** some rooms could use updating; complaints of inadequate amount of and attitude of staff. ⑤ *Rooms from: C$240* ⊠ *181 rue Richelieu, Pointe-au-Pic* ☎ *418/665–3703, 800/463–2613* ⊕ *www.fairmont.com/richelieu-charlevoix/* ⇌ *422 rooms* ◎ *Free breakfast.*

⊙ Performing Arts

Domaine Forget

DANCE | This music and dance academy has a 604-seat hall in Ste-Irenée, 15 km (9 miles) south of La Malbaie. Musicians from around the world, many of whom teach or study at the school, perform during its International Festival. The festival, which runs from mid-June to late August, includes Sunday brunches with music, a buffet, and a view of the St. Lawrence. Some weekend concerts are also held in the fall and spring. ⊠ *5 rang St-Antoine, St-Irénée* ☎ *418/452–3535, 888/336–7438* ⊕ *www.domaineforget. com.*

 ## Activities

GOLF

⭐ **Club de Golf Fairmont Le Manoir Richelieu**

GOLF | Be warned: if you play this course, you'll have to work hard to focus on the game and not the gorgeous scenery overlooking the St. Lawrence River. Originally established in 1925 and recently restored and expanded, this is a links-style course with three 9-hole courses that offers quite a bit of challenge, thanks to the design (the fairways are relatively wide but feature a number of strategically placed bunkers, trees, and mounds) and to the course's hilltop undulations. ⊠ *181 rue Richelieu, Pointe-au-Pic* ☎ *418/665–2526, 800/665–8082* ⊕ *www. fairmont.com/richelieu-charlevoix/golf* ⊒ *C$59–C$115 for all courses* ⅄ *St-Laurent Course: 9 holes, 3178 yards, par 36; Richelieu Course: 9 holes, 3148 yards, par 36; Tadoussac Course: 9 holes, 2918 yards, par 35* ☞ *Facilities: driving range, putting green, golf carts, rental clubs, restaurant, bar.*

SKIING

Mont-Grand Fonds

SKIING/SNOWBOARDING | This winter-sports center 12 km (7 miles) north of La Malbaie has 20 downhill slopes (including four recently opened glades in an area called The Lynx), an 1,105-foot vertical drop, and three lifts. It also has 184 km (113 miles) of cross-country trails. Two trails meet International Ski Federation standards, and the ski center occasionally hosts major competitions. You can also go dog sledding, sleigh riding, ice-skating, and tobogganing here. ⊠ *1000 chemin des Loisirs* ☎ *418/665–0095, 877/665–0095* ⊕ *www.montgrand-fonds.com* ⊒ *Full day tickets: C$50.*

Tadoussac

71 km (44 miles) north of La Malbaie.

Most people come to Tadoussac for the whale-watching excursions and cruises along the magnificent Saguenay Fjord. Beluga whales, highly recognizable because of their all-white color, small size, and high-pitch call, live here year-round and breed in the lower portion of the Saguenay in summer. The many marine species that live at the confluence of the fjord and the seaway attract other whales, too, such as pilots, finbacks, and humpbacks.

Sadly, the beluga is endangered; the whales, together with 35 other species of mammals and birds and 21 species of fish, are threatened by pollution in the St. Lawrence River. This has spurred a C$100 million project (funded by the federal and provincial governments) aimed at removing or capping sediment in the most polluted areas, stopping industrial and residential emissions into the river, and restoring natural habitat. There's still much work to be done, but greater attention is being given to this unique ecosystem, now a National Marine Conservation Area.

The short drive here from La Malbaie leads past lovely villages and views along the St. Lawrence. Jacques Cartier made a stop at this point in 1535, and from 1600 to the mid-19th century it was an important meeting site for fur traders. As the Saguenay River flows south from Lac St-Jean, it has a dual character: between Alma and Chicoutimi, the once rapidly flowing river has been harnessed for hydroelectric power; in its lower section, it becomes wider and deeper and flows by steep mountains and cliffs en route to the St. Lawrence.

GETTING HERE AND AROUND
From La Malbaie, drive northeast on Route 138. You must take a free 10-minute ferry ride from Baie-Ste-Catherine to get to Tadoussac. The ferries leave every 20 minutes, from 4 am to midnight, then every half hour until 4 am. For more information on ferry schedules, call *418/643–2019.*

VISITOR INFORMATION
CONTACT Tourist Information Center Tadoussac. ⊠ *197 rue des Pionniers* ☎ *418/235–4744, 866/235–4744.*

 Sights

Centre d'Interprétation des Mammifères Marins
INFO CENTER | You can learn more about the whales and their habitat at this interpretation center run by a locally based research team. They're only too glad to answer questions. In addition, explanatory videos and exhibits (including a collection of whale skeletons) serve as a good introduction to the mighty but endangered cetaceans. ⊠ *108 rue de la Cale-Sèche* ☎ *418/235–4701* ⊕ *www. baleinesendirect.org/en* ☜ *C$12.*

Parc Marin du Saguenay–St-Laurent
NATIONAL/STATE PARK | The 800-square-km (309-square-mile) marine park, at the confluence of the Saguenay and St. Lawrence rivers, has been created to protect this marine area's three fragile ecosystems. ⊠ *Park office, 182 rue de l'Église* ☎ *418/235–4703, 888/773–8888* ⊕ *parcmarin.qc.ca/home.*

 Hotels

Hôtel Tadoussac
$$ | **HOTEL** | **FAMILY** | A stunning natural environment and the 1942 Victorian-style building make this an equally great choice for an active or romantic stay. **Pros:** views over the bay; summer kids'

club with day care; good spa. **Cons:** no air-conditioning in rooms; service can be slow in the restaurant; walls very thin. Ⓢ *Rooms from: C$180* ⊠ *165 rue du Bord de l'Eau* ☎ *418/235–4421, 800/561–0718* ⊕ *www.hoteltadoussac.com* ☉ *Closed Nov.–mid-May* ☜ *149 rooms* ⦿⦿ *Free breakfast.*

🏃 Activities

WHALE-WATCHING
The best months for seeing whales are August and September, although some operators extend the season at either end if whales are around. Fjord tours are also available.

Croisières AML
WHALE-WATCHING | This outfitter offers two- and three-hour whale-watching cruises starting at C$69.95. The tours, in Zodiacs or larger boats, depart from Tadoussac pier. Tours of the Saguenay Fjord are available, and you can also take a daylong excursion on a chartered bus from Québec City, including a three-hour whale-watching cruise. ⊠ *Tadoussac* ☎ *418/692–1159, 800/463–1292* ⊕ *www. croisieresaml.com.*

Port Saguenay

This seaport is appreciated more for its natural beauty than for its shipping industry. Although it's interesting to see the big vessels and the huge equipment used to load and unload them, the scenes simply can't compete with the surrounding wilderness of cliffs, fjords, and the bare rock faces of the Canadian shield, not to mention the whales that inhabit the waters seasonally.

👁 Sights

★ Parc National du Fjord-du-Saguenay
NATURE SITE | Colossal rock cliffs and forest-covered mountains meet the still waters of the Saguenay Fjord, one of the

In Tadoussac from May to October, you can see whales living in the Saguenay River.

longest in the world, and the namesake national park runs its entire 105-km (65-mile) length. Of the park's three regions, the Baie-Éternité, which hosts the visitor center, is about 60 km (37 miles) south of the city of Saguenay, where you can visit the Fjord Museum (Musée du Fjord). Outdoor enthusiasts have much to do here, including kayaking, fishing, hiking, camping, bird-watching, whale-watching, and mountain biking, and the park can supply equipment and guides. The spectacular Baie-Éternité escarpments provide thrilling climbs and a via ferrata. Or you can take it easy on sailboat and sightseeing boat cruises, or enjoy a thrilling whale-watching experience. ☎ 418/272–1556 ⊕ www.sepaq.com/pq/sag/index.dot?language_id=1 ✉ C$9.

★ **Village historique de Val-Jalbert**
HISTORIC SITE | FAMILY | Powerful Oui-atchouan Falls, higher than Niagara Falls, overlook and long ago powered this once thriving mill town. Ultramodern in its day, the village had electricity and running water 25 years before the rest of

Québec, but administrative and production pitfalls closed the mill and by 1927 all the residents had departed. Today, you can see the beautifully restored mill, post office, general store, and butcher shop, then hike to the top of the falls, where a glass platform puts you directly over the center of the cascade. Modern accommodations are available within the general store and some restored period houses, and campgrounds and rustic cottages to rent are other options. ✉ 95 rue St.-Georges, Chambord ☎ 418/275–3132 ⊕ valjalbert.com/en ✉ C$29.

★ **Zoo Sauvage de Saint-Felicien**
ZOO | FAMILY | Cougars, polar bears, grizzly bears, Canadian lynx, American bison, and Japanese macaques are among the 75 species that roam open environments here. Between June and October, guides lead overnight tours in The Land of the Caribou, including hiking, a campfire meal, and canoeing on Lac Montagnais, where caribou may swim right by your boat. ✉ 2230 boul. du Jardin, St-Félicien

☎ 418/679–0543 ⊕ zoosauvage.org/en/ ✉ C$42; Land of the Caribou tour C$360.

🍴 Restaurants

Boucherie Davis Ltee

$$ | CANADIAN | Come hungry—really hungry—to this foodie destination, where the full-service, family butcher shop dating back to 1943 also hosts a café and gourmet food market featuring locally made artisanal products. Tuck into a thick rib steak with a local *saison* beer, select from the hot and cold buffets, or go for the "menu of the day" and watch butchers in action as you dine. **Known for:** high-quality produce and products; warm welcoming environment; wide variety of products available for purchase on-site. ⑤ *Average main: C$20* ✉ *1959 rue Davis, Jonquière* ☎ *418/548–5243* ▭ *No credit cards.*

Le Restaurant La Cuisine

$$$ | ECLECTIC | World cuisines influence chefs who are well-versed in French techniques and fond of using local ingredients. Thai cuisine inspires five-spice chicken with cashew nuts, rice noodles, vegetables, and sweet chili sauce; a taste of Italy is clearly evident in the veal flank with mushrooms, truffle oil, and Parmesan risotto. **Known for:** local produce; chic decor; good selection of beer and wine. ⑤ *Average main: C$25* ✉ *387 rue Racine E, Chicoutimi* ☎ *418/698–2822* ⊕ *www.restaurantlacuisine.ca* ☾ *No lunch weekends.*

Rouge Burger Bar

$$ | BURGER | Towering gourmet burgers are made exactly to order with a choice of lamb, chicken, salmon, local beef, or a vegetarian patty. Dress it up with one of several cheeses (maybe fresh chevre), various garnishes (how about caramelized onions and smoked bacon?), and a range of sauces (a dab of citrus tarragon mayonnaise?). **Known for:** their own line of barbecue and other sauces ; popular so reservations necessary; several TVs make it perfect for sports fans. ⑤ *Average main: C$15* ✉ *460 rue Racine E, Chicoutimi* ☎ *418/690–5029* ⊕ *www.rougeburgerbar.ca* ☾ *Closed Mondays.*

🏨 Hotels

Auberge de la Riviere Saguenay

$ | B&B/INN | Set on a slope overlooking the Saguenay Fjord, this lovely inn is a fine launching place for waterway or mountain adventures. **Pros:** most rooms have stunning fjord views; convenient base for exploring; beach access. **Cons:** no air-conditioning; decor is a little dated; breakfast is not included. ⑤ *Rooms from: C$115* ✉ *9122 chemin de la Batture, La Baie* ☎ *418/697–0222, 866/697-0222 toll-free number* ⊕ *www.aubergesaguenay.com* ▭ *No credit cards* ☞ *15 rooms* ⊚ *Free breakfast.*

🛍 Shopping

Bons Délices et Péchés

FOOD/CANDY | Chocolatiers here make truffles, cream-filled chocolates, spirits-spiked bonbons, chocolate-dipped ice cream in chocolate-dipped cones and dark, white, and milk chocolate. Fancy cookies and custom cakes are sold, too. ✉ *244 rue La Fontaine, Chicoutimi* ☎ *418/545–1660.*

Domaine de la Savonnière

GIFTS/SOUVENIRS | FAMILY | Herbs, flowers, fruit, spices, and essential oils are used to make soaps prepared on the premises. The soap maker is usually in and happy to explain the process and answer questions about the soaps' healthful properties. Soap-making workshops are available for adults and kids. ✉ *3289 boul. de la Grande-Baie Sud, La Baie* ☎ *418/544–8484.*

The Sanctuaire Notre-Dame-du-Cap in Trois-Rivières has been a place of pilgrimage and prayer since 1888.

Trois-Rivières

Where the Rivière St. Maurice divides into three channels, the town that grew up around it came to be known as Trois-Rivières (Three Rivers). Today it's a busy industrial hub but still retains pleasant shady streets and historical sites; a bygone iron and steel mill are worth a look. The town is also a good base for exploring the waterfalls and rock faces of the Parc National de la Mauricie, just 64 km (40 miles) away.

👁 Sights

Boréalis

FACTORY | FAMILY | Back when Trois-Rivieres was a lumber, paper, and pulp industry leader, this plant's machinery whizzed and whirled. Built in the early 1920s, it pumped, filtered, and stored water for the paper mill. By the mid-1950s, the plant filtered more than 20 million gallons of water a day that was used to produce 1,000 tons of newsprint.

Today, it is eerily quiet, especially the long-abandoned underground vaults, which are part of the original architecture and machinery that's on display. ✉ 200 av. des Draveur ☎ 819/372–4633 ⊕ www. borealis3r.ca 🖃 C$14.

Sanctuaire Notre-Dame-du-Cap

RELIGIOUS SITE | Built in 1955, on the site of earlier churches dating back to 1659, this is Canada's national shrine to Notre Dame (Our Blessed Mother) and an important pilgrimage site. As impressive as the great European cathedrals, this white granite, octagonal building hosts up to 1,660 people, and its lofty dome is topped by a pyramid and cross 258 feet above the ground. Reinforced concrete arches outline the building. Five bells ring A, Bb, D, F, and G notes, and the sanctuary's organ has 5,425 pipes. Inside, the altar is a single block of marble, and nary a pillar blocks views of magnificent architecture and stained glass masterpieces. ✉ 626 rue Notre-Dame E ☎ 819/374–2441 ⊕ www.sanctuaire-ndc.ca 🖃 Free.

Vieille Prison de Trois-Rivières

HISTORIC SITE | Dating to the early 1800s, this was the oldest continuously operating prison in Canada prior to its closure in 1986. The stark, stone structure with thick bars on the windows makes it clear that nobody is getting out. Originally built to house 40 inmates, the facility at times hosted up to 100 convicted criminals. If only the old doors and cedar basement joists could talk, what tales of mayhem might they tell? Tour guides share a few. The prison is attached to the Musée Quebecois de Culture Populaire. The museum's collection of more than 70,000 objects, plus traveling and changing exhibitions, showcase Québec's history and culture, including crime and prison life. ✉ *200 rue Laviolette* ☎ *819/372–0406* ⊕ *www.culturepop. qc.ca* ⚲ *C$17 for jail; C$15 for museum; C$24 combined ticket.*

 Restaurants

Le Sacristain

$$ | ECLECTIC | What was once a Wesleyan church has become a sanctuary for salads and grilled sandwiches. Ingredients stretch beyond ham and cheese; choose capers, smoked salmon, grilled mango, and hearts of palm. **Known for:** great stop between Montréal and Québec City; English-speaking staff; unique location in a converted church. ⑤ *Average main: C$14* ✉ *300 rue Bonaventure* ☎ *819/694–1344* ⊕ *www.lesacristain.ca* ⊘ *Not open for supper dining.*

Poivre Noir

$$$ | FRENCH | Sleek and modern, this friendly restaurant hits all the right spots—it's devoted to local ingredients and its dining room and deck overlook the St. Lawrence River. Expect creative plates: bison tartar, pickled mushrooms and salt foie gras; sablefish, lime mousseline, and clementine white butter; and savarin, elderberry, and white chocolate chantilly as dessert. **Known for:** creative cocktails; outside bar and terrasse overlooking the St-Lawrence; accommodating to food allergies. ⑤ *Average main: C$30* ✉ *1300 rue du Fleuve* ☎ *819/378–5772* ⊕ *www.poivrenoir.com* ⊘ *Closed Mon.*

Restaurant le St-Antoine

$$$ | BISTRO | This family-owned restaurant is rooted in French classics but has a taste for pizza and pasta, too. Escargots, steak tartare, veal scallops with mushroom cream sauce, grilled steaks, and various steamed mussel presentations join numerous Italian-style linguini dishes including alfredo, Bolognese, and carbonara. **Known for:** bring-your-own alcoholic beverage; seafood and pasta dishes; pleasant terrasse. ⑤ *Average main: C$25* ✉ *151 rue St.-Antoine* ☎ *819/378–6420* ⊕ *www.lestantoine.ca* ▤ *No credit cards* ⊘ *Closed Mon. and Tues. No lunch.*

🛏 Hotels

Le Gîte Loiselle

$ | B&B/INN | Beautiful woodwork and eye-catching architectural elements mark this late-19th-century neoclassical home. **Pros:** free Wi-Fi throughout the inn; garage available for bikes and motorcycles; walking distance to many attractions. **Cons:** no pets; early checkout time (10 am); late check-in time (4 pm); Victorian style may be too busy for some. ⑤ *Rooms from: C$95* ✉ *836 rue des Ursulines* ☎ *819/375–2121* ⊕ *www. giteloiselle.com* ▤ *No credit cards* ⇄ *4 rooms* ⊚ *Free breakfast.*

Motel Canadien

$ | HOTEL | A nice cross between a hotel and an inn, the rooms are not fancy but well appointed and clean, and the innkeepers are friendly and helpful. **Pros:** electric fireplaces in rooms; free Wi-Fi; air-conditioning; late checkout time (noon). **Cons:** 50% deposit required when booking; small rooms; interior design feels dated. ⑤ *Rooms from: C$75* ✉ *1821 rue Notre-Dame E* ☎ *819/375–5542*

⊕ *www.motelcanadien.ca* ⊟ *No credit cards* ⇆ *10 rooms* ¶⊙¶ *Free breakfast.*

Motel le Marquis

$ | **HOTEL** | **FAMILY** | On the historic Chemin de Roy linking Québec to Montréal, this motel offers comfortable, good value close to attractions like the charming sanctuary and lovely gardens of Ste-Marthe-du-Cap church. **Pros:** family-friendly; hearty breakfast; free Wi-Fi. **Cons:** innkeepers don't speak much English; small rooms; few decorative touches. ⑤ *Rooms from: C$79* ⊠ *989 rue Notre-Dame E* ☎ *819/378–7130* ⊕ *www. motelmarquis.com* ⊟ *No credit cards* ⇆ *12 rooms* ¶⊙¶ *Free breakfast.*

⑪ Shopping

Cabane à Sucre Chez Dany

LOCAL SPECIALTIES | **FAMILY** | Maple syrup, maple taffy, maple candy, maple everything—when it's "sugaring time" in Québec, this shack is busy. Visitors get to not only purchase the fruits of this labor, they may also see how maple sap becomes syrup and how to make taffy in the snow. There's an all-you-can-eat restaurant with a maple-centric menu, and live music of the region. ⊠ *195 rue de la Sablière* ☎ *819/370–4769* ⊕ *www. cabanechezdany.com.*

Les Jardins Dugré

FOOD/CANDY | Just a few minutes from downtown, the Dugré family tends a large vegetable farm. Besides selling their own berries, asparagus, and sweet corn, among other produce, the farm market offers various other local choices, including baked goods, cheeses, jams, pickles, honey, vinaigrettes, fresh pasta, maple products, and more. Arrive in the right season and you may pick your own strawberries. ⊠ *3861 rang St-Charles* ☎ *819/377–3108* ⊕ *www.jardinsdugre.ca.*

Index

Index

*Every effort has been made to trace the copyright holders, and we apologize in advance for any accidental errors. We would be happy to apply the corrections in the following edition of this publication.

Notes

Notes

Notes

Notes

Fodor's MONTRÉAL & QUÉBEC CITY

Publisher: Stephen Horowitz, *General Manager*

Editorial: Douglas Stallings, *Editorial Director;* Jill Fergus, Jacinta O'Halloran, Amanda Sadlowski, *Senior Editors;* Kayla Becker, Alexis Kelly, Rachael Roth, *Editors*

Design: Tina Malaney, *Director of Design and Production;* Jessica Gonzalez, *Graphic Designer;* Mariana Tabares, *Design & Production Intern*

Production: Jennifer DePrima, *Editorial Production Manager;* Carrie Parker, *Senior Production Editor;* Elyse Rozelle, *Production Editor;* Jackson Pranica, *Editorial Production Assistant*

Maps: Rebecca Baer, *Senior Map Editor;* Mark Stroud (Moon Street Cartography), David Lindroth, *Cartographers*

Photography: Viviane Teles, *Senior Photo Editor;* Namrata Aggarwal, Ashok Kumar, Carl Yu, *Photo Editors;* Rebecca Rimmer, *Photo Intern*

Business & Operations: Chuck Hoover, *Chief Marketing Officer;* Robert Ames, *Group General Manager;* Devin Duckworth, *Director of Print Publishing;* Victor Bernal, *Business Analyst*

Public Relations and Marketing: Joe Ewaskiw, *Senior Director Communications & Public Relations;* Esther Su, *Senior Marketing Manager*

Fodors.com: Jeremy Tarr, *Editorial Director;* Rachael Levitt, *Managing Editor;* Teddy Minford, *Editor*

Technology: Jon Atkinson, *Director of Technology;* Rudresh Teotia, *Lead Developer;* Jacob Ashpis, *Content Operations Manager*

Writers: Chris Barry, Marie-Eve Vallieres, Elizabeth Warkentin, Barbara Woolsey

Editor: Jacinta O'Halloran, Debbie Harmsen

Production Editor: Elyse Rozelle

30th edition

ISBN 978-1-64097-244-5

ISSN 1525-5867

All details in this book are based on information supplied to us at press time. Always confirm information when it matters, especially if you're making a detour to visit a specific place. Fodor's expressly disclaims any liability, loss, or risk, personal or otherwise, that is incurred as a consequence of the use of any of the contents of this book.

SPECIAL SALES
This book is available at special discounts for bulk purchases for sales promotions or premiums. For more information, e-mail SpecialMarkets@fodors.com.

PRINTED IN CANADA

10 9 8 7 6 5 4 3 2 1

About Our Writers

 Chris Barry is a native Montrealer and freelance journalist who has contributed to scores of publications over the years and has been writing for the *Fodor's Montréal and Québec City* guide since 2002. He's currently finishing a book documenting his years as a professional rock-and-roll musician in the 1970s, '80s, and '90s. Chris updated the Side Trips from Montréal and Side Trips from Québec City chapters for this edition.

 Marie-Eve Vallieres Born and raised in Montréal, Marie-Eve Vallieres knows the city like the back of her hand, despite that it is constantly evolving. Marie-Eve has written for *AFAR Magazine,* Expedia Canada, and Viator, and she has been interviewed regularly on CBC Radio One. Her blog is called To Europe And Beyond (⊕ *http://toeurope-andbeyond.com*). Marie-Eve updated the Québec City chapter for this edition.

 Elizabeth Warkentin is a freelance writer who was born and raised in Montréal and is enjoying getting reacquainted with her native city after a 20-year absence. She is an avid photographer and freelance journalist and has contributed to a variety of publications including BBC Travel, the *Boston Globe,* the *Toronto Star,* and the *Vancouver Sun.* She updated the Montréal chapter for this edition.

 Barbara Woolsey is a Canadian journalist who's trekked across the world by plane, train, and motorbike. She currently spends most of her time in Berlin, producing for Reuters TV and contributing to publications such as *The Guardian, The Telegraph,* and *Thrillist.* Barbara studied French at the Université de Montréal and has returned regularly to cover the city for different outlets. Barbara updated the Travel Smart chapter for this edition.

Montréal métro